THE SPIRITUAL JOURNEY OF A SHOWBUSINESS PRIEST

The Spiritual Journey of a Showbusiness Priest

Ellwood E. Kieser

PAULIST PRESS
New York, NY   Mahwah, NJ

Cover photos by John P. Johnson. Cover design by Morris Berman Studios.

LIBRARY OF CONGRESS CATALOGING-IN-PUBLICATION DATA

Kieser, Ellwood E.
[Hollywood priest]
The spiritual journey of a showbusiness priest/by Ellwood E. Kieser.
p. cm.
Includes index.
ISBN 0-8091-3587-6 (alk. paper)
1. Kieser, Ellwood E. 2. Catholic Church—United States—Clergy—Biography. 3. Screenwriters—United States—Biography. 4. Motion picture producers and directors—United States—Biography.
I. Title.
282'.092—dc20
[B]
95-44285
CIP

Published by Paulist Press
997 Macarthur Boulevard
Mahwah, New Jersey 07430

Printed and bound in the
Unites States of America

TO THOSE WHO

SEEK THE TRUTH

WITH PASSION

The important thing
is not success.
The important thing is
to be in history
bearing the witness.

—JACQUES MARITAIN

Contents

INTRODUCTION

I was frightened.

It was March 1983, and I had hired John Sacret Young to write the screenplay for a theatrical motion picture on Oscar Romero, the assassinated archbishop of San Salvador. Together we had decided to fly to El Salvador, so that we could talk firsthand with all those involved, both Romero's friends and his enemies. We made the decision without thinking about the consequences.

But then Jenny, John's wife, began to worry about the things we should have thought of but didn't: the guerrilla war, the death squads, the murder of forty thousand people, most of whom were civilians, some of whom were Americans.

I talked it over with John. He thought the dangers were manageable. I told Jenny I had no desire to be a martyr. John promised to call her every evening. I promised we would be careful and take no unnecessary chances. This seemed to reassure her. But in allaying her anxieties, I triggered some of my own.

I decided to take out insurance, although it turned out to be terribly expensive. "The most dangerous piece of real estate in the world," the agent explained. If anything should happen, at least John's children would be provided for.

Paul Weber, the general manager of Paulist Productions, came into my office and began to make nervous small talk. This was out of character for him, so I asked what was bothering him. "What do I do if you don't come back?" he blurted out.

I could no longer ignore the consequences of what I was doing.

I decided to go to the Benedictine monastery at Valermo for a couple of days to think it through. While there, anxiety-ridden questions popped into my consciousness. What have I gotten myself into? Can I call this responsible stewardship? Risking John's life? And my own? Is this an ego trip? A test of virility? A surrender to some kind of death wish?

I prayed. I tried to turn the whole thing over to the Lord. I asked Him to tell me what He wanted. No movie is worth dying for, I said to myself. But then I realized that peace and justice and freedom for the people of El Salvador—which this movie could promote—were worth taking some risks for.

With that, my fears began to evaporate.

In El Salvador John and I spent extensive time with those closest to Romero.

But we also spent time with his enemies.

We visited a member of the oligarchy—that minuscule group of Salvadoran aristocrats who own such a disproportionately large share of the nation's resources—whose law office was guarded by two soldiers with automatic weapons. Despite the fact that he had been educated in the United States and spoke English fluently, he refused to talk with us until his wife arrived to translate. They were both very polite and called me "Father" repeatedly. Yet they were also very nervous. The room was heavy with fear.

I had heard they were bitter critics of Romero—that they had, in fact, thrown a party of celebration the night he was killed—so, after the initial pleasantries, I asked them why they so disliked the archbishop.

"He preached hatred and class warfare," said the lawyer succinctly.

"He said it was no sin for the poor to steal from the rich," declared his wife.

I could feel a rising vehemence as their words began to tumble out.

"He was manipulated by the Jesuits," said the lawyer.

"He was brainwashed by a psychologist in Costa Rica," said his wife.

"He was a tool of the Marxists," summed up the lawyer.

"And he forbade private baptisms," concluded his wife, with barely disguised venom. "Imagine my child being baptized with a bunch of Indians."

* * *

We also spent ninety minutes with one of the commanding generals of the Salvadoran army. Not wanting to be patronized, and itching to put the tough questions to him, I did not wear my roman collar. Press credentials hung from my safari jacket.

In the opinion of some Salvadorans, the general was the originator of the death squads. He was short, barrel-chested, with a pockmarked face, energetic, bright and articulate in speech, given to Napoleonic gestures and rhetoric. For most questions he had canned answers; portions of speeches, I would guess, he had given many times. When we pressed him on the murders committed by his troops, he was apologetic, saying he was trying to control the death squads and punish those responsible. He became defensive when we asked him about the murder of the American nuns and quiet, almost tender, when we pressed him about Archbishop Romero.

He knew Romero well. On more than one occasion, Romero had asked him to resign, and on more than one occasion, he had asked Romero to pull back, to moderate his denunciations of the exploitation and terrorism. Each man had rejected the other's request.

As I listened to the general, I kept asking myself, Does this man really believe what he is saying? Is he as evil as I have heard?

He knew how to say what he thought Americans wanted to hear—that he was fighting our war against the Communists, that if El Salvador went Marxist so would all of Central America and Mexico, that he was so grateful for American help, that victory would be theirs because the people were so wholeheartedly behind them.

"Not the people I've been talking to," I cut in.

"What people?" he asked.

"The ones who tell me they have to flee their homes because they are afraid your soldiers will kill them."

"*¿Dónde, dónde?*" he thundered, his fist pounding the table. "Where are the people saying these things?"

I had the answers to my questions.

Two days later I was able to see why the people were so afraid. At five one morning we went out with one of the human rights agencies to look for the bodies of the people who had been murdered the night before. We went to a ravine on the outskirts of town. Lots of dumped garbage there. But no bodies. Part of me was relieved. Part was disappointed. But I would not be disappointed long. We went next to El Playon, a lava field ten miles outside San Salvador. Walking over the mounds of volcanic ash, the cinders crunching under my feet, I was startled as four giant vultures lifted off and flew to a nearby tree. As I walked toward their point of departure, two more lifted off, their wings beating noisily against the early morning air. Then I could see where they had come from and what they had been doing. It was a mass grave. They had been having their breakfast. I counted eleven bodies. To one side I saw another, smaller grave. It contained four bodies. More skeletons than bodies. The vultures had stripped off most of the flesh. Yet I could see the thumbs tied together behind the backs with piano wire. And I could see the three-inch hole in the back of each person's skull where their brains had been blown out by the murderer's bullet.

If the Devil is, as Jesus tells us, the father of lies and a murderer, it would seem he was having a field day in El Salvador.

I made the sign of the cross over the bodies and murmured the words of absolution. The human rights people snapped photos and took notes. John just drank it in.

Nobody said anything, probably because we were feeling so much. How does one assimilate that kind of horror?

So this is how we will end up, I thought to myself. A corpse. A skeleton. That was part of it. But not all. I had been a hospital chaplain. I knew what it was like to have my nose rubbed in my own mortality. This was more than that. This was the depravity of which we are capable. This was not only death. This was pure hatred, an abhorrence of human life, a cold-blooded assault upon it. A kind of evil I had not encountered before. It would have been easy for me to say it was all the oligarchy's fault, the Salvadoran army's fault, the American government's fault, the death squads' fault. But I knew better. The sickness was in them. But a susceptibility to it was also in me. No use denying it.

The human rights people were used to this. They prepared to move on. I did not want to go. Neither did John. We signaled our driver we would remain.

We needed time to contemplate the face of the Devil.

Off in the distance, the vultures sat in the tree branches and patiently awaited the next delivery of human carrion.

* * *

Not that the situation in El Salvador in 1983 was purely demonic. Far from it.

In a village outside San Salvador, we met a young nun—she could not have been more than twenty-five—setting up for a base community meeting that evening. These gatherings of campesinos to discuss the Bible and apply it to their daily lives have provided much of the impetus behind the grassroots efforts to transform the economic and political structures of Latin America in recent years. In El Salvador, in 1983, anybody connected with a base community was liable to be kidnapped, tortured, and killed.

"You must be careful, Sister," I said. "Aren't you afraid?"

"No more than any other Salvadoran," she replied simply.

A couple more questions and she told us her story.

"When I graduated from high school seven years ago, I joined one of the established religious orders. But as a novice, I came to realize that if I stayed in that order, I would spend the rest of my life serving the rich. I wanted to serve the poor. So, with six other novices, including my own blood sister, I left that order, and with Archbishop Romero's help we established a new order to work with the campesinos."

"How did his death affect you?" I asked.

"It upset us, of course," she replied. "We felt so discouraged that my sister left us and went into the hills because the guerrillas needed someone to nurse their wounded."

"Is she still with them?" I asked as gently as I could.

"No," she replied, her eyes filling with tears. "She got caught in crossfire and was killed two years ago."

"I am so sorry," I said, seeing the pain on her face. "Have you ever thought of doing some other kind of work, living a life that might be safer, more comfortable?"

"I have thought about it," she said, a note of sadness in her voice, "but then I think, these people give me so much and they have no one else and this is what God wants me to do—to let them know someone cares. This is where the Church should be. With the poor."

There was a gentleness about her, but I could feel the fire inside of her. It flashed in her eyes and resonated in her words.

Fortunately, in Salvador, there were many like her.

* * *

Two days after our arrival, the Pope visited El Salvador.

After the morning Mass, fifteen hundred nuns, priests, brothers, and seminarians crowded a high school gym to hear him talk.

While they awaited his arrival, there was much backslapping and good cheer. Old friends glad to see each other again. I joined them, privileged to be part of their family reunion.

Because the Pope was delayed, the seminarians began to sing Salvadoran folk songs, and the whole group picked up the melodies.

By this time I had a pretty good picture of what these people had been through. Already three nuns, eleven priests, and more than three thousand lay church workers had been killed by the death squads. Their only crime was working with the poor and joining them in their struggle for justice and freedom.

At a certain point someone struck up Beethoven's *Ode to Joy* and the whole crowd—fifteen hundred strong—stood up and bellowed out that celebration of human life, that triumphant hymn to the Author of that life.

I could not join in. I was crying like a baby.

That these people—who had seen their friends and co-workers cut down by the score, who had to face the same prospect for themselves if they continued to challenge the status quo, which the overwhelming majority of them had decided to do—that these people could say hurrah for life, hurrah for God, I found an overwhelming sign of faith, courage, and resurrection.

Salvador in 1983 was the worst and the best that humankind has to offer.

I saw a disdain for human life, for human rights and human dignity—an idolatry of violence, force, and naked power—a malevolent destructiveness that frequently reached the point of frenzy.

I also saw a church community so spirit-filled that it had opted for the poor and wholeheartedly committed itself to their continuing battle for peace and human dignity. I had also seen many, many people who had so transcended their egos that they were ready to die that other people might live full and free.

John and I did not talk much on the flight back to Los Angeles. Mentally and emotionally we were drained. We needed time to digest what we had seen and heard. I needed time to decide what I was going to do about what I had experienced and that meant bringing to that decision everything that had gone before.

My mind flashed to June 1950. I had just graduated from college, and I was arguing with God. He wanted me to be a priest. I didn't want to be a priest. Maybe a novelist. My father was on my side. He suggested I go to Europe for a month to sort things out. "Sow some wild oats," he said. I thought it was a great idea.

With my plane ticket in my pocket, I wandered around Manhattan's Lower East Side before going out to the airport. An unshaven and disheveled-looking man approached me and said, "Please, I'm no bum. But I haven't eaten in three days. Can you help me?"

I looked at him and figured what I had and what I needed. It was going to be tight, so I hardened my heart and said, "No, I'm sorry."

Crestfallen, he started to walk away, then spun on his heel and, with a hoarse bitterness in his voice, shouted, "Are you a Christian?"

"Yes," I replied. "I try to be."

"Well, I'm glad I'm an atheist," he shot back.

He walked away. I was stunned. I have never been able to forget the anguished look on his face and the despair in his voice. Nor the terrible cogency of his words.

It was August 1959, and I had been a priest for three years, living and working in a parish in Los Angeles.

Home on vacation in Philadelphia, I decided to go over to New York City for several days.

"I'll be back Thursday night," I told my stepmother on Monday afternoon as I kissed her good-bye.

"Will you be back for dinner?" she asked.

"Yes," I replied. "What time will dinner be?"

"Six-thirty," she said.

My stepmother was an excellent cook. Of German descent, she organized a meal like General Rommel organized a battle. Everything was perfectly synchronized, so when she said dinner would be at six-thirty, she meant six-thirty on the dot, not three minutes before or three minutes after.

I drove the ninety miles to New York, saw my friends, did my business, and was all set to leave the rectory there at four-thirty for the leisurely drive to Philadelphia, when I ran into a friend whom I had not seen since the seminary. It was five-fifteen by the time I got on the road.

That meant I had just seventy-five minutes to get through Manhattan's rush hour traffic and navigate ninety miles of turnpike if I was going to get home in time for dinner.

It had been a miserably humid day, and as soon as I got onto the Jersey turnpike I peeled off my black coat and roman collar to reveal the Hawaiian shirt underneath.

I was speeding along at eighty-five miles per hour in my Hawaiian shirt when it started to rain; not a heavy rain, just a drizzle that covered my windshield with a mist. I turned on my wipers and continued to speed along at eighty-five, looking for the radar traps. I had had experience with the New Jersey police before.

I spotted this radar trap, but I did not see it soon enough, and I was pulled over to the side of the road with three other cars by two motorcycle policemen.

Working from the two ends, they began to write us up. As usual I was in the middle. I got out of my car and debated with myself which license I would show the cop. I had two—the Pennsylvania one, which I received when I was in high school, and the California one, which I got when I went to Los Angeles in September of 1956. Unlike the Pennsylvania one, it had my picture on it, in roman collar, in living color.

As the policeman on my right began to walk toward me, it began to lightning. What I am about to tell you really happened. Priest's honor. Three fingers. As he walked toward me, the lightning struck the soggy ground between us. I had never been so close to lightning before. I could not only see and hear it; I could smell it. And I was jolted, as if I had been hit on the head with a hammer. But I was not hurt. The policeman was not so fortunate. He was knocked on his fanny and badly shaken up. But he, too, was not seriously injured. He picked himself up, dusted himself off, and came over to write me up.

By this time I had decided to show him my California license.

He took one look at the roman collar on the California license and said, "Hell, Father, I'm not gonna bother you."

The Lord sometimes takes best care of us when we least deserve it.

It was October 1960. The team with which I worked in adult education decided to put my theological lectures on television.

Called "Insight," the thirteen-week series drew three hundred letters a week and very respectable ratings.

Reflecting on the experience afterward, we came to two conclusions:

1. Television gave us a great opportunity to enrich people.
2. We had a dreadful series. Dreadful not because the first "Insight" series had not worked, but because it had not tapped the visual and emotional potential of television. It was cerebral, touching the mind, ignoring the heart. And despite our best efforts, it was all talk; so much to hear, so little to see.

We decided to make radical changes. The second year we used a documentary format and explored the theological issues of the cold war.

The third year we went to drama, which was the format we retained for the next twenty years.

It was May 1965, and I was having lunch at the studio with a well-known Jewish actor. We were shooting our fifth "Insight" series. The idea of value-oriented drama had really caught on. The best writers, directors, and actors in Hollywood were gravitating toward the series, which was now playing on more than one hundred TV stations a week. "Insight" had become the experimental theater for Hollywood television.

The actor leaned across the table and said to me, "Something that's always puzzled me—why do your people hate my people?"

I was taken aback. How could I respond to a question like that?

"Most don't," I finally answered. "Those who do are usually ignorant and afraid. They're jealous of your brains and drive. But they can hate only by suppressing their Christianity. Contradicting it, really."

"You think we ask for it?" he went on.

"Nobody's perfect," I replied, "but nothing can justify what's been done. Nothing!"

"You think we killed Christ?"

"I think we all killed Him. And I think we continue to do it every time we close our hearts and hate any other human being, Jew or Gentile."

He reached across the table and we locked hands. There were tears in his eyes.

* * *

It was March 1967. The radical changes launched by the Vatican Council created much media interest in things Catholic. Having been a correspondent at the Council, I found myself one evening on the Johnny Carson show.

Johnny made some jokes about my six-foot-six frame and then asked, "What exactly do the Paulist Fathers do?"

"We're in the construction business," I answered.

Johnny did a double take.

"We try to demolish the walls of ignorance and distrust that separate one religious community from another, and we try to build bridges of understanding and respect between the various faith communities."

"Does that mean conversion is out? You've given up proselytizing?" interrupted the standup comic who was the previous guest. There was an edge to his voice.

"That all depends on what you mean by conversion," I answered. "If you mean a change of labels, from Presbyterian to Methodist, from Baptist to Jewish, from Protestant to Catholic, we don't feel labels are important. But if by conversion you mean a turning from ego, pleasure, and the acquisition of things to the service of God as He lives in other people, we feel that kind of conversion is a desirable thing, and we do everything we can to promote it."

"I'm glad I don't have to play basketball against you," said the comic, the edge gone from his voice.

It was August 1967. To those outside the Church, the changes happening within the Church were very exciting. But to those inside, the changes were sometimes confusing. And those in authority were not always happy with those of us who were experimenting.

"Bud," barked Monsignor Ben Hawkes, Cardinal McIntyre's arch-conservative hatchet man, into the phone. "I am shocked."

"About what?" I asked, on guard not to get sucked into his game.

"I have before me a photo of you concelebrating Mass, allegedly with the Immaculate Hearts, allegedly on August 15, and you are wearing a crepe-paper chasuble."

"So?" I said as nonchalantly as I could.

"So what can I tell the cardinal? He'll be very upset. It's against the rules."

"Tell him anything you want, Ben. The atmosphere was very celebrative. Like a party. Crepe-paper vestments seemed very appropriate. Besides, there were not enough conventional ones to go around."

"Appropriate, my eye. You're supposed to wear cloth vestments. That's what Rome wants."

"Really, Ben," I answered, my blood pressure starting to go up, "with kids starving to death and the world getting ready to blow itself up, do you think Jesus wants us worrying about the kind of vestments we wear?" I was playing dirty, but he deserved it.

"You guys are all the same," he retorted. "You start out playing around with the liturgy. Next you question church doctrine. You end up dating nuns."

By this time I was furious; partially, I guess, because I was doing all three.

It was December 1978, and I was starting to burn out, so I took a sabbatical and gave a series of workshops in India on the humanizing capacities of radio and television. The schedule was such that I had plenty of time to wander the streets and visit the historical monuments.

One day, in khaki slacks and jacket, I was walking through the Red Fort in New Delhi when I encountered a large group of tourists whom I took to be Polish because of their blondish hair, red cheeks, and peasant builds. I decided to start a conversation.

"Polski?" I asked one of them.

"No," he replied emphatically, "Russki."

"Russki," I repeated, to give myself time to shift gears.

"Swedski?" he asked me with a smile.

"No," I said, "Amerski."

"Oh, oh," he said, "Amerski." He, too, was shifting gears. Then a bigger smile lit up his face, and he stuck out his hand. We shook several times. We bowed to each other. Neither of us knew what else to do since neither of us spoke the other's language. Yet, somehow, it did not seem adequate. Finally we said good-bye, and he rejoined his group.

A moment later he was back. He wanted to give me a present. It was a Lenin pin, which he had just removed from his lapel. I put it in my lapel, and we hugged. It was an awkward hug—I was eighteen inches taller—but it said what each of us wanted to say:

We are both human beings, brothers, a part of each other. Never, under any conditions, do we want to make war on each other.

In India I also experienced as never before the presence of God in the desperately poor. I found they had so much more to give to me than I had to give to them.

It was October 1980, and John Amos and I were visiting the refugee camps of Somalia and the famine-ravaged areas of Kenya. Our task: to immerse ourselves in the situation of the hungry people, let them know we care, capture as much of it as possible on film, and then return to do the news and talk shows, so as to inform the American people of the problem and mobilize support for its solution.

It was one of the most beautiful and most devastating experiences of my life.

Early one morning in Somalia, while we were filming, a tall, handsome woman with a child in her arms burst through the crowd and angrily shouted, "We don't need pictures. We need food. Look, my child is dying and my breasts are empty. I have no milk to give him."

I could have tried to explain to her that the pictures were an important first step in getting massive amounts of food to her camp, but she would not have been able to understand.

More to the point, I knew she was right. I sent the crew on ahead and together we sat down and, with the help of an interpreter, she told me her story. It was a heartrending one. She had lost her husband in the war and her older child to measles. Now she was afraid her younger child would die.

In time her anger subsided, and she started to cry. I felt like putting my arms around her. But I did not, knowing that would be misinterpreted in a Moslem country. But she got the message. I cared. I wanted to understand. I wanted to help.

I got her some food. I gave her some money. But I think my listening to her was almost as important.

When we got back, John and I did the news and talk shows, and we joined Valerie Harper and Liv Ullmann to testify before the House Subcommittee on Africa, hoping to get Congress to boost its allocation for famine relief.

Liv began by describing the desperate plight of the people she had met on her travels in the Horn of Africa. It was low-key, heartfelt, and very effective. I decided to take a different approach.

"We are a generous people who have a stingy foreign aid policy," I said. "As an American I find that unacceptable. Hundreds of thousands of our brother and sister human beings are dying of starvation. I think that's intolerable. Hunger is a moral imperative. Each of us, and all of us, must do whatever is necessary, at whatever personal cost, to remedy it. As individuals we must take decisive action. So must the Congress of the United States."

The galleries responded with sustained applause. Liv looked around quizzically. Apparently they did not do that in Sweden. I leaned over and said to her, "You are prettier, but I was louder."

The "CBS Evening News" carried the hearing, and Congress did respond, significantly increasing its allocation for famine relief.

I was beginning to see that Third World poverty had a political dimension, that living out the Gospel in the latter part of the twentieth century necessitated sustained political involvement.

John Sacret Young seemed to be sleeping in the seat beside me. It was a five-and-a-half-hour flight from San Salvador to Los Angeles. He shifted position. I looked out the window. That must be Mexico down there.

I went back to my reverie. I was a priest, trying to be a good one. I was a producer, some people thought a creative one. I needed to decide how I could better integrate the two and what I wanted to do about what I had just seen and heard in El Salvador.

If I was able to forget, I might not have to do anything. But I knew that was not possible. The shattered skulls. The tied thumbs. The strains of the *Ode to Joy* from the throats of those heroic people. These things had been etched into my consciousness.

But if I could not forget, I had to act. How could I best say *no* to the death squads and to the system of lies and racism, injustice and grinding poverty, they support? And how could I best say *yes* to the Salvadoran people and to their struggle for justice and human dignity?

Slowly, by no logical process, the decision made itself.

I went to El Salvador feeling *Romero* was a movie I would like to make. I came back from El Salvador knowing *Romero* was a movie I had to make. John was coming to a similar conclusion.

No matter how long it took, no matter how many times we were turned down, no matter how discouraging it got, we had to make this movie.

So we did.

It took five years to put together all the pieces. We did get turned down repeatedly, and sometimes we did get very discouraged, but we hung in there because of the decision we made on the plane coming back from El Salvador in March of 1983.

In ways that I do not quite understand, this book also flowed from that decision.

By the summer of 1987 the *Romero* script was in good shape, the board had voted unanimously to make the picture, most of the budget was in hand, and I was aggressively seeking the right director. This left me with blocks of leisure time while I waited for someone to read the script and make up his mind. That's when I started this book.

I remember telling the priests with whom I live that it was my hobby, something I did for a change of pace when *Romero* did not demand all my time. That was accurate. But before long the hobby had become a passion, something I felt compelled to do.

It enabled me to relive my whole life—from start to present—so I could grapple with its mystery and seek out its meaning, explore its secrets, examine its facets, see how its various segments fit together, and discern how God was leading me and where.

I had lived out my life as a priest and a television producer during a very special time in human history. I was a boy during the Depression, a teenager during World War II, a college student when the Cold War began, a seminarian during the McCarthy era, a parish priest during Eisenhower's second term, a television producer during the sixties, seventies, and eighties. I made the first of twenty-three "Insight" series the year Jack Kennedy was elected; the second, the year of the Cuban missile crisis; the third, the year Kennedy was killed; the last, in 1983, the year the Soviets shot down the Korean jetliner. I was a correspondent at the Vatican Council in 1965, a teacher of theology in 1968 when Martin Luther King and Bobby Kennedy were assassinated and it seemed the country would come apart, a Ph.D. candidate during Watergate, a visiting lecturer in India when Jimmy Carter established diplomatic relations with Red China, a media spokesman for the world's hungry and oppressed during the Reagan years, and a producer of two network specials and a feature film during the latter part of the eighties, when Gorbachev launched *perestroika*, the peoples of Eastern Europe overthrew their Communist masters, and the Cold War came to an end.

I felt fortunate that my years on this planet had coincided with this unique period in human history. I felt doubly fortunate to have been a priest and a motion picture producer during this time. But once I began to write, I discovered the interfacing of priest and producer—a strange combination, but not an impossible one—was an important part of my story but not all of it. And the historical flow of which I was a part, which enriched me in so many ways and to which I tried to contribute in my own way, provided the context of my story but was not its central focus.

That focus was deeper. It was and is my spiritual journey—my struggle to say yes to myself, get beyond my ego, and find the best way to give myself to God as He lives in other people.

In my sixty years I have done many things. But what I have done outside only remotely reflects the far more important things that have taken place inside.

I have traveled to Europe and Asia, Africa, Australia, and Latin America. But the most exciting journey I have taken has been into myself and toward God.

I have wrestled with scripts and budgets, schedules and organizational tables. But I have always found it more challenging—as well as more difficult and satisfying—to wrestle with God and those I love on the deepest and most intimate of levels.

This journey and this struggle have been central to my life. In a real sense they have been my life, and they have propelled me into the world, in search of the God who lives in other people, but also into the center of myself and through that center in search of the same God who lives in the depths on the other side.

"What persona are you going to present?" asked John Sacret Young, when I told him what I was doing.

"No persona. Just me, as I am," I replied.

"The naked truth?" he asked skeptically. "Are you ready for that?"

Good question. Did I want to drop my defenses, step out of role, and share my most intimate thoughts and feelings—the kinds of things I told only my confessor and closest friends—with my readers? Would they be interested in such things? Wouldn't some people be scandalized? A priest who falls in love. A man of God in psychotherapy. A minister of the Gospel with murderous thoughts. A celibate with erotic desires.

The more I thought about it, the more I realized there was only one way to write this kind of book—go deep, reach for the truth about myself in all its dark and luminous mystery, and then struggle to find the words to express that truth as clearly and as honestly as I could. I found it a rigorous and demanding process. I could allow myself only one concern: what's real, what's true, what's honest. Nothing else was important. Nothing. I had neither the energy nor the inclination to look over my shoulder to worry what other people would think.

So, if you like your priests perfect and think most of them are saints, this is probably not your kind of book. For my sake as well as your own, please put it away.

But if you sometimes ache with loneliness and fear, emptiness and guilt, and journey you know not where, in search of you know not what, because you hunger for something bigger, something better to give yourself to, then you may find this book of interest.

At least it will tell you that you are not alone.

Where do we begin? At the beginning, of course.

PART ONE

BREAKING AWAY

CHAPTER 1

BOY

I was born midway between the great wars, in the year of the great stock market crash, at that place on the Middle Atlantic coastal plane where the Delaware and Schuylkill rivers come together and bolt for the sea, in the city that Billy Penn dedicated to brotherly love, to a father who was so delighted to have a son that he went out and bought himself a derby, and to a mother who was exhausted and exhilarated and so happy to see him so happy.

I was the second of four children. Shirley was born three years before; Bill and Don, twenty months and six years later respectively.

That was March of 1929. The disaster on Wall Street did not come until October. Most of the middle class were in the market then, my mother and father included. They were crimped by the crash but not wiped out. Crimped enough that they would never go near the market again. But not crimped enough that it seriously affected their way of life, which, for the time, was quite comfortable.

My Dad, who was almost twenty-nine when I was born, was in the car storage business. He had converted my grandfather's slaughterhouse into a garage and had rented an even larger one in the same neighborhood. In those days people did not have garages of their own, nor did they leave their cars on the street overnight. For a monthly fee, they parked them in public garages, like my Dad's. It was a good business, for only the wealthy had cars.

As Henry Ford's revolution progressed and the family car became a fixture of the American middle class, my Dad branched out into gas stations; and finally he went into the wholesale automobile accessory business, supplying tires, batteries, spark plugs, and oil filters to the Atlantic stations in the Philadelphia area. Hardworking and fun-loving, an entrepreneur and a showman, his motto was always "Let's do it bigger and better."

Those were the Depression years. Sometimes my Dad worried about paying the bills. But at home we never lacked anything we needed. And most of the time we had domestic help and spent the summers at Ocean City on the New Jersey coast. None of our relatives and few of our neighbors were so fortunate.

When I was born, we lived in Lansdowne, a suburb of Philadelphia. But sometime between then and the time I entered kindergarten, we moved to a big old three-story house in the center of Philadelphia, just two blocks from my Dad's garages. Ours was a solidly white street. The next one over was solidly black. A worry of my early years was that the curly-headed kids would move onto our block.

In the mid-thirties, my Dad was very active in Franklin Roosevelt's National Recovery Administration and was president of the garage dealers' association. In those capacities he did considerable traveling and made a lot of speeches, one of which, on the nation's economy, was reported on the front page of the *New York Times.* He loved the limelight and relished the applause, a quality he bequeathed to his oldest son.

My mother was the only girl my father ever dated. He made up his mind on that first date that this was the lady for him. He proposed shortly thereafter. I guess she had similar feelings, because after a suitable period of hesitation, she accepted.

There was, of course, the religious question to be worked out. Mother was a Catholic, Irish on her mother's side, German on her father's. Her faith was a very important part of her life. Dad was German Lutheran. He also believed deeply. He had a particularly keen sense of the sacred. But he did not go to church regularly. "No problem," my father said. "I will become a Catholic." And he did.

It was a little too easy and would cause tensions later on.

But their marriage worked. Their love was deep, and they gave each other great happiness. They liked to go off alone, just the two of them, for a private talk. "There was not a selfish bone in her body," my father was to tell me after she died.

Theirs was a good marriage, even if, by today's standards, my father was a chauvinist. "No wife of mine will ever work," he said more than once. Yet religion was my mother's province, and he was more or less content to let her make the decisions in that area.

Even after Dad entered the Church, he was not free of the anti-Catholic prejudice that characterized certain segments of Protestantism in those days. "Catholics are Irish," he once told me. "They are either cops or streetcar conductors. And they get drunk on Saturday nights."

But that was nothing compared to what he said about the Jews and the blacks. "A kike is a nigger turned inside out, and a nigger is a kike turned inside out."

Hearing remarks like that, my mother would wince. "His conversion," she once said, "was less than complete." Yet she also knew a different side of my Dad—how generous, if paternalistic, he was with his black employees; how one of them—Jeff—worked for my Dad for forty-five years and was a loved member of our family; how his crews were always evenly split, half white, half black; how easy a touch he was for the black ministers in the area. When the race riots hit our section of Philadelphia in the summer of 1944, ours was the only white business that was neither looted nor burned. The blacks in the area knew whose side he was on.

My mother also knew of Dad's deep and genuine friendship with many of our Jewish neighbors and customers.

Why, then, would he make such bigoted remarks? Was this his way of asserting himself and venting his frustrations, an exercise in flamboyance, a device to shock or get a laugh? I do not know. But I do know that what he sometimes said and what he quite consistently did—in his personal relations and in his business practices—were not the same thing.

When it came time to send my sister and me to school, my parents choose an elite public school with a student body that was predominantly Jewish.

My mother would probably have preferred a Catholic school, but her prerogatives in the religious field did not go that far. Dad thought a Catholic school education might be fine for saving one's soul but less than adequate for the more mundane process of making a living. "What could a nun know about making a buck?" he asked with a chuckle. Years later his children were to shatter this illusion.

Both my parents valued education. Dad had attended Temple University at night, taking a variety of business courses. Mother was a high school graduate who worked as a secretary prior to her marriage. Thereafter she focused her considerable energies on being wife, mother, and homemaker. At all three, she was superlatively successful.

Mother and Dad were always present to each other, tuned in to what the other was feeling, aware of where the other was. He may have dominated her (or thought he did), but there is no doubt in my mind that pleasing her was the underlying motive for all he did. As I grew up, I never had the slightest doubt about their love for one another, nor any fear about the stability of their marriage. When the parents of one of my friends got divorced, I was shaken. "You never have to worry," my father told me quite solemnly. "Your mother and I have loved each other too much, too long, for anything like that ever to happen to us."

Nor did I ever question their love for me. It was an affectionate family. We hugged and kissed to say hello, and we hugged and kissed to say good-bye. As a young boy, I always got kissed and tucked into bed at night.

When we were at Ocean City for the summer, we would almost always meet my father's train. I can still remember racing Shirley and Bill down the platform to see who could get the first hug. Dad made a great ritual of this, flamboyantly tossing aside his newspaper to give us his undivided attention. He taught me how to fish and catch crabs. We went to boxing matches and baseball games together. When I was sick, he made me beef tea. Dinner was always an event. It was never catch as catch can. Everybody was expected to be there, and everybody was, even if afterward my father went back to work. Conversation was freewheeling, and there were no holds barred.

Sundays we sometimes took a ride in the family car or went to the duck pond at Swarthmore or frolicked in Fairmont Park.

I was a sapling of a boy, taller and skinnier than most, doing what saplings usually do—reaching for the sun, putting down roots, opening up to breathe in the air, bending with the wind, trying not to break, with no layer of bark to keep me warm in winter or cool in summer. I did not always know what was expected of me, and when I did, I did not always do it. But I liked to please, and I responded to praise.

Mother was always there when I needed her. She picked me up after school and had the cookies and milk waiting when I got home. She always wanted to know how the day went and what I had learned. She liked soul talk and was a good listener. She knew about positive reinforcement. "You're the kindest boy I've ever met," she once told me. But she also knew how to respect my privacy and affirm my independence. She nurtured and unconditionally accepted. She was always there—present, loving, listening.

She created the atmosphere in which my sister, brothers, and I could relate. We fought a lot. But we always communicated. And we always protected each other.

Sometimes now, when my sister and two brothers get together and I listen to their table talk, I marvel at their emotional health, and I think Mother deserves most of the credit. In the beginning she was our only reality, and for years she was our primary reality, and from her we learned that life is good, that it can be trusted, that even when it is shot full with pain and frustration, it is permeated by meaning and purpose, that you can take chances because, even if you fail, in the end it will all work out. At its deepest level, she taught us life is loving, that it can be embraced unconditionally and enjoyed wholeheartedly.

I don't think there is anything more important for a child to learn.

There was nothing passive about my mother. There was a restlessness in her that made her hunger for new and different experiences. She took me deep-sea fishing and got terribly seasick herself. She insisted on holding my head and my hand as the doctor lanced the boils I developed on my scalp one summer. She loved the mothers' clubs at the schools where I went. She not only fed the beggars who came to our door, she enjoyed talking to them. She liked to shop on Marshall Street, a portion of the Jewish ghetto where produce and clothing were sold from carts by the newly arrived. She loved the Eastern European ambience and the medley of diverse tongues. She also loved the bargains. Mother was ambitious for herself, but mostly she was ambitious for us. This gave her an agenda—an unselfish one—and she was not above manipulating my father, or waiting him out, or wearing him down, to fulfill it. Like him, she had an engine that was always throttled up and in gear. She wanted the very best for us.

My father was generous to a fault. One Christmas he handed my mother a roll of ten-dollar bills and said, "You better keep this. If I have it, I will give it away."

My mother took it and, knowing my father's proclivity, she regularly siphoned off other money, until, when it came time to buy another house, she could announce, much to my father's surprise, that she had most of the purchase price. Quietly she had squirreled it away.

How religious faith is transmitted from one generation to another is something of a mystery to me, but somehow or other, my parents succeeded in doing it, despite their differing backgrounds.

My mother usually heard our prayers, but if she was busy, my father happily filled in. We said the Lord's Prayer and the Hail Mary and then prayed for the different members of our family and for our friends by name.

Implicit in all this was the loving closeness of God. He was always there. He cared and He listened. He could be talked to anytime we wanted.

For a time I thought I had to make the sign of the cross in order to tune in; so when I wanted to pray and there were other people around, I developed a sneaky way of doing it so as not to be noticed. But Shirley noticed what I was doing and informed me that making the sign of the cross on the palm of your hand with your thumb worked just as well and could be done so nobody would notice. I tried it and it did work.

Sometimes fear drove me to prayer. I said scared prayers when Mother was late getting home from the store and it was lightning and thundering out and I was afraid she had had an accident with the car. I also said scared prayers the time I went down in a leaky rowboat in Chesapeake Bay and almost drowned because I did not have enough sense to slip out of the clodhoppers I was wearing.

But sometimes I prayed when I was lonely and needed somebody to talk to, and sometimes I prayed when I was happy and just needed to say thank you.

And sometimes I misused prayer. One time Billy and I were raising hell, and Dad chased us through the house to punish us. We barreled into our room and, by the time Dad arrived, we were plopped down by the beds, on our knees, in the position of prayer. In exasperation he threw up his hands and walked out, muttering, "What the hell am I supposed to do about that."

Prayer has always been an important part of my life, because God has always been a significant reality for me. He loves. But He also demands. How I respond to His love and answer His demands, I realized, is deadly serious business, for our actions in this world have eternal consequences in the next one. I learned about heaven and hell at a very early age.

I was seldom spanked by my parents, but they were very clear about the difference between right and wrong and insistent that I act accordingly. I remember after one incident of lying, Dad gave me a good talking-to about telling the truth, no matter what the cost. Another time he made me apologize to someone whom I had treated shabbily.

When I got older, I attended religious instruction classes for public school students at Our Lady of Mercy parish, in preparation for first communion and confession. I didn't like these classes, partially because they cut into my playtime, partially because I was frightened by the nuns, and partially because they were taught catechism-style—memorized answers to pat questions.

But something must have taken, since I have gone to confession and communion regularly ever since.

We used to go to the Saturday matinee at a local moviehouse on Broad Street and then stop off at Our Lady of Mercy church on the way home to go to confession.

Somewhere along the line, I developed a severe case of scruples. Compulsively I began to confess things that weren't sins and to worry that the real sins I had already confessed weren't really forgiven. I was stricken with fear and sometimes went to confession more than once in the same day.

In exasperation one of the priests to whom I confessed said to me, "Look, God's not out to get you. He loves you. Stop this or you'll drive yourself nuts." I stopped.

A functioning family? Yes. An idyllic childhood? Hardly. One uncle committed suicide. Another stole from my father. Still another left his wife and got divorced. On both my mother's and my father's side, uncles were out of work. A number of the neighbors were on relief. Dad frequently had trouble paying the bills. Drunks could be seen weaving down the street, and the druggist on the corner was shot dead during a holdup. The Depression was in full swing, and Joe Louis, the Brown Bomber, was heavyweight champion of the world. Every time he won a fight, the black kids on the next street over would race up and down ours in celebration, throwing milk bottles into the air, while upstairs in bed we pulled the blankets over our heads.

My sister and I were sent to Stephen's Practice School, so named because the student teachers from the adjoining teachers college came there to observe its master teachers in action and, on occasion, to practice on its pupils. My parents chose it because its teachers were the best in the system and its student body especially selected.

At home, I was called Bud or Buddy, a nickname that has clung to me throughout life. But at Stephen's I was called Ellwood, the name I had been baptized and which I shared with my father.

I was a mediocre student until the fifth grade. Then I lucked out. My teacher—a Miss Jesse Grey—was that rarity, a teacher who knew how to inform, stimulate, and inspire, all at the same time.

My year with her did not begin auspiciously. Early in the term, I neglected to do a homework assignment. What was I going to do? Tell her the truth? Not on your life. I decided to steal another kid's homework, erase his name, replace it with mine, and then turn it in. Naturally I got caught. How could I not have been caught? Miss Grey looked me square in the eyes and asked, "Ellwood, why did you do that?" I mumbled that I did not know. I suspect she told my mother at the next parent-teacher meeting. But I never heard another word about it. I expected my mother to rebuke and punish me, but she never did.

That was the low point of my life at Stephen's Practice. I think Miss Grey took me as a special challenge, because she gave me a great deal of attention after that. With her learning became fun. From her I learned that I could excel, that I enjoyed excelling, that to excel I needed to position myself and work hard. She taught me that there were few things I couldn't do if I set my mind to them. "Aim high" was her constant challenge. She believed in me. She motivated and stimulated me. Obviously she saw something in me that I didn't see in myself. She called that something into life, then nurtured, cajoled, and challenged it. She demanded my best, and I did everything I could to give it to her. I was never able to be a mediocre student again.

By eighth grade Mother's persistence paid off, and I made the transition to Catholic school. First, Melrose Academy; then, La Salle High. The years that followed were intellectually uneventful. The Christian Brothers who ran La Salle were good teachers who cared about their students. But I was not really engaged.

I was an adolescent. I had always been tall. But now I sprouted skyward. I was six feet five and a half inches tall by my senior year. Sexual hormones began to course through my body, mystifying, scaring, and delighting me. I began to look at girls in a brand-new way.

Teenage mores were very different in those days. There was no dope. Students might drink beer or wine at home, but nowhere else and never anything stronger. The parishes held weekly dances, but there was a minimum of sexual experimentation. A consistent question in religion class was: Is it wrong to kiss a girl good night? "Snapshot kisses are OK," the Brother answered. "Time exposures can be trouble."

My parents never sat me down for a talk about the birds and the bees. But their rapport with each other made their attitude toward sex crystal clear: It's good, special, to be enjoyed, but only in the context of that permanent and exclusive covenant of love that is marriage. The biological specifics I got on the street corner and from the encyclopedia.

In high school I did not date much. Neither did most of the other kids. Girls were mysterious creatures with bumps who were always giggling. I was a little afraid of them, except for Shirley's classmates, who were a lot of fun, even if they did borrow my clothes for their plays and leave their bobby pins in the pockets. It would be several years before I would be irresistibly drawn to them. During the early years of high school, I was more interested in basketball.

I started to work at one of my father's gas stations the summer I graduated from eighth grade. In varying capacities, I continued to do so for the next eight years. I pumped gas, checking oil and filling radiators, and soon graduated to repairing tires, changing oil, and lubricating cars. I was learning the business from the ground up. I was also learning how to hustle tips. At work I wore overalls, which sometimes became dirty, very dirty. At times I had grease, not only on my hands and under my nails, but on my face and in my hair. I loved getting dirty. My mother hated it, but somehow she resigned herself to it as part of my special rite of passage.

The station where I worked—16th and Fairmount—was located in a business district of Philadelphia's inner city. Two blocks south was Greene Street, at that time the toughest of the poor white sections. Two blocks north was Ridge Avenue, the heart of the black ghetto. Our customers—and my fellow workers—reflected the neighborhood. I loved the mix of people and their colorful earthiness.

There was Ginger, an old circus ventriloquist who operated a cab out of our station. One day, while we were lubricating a hearse, Ginger threw his voice into the coffin carrying back, saying, "Let me out. Let me out." Its driver would not let us finish, he was in such a hurry to get away.

Sometimes when business was slow we would sit around and tell stories. The funniest at this was Slim, a black Alabaman who could neither read nor write but who could wash forty cars a day in his bare feet and recite chapter after chapter of the New Testament.

It was an education in humanity for me, a shattering of naivete, a crash course in the seamier side of the human condition. One day, on a sidewalk in front of our station, a man was pummeling his wife with his fists. I picked up a tire iron, stepped between them, and ordered him to stop. She pushed me away, telling me to mind my own business.

Another time I was propositioned by a pimp for a group of homosexuals. When he came back a second time, I growled, "If you ever come in here again, I'll break every bone in your body."

My father caught the last part of the exchange and said, "That's no way to treat a customer."

As the years went on, I assumed new responsibilities and exercised more and more leadership. I learned how to sell, how to increase business without increasing overhead, how to motivate crews and please customers.

I was having an experience not shared by my classmates, and I was making lots of money. I was good at what I did—I had results to prove it—and I knew it. It was great for a gangling teenage kid who was struggling to say yes to himself.

But the best part of working at the gas station was the relationship with my father that grew out of it.

One day, shortly after I began, my father told off a particularly obnoxious customer with a great burst of obscene eloquence. Then his eyes lighted on me. In troubled surprise, his chin dropped. He recovered and said, with a twinkle in his eye, "Don't you dare tell your mother."

Most often he worked the wholesale warehouse, which was about two miles from the station. But we always drove to and from work together, and he always came down to the station so that we could have lunch together. He was delighted that I plunged into the business and made it my own. He took pleasure in answering my questions, which were usually an incessant string of "whys." He was proud of me and liked to introduce me to his friends. "A chip off the old block," he used to say.

I felt needed, valued, loved. What more could a teenage kid want?

These were the years of World War II.

I sold copies of an extra edition of the newspaper the day Pearl Harbor was bombed and hung on every word of Roosevelt's declaration of war. I plotted the battlefield positions in each theater and studied the silhouettes of the planes flying for both sides. I read everything I could on the conflict and committed to memory the number of divisions, ships, planes, and tanks each side had. I was elated when our side was doing well and sickened when it wasn't.

This was a special time in the United States. Heroism was in the air. The newspapers, radio broadcasts, films, and songs were full of it. Roosevelt and Churchill, De Gaulle and MacArthur both articulated and symbolized it. The young men who were risking their lives on the battlefield were practicing it. And those of us who remained at home were challenged to imitate their selflessness, to give whatever was necessary to spur forward the war effort.

I was not old enough to go into the armed forces. Three of my cousins and one of my uncles did. The sacrifices I was asked to make were minimal by comparison. Yet the demand to give everything, to love to the point of sacrifice, to lay down one's life for something beyond oneself, resonated deep within me. It activated something—Jung would call it the heroic archetype—I have never since been able to shake off.

"There is nothing man desires more than a heroic life," Maritain says. "There is nothing less common to man than heroism."

I do not know what would have happened if I had gone to war. As it is, I still, on quite regular occasions, hear the staccato beat of the hero's drum. I rouse myself and join the march. For a time I am energized by my own enthusiasm and the example of my fellow marchers. Who would not be energized by Gandhi and King, Romero and Popieluszko, Ita Ford and Maura Clark? But then I become tired, and suddenly the other marchers have sprouted warts.

I try to remind myself of that which as an adolescent I could only sense but which as an adult I have learned to articulate: that there are profound psychological, philosophical, and theological truths implicit in the call to heroism; that nothing else can so completely and permanently shatter the stultifying and joyless hammerlock of narcissism on the human psyche; that we find our happiness and fulfillment not by seeking them but by forgetting all about them in seeking the happiness and fulfillment of other people; that we are never so alive as when we are ready to die to promote that which is bigger and more important than ourselves; that the only life worth living is the committed one; that, in short, we find ourselves by giving ourselves.

All my life I have struggled with this challenge and with the fundamental question that underlies it: If living means giving and living fully means giving totally, even to the point of sacrificing one's life, then to what could I give myself? What reality deserves such a total gift? What could justly demand such a sacrifice?

These questions took on a new significance in the light of an experience I had in January of 1944.

I was almost fifteen, midway through my sophomore year of high school. It was about ten-thirty on a cold winter night. After helping with the dinner dishes, I had tackled my homework at the desk in my room. First the geometry, which I liked, then the Shakespearean play, which I tried to get into but couldn't. I gave up fighting the nod and went downstairs to say good night to my parents. Mother was folding clothes. Dad was writing up invoices. I returned to my room, pulled off my clothes, threw them on the chair by the desk, and slipped into my pajamas. With a jolt I opened the frosted-over window and felt the arctic air hit my face. Looking out, I could see most of the windows were dark in the houses across the driveway. A trolley rattled along the tracks on Ogontz Avenue. In the shadows of our yard, I could see the next-door neighbor's dog taking a leak against the tree. I turned back and pulled down the covers on my bed. At its head was a crucifix. On the walls were maps of Europe and the Pacific; pictures of General George Patton, the conqueror of Sicily; Admiral Bill Halsey, the victor at Midway; West Point's All-American running backs, Doc Blanchard and Glenn Davis; and World War II posters. One of the posters contained a picture of a freighter going down in the Atlantic with a U-boat's periscope in the foreground and a finger pointing accusingly at the onlooker with the caption "Who blabbed?"

I turned off the radiator, which was hissing. On its cover were some beakers and glass tubing I had just bought for my chemistry lab in the cellar. By it, on the floor, was a sweaty Marine Corps T-shirt, which we used for basketball uniforms.

I switched off the overhead light and was about to kneel by my bed to say my night prayers when it happened. Suddenly I seemed surrounded by an all-encompassing silence. I felt the presence of something greater than myself. Wonder and awe suffused my body and lit up my face. I went to my knees and turned inside. How to describe what happened then? An earthquake within me. A bursting into consciousness of what had apparently long been in my unconscious. An eruption of the Ground of Being, surfacing from the depths so as to grasp hold of me. A speaking of His Word within me. A breathing forth of His Spirit inside me. And words that surfaced into consciousness, clear as a bell. "I am called." Not "You are called," as if someone outside of me were telling me something. But "I am called," because the words did not come from outside me but from such a depth within me that they came from beyond me. Subject communicating with subject as hand in glove.

The fundamentalists would say I was being born again, the Pentecostals that I was being baptized in the Holy Spirit.

There was no doubt in my mind then, nor is there now, that God was the author of this experience: He was drawing me to Himself in a new and fuller way, and He was giving me a job to do; just what I didn't quite know.

God's ways are not our ways, and His dealings with us are full of mysterious surprises. But this was more than a mysterious surprise. It was to be surprised by a Mystery. It was to be grasped hold of by *the* Mystery, in whom we all live and move and have our being.

I could not understand the Mystery then, nor can I now. But what was being asked of me then—and now—was not understanding. It was surrender—a letting go—an acceptance of the Mystery's love for me, a response to it, a giving of myself in love to the Mystery, a blank check for the Mystery to work in me and through me.

At the time the experience was so powerful that I seemed to

have little choice about saying yes. But like all ecstatic experiences in this world, this one was transitory. It passed, and once it did I had the hard job of ratifying it, of incorporating this new realization into my day-to-day living. I had said yes. I would continue to try to say yes. But sometimes it became a "yes, but," or a "yes and no," or "it all depends"—and sometimes it became a straight "No! You're asking too much."

It was a blessing—I have no doubt of that—but there would be times in the future when it would feel like a curse. In some radical way it marked me, made me special. I was never to be the same again.

Several weeks later I told my mother I wanted to be a priest. She gulped and said, "You better not tell your Dad."

As a child my mother had contracted rheumatic fever and it had left her heart with severe mitral valve damage. At that time the doctors had told her she would never be able to bear children. She fooled them. But now, in the spring and summer of 1944, in her forty-fifth year, the inefficiencies of a damaged heart began to take their toll. Twice that summer the doctor was forced to put her in the hospital. Twice she snapped back. In between she and my father had purchased a new and better house and had organized the moving process. Then it was necessary to put her in the hospital a third time. Even after her ankles began to swell, I had no realization how sick she was. On the evening of September 14, my father and I were visiting her in the hospital. She was sitting on the edge of the bed, chatting with us, when she simply keeled over and was gone.

Writing this more than forty years later, I remember being asked to leave the room while the young intern examined her. I remember a young priest in sneakers sprinting down the corridor to give her the sacrament of the sick. And I remember my Dad telling me she was dead.

I also remember that I did not—could not—cry. I did not cry then, nor when we went home and told Shirley, Bill, and Don. Nor did I cry during the wake or funeral. I wanted to cry. I had always cried in the past. Now I felt guilty because everybody else was crying and I could not. Was there something wrong with me? Didn't I love my mother?

I still do not understand why. Crying would have been such a release, a cleansing of my emotions. But for some reason, I could not do it. I know there is a sorrow too deep for tears. I know it is possible to be so stunned by a calamity that one is unable to respond emotionally. Was I traumatized by the loss, in a state of shock? Did I feel I had to suppress the emotion in order to keep going? I do not know. What I do know is that I was not able to cry. Nor was I able to cry at any time for the next thirty-five years. And then the tears would come only after I had traveled to the other side of this planet and been immersed in a tragedy of catastrophic proportions. It was not that I could not feel pain. I felt plenty. But I just could not express it in that way.

Mother had poured her love and tenderness, support and affirmation, encouragement and affection into me. You might think she gave me enough nurturing for a lifetime, and in a way she did. But it did not feel that way at the time. Her death left a gaping hole within me.

But my sense of loss was minuscule when compared to my father's.

His friends, customers, and neighbors rallied around him. One of his Jewish customers gave him a signed check with the amount left blank and told him, "I know this is a tough time. Use this any way you want."

But they could not give him what she did. They could not fill his heart, share his life, or focus his energies as she had. Mother was the foundation on which Dad's psyche rested. Because of her, he could be buoyant, vibrant, full of confidence. Deprived of her, he collapsed inside.

My father was a giant redwood. But he was totally dependent on the bed of roots that was my mother, a bed of roots that was sunk deeply in the ground, nourishing him and giving him security, strength, and vitality. When the bed died, the tree wilted. My father, who had always seemed so strong, now faltered. Consumed by grief, it seemed he might come apart.

That fall I worried about him a great deal. Somehow I felt I needed to be strong because he no longer seemed to be that way. Was my appearance of strength authentic? Not really. How could it be? I was an adolescent—more boy than man. It conveyed what I wanted to be, not what I was. Certainly I was pulled into the vacuum left by my mother's death and my father's collapse and asked to assume new and fuller responsibilities.

On one occasion, not knowing the full implications of what I was saying, I asked him if crying might not help him handle his grief. He put an arm around me and said, "Bud, I cry every day. Sometimes for hours. I just don't let anybody see it." One weekend he felt he had reached the breaking point and had to get away —to what? a binge, a nightclub, a woman—I do not know. But then I got sick and he had to care for me and the moment passed. Some strong man.

I had good friends at school and in the neighborhood, but it was a hard time. Very hard.

My younger brother Don was sent to Norwood Academy, a private Catholic boarding school, and my sister Shirley was away at Chestnut Hill College, coming home only on weekends, so I was in charge of the house and usually, with Bill's help, did most of the cooking.

Externally I was being stretched. But internally chasms were opening up within me as I became aware of huge new areas of myself that previously I had not known existed. Gone were the comfortable complacencies of the past. I was forced to look at things that before I had blocked from consciousness. I was also forced to let go of things that I had taken for granted but which now no longer seemed real. And I was forced to go places inside myself that before I had shunned.

What could I depend on? Nothing. This realization forced me to look at myself in a new way. We exist. That's certain. But like the most fragile of cobwebs, we needn't exist. That's also certain. Our hold on life is very precarious, so nothing is safe, sure, secure.

This realization caused new feelings to burst into my consciousness—not only loneliness and fear, guilt and futility, but also doubt and despair, need and desire, frustration and yearning.

I had more questions than answers.

I had more desires than objects to fulfill them.

I had more needs, deeper ones, than things to satisfy them.

I was in pieces. I needed a center about which all else could revolve.

I was tossed this way and that. I needed something in which I could root my life.

Like the streetcar, my name was desire. I ached with incompleteness. I felt empty, alone, insecure, scared, and confused. I groped for something to fulfill me.

The birth of subjectivity? Yes, and more. I was growing up. I was starting to deal with the reality of the human condition, *my* human condition. I was becoming a person, a frustrated and needy one, for sure, but a person nevertheless.

But what did I need? What could satisfy me? Could anything give me the completion, the fulfillment, the wholeness I desired? These were the questions that preoccupied me as I graduated from La Salle High School and entered La Salle College.

CHAPTER 2

COLLEGE STUDENT

My going to La Salle College was the result of a nondecision.

I was still very worried about my father. Some months after my mother's death, he started to go out with Anne Weber, whom he had known as a girl in the neighborhood where they had both grown up. Their friendship blossomed into romance, and for a time their love for each other picked him up and restored his zest in life.

I was their best man when they were married by a Protestant minister on October 20, 1945.

Immediately after the ceremony, my father suggested I call her "Mother." I refused, as did my sister and brothers. We had only one mother, and Anne Weber wasn't she.

We did not make it easy for her. But she did not make it easy for us either. A professional woman, rigidly set in her ways, Lutheran and very, very Germanic—it takes one to know one—she was forty-six years old when she married my father. This was her first marriage and so her first experience of family life since her own girlhood.

How could anyone have realistically expected her to adjust gracefully, not only to my father but to his four unruly kids, all of whom had minds of their own and argued just for the hell of it? It would have taken the flexibility and selflessness of a saint, and Anne was blessed with neither quality.

She liked things neat, clean, and orderly. The only trouble was, teenage kids are never neat, clean, and orderly and we were worse than most. She did not like us to come home from work in our overalls. "Do you have to get so dirty?" she asked impatiently.

Mud on the shoes was a mortal sin. If cleanliness was next to godliness, we were already deep in hell.

She bought new rugs and furniture for the house. It looked nice. But then she did not want us walking on the new rug or sitting in the new furniture. The living room was no longer for living. It was for looking. She loved to show it off to her friends. We were told to come in through the cellar, where she installed a shower.

We loved to argue at the dinner table. Along with Ping-Pong, it was our favorite indoor sport. She had trouble understanding a clash of ideas and treated every disagreement as mortally serious. It was possible to get her to laugh, but it took a major effort. No one would ever accuse her of being jolly.

All of which is to say that we did not have much in common. Dad was a Roosevelt Democrat. By the end of high school, I liked Henry Wallace. Shirley was somewhere in between. Anne was a right-wing Republican, an isolationist in the manner of Robert Taft. She hated Roosevelt. She sold Roosevelt dimes for a nickel, and the night he died, she invited her friends over to celebrate.

Dad did not seem able to address the situation. He was good at telling off obnoxious customers, but he seemed incapable of confronting those he loved. If he wanted to tell me to shape up, he usually did so through my sister. I was the conduit for similar messages to her and my brothers. Apparently he had no way to communicate with Anne about the things that were causing problems. It was not a healthy situation. Tensions increased, especially between Shirley and Anne, until finally in the spring of 1946, caught in the middle, my father suffered a kind of emotional collapse.

He went to see a psychiatrist. He did not think much of the advice he got until the doctor charged him twenty-five dollars—an astronomical sum in those days. Then he felt he had better follow it, just to get his money's worth.

I took over the running of the business while he tried to recoup his energies.

It was not an ideal situation in which to choose the site of my higher education. There was no question about my going on to college. That was a given. But where? I could hardly leave home, given the family situation. And this was 1946. The veterans were returning en masse from the war, and many were using the GI Bill of Rights to enter the nation's colleges and universities. Most were swamped. Admission was far from automatic. Why not just cross the campus and matriculate at La Salle College? It was the easy way out. But, providentially, it was also the smartest thing I could have done. For me, La Salle was the right school at the right time, partially because it was so similar to, yet so radically different from, anything I had ever known before.

La Salle High was a superbly organized elite prep school taught exclusively by the Christian Brothers and attended by upper-middle-class kids who were required to wear a coat and tie and got a report card every week. La Salle College in 1946 was just the opposite. Trying frantically to cope with a student body that was mushrooming from two hundred to two thousand, it was anything but organized. The faculty was almost exclusively lay. Most of the students were recently discharged veterans from lower-middle-class or poor homes.

But what they lacked in folding money, they made up in life experience. Plucked from their families and bonded with men from vastly different backgrounds, they had been plunked down in all parts of the world and forced to immerse themselves in its variety of cultures. And they had fought a war, many of them having seen combat, some having been wounded, others having killed or seen their buddies killed beside them. One of my classmates, a Marine tank driver, had the brains of his best friend sprayed all over him when their tank was hit on the second day of the invasion of Okinawa. The emotions they had known ran the gamut from horror and revulsion to intense camaraderie and joyful exultation, and the compressed emotional charges they carried within their unconsciousnesses were deep, potent, and itching for outlet.

Most were not prepared for school. And the way they expressed their maladjustment and released those emotional charges was through storytelling. They loved to tell stories. And I loved to listen to them. We sat in the cafeteria by the hour, smoked dozens of cigarettes, and drank quarts of coffee as they swapped stories. Funny stories. Stories filled with pathos. Stories that could only be called tragic.

It was their way of making sense of what they had been through and as a green eighteen-year-old kid, it was my way of tapping into their reservoir of experience and nurturing myself with it.

I cut few classes my freshman and sophomore years, and I had some excellent teachers, but my great learning experiences were not in the classroom, nor in the library where I did my reading, but in the cafeteria, where I feasted upon their stories.

I could only sense then what now I can articulate—that experience precedes reflection, that life is prior to thought, that the question must be asked before the answer can be heard, that books are a good way to discover the meaning of life but are no substitute for living it, and that, not infrequently, stories are the most effective way to discern, distill, and communicate the whys of human existence.

With these stories, life flooded in on me. So did reality. Sometimes it seemed more than I could handle, and my system went on overload. Once in class I must have had a look of consternation on my face, because the teacher said to me, "Ellwood, what's wrong?"

"I'm confused," I replied.

"Oh ho," he shot back, rubbing his hands together enthusiastically. "We're making progress."

Confusion was something I felt a lot of during those first two years of college. I was not alone in this respect. Most of my classmates were also confused. They were trying to sort out and assimilate their wartime experiences and the new academic environment in which they found themselves. Their adjustment was certainly more difficult than mine, and so their confusion was frequently deeper and more pervasive. But I had my hands full. I tried to figure them out, and I struggled to make sense of the wider and more penetrating view of the world that they were sharing with me. I was also trying to integrate the things I was learning in class, my new responsibilities at home and at work, an awakening sexuality, an ambivalent awareness of being called to the priesthood, the collapse of the parental supports of my psychic security, as well as the usual adolescent concerns about who I was, what I wanted to live for, how I was going to seek acceptance and achievement.

Coping with reality is no laughing matter, and confusion is no fun. I did not like it then. I do not like it now. I was able to work my way through it only because I was part of a community—a network of concerned and truth-seeking people who understood what I was going through, encouraged me when I faltered, yet who challenged me to be honest with myself at every step along the way.

La Salle supplied me with that kind of community. Its lifeblood was free and open dialogue. Any problem could be raised and any question could be asked. "Tell it like it is" was its modus operandi. Only pretense, pomposity, and phoniness were not tolerated. This applied to the bull sessions in the cafeteria and lounge. But it also applied to the classroom. Nothing was off-limits. We were filled with questions, mostly the personal, existential kind: Who am I? Where did I come from? Where am I going? What am I supposed to be doing with this life of mine? Where can I find the happiness and fulfillment I desire?—and we sought answers with a persistence and intensity that must have exhausted our teachers.

If religion is the deepest dimension of the human situation, as Paul Tillich tells us, and if the religious person is the person who is concerned about ultimate things, then I think we must say that religion was the essence of these discussions.

This was not because of the religion classes we were required to take. They were dreadful. Most were taught by Christian Brothers, who were good and holy men but not the professionally trained theologians we needed. It was because of the nature of the questions themselves, the depths from which they sprang, and the anguish with which we asked them. And it was because of the preexistent faith of most of those articulating the questions and groping for the answers, whether students or teachers. We believed in God, and so we wanted to understand our relationship to Him. The deeper our faith, the livelier and more persistent our questions.

Not that there were not times when we doubted. There were plenty of those. When I was depressed, God seemed very far away. When I was lonely, His love seemed a mirage. When I did something I shouldn't, He seemed like a stern old tyrant with darting eyes who was looking for an excuse to send me to hell. There were times I seriously questioned the existence of God, times when I wondered if He could really care about me, times when I doubted that the priests, nuns, and brothers knew what they were talking about when they told me about Him.

God was up for grabs at La Salle in those years. But He was part of the mix. We argued with Him. We told Him off. We put him on trial. Sometimes we insulted Him to His face. But we did not ignore Him. He was the hub about which so many of our bull sessions revolved.

In this communal atmosphere of free dialogue and honest questioning, I became ravenous for the truth. Not just any truth. But the truth about people, the human truth, and in the most intimate and personal sense, the truth about me. I wanted to understand myself, to discover who I was and why I was feeling the things I was. My emotions ran wild. Sometimes I was elated; at other times, discouraged and depressed. Often I felt in pieces inside, one facet of my being wanting this, a contrary facet wanting that. Yet I could not have both, for they were incompatible. So I felt much tension and inner conflict.

I was incomplete. But I did not know what could complete me. I was empty. Yet I did not know what could fulfill me. I needed something. But I did not know what. I had something to give. But I didn't know what it was, or how to give it, or to whom. I felt a capacity for commitment, an ability to give myself in a total and absolute way. Yet I did not know how to actualize this capacity or to what I could authentically give myself. I felt an intense and compelling desire. But for what? What could satisfy these cravings of mine? To what could I deservedly give myself? These were the questions I wrestled with.

And then, in the spring of 1947, two things happened that were to prove of decisive importance. Charles Kelly, my teacher in English composition, assigned a term paper. Three thousand words in length, it could be on anything we felt deeply about.

Looking for something to write about, I shared my questions with Shirley, who was now a senior at Chestnut Hill College. Afraid that I was becoming an agnostic, she suggested I read one of her philosophy books, Étienne Gilson's *The Spirit of Medieval Philosophy*. It was heavy going but worth the effort, until I came to one of its later chapters, "Love and Its Object," which I found captivating. It spoke to me right where I was. It directly addressed the questions I wrestled with, and it answered them with an intellectual cogency that I found irresistible.

Tapping the best of the medieval philosophers, Gilson argued that we have been made in such a way that only a God of Infinite Being could satisfy the infinite desires we find within ourselves; that only a God who is Pure Existence could actualize the existential capacities that stalk about in restless need inside our hearts; that only a God who is absolute love could give us the love we need and want; that only a transcendent God could honestly demand and deserve the absolute gift, the unconditional love we need to give if we are to fulfill ourselves; that every love of ours for a creature, even the most debased, is a love of God, a craving for the absolute, a reaching for the infinite in and through that creature, even if, at the time, we are unaware of what it is that is our love's ultimate object; that apart from God, alienated from Him, we are condemned to frustration and nonfulfillment.

Gilson quoted St. Augustine's prayer, "Thou has made us for Thyself, O Lord, and our hearts are restless until they rest in Thee," and I heard echoes of Jesus' words: "The man who loses his life will find it; the man who seeks to save his life will lose it."

I wrote the term paper on what Gilson helped me discover—that God alone can fill the aching void we find within ourselves, that we need Him, that apart from Him, we are incomplete and unhappy.

Reading it over now, forty years later, I realize that studying Gilson and writing that paper were providential for me. With it things began to come together, and a new synthesis took form. In that paper I was honing in on the central insight of my life and beginning to construct a framework that would give shape to everything else. I was articulating the theme that would pervade everything I would do, a motif that would recur again and again in different forms in the years ahead.

Another thing happened that first year at La Salle. I fell in love. Her name was Clair. Pretty, with dark hair and an extremely sensitive face atop a well-proportioned body, she was dating a friend of mine. I started taking her out to lunch. Then he dropped away, and I began to see a great deal of her.

I always tried to be honest with her. I shared my questions and my doubts. But also my intentions concerning the priesthood. That was the context in which we related, at least on the conscious level. What was going on in each of our unconsciousnesses, I am not sure. But I suspect much more than either of us knew at the time.

I did not fall in love with her all at once. It happened in stages. At first I think I was in love with love. But before long my love became completely centered on her. I began to feel things I had never felt before. They were gloriously exuberant feelings, and I rejoiced in them.

She was bright and sensitive and idealistic and liked to talk about the things I did. I could share with her what I was thinking and reading and feeling, and she understood and reciprocated.

She was Italian and only nominally Catholic, so one of my challenges was to sort through her ambivalence. We complemented each other. I was high-energy and aggressive and she was laid-back and serene, so she seemed to possess the very qualities I most lacked. I projected my ideal woman upon her, and she gracefully tried to carry that unfair load.

In the fall of 1947, she went away to Penn State. As a result, over the next three years, our relating was limited to the summers, holidays, the U.S. mails, and telephone calls. Absence only made the heart grow fonder.

I dated other women during this period. Clair dated other men as well. But she was my emotional center of gravity, *the* woman in my life. We wrote and we talked on the phone and when I got too lonely, I would go to see her folks, who accepted me as a son. I eagerly anticipated her visits and peaked emotionally when she came home. Sometimes we went to the theater, but most often we stayed home and talked. With her I felt complete, alive, whole. Apart from her, I felt incomplete. My emotional swings were wilder than usual—intense joy when we were together, despondency the first couple of days after she left. Was I depressed or just exhausted? I don't know. What I do know is I was in love and it was wonderful.

Somehow she put the seal of authenticity on Gilson's thesis. What he was talking about philosophically, she was helping me experience emotionally. In loving her I was loving God, in her and through her. In opening myself to her love, I was allowing God to love me in her and through her. She was my point of contact with God, my entree into His life, the flash point where I experienced His love. For hours on end I spoke of these feelings to her. It was our way of sharing affection and making love. Sometimes I couldn't tell where my feelings for her ended and prayer began. Both were of a piece. Reverence was one of the emotions I consistently felt in her presence.

Was this sublimated sex? Of course. But none the less authentic for that reason. We were not sleeping together. Which meant our erotic energies were not being given that outlet. So they sought out this other avenue of expression. Was this unhealthy? I don't think so. We found great freedom and joy as a consequence.

By the end of sophomore year, I began to settle down. So did most of my peers. We had adjusted to college life. And the college had learned to cope with us in a reasonably ordered way.

But, saturated with war stories, I began to look around for some new outlet for my energies.

I started to write for the college newspaper—*The Collegian*—usually book reviews and editorials, and I became active in student politics by joining La Salle's chapter of the National Student Association. In the spring of 1949 I was elected chairman of La Salle's NSA committee, which gave me the platform, the position of leadership, and the sense of achievement I had been craving. It also gave me a lab in the give-and-take of political action—a place where I learned that authority means service, that power follows contribution, that the secret of success in leading people is to find out what they need and do your best to give it to them.

At the end of my sophomore year, I had to select a major. Philosophy was my first choice, but La Salle at that time had no such major, so I chose to major in English yet take every philosophy course La Salle offered. I chose English because, like philosophy, it addressed the questions that haunted me, because the English faculty was especially good, and because it was La Salle's most demanding major. At the core of its curriculum was the reading list course, which meant that over two years, starting with Beowulf and ending with Hemingway and Faulkner, I would be required to read almost everything of quality that had ever been written in the English language. It averaged out to four books a week. I wanted a challenge, and I hoped this would give it to me. It was an inspired choice.

Gone was the drudgery of the past. Every course had its own excitement, and each one spoke to me where I lived. Each fed into the bull sessions that continued late into the night in the cafeteria, *The Collegian* office, and my room. Many of these discussions concerned the restructuring of society so that it could be more responsive to the dignity of its members.

The classroom and the bull sessions were my most authentic experience of church in those days. We would not have called it that, but now I recognize it for what it was. The Spirit of God was there, and we were wrestling with Him. We believed. But we needed to work out what that meant, what God was asking of us, what the world needed from us.

My parish at the time—St. Theresa's—was little more than a sacramental filling station. I went to Mass there on Sundays and sometimes during the week and I went to confession there. But that was it. There was no sense of community, the old-fashioned liturgy was deadening, and more often than not the sermons were appalling. I swore then that if I ever became a priest, I would do my best never to give sermons like those.

Then I made a startling discovery. The best of my philosophy teachers—Yvonne Blanchard—had taken his doctorate in France and was filled with the intellectual and pastoral ferment that characterized the French Church at that time. Emerging from the Nazi occupation, the concentration camps, and the Resistance, the French Church had been forced to face some unpleasant realities. It had lost a good portion of the educated elite to the atheistic existentialism of Sartre and de Beauvoir. It had lost most of the working class to the militant Marxists. Only the peasants were still loyal to the Church, and there were fewer and fewer of them as France became more and more urbanized. The eldest daughter of the Church had become a pagan.

It was a shocking realization, but to its credit, the French Church did not try to duck it. It mobilized its not inconsiderable resources for a counterattack. On the intellectual front, the priest theologians Henri De Lubac, Yves Congar, and Teilhard de Chardin and the philosophers Jacques Maritain, Gabriel Marcel, and Étienne Gilson led the charge. Their approach was more irenic than polemical. They listened to their opponents with sympathy and tried to get inside their minds and hearts, so as to understand what they saw and why they saw it the way they did. Whether the opponent was an existentialist or a Marxist, they always sought out the common ground, affirming that portion of their opponent's truth with which they could agree and those values of his which they could call authentically human. Starting from the areas of agreement, they would then move on to the areas of disagreement, presuming the very best intentions in their adversaries and giving them the benefit of the doubt at every step along the way. They not only taught Christianity, but they did so in a very Christian way.

This was particularly true of Maritain. A French Protestant who had studied under Bergson, he and his wife Raïssa were helped into the Church by the novelist Léon Bloy. Maritain's were the books that provided the inspiration for the Christian Democratic politicians of Europe—Alcide de Gasperi of Italy, Georges Bidault of France, and Konrad Adenauer of Germany—in the immediate postwar period. A later generation of Christian Democratic politicians in Latin America drew upon him. He became my philosophic mentor. I devoured his books. Whether he wrote on metaphysics or politics, aesthetics, education, or prayer, he did so with a breadth of vision and depth of insight that I found compelling. Unlike Gilson, whose style was objective and abstractly conceptual, he had an experiential way of writing that not only fed my mind but nurtured my soul. With the reader he shared not only his ideas, but his search for the truth, his excitement at discovering it, and his experience of integrating it into his overall vision. Maritain not only saw the truth, but he loved it and he helped his readers, especially this one, love it, too.

When I was ordained, I wrote to Maritain, who was then retired at Princeton, telling him of my indebtedness, inviting him to my first Mass, and letting him know he would be part of any good I might be able to accomplish. He responded, declining the invitation but warmly wishing me well.

Passing through Princeton several weeks later, I got off the turnpike and called him.

"I am in town," I said tentatively, "and wondered if I might drop over."

"Of course. Of course," he replied. "But Raïssa is ill. She would so much like to meet you."

A servant answered the door and invited me in. The living room looked lived in. It was warm, human, with French provincial furniture and line drawings on the walls. Books were everywhere. I was a little nervous. After reading so many of his books, looking at life through his eyes, nourishing my mind on his, I did not know what to expect.

We shook hands when he entered and took a long look at each other. Perhaps a long look *into* each other would be more accurate. He was reading me, and I was trying to do the same to him. Physically, he was not impressive—short, stoop-shouldered, with white hair and a goatee. But in manner, he was genial, almost pixie-like, with an easy smile and a sweetness of spirit I found attractive. As we talked I could see he was a luminous person who gave off a light that resided in him but which came from beyond him. He also radiated peace and joy. He was worried about Raïssa, but he was not torn up about her condition. I had the impression that somehow he had come to terms with both life and death, with all of reality, and with God. In no way was his surrender to the Lord ambivalent. He was whole and holy—a transparent person.

We talked about prayer—about when in the interior life it is advisable to abandon the practice of active meditation in favor of the passivity of contemplative prayer.

"There's no objectively certain way to tell," he said, shaking his head. "Just the individual's own sense of where the Spirit is leading. And, of course, how he's fulfilling the duties of his state in life. Is he more faithful and hardworking, humbler and more loving as a result?"

He told me a story of a Russian saint who was called in to consult about a monk who was having visions. The monk's superiors did not know what to make of him. Were the visions authentic or not? The saint went to see him. Arriving at the monastery, he asked the monk with the visions to help him off with his boots.

"Humpf," said the monk. "What do you think I am? Take off your own boots."

"With that," Maritain said with a chuckle, "the saint had the answer to his question."

As we said good-bye, he dropped to his knees and asked for my blessing. A humbling thrill for a young priest who owed so much to the man who knelt before him.

Bloy was also very important to me. His books—*The Woman Who Was Poor* and *The Pilgrim of the Absolute*—preached the kind of radical Christianity I was looking for.

The second thrust of the French Church's counterattack was pastoral. If the workers wouldn't come to the Church, the Church would go to the workers. With the enthusiastic support of Cardinal Suhard, scores of French priests doffed their cassocks and collars and took jobs in the factories, mills, and mines of France. Their purpose: to create a presence for the Church in the workplace and establish rapport with the workers on their own turf. Thus was born the priest worker movement.

It was an audacious move. Although ultimately destined for tragedy, it captured the imagination of the world. I was fascinated by it, gobbled up everything that was written about the priest workers, and wrote an article for *The Collegian* on them.

I cannot walk the streets of Paris today without being haunted by the ghosts of those courageous men and of the philosophers, theologians, poets, and novelists who inspired them—Jacques and Raïssa Maritain, Charles Peguy, Léon Bloy, François Mauriac, Teilhard de Chardin, Cardinal Suhard, Henri De Lubac, and Yves Congar. They were to join the German, Austrian, and Swiss theologians who conquered the universal Church in Vatican II. But first they conquered me. I am a child of the postwar, radicalized French Church.

If Jacques Maritain was my philosophic mentor, Thomas Merton was my spiritual one. Born in France of American parents, he studied at Cambridge early in World War II, took a master's degree at Columbia under Mark Van Doren, became a Catholic, and entered the Trappist monastery at Gethsemane, whence he wrote his autobiographical book *The Seven Storey Mountain,* which I reviewed for *The Collegian* shortly after it was published in 1948. Intensely introspective and acutely sensitive by temperament, he brought the gifts of the poet and novelist to the description of the spiritual search and the analysis of spiritual experience.

His approach, like Maritain's, was wholistic. He was not content to see the realities of the spiritual world. He wanted to experience them. Once he had done so, he was able to write about those realities in such a way that his readers could experience them, too.

Merton was in so many ways such a contemporary man, but he was also a mystic who chose to work at his mysticism in the Trappists, which is one of the Church's strictest and most traditional orders. I had to ask why. The choice was obviously the right one for him, since he had found great joy in it. Couldn't I perhaps do the same thing?

For two decades it seemed he would face a crisis, work it through, and write a book about it just in time to help me weather a similar storm. His accidental death in Bangkok in 1968 has left a hole in my life. I miss Thomas Merton. He was my older brother, and we were traveling companions. No other spiritual writer has meant so much. None has been able to take his place.

Another hero of mine during this period was Bishop Fulton J. Sheen. Superbly educated, theatrical by temperament, Sheen was a pulpit orator of rare eloquence, an apologist of great persuasiveness, an aggressive polemicist with those he considered the Church's enemies—Marxist-leaning liberals and religiously closed intellectuals. He was *the* priest of the rich, the famous, and the powerful, both those inside and those outside the Church; the author of consistently bestselling books; the convert maker par excellence, who helped hundreds of influential people into the Church; and the first and perhaps the greatest of the TV evangelists, whose weekly show "Life Is Worth Living" topped the Nielsens when it played on the old DuMont network in prime time against Milton Berle.

Undoubtedly some of his popularity was due to the inferiority complex that afflicted the Catholic population during that period. The sentiments of my sociology teacher were typical: "We may not be as educated as the liberals, as powerful as the Protestant establishment, as rich and cultivated as the snobs from the Main Line, Westchester, and Silver Springs, and they may think we are not fully American because we're Irish or Italian or German or Polish, but Fulton Sheen is our boy, and he is smarter than they are and more cultivated and glamorous and powerful and more patriotic, too, because he's more anti-Communist. He can take the competition into their own backyards—meeting the rich and famous and powerful on their own turf—and he can beat them. He does beat them. Look at all those converts."

Jack Kennedy benefited from the same psychology. Thank God it has now passed into history, but it was a real factor in the early fifties.

I liked Sheen because he carried the Gospel into the heart of the secular. He addressed the world on its own terms. He may have been overly theatrical, but there was nothing churchy about him. He was a missionary.

In retrospect, I can see that there was something of the apostolic warrior bent on spiritual conquest in all of this, a touch of aggressive and self-righteous religious imperialism. But I bought into it—all the way. Bishop Sheen was a very important role model in my life during those days. If I was to become a priest, I wanted to be like him.

I tried but I couldn't forget that experience in my sophomore year of high school when those words—"I am called"—surfaced from the deepest levels of my unconscious. I couldn't forget because my soul still resonated to them. But I wanted to forget them, I tried to forget them, because there were many times when the whole idea of a priestly vocation was abhorrent to me. In the journal I kept at the time I remember calling it a "scourge." This was something God wanted. But it was not something I wanted. I wanted to be just like everybody else. I wanted a career. I wanted to write novels and become famous and make lots of money. I wanted a home and children, and most of all I wanted a wife to share my life with, to be there for me, to understand me and pull me outside myself and give me the joy of forgetting all about myself in seeking the happiness of someone else. I wanted a warm body beside me in bed, someone to make love with, someone I could touch and caress and fondle, someone who would touch and caress and fondle me, someone I could give myself to physically, someone who would physically give herself to me.

I wanted someone to sleep with. I needed someone to sleep with. I was not at all sure I could live out my whole life in fullness without that someone to sleep with. I was not at all sure I wanted to.

So I was in great conflict, torn this way and that.

My family knew it. My Dad was very respectful of my freedom. He would support me in anything I chose. But silently, I am sure, he was hoping I would decide against the priesthood. Once he told me that Catholic seminaries were filled with poor kids who were there because it was the only way they could get an education. Once he told my sister that I must have decided to become a priest because I had promised my mother I would. Little did he know that she had discouraged me.

My friends also knew I was deeply conflicted. They sympathized and supported and sometimes they protected me in ways I did not want.

Once, during my senior year, with Clair unable to come down from Penn State, I took a lovely senior from Chestnut Hill College to one of our school dances. She was beautiful and charming, and there was a great deal of chemistry between us. I made no secret of my attraction, and she was ardent in her response.

But after intermission, during which time she went to the ladies' room, I noticed a considerable cooling of her ardor. Days later, I learned that one of our mutual friends, noticing the attraction between us, had told her of my dilemma. A devout Catholic, she was not about to get between me and God.

But what to do? God seemed to want one thing. I seemed to want something else. We argued a lot. He wouldn't budge. Neither would I. It seemed like a standoff. Yet the more I argued with God, the more unhappy I became. What was I going to do?

Sometime early in my college career, I came across a pamphlet on the Paulists, an American religious community that had been founded by Isaac Hecker, a friend of Emerson's and Thoreau's who had become a Catholic and joined four other American converts to establish the Paulists as an American order dedicated to the service of American unbelievers, carrying the Good News to those who have yet to hear it, reaching for the lonely, alienated, and rejected, establishing friendly relationships with the Protestants and Jews.

The spirituality of the Paulists is characteristically American. The stress is on individual initiative and freedom. The Holy Spirit works in the individual's soul, leading him to greater intimacy with God and new and more creative ways of spearheading the Church's thrust of love and service to the secular world.

I read the pamphlet and knew intuitively that if the priesthood was right for me, then the Paulists were the right communal context for me to live and work as a missionary priest.

It was a providential realization. The Paulists were right for me; how fully right I would only know as the years went on. In retrospect I don't think I could have survived the chaos of the post–Vatican II period in the secular clergy or in any other religious order. Nor, I suspect, would any other order have been able to survive me.

I also think I gravitated toward the Paulists because I sensed that they would appeal to my father, that he would understand and appreciate their spirit, style of living, and work more fully than he could any other order.

But still the question remained: What did I want to do? What did God want me to do? How could I reconcile the difference?

I prayed and I prayed, and I began to realize that when you argue with God, you lose. You always lose, because He knows what's best for us, better than we do. He wants our happiness more than we do. So, instead of arguing, I tried to listen and let go and turn it over and surrender. But I didn't succeed. Like the "Indian giver" I am, I kept taking back the gift. But then I would try to make it again. I visited the Paulist House of Studies in Washington and liked what I saw. I visited the novitiate at Oak Ridge, New Jersey, the spring of my senior year and told the novice master—Father Bob Murphy—of my ambivalence. He did not seem surprised. "If I enter in August," I asked, "how long will it take for me to know whether or not I have this thing?"

"You'll know by Christmas," he replied.

I decided to give it a try. I knew of no other way to resolve the ambivalence. But the decision brought me no peace. I was not really surrendering.

I went to Europe that summer, hitchhiked through Germany and Austria, traveled by train through Italy—from Innsbruck to

Florence and Rome and back again to Genoa, and on to Nice and Lourdes and Paris in France. I couldn't get enough of it.

I returned from Europe two weeks before I was to enter the novitiate. Every other evening I spent with Clair. One day we drove over to New York City to see *Annie Get Your Gun.* It was a bittersweet time for us. Our last evening—a Friday—was particularly sad. As two o'clock approached, and it was time to go, she asked me not to do anything dramatic. I didn't. I simply kissed her good-bye and left.

I spent most of Saturday writing her a long letter. I signed it, "All the love a guy like me can give."

Saturday night I spent with my parents. Sunday morning I left for the novitiate. My Dad's last words were: "Be happy."

CHAPTER 3

NOVICE

I went to the novitiate determined to give it everything I had. But during the first several weeks, that determination was to be severely tested.

My fellow novices were not the problem. Twenty-eight in number, they came from all parts of the continent and spanned the economic and educational spectrums. Some were from big-city slums. Others were Midwest farm kids. One came from an aristocratic family in Canada. About half were graduates of the Paulist minor seminary, so they had some experience of the Paulist way of life. The other half were as green as I was. Many were GIs, one an army captain who had part of his face shot away in the Battle of the Bulge. All had finished two years of college, most four, and one had completed law school. I liked them.

Nor was the problem the locale. Situated in the wooded hills of northern New Jersey, about forty miles west of New York City, the novitiate building was an old hunting lodge that was perched on the shore of a sizable lake. About two miles from the closest road, it was very secluded. There was a farm on the property, as well as a ball field. I could hardly have asked for a more beautiful spot.

In retrospect, part of my problem was letdown. Europe had been six weeks of intense stimulation. I had been enthralled. But it had taken its toll. And those last two weeks with Clair were emotionally charged. Saying good-bye to her was the most difficult thing I had ever done. I arrived at the novitiate physically spent and emotionally exhausted, and, once the initial excitement was over, despondent in both body and spirit.

But my principal problem was: I did not understand anything

we were doing. Nothing made any sense. The eating and the sleeping I understood. But that was about it. About meditating, scrutinizing my conscience, spiritual reading, manual labor, recollection, silence, common recreation, I did not have a clue.

The novice master—Father Bob Murphy—tried to orient us. But he was not getting through. I was very confused.

One novice arrived, stayed overnight, and left the next morning. When I found out, I felt like running after him shouting, "Hey, wait for me."

Bob Nugent, a fellow novice, took one look at the depressed expression on my face and said, "They'll have to throw me out." It was what I needed to hear.

As the days turned into weeks, the mists of confusion began to lift, and I started to take hold. At first I found the place too quiet. The silence was deafening. But after a time, I got used to it, and before long I began to like it.

We were awakened at 5:30 A.M. by a knock on the door and "*Benedicamas Domino.*" From then until lights out at 10 P.M., we were kept pretty busy.

The schedule:

5:30—Awake
5:45—Meditation
6:15—Mass
6:45—Thanksgiving
7:15—Clean room
7:30—Breakfast and free time
8:30—Manual labor
10:30—Study or write
12:00—Examination of conscience
12:15—Lunch and common recreation
1:15—Nap
2:00—Recreation
4:00—Rosary
4:30—Study or spiritual reading
5:30—Meditation
6:00—Dinner and common recreation
7:00—Free time
7:30—Scripture reading
8:00—Spiritual reading

9:00—Night prayers
10:00—Lights out

We talked during recreation periods but only when necessary during manual labor. The remainder of the time we kept silent. There was reading during meals and no eating betweentimes. No beer, wine, or whiskey, no smoking, and, of course, no drugs.

Thursday and Sunday afternoons were completely free, and once a month we had a day of recollection during which we did not talk at all.

Contact with the outside world was cut to a minimum. There were no newspapers, radio, or television. We could write one letter home a week. Every three months, visitors were welcome.

Several times a week, Father Murphy would give a conference, usually during the afternoon study period. In one of these, he told us that as long as we were novices, the novitiate rule and its schedule defined the will of God for us. "Keep the rule," he said, "and the rule will keep you." I bought it. It would be nice if life were always that simple.

He also said, "This is the one year in your life when you will have complete freedom to get to know yourself and work at intimacy with God. I hope you will take full advantage of it."

I decided to try.

The schedule was tight but not rigid. Once I adapted to it, I found it had a rhythm of its own. I liked the discipline it imposed upon me. And I liked the peace and the freedom it gave me.

The discipline was external. The peace and the freedom were internal.

I was a body of broken bones, and the novitiate schedule was the body cast within which I could be quiet, get in touch with myself, and heal.

Gone were so many of the sensations and stimulations of the past: the nerve-wrenching stop and start of traffic when you are late and hurrying through clogged city streets; the pouring of students into college corridors blowing verbal steam after the ringing of the bell releases them from the pent-up pressures of the classroom; the graceful flow of female bodies, their clothes swishing as they walk; the press and swell and roar of the crowd when the home team quarterback unleashes a bomb for the tie-breaking touchdown; the lovely feel of a woman in your arms when she looks into your eyes and you know she loves you.

Sensations that soothed and assaulted, enriched and exhausted, enlivened and deadened—they were gone. At first it seemed there was nothing to take their place. I felt both relief and nostalgia. But then I became aware of a whole new range of sensations; on the whole, gentler, quieter ones: whitecaps on the lake when the wind is up and whistling through the trees; the feel and smell of wet earth when you crush it between your fingers; the clinging of a sweat-filled shirt to your body when you've been chopping wood; the exhilaration of plunging into the cold lake right afterward; the slow changing of the trees from green to red and yellow before the leaves fall and death covers the earth; the rhythmic cadence of the rosary at the outdoor grotto of Our Lady; the glistening of sunlight through pine needles on a crisp fall day; stars so close you can almost reach up and touch them; the shifting of cassocked bodies from knee to knee during morning meditation; all the wondrous yet terrifying facets of the hurricane that struck us in November—the snakes of lightning, the explosions of thunder, the sheets of rain, winds of such velocity that scores of trees were knocked over and we lost our electricity and lived by candlelight for ten days and I learned to love the crackling of pine logs in the fireplace.

I tuned in to nature and rejoiced in it. I made friends with the lake and the hills and the trees and the rocks, the soil and the shrubs, the squirrels, the rabbits and the deer. I felt loved by them. Sometimes they seemed translucent. God nurtured me through them.

Wrapped in the silence that pervaded the area and emboldened by the security that its beauty engendered, I was ready to move out and take some chances. I let go and went deep within myself, and with ears that were not attached to the outside of my body, I began to pick up the symphony that permeates the depths of all creation. The Fiddler may be on the roof, but I first heard His sweet melody—and His invitation to dance—in the depths of myself when I allowed myself to experience my oneness with His creation and entered into communion with Him through it.

Not that I was a complete stranger to inner experience or to the ramifications of an interior life. As a boy, my imagination had always been ready for a romp. My fantasy life was multifaceted. I enjoyed daydreaming. On a rainy day, when I could not go outside to play ball, I would frequently lie on my bed and create movies in my head. Usually I was the lead character. When I entered adolescence, some of the movies became X-rated.

I was also good at talking to myself. At first I used to get caught moving my lips, and the other guys would laugh at me. They thought anybody who talked to himself was either crazy or in love, and sometimes they made no distinction between the two. They did not know—or had yet to admit to themselves—that all healthy people talk to themselves. We learn by asking ourselves questions. We decide by listening to the arguments on both sides. When we love somebody, we allow that person to take up residence inside ourselves, so that we can have a conversation with them anytime we want. As soon as we stop talking to the people outside us, we begin to talk to the people inside us, or directly to ourselves, usually about what concerns us most. Which is just another way of saying we are creatures of dialogue. We talk to other people and we listen to them. We talk to ourselves and we listen to ourselves.

Sometimes this inner dialogue is carried on by means of words. Sometimes, like two lovers resting in each other's arms, it is wordless, a silent communion.

Either way, the interior conversation that we all hold with ourselves is how we grow and discover who we are. It is *the* pathway to self-awareness, self-acceptance, self-possession, and self-giving. It is what makes us human.

Built into the dynamism of this interior conversation, especially as self-awareness and self-possession increase, is a tendency to spiral upward, to go beyond the particular human being we are talking to and reach for the horizon. We begin by talking to ourselves. Not infrequently we end up talking to God.

I am not sure how this happens. But I do know it does happen and that the process by which it does is as natural and as spontaneous as breathing. Talking to God, listening to God, silently communing with God, are normal activities for the developing psyche. We may use different words to describe what we are doing and with whom we are doing it, but the reality is the same. We do not need to make it happen. All we need to do is get out of the way and let it happen.

Time at the novitiate was structured in such a way as to facilitate this process, to stimulate and nurture it. Its purpose was to create in us the space needed for this to happen.

Throughout the centuries, the desert has been the place where people have gone to take stock of themselves, think things through, and make contact with God. In spiritual need we are attracted by the desert because in a desert there is nothing to distract us from ourselves—or from God. No vegetation. No wildlife. No people. Nothing. In the silence of the desert, we are free to turn inward and listen to all the different people who live within us. Initially some of them may yell and bark and bellow, but, like unruly children, once they know they are being listened to, they quiet down. And then, beneath them, and in between them, we pick up the voice of God. Deserts are hostile to physical life. But, paradoxically, they stimulate the spiritual life. The very emptiness of the desert sets the stage for an enrichment of spirit, a fullness of soul. The purity of the air is part of it. But not all.

I think it is no accident that Moses and John the Baptist and Jesus and Paul and the fathers of the Church and holy people throughout the ages have gravitated toward deserts and had major spiritual experiences there. Nor is it any accident that three of the world's major religions—Judaism, Christianity, and Islam—arose among desert peoples.

When I went to the novitiate, I had never seen a desert. And geographically, in terrain, flora, and fauna, northern New Jersey is anything but a desert. Yet, for me, spiritually, emotionally, psychologically, the manner of living at the novitiate functioned like a desert—a place of freedom where nothing violated my psychic space, nothing distracted me from myself, nothing prevented me from going deep, nothing kept me away from the center of myself. Nothing, that is, except myself.

And that, of course, is always the central problem.

So much of the popular culture I had just left (and which I carried, full-blown, within my psyche) was oriented in the opposite direction. Its approach was intrusive and its aim was escapist; to distract us from ourselves, to draw us from the center to the periphery, from the depths to the surface.

American television both reflected and created this orientation. Its commercials told us that material things were central to the success of our lives, that unless I got certain things I would be a nobody. I did not completely believe them. Neither did most of my peers. But we did not completely disbelieve them either. And so the tendency was to play it safe and go after those things—cars, clothes, gadgets—sometimes with an intensity that made rat races of our lives. In most cases the things we sought were quite innocent, but the desire for them, the preoccupation with them, the desperation with which we sought them, pulled us from the depths to the surface and made superficial people of us.

The popular media also repeatedly told us that certain pleasures—particularly sex—were essential for the good life, that we would be failures if we did not experience them on a regular basis. But their approach to sexuality was one-dimensional. It was more concerned with the coupling of bodies than with the fusion of souls, and so preoccupied with orgasm that it neglected emotional rapport, honest caring, and profound sharing. It massaged the senses and allowed the deeper reaches of the human soul to atrophy. If followed, it would pull us from the center to the periphery of ourselves and make dissipated people of us.

Implicit in this emphasis on the acquisition of things and the pursuit of pleasure was the cult of success. "You gotta get ahead, lead the pack, be number one. How else are you going to buy the things that'll get you the woman you want? So don't let anything —or anybody—stand in your way. Just keep telling yourself: 'It's worth it. It's worth it. There's nothing else.' "

Underlying this cult of success is a deep-seated narcissism, a fixation with the self, a vision of human life that stops with the four walls of the individual's ego.

There's nothing wrong with ego. A strong ego is a part of every healthy psyche. But there is something terribly wrong when we confuse ego with the center of ourselves and identify it with our true selves. There is also something terribly wrong when we so exaggerate the ego's importance that we care only about ourselves.

If the American culture from which I had just emerged tended to the superficiality of the acquisitive rat race, the dissipation of the frenetic pursuit of one-dimensional sexual pleasure, and the narcissistic self-absorption that flows from always taking care of number one, then the life-style of the novitiate tended strongly in the opposite direction. Organized along the lines of the evangelical counsels—poverty, chastity, and obedience—it struck at the root of the contemporary preoccupation with possessions, pleasure, and self. It attacked, not the things or the pleasures or the self, all of which are gifts of God and very good in themselves, but the desire, the need, the preoccupation with these things. It sought to free us from whatever intruded on our inner space. It removed the clutter from our lives, the distractions, the noise. Its aim was freedom—and peace.

Certainly things had only a minor place in our lives. We had the clothes we had brought with us—mostly of the work variety—and could get from the common stock anything we lacked. We had the novitiate library and our own personal books to fill in our free time and could write home for any others we might need and could not borrow.

There was always enough to eat. Our rooms were spartan but adequate. We lacked nothing that we really needed. This is why poverty is not the most accurate description of the way we lived. Simplicity says it better, I think. We were encouraged to cut back on our desires, to be detached from our possessions, to share what we had. "Not to want something," a wise man has said, "is frequently better than to have it."

For Christmas that year my parents had given me a leather jacket. I liked it—partially because of the love it expressed, partially because it was so nice and warm. But I did not really need it. I had a heavy sweater.

In January, Rocky, a knight of the road, stopped off and spent several weeks with us, as was his habit. He had neither heavy sweater nor jacket. I agonized over whether or not to give him mine. Finally I decided. He was delighted. But that was nothing compared to the freedom and the joy I felt in giving it to him.

Most of the pleasures of the novitiate were of the spiritual variety. The physical pleasures were much more limited. We had little contact with women—the sisters of our classmates on visiting days, the mothers of the kids to whom we taught catechism on Saturday afternoons. Not exactly the stuff of wild sexual fantasies.

That left food. In moderation, it is, of course, a very legitimate pleasure, and we had a decent cook. But we were encouraged to deny ourselves in this area. During Advent and Lent, we fasted—which means we ate only one full meal a day. Some of the guys lost weight. Some gained. I stayed about the same. Bob Martin took Father Murphy's recommendations the most seriously. He worked hard and ate very little. But on one feast day, he decided to enjoy himself. His stomach had shrunk so he got terribly sick. Very embarrassing for the most ascetical member of our class. Apparently Lou Colonese, in his letters home, said something about losing weight, because on our next visiting day, his family showed up with enough pasta to feed an army.

I don't know whether the talk of physical self-denial did any good. I guess we learned something about delaying gratification, an important facet of self-discipline. But I do know that neither before nor since have I ever thought so much about food.

Obedience is the toughest of the evangelical counsels because it attacks the narcissism, the self-centeredness, the ego fixation that are the most deeply rooted and persistent of the enemies of spiritual growth. Obedience to whom? To God, of course, absolutely and unconditionally. But how does God let us know what He wants? He speaks in prayer. He speaks in the responsibilities of one's calling in life—whether husband or wife, lawyer or pipe fitter, priest or short-order cook. He speaks through the orders of legitimate authority. And He speaks through the needs of other people.

Life at the novitiate was life in community and that, as anyone who has ever tried it can tell you, is never easy. In community, as in a family, the important thing is not *my* welfare, growth, and happiness, but *our* welfare, growth, and happiness. Not a small adjustment for someone raised to be a high achiever and a rugged individualist.

I liked my fellow novices. But as the weeks turned into months and cabin fever set in, I became painfully aware of their imperfections, and they became painfully aware of mine. I'm not sure which I hated more. We began to grate on each other's nerves. Suddenly the honeymoon was over, and I needed patience, self-control, and a keen sense of humor, especially about myself.

I was frequently tempted to deny, at least implicitly, my own faults while expecting perfection of everyone else. The remedy, I learned, was to keep in close touch with my own faults. That way I would be less likely to expect perfection from anyone else. Easy to say. Hard to do. Sometimes common recreation was the most penitential period of the day. I was frequently grateful when we did not talk at meals.

Both the solitude and the communal living of the novitiate forced me to take a long, hard look at myself. So did the twice daily examination of conscience and the weekly confession.

Our weekly confessor—Father Henry Flautt—was a kind and zealous man who systematically visited all the people in the neighborhood. Our extraordinary confessor—Father Jim Buckley, who came out from New York City every couple of months—was a holy man whose physical blindness only enhanced his spiritual impact upon us. Neither man was psychologically sophisticated, but both men, by word and manner, made sure our exploration of self was carried on in the presence of a demanding yet unconditionally loving God.

"To experience the misery of man without the mercy of God," Pascal says, "is to despair. To experience the mercy of God without the misery of man is to sin by presumption. But to experience both is the beginning of wisdom."

The confrontation with self that the novitiate provoked, the long journey through the shadow side of my psyche that it involved, and the frequently devastating data it unearthed did not produce in me the crisis of self-acceptance that has since become so common in our culture. This was partially because of the emotional health my mother and father bequeathed to me. But it was primarily because the confrontation and the journey were always carried on in the context of God's unconditional love for us. I continued to say yes to myself because God did. I came to look at myself through His eyes, and, in this light, my faults did not diminish in severity, but they did not make me unlovable either. I came to the conclusion I was a lovable slob.

What did I learn about myself on this journey?

That I am not what I would like to be.

That I am not even what I seem.

That sometimes, under the guise of doing something unselfish, I am really being quite selfish.

That God isn't particularly lucky to have somebody like me working for Him.

That, despite appearances, I am insecure and frightened.

Insecure about being accepted by those important to me.

Frightened of going before the judgment seat of God and having to admit I blew it, that I wasted the time and the talent He gave me, that I did not give what I had to give, that the people I was supposed to give it to might well go without because of my failure.

That in no sense do I have it made, that I am incomplete and needy, that what I need is integration and healing, completion and fulfillment; that, most of all, I need to love and be loved. Not in a calculated or niggardly fashion, but totally, passionately, with abandon. Which is just another way of saying I need to love and be loved by God.

This was not a new realization for me. But it was a deeper and more intense experience of the same dynamic I had explored in that freshman-year term paper: I am incomplete. God is the only reality that can complete me. I need to go to Him to find the fulfillment I desire.

In college I had acted this out by going to God through Clair, by allowing Him to come to me through her. For me she was a sacrament of the tenderness of God. I loved God in her and through her. He loved me in her and through her.

Clair taught me how to forget about myself, how to go beyond myself, how to so identify myself with another human being that she became for me an alter ego—another self—so that whatever made her happy made me happy, that whatever hurt her, hurt me. Clair taught me both the price and the joy of loving.

Clair also caused me to bring to our relationship a concentration of my sexual-affective energies. She turned me on. But now, separated from her, where could these energies go? What was to be their focal point?

In the beginning it was touch and go. When Clair's first letter arrived, my emotions ran riot. I shook all over. I took my turbulence to God in prayer. I asked Him what He wanted me to do with my love for her. He did not seem to answer. But I continued to feel especially loved by Him. Which, I guess, was answer enough.

She sent word through my parents that she would like to come for a visit. I should have said yes. But I was too unsure of myself to risk it. I replied that I had better stay in a vacuum for a while longer.

Slowly, sometimes painfully, I made the transition. The key, I understand now but did not then, was not repression—turning off my sexual-affective energies or driving them down into the unconscious—but sublimation; directing them on to a more elevated plane, transforming them from erotic into spiritual energy. To the extent to which I succeeded in doing this, prayer became an exciting form of communication for me. God was close. He was loving. He had what I needed. He was ready to share Himself with me. So I went to Him. I opened to Him. I communicated with Him. I did more than that. I made love to Him.

Clair also made her adjustment. A year later she announced

her engagement. I knew and liked her fiancé. I was not able to attend their wedding. It was probably just as well. I would have been celebrating their happiness but also mourning my own loss. The night of their wedding I was painfully aware that someone else was enjoying that lovely body of hers.

Everything has its price. Clair made concrete the price I was paying for the priesthood. During the latter part of the novitiate year, a visiting priest, Father John Cleary, gave us a conference on the spiritual and psychological benefits of Paulist life, in the course of which he oversimplified and said, "You men haven't given up a thing." I was infuriated. In no way did I regret the choice I had made. But I was not about to allow anyone to minimize the price.

Clair and I have remained good friends over the years, exchanging letters and visits.

At a very crucial time, we had entered each other's lives, made our contributions, and then, in obedience to what we perceived as God's will, moved on. I am grateful for what we shared together, what we have been—and are—to each other.

Once I made the adjustment to the novitiate and bought into its way of life, I could not get enough of its contemplative side. I spent every spare moment in one form of prayer or another.

We were taught two different systems of meditation—the Ignatian and the Sulpician—and encouraged to pick and choose whatever worked for us. The important thing was to enter into loving communion with God, and whatever helped us do that was good, whatever did not was to be discarded.

In retrospect the two systems we were taught seem too complicated, too concerned with the conscious mind, too rational and voluntaristic. But pretty soon I developed my own, which has continued to evolve over the years. Zen and yoga have contributed to this evolution.

At the novitiate my prayer was active. I was going to God. I wanted to give myself to Him. There was great energy and gusto about it, almost as if I were taking God by storm. God was out there—transcendent—and I was going to fight my way to Him and then tell Him how much I loved Him and how ready I was to do whatever He wanted. I did more talking than listening.

Since the novitiate my system of meditation has simplified considerably, and now the focus is on the God who lives within me. I don't need to make God present. He already is present. I just need to become aware of His presence, pay attention to Him, be present to Him as He is to me. I try to accept His love and respond to it in kind. I listen more, talk less. And when I do talk, it usually takes the form of a simple mantra:

"Lord, speak your Word in me."
"Put me together again."
"Show me what you want me to do."
"Come, my beloved."
"Whatever you want is OK with me."

More often than not, the communion is wordless. It takes place deep within me, more in the unconscious than the conscious mind. I am more passive than active, more receiving than giving, more responding than initiating. What's most asked of me in prayer is the surrender, the letting go, the turning over, the giving of myself to God so He has complete freedom to work in me and through me.

Sometimes this comes easily. Sometimes it doesn't come at all. Most of the time, it is somewhere in between.

The spiritual pacesetter of our class—Bob Martin—was so taken with the inner life that he decided to transfer to the Trappists, a purely contemplative order.

For a time I was afraid God was leading me in the same direction, so once again I started to set limits and argue with Him. Some people never learn. The result was the same: Prayer became blocked and I became unhappy. So I decided to open up and take a chance on what God might want. I also discussed the matter with Father Murphy. His response was blunt and to the point. "Ellwood, you could never be Trappist. You like to talk too much." After a time I got the same answer in prayer. I was where I was supposed to be. But being there, I needed to be open to whatever God wanted of me.

In the early weeks of the novitiate I discovered scripture, and it spoke to me as it never had before. Sometimes a single chapter of the New Testament would feed my prayer for days. I read every life of Christ I could get my hands on, and during study period I began to write one of my own.

Suddenly God had a human face, and His name was Jesus.

My relationship with Jesus in prayer activated something within me, and I began to become aware that there was a place deep in my psyche where all the different strands of my personality came together and around which—mandala-like—every facet of my life could revolve, a communications and command center where I could be in charge and from which I could plot the direction of my life.

In this place I began to see that the Word of God is my true self. In being faithful to myself, I am being faithful to Him. In finding Him, I find myself, for He is the image of the God in whose likeness I have been made. He is the center of my center, the mysterious ground of my depths, the divine self in whom I live and move and have my being.

The Spirit of the Word of God lives in this place, and I can commune with Him there. And there I am confronted with His challenge: that I say yes to Him, that I allow Him to pour His light and life and love into me and through me into the lives of the people around me.

Over the years I have had to struggle to stay in the center of myself. Sometimes I have failed, and it has always been because I have allowed other things to crowd out my daily hour of meditation.

Outside this place, I am not myself. Alienated and estranged from the center, I am a very unhappy human being. I am also a very inefficient one. Not being present to myself, I cannot be present to other people, or to the job at hand. I am no fun to be around.

For these reasons, and for some others, I have had to be rigorously tough with myself about the hour a day. No matter what the problem or the demands upon me, I have to get that hour with the Lord in every day. I must because without it I lose contact with myself and with God. I die inside. I need it because I need Him. So I get it. No excuses allowed.

Running through all Father Murphy's conferences was a simple theme: Prayer is the foundation of the Christian life; contemplation is essential for a happy and fruitful priesthood.

I bought it. Nothing that has happened since has caused me to doubt in any way his central insight. If I have been able to accomplish anything in the intervening years, it is because I have tried, sometimes successfully, sometimes not, to live out the ideal he articulated so well.

As the months passed, and I was able to move more and more fully into a loving relationship with God, my ambivalence about being a priest dissolved. Now it was not only what God wanted. It was also what I wanted—very badly.

At the end of the novitiate year, on September 8, 1951, just before going on to St. Paul's College in Washington, D.C., for advanced studies in philosophy and theology, eighteen of us formally affiliated ourselves with the Paulists and made temporary promises of poverty, chastity, and obedience. Receiving our promises and bestowing the habit was Father Jim Cunningham, the Paulist Superior General.

The punch line of his welcoming address was "I can buy brains. What we need is sanctity."

Afterward, Dave O'Brien, one of the sharpest of our class wags, said, "About the sanctity, I don't know. But he's sure as hell going to have to buy the brains."

The next day we left for Washington.

CHAPTER 4

SEMINARIAN

My folks picked me up at the novitiate, and together we drove to Ocean City, New Jersey, for a couple of days at the seashore before heading on to Washington, D.C. The first night, with a measure of pride, I showed my stepmother the especially tailored black cassock with the five buttons across the left shoulder that is the Paulist habit—the uniform of the ecclesiastical outfit I had just joined. She responded with a complete lack of enthusiasm. I was to understand why only some months later.

Unlike a number of my classmates, I had visited St. Paul's College before. But now I had come to stay. The forty-two upper classmen who were waiting to greet us made the adjustment easy. Their welcome was warm and enthusiastic, partially because that is the Paulist tradition; partially, too, because we symbolized the vitality of the Paulist future; but most of all, I think, because we represented new faces, new stories, and a whole new range of experiences and outlooks to add spice to the community cauldron, a heaven-sent antidote for the claustrophobia that afflicted seminary life at that time.

In short order we were introduced to the faculty and given a tour of the building, which is an ivy-covered granite structure resembling, more than anything else, a fortress; in retrospect, a fitting symbol of the life there. Situated just four miles from the White House and Capitol and five hundred yards from the campus of Catholic University, it was, at the time of our arrival, one of perhaps thirty such colleges that were clustered around the university and that were operated by various religious orders for the education of their own members. Its three stories and basement contained four classrooms of varying sizes, a library well stocked with the classics of Catholic philosophy and theology along with the latest scholarly periodicals, a warm and beautiful chapel done in dark brown polished wood with pews that fit the curvature of the spine and rubber linings on the kneelers that made morning meditation less of an endurance test, a music room with record collection and phonograph, a homey common room for the students and a homier one for the faculty, a rather bare dining room and kitchen, and living quarters for sixty students and twelve priests. The students' rooms were just large enough for their furnishings—a bed, a desk, a straight-backed chair, a closet, a chest of drawers, and a bookcase. The priests' rooms were somewhat larger and had throw rugs on the floor. On the land adjacent to the building were two handball courts, a baseball diamond, a touch football field, and a basketball court.

Remarkably self-contained, St. Paul's seemed to have everything that was necessary and nothing that was not. I gloried in its compactness and in the efficiency that flowed from it.

The student rule regulated our activities and reinforced the atmosphere of prayer and study. We talked during recreation and at some meals. But we did not talk in the corridors, and we were not supposed to visit each other's rooms. Nor were we encouraged to seek out the company of those outside the community. We had an important job to do—educating ourselves for the priesthood—and all our energies had to be directed toward that objective.

The curriculum at St. Paul's covered six years, two for philosophy and four for theology. We began our philosophy classes—metaphysics, epistemology, and the philosophy of science—shortly after we arrived, with Father Ben Hunt, the principal lecturer. Small and slight of stature, Ben was a Texan who had converted to Catholicism. With his sensitive face, floppy black hair, folksy voice, meek manner, and gentle smile, he was not your stereotypical Texan. Intellectually intense, physically relaxed, he was given to soaring flights of rhetoric. He was not the most organized of teachers, and he was called impractical by some of my classmates who did not have the background to follow his speculative flights into the realm of metaphysics. "What does all this being stuff have to do with making converts?" they asked in consternation. But I loved to take an intellectual romp with him, and even more I loved to look at reality through his eyes; primarily, I think, because he had such enthusiasm for it. He loved to explore it, to penetrate its depths and mine its secrets. He loved, too, the give-and-take of philosophical debate and frequently challenged us to take him on. He knew the pedagogical value of controversy. I always found his classes alive and exciting. If a good teacher is someone who stimulates, inspires, and informs, then Ben Hunt was, for me, a superlative teacher, one of the best I have ever had—certainly the best I had at St. Paul's—because he did all three so very well. He helped me intuit reality in some kind of pure and deep way and grasp the laws that flow from its nature.

Not only was he brilliant; he was also deeply caring. He was easily accessible and always made time for me. He listened well, and every conversation began with an acceptance of where I was and what I wanted to do. He was one of the most selfless human beings I have ever met.

Whenever I would go to his room, no matter how much heat the furnace was putting out, I would find him at his desk, in overcoat and hat, sometimes shivering. It seems he had a circulatory problem and was perpetually cold. Perhaps in his body but certainly not in his heart. We were to become close friends in the years ahead.

In that first year, Father James McVann taught us public speaking—everything from diaphragmatic breathing to the building of an oratorical climax. Jimmy's persona was that of a gloomy gus. He always spoke in somber tones, and, despite his habit of lacing his lectures with humorous anecdotes, he seemed to have no playful side. Which, of course, made him the frequent butt of our jokes. We called him "Jazz."

Dave O'Brien, in particular, loved to mimic him, saying if we were ever persecuted and forced to form an underground church, going about in disguise, as the priests did in China and Russia, he would be a natural for funeral director.

Each year in April, the underclassmen put on a show to skewer those about to be ordained. Who was the surprise choice to play Dave O'Brien the year we were ordained? Not another student but Jazz McVann—to a thunderous ovation from the delighted student body.

Jazz McVann was also to teach us upperclassmen canon law. Perhaps his studies in that field produced his dour exterior. Or perhaps he was putting us on, laughing at us behind that somber mask of his.

Because I had taken considerable philosophy at La Salle, I was able to skip the second year of that subject and move directly into theology. I had enjoyed philosophy. I thought theology was going to be even better, more stimulating, nurturing, exciting. It was a reasonable expectation, but unfortunately a mistaken one.

Part of the problem was the approach to theology in those days. Instead of reflecting on the experience of the Christian community as it grappled with the presence of the Risen Jesus in its midst—which I think is the task of authentic theology—it sought to construct an interlocking system of clearly defined concepts arranged into syllogisms that would prove the existence of God, the divinity of Christ, the veracity of the Church's teaching authority (apologetics or fundamental theology), and then illumine the Church's authoritative teaching on God, Jesus, the Church, the human situation, faith, grace, the sacraments, etc. (dogmatic or systematic theology) in such a way that any open-minded person would be compelled to accept them. The emphasis was on clarity rather than mystery, logic rather than experience, the clear and abstract idea of philosophy rather than the emotionally evocative image of scripture. There seemed no place for the subjective, the intuitive, the experiential; only for the objective, the rational, the abstract. It was as if the conscious mind were the totality of the human person; as if the unconscious mind did not exist; as if feeling were an abdication of one's human dignity.

This kind of theology was strongly encouraged by the Council of Trent and betrayed the anti-Protestant bias of that Counter-Reformation phenomenon.

Part of the problem, too, was the way in which this theology was presented. Most of the classes consisted of a lecture in which the teacher presented a portion of the schema that he had compiled from his own graduate studies, personal research, and the perusal of the classic textbooks, most of which were in Latin. Its core was a series of theses articulating essential church teaching in the area, together with the testimony of scripture and tradition, authoritative statements of the popes and bishops, the opinions of theologians, and both sides of any controverted issues.

The priest who taught fundamental theology seemed chained to his notes. A methodical and almost officious man who was always well prepared, he set himself to cover in each class a portion of the schema he had drawn up. This was his goal, and he did not want to deviate from it. He did not like interruptions. He made no attempt to elicit questions or stimulate discussion. His classes always seemed hurried, as if he had so much to cover and so little time in which to cover it.

While he lectured, we were expected to take notes. By the end of the course, we were to have in our notebooks a facsimile of the notes with which he had begun the course. Why he didn't simply mimeograph and distribute them to us, I don't know. It would have saved all of us a great deal of time, energy, and frustration.

Our scripture teacher was even worse. A genial, outgoing man with an inferiority complex to match his extended girth, he would have made a great parish priest. But the Paulists needed somebody to teach scripture, so they asked him to go to graduate school in that area. He did not have enough sense to say no.

In class he would simply read his notes to us, and as the year went on, he did so in a more and more inaudible voice. After a while he stopped looking up. He did not want to see that we were not listening, that we had written him off, that we were studying something else on our own.

This was tough on us. It was even tougher on him. Periodically he would explode in self-pitying outrage, the subtext of which was "Look at all I'm doing for you. Why don't you love me?" A pitiful figure, he needed a lot of strokes and got very few from us.

Unfortunately our apologetics and scripture teachers were typical of the other teachers at St. Paul's. This was an agonizingly difficult time for me. Sometimes I wondered if they understood what they were teaching, if the words they spoke so glibly were associated in their minds with any of the awesome realities of which they spoke, if their method of teaching did not involve the transmission of the teachers' notes to the students' notes without passing through the mind of either. Was their pedagogical method a cover for insecurity? Was their faith more blind obedience than informed intellectual assent? Did they not know, or had they forgotten, what Maritain had said so well, that the faith that is not inquiring and curious, not asking questions, not seeking vision, is sick? I do not know the answers to these questions. But I do know I found in their classes none of the emotional resonance we usually associate with a feeling for the holy, the experience of the sacred. The material was presented in bloodless fashion. It might just as well have been geometry or physics. And the tone was authoritative. The subtext was: This is what the Church teaches;

this is what a good Catholic believes. It was as if asking questions were a sign of feeble faith; as if accepting what was taught were more important than understanding it; as if the Holy Spirit spoke through the authoritative pronouncements of our teachers but not in the dialogue of their students who were also the Lord's disciples and who had gathered together in His name to explore what He said and what He meant.

"The worst thing a teacher can do," said Paul Tillich, "is to answer a question that has never been asked." Our theology teachers made that mistake repeatedly. At communicating the necessary material, I would have to give them an A for effort, but at stimulating us to probe the multiple facets of God's presence in the human, at inspiring us to explore the Mystery of Jesus in us and between us, they failed miserably.

Some of my classmates had no difficulty with their approach. By temperament they were rational and objective. They breezed through. I was not so fortunate. The intuitive, subjective, and experiential side of my nature did not like being ignored. It needed nurturing. It was not going to allow itself to atrophy. I became restless and found many of the classes painful. The only way out was to turn off my mind and take notes frantically. I could not bring myself to do that. But at least the pain was better than the boredom, which was just as frequent an occurrence. The real danger, of course, was not the pain or the boredom but the tendency, built into this type of pedagogy, to reduce mystery to formula; sanctity to perfectionism; scripture to exegesis; moral theology to casuistry; liturgy to rubrics; sacraments to magic; canon law to pharisaism; intellectuality to rationalism; Catholicism to sectarianism. This is the perennial temptation for a professionally religious person, but somehow the climate of rationalistic theology and the nondialogical pedagogical methods at St. Paul's did not help us resist it.

There was a time when I was very angry at the pain and frustration this approach caused me and at the intellectual enrichment it could have given me and did not. Now, with perspective, I have more of a sense of humor about the situation. I'm also aware that such resentment is a terrible waste of energy. We are all creatures of our time. Like it or not, we are not only the beneficiaries of history but also its casualties. And the deprivation we suffered was not ours alone. My tales of pedagogical ineptitude pale in comparison to the horror stories told by some of my colleagues from the medical, engineering, and law schools of the time.

Certainly the hardworking and caring men who taught us did the best they could under the circumstances. They were limited by their situation as we are limited by ours. But they also made me painfully aware that their limitations did not have to be mine, that I could educate myself, that my education need be limited only by my own intelligence, drive, and desire to know. In the final analysis, we all educate ourselves. Nobody can do it for us. We neither can nor should shift that responsibility to someone else.

Besides Ben Hunt, two priests guided and encouraged me in this direction; they mentored me and made an admittedly difficult situation much more bearable.

I first met Father Gene Burke, a tall, gangling Paulist with the gnarled face of an aged prizefighter, at second table, which was where the waiters ate. And any priests who were late for breakfast.

Gene was then professor of systematic theology at Catholic University, and he was always late. Perhaps because he worked late. Or because in those days, breakfast was in silence and second table was not.

Gene loved to talk. Theology. Philosophy. History. Politics. Sports. Music. Movies. You name it, Gene knew all about it. He had an opinion on everything. And on everyone.

He had advice for Maritain, Gilson, and Garriou La Grange. He knew exactly where Rahner, De Lubac, and Teilhard had achieved their great theological breakthroughs. And where they had made their mistakes.

He had suggestions for everyone—including the Pope—and on more than one occasion he was known to compliment the Lord for articulating so well an insight they shared in common. Gene was not shy. And no one ever accused him of humility.

Gene and I liked each other. I was attracted by his insatiable curiosity, his renaissance interests, and the fascination which every facet of the human situation inspired in him. His braggadocio did not bother me. Perhaps even then I sensed what later I would see clearly. It was his way of handling his intense loneliness.

I was also attracted by Gene's depth—he had suffered much—and by the passion that flowed from that depth with a power I have seen in few others. From his mouth came none of the bloodless abstractions that characterized so many of my teachers. When he spoke, whether about God or Jesus or the Church, his guts were on the line, and you knew he believed. He was a lion of a man, a passionate witness to the faith.

We spent time together, discussing not only theology and philosophy, history and psychology, but also ourselves. I could share my anger and frustration with him, and he could understand because he felt much of the same. He knew he could not fight my battles. Nor make my decisions for me. He never tried, but all along the way he did give me what I needed most—support and affirmation—as I fought those battles and made those tough decisions. He was always there when I needed him.

The second mentor was Father John Carr. He taught systematic theology at St. Paul's. An intensely private person, his post-ordination graduate work had been, not in theology, but in psychology. As a result, in class he was constantly playing catch-up. Sometimes it seemed he was only a couple of chapters ahead of us in the textbook, and sometimes we had read books in the field that he had not. His was a difficult position, and this made him, on occasion, very tense.

But if John Carr was not the very best of teachers, he was a superb confessor—a good listener, an insightful counselor, a wise and caring human being. In him I found the spiritual sensitivity, sense of the sacred, and feeling for the holy I was yearning for. At some very low moments, he gave me much support and some excellent advice—about prayer, studies, ministry. We, too, have remained lifelong friends.

Both Gene Burke and John Carr helped me realize the system then operative at St. Paul's (it has since changed radically) had one great advantage: It made few demands. It intruded little on my free time. It afforded me the space I needed to give my curiosity free rein. So I read widely. I probed deeply. I wrote some newspaper and magazine articles. I also wrote some essays just because I was interested in the subject and wanted to organize my thoughts about it. I continued to devour Maritain, Gilson, and Merton, and I discovered Karl Adam and Romano Guardini, two of the new breed of German theologians. In them I found the resonance of subjectivity, the intuitive insights, and the passion for God that I missed in the lectures I heard in the classroom. And I wrote a dissertation for my master's degree entitled "The Principle of Finality and Human Nature." Derived from the

Prima Secundae of St. Thomas's *Summa Theologica,* it took up the same theme as that chapter I had read in Gilson's *Spirit of Medieval Philosophy* six years before—our need for God, our incompleteness apart from Him.

Now, too, I began to probe further in an attempt to identify those particular needs of the human person that God alone can satisfy. Classical apologetics proved the existence of God, the divinity of Christ, and the authority of the Church. It appealed to the conscious mind. I was not interested in proving anything. I wanted to help people experience God, Jesus, and the Church, as the fulfillment of the needs they already found within themselves. I wanted to appeal to the whole person: mind and heart, reason and emotions, conscious and unconscious minds. In doing so, without fully knowing it, I was creating a subjective kind of apologetics for myself in the tradition of Isaac Hecker, Henri De Lubac, and Cardinal Newman.

I also engaged at this time in social analysis, trying to sort out the dynamics of contemporary American society so as to isolate where its needs and the Gospel intersected. Years later Pope John XXIII was to call this "reading the signs of the times."

I was able to try some of this out when I joined the Catholic Evidence Guild and did street preaching at the "Pitch" on Sunday afternoons in the city's parks and on the mall near the Capitol. The trick, of course, was to draw a crowd, and the best way to do that was to get attacked. A fallen-away Catholic whose name was Quirk (really) obliged us week after week.

"You say the Pope is infallible. Every Pope. How about Pope Alexander VI? He had an assortment of mistresses and more bastard kids than you can shake a stick at, one of whom he made a bishop. You saying God speaks to the world through a jerk like that?

"And how about Boniface VIII? He said, and I quote, 'There is no salvation outside the Church.' That means all Protestants, Jews, Hindus, Moslems, and Buddhists are going to burn in hell. Gonna be a terribly crowded place. Think of the fuel bill."

Quirk knew every mistake the Church had made in nineteen hundred years, every sin any Pope had ever succumbed to, and he threw them all at us. It was great fun.

After one particularly exciting session, I offered Quirk a ride home. In the car he winked at me and said, "You know . . . I think we have the best Pitch in the country."

I am not sure how much I gave the people who came to the Pitch, but I do know this was a useful lab for me, a place where I could refine my thinking and experiment with various approaches. It was also the most difficult kind of public speaking. After it, everything else would seem easy.

Community life with the other students at St. Paul's was a mixed blessing. Early on I realized I was living side by side with a number of people whom I really did not know and who really did not know me. Some of these men seemed uninterested in friendship. But these were the exception rather than the rule. With most there was a wide range of shared interests, and we had much fun together. We went to the plays and lectures at the university. On days off we would attend sessions of the Supreme Court, go to congressional hearings, sit in on the debates in the Senate, trek through the Mellon Art Gallery, settle in for a read at the Library of Congress, or hike together in Rock Creek Park or along the old canal.

Sometimes, too, we played pranks on the priests. Late at night, on the eve of one Ash Wednesday, we padlocked the refrigerator in their common room and put a penitential purple drape over their TV. Some of the priests did not see the humor in it.

We also played pranks on each other. Jack Kelly hated snakes. Once we tied a live garter snake to the light cord in his room. Entering in the dark, he reached for the cord. His shriek was earsplitting.

In twos and threes, we also critiqued each other's sermons. On one occasion Henry Noyes was particularly scathing with one of Jim Gollner's, who, in exasperation, shot back, "Henry, you wouldn't know a good sermon if lightning came out my ass."

"Sure I would," Henry replied drolly. "It would simply mean you had switched power sources—from gas to electricity."

So the process of bonding happened at St. Paul's. But it happened even more at Lake George, where we spent a portion of each summer. There we fished, swam, camped, sailed, and climbed mountains together, and there we had the leisure for extended conversations and common prayer. I became very close to a number of the guys. On some deep level, we became brothers.

Lake George was also where we made our annual eight-day retreat. These were times of intensive prayer, of listening for the Holy Spirit's voice within us, of reflecting on how we were doing and where we wanted to go. Sometimes I seemed to take spiritual flight during these retreats, basking in God's love. At other times I only seemed able to slog through the mud of my own emptiness.

I did have some nasty sieges of an unhealthy kind of narcissism. Sometimes I was so self-conscious that I ceased to be God conscious, so concerned with myself and my "perfection" that I lost all consciousness of the God who alone could give me a share in His perfection. This was a painful exercise in futility for me, not unlike a dog chasing his own tail.

In the beginning I used to make a long list of resolutions during these retreats. As the years rolled by, the resolutions became fewer and fewer as I realized I could not make myself into the kind of person I wanted to be, let alone the kind of person God wanted me to be. If the job was going to get done, God had to do it. What I could do, what was important for me to do, was to recognize my own impotence and turn the whole job—and myself—over to Him with the earnest prayer that He get busy—and soon.

Part of the problem was me. I spent so much time thinking and reading about perfection, so much energy willing and working at perfection, that I began to believe I was approaching it. Which made the shock of my not being perfect all the more devastating. It would be years before I would be able to accept myself as profoundly flawed, before I realized that being imperfect is OK, that God loves us as we are, sins and all. But part of the problem was also the seminary life-style—not just the type of theology we were being taught and the mode of its presentation, but our whole situation. We wanted to be a Christian community, a people of God, a church—a religious reality that by its nature must be open to the world, in dialogue with the world, responding to the needs of the world, sharing the Good News of God's healing love with that world. Yet the reality was we were isolated from the world. We had little contact with it. We did not feel its pain, wrestle with its confusions, share its anguish. And this by design. In the spirituality of the time, worldliness was a dirty word, the first step, for a priest, on the slippery slope to corruption. In *The Imitation of Christ,* Thomas à Kempis says that every time he went out among men, he came back less a man.

And not only were we isolated from the world, but we were almost completely isolated from women. That is not healthy, for the integrally human is not man alone, nor woman alone, but men and women, the masculine and feminine in relationship. For the sake of the Kingdom, I was ready to give up the emotional security the marital commitment can give, and I was ready to give up the sexual act. But I was not ready to give up friendship with women nor a collaborative working relationship with them, because I knew that would stunt my growth and cut me off from half the human race. I knew I needed rapport with women to be fully masculine, fully human, fully myself. For the celibate, women friends can be mirrors in which the femininity of God is reflected. They can be sacraments of the tenderness of God.

Isolated from the world and cut off from the feminine, we found it easy at St. Paul's to turn in on ourselves, allow our horizons to contract to the seventy-five men with whom we were living. Our preoccupation tended to be with our own growth and development.

There is nothing wrong with seeking one's own growth and development. God wants us to do that. But there is something terribly wrong when we seek only our own growth and development.

I think I was sincere when I said I was seeking these things so that I would later be a more effective servant of the world, sharing with it the light and life and love of God. But the immediate focus was still on myself, and that spelled trouble.

I needed something to pull me outside myself, something to engage my heart, activate my emotions, and help me experience God's presence in the human; something to balance the task orientation of my Teutonic temperament and involve me on a deep level with other people; something to ground me in the real world and remind me that love—not perfection—is where joy and the fulfillment of the human personality are to be found.

I did not find that something at St. Paul's College. As the months rolled past, I suffered from its absence. I felt confined and imprisoned, isolated from life, from reality, from human experience. So did many of my classmates. "Hang on" was our frequent greeting to each other. We were hanging on, enduring a situation we did not like, a situation that was not entirely healthy for us. We could hardly wait to get out.

The countdown to ordination began two years before, with the rite of tonsure, which initiated us into the clerical state. In this ceremony we committed ourselves, in the words of the psalmist, to make God our portion, to seek the meaning and purpose of our lives in Him. Subdiaconate was the point of no return, since it carried with it the obligation of celibacy and the praying of the Office. Diaconate gave us the license to preach. But these things were for us just stepping-stones. We wanted the priesthood. That's what we had dreamed about, worked for, and felt called to. We could not wait. We were no longer living in the present. We were living for the future. We practiced saying Mass, hearing confessions, and administering the other sacraments. We planned with our families our first Masses when all our relatives and friends would come together to celebrate with us.

My first Mass created a special problem for my father. He had left the Catholic Church when he had married my stepmother. Would he now return? He considered it, talked to some of his Catholic friends about it, one of whom made an appointment for him to discuss the matter with a priest. He did not keep the appointment, and, after much soul-searching, finally decided against it. Years later he told me the reason was my stepmother. "There would be no living with her if I did," he said.

Their marriage had been up and down, times of great love and tenderness interspersed with times of hurt and barely suppressed anger. She had been an inactive Lutheran when she had married my father. She drank and smoked and loved to go to the theater for the musicals my Dad enjoyed so much. Shortly after I went into the novitiate, she joined a fundamentalist church that was bitterly anti-Catholic and allowed none of these things. My father was appalled. He loved the theater and he loved to drink and smoke and now he had to do all these things alone. He said I was the reason for her move to the fundamentalists. I had made Catholicism so attractive, he told me, that she felt she had to join them in order to resist the Church's gravitational pull. Maybe. Maybe not. It may have been just one more maneuver in their intermittent war with each other.

Complicating my Dad's feelings about my first Mass was his own attitude toward my priesthood. He had always respected my freedom. But initially he would have been delighted if I had decided to do something else with my life, preferably go into the automobile business and work side by side with him, something both my brothers decided to do.

But by the time of my ordination, his attitude had changed. Part of the reason was my happiness. But part, too, was the attitude of his customers. One incident in particular was decisive for him.

A group of Jewish clothiers had their factory across from one of Dad's gas stations. They bought their gas from him, and in exchange he made parking available to them. But frequently, especially when they were pressed for time and the station was crowded with customers, they would simply drop their cars anywhere they could and rely on Dad's men to put them away. He thought this was imposing and grumbled vociferously about it. So did his men.

But one day he noticed the clothiers had begun to park their own cars. He also noticed they had become more patient, more considerate. Dad was so struck by the change of attitude that he asked about its cause. They were very blunt. "Your having a boy who's going to be a priest makes you a different kind of man than we thought you were."

Finally the agonizing wait was drawing to a close, and we could see the end in sight. After a seven-day retreat, we were given a rousing send-off by the faculty and underclassmen of St. Paul's. They stood on the front steps of the college and clapped as the bells tolled and we boarded the cars for the ride to Union Station and the train to New York City.

We were to be ordained by Cardinal Spellman in the Church of St. Paul the Apostle—the mother church of the Paulist Fathers on Manhattan's West Side—on May 3, 1956. As we slipped our bloodred vestments over our white albs in the sacristy beforehand, the Cardinal arrived, looking like he had been sucking on a lemon. I was struck by the incongruity of the situation. Why should he be tense? He had done this a hundred times. We had a right to be tense. But we were too overwhelmed, too excited to be tense.

Processing down the main aisle of the mammoth church, I could feel the gravitational pull of the seventeen hundred people who were crowded into the pews, and I wondered where my father and stepmother, my brothers and sister, were. I also wondered what was going on inside these people as they stretched their necks to get a better look at us. Some, I could see, were crying, men as well as women.

I could also feel the tradition of the place, the generations of people who had worshiped here. Father Hecker had regularly celebrated Mass and preached here. Now he was buried here. Bishop Sheen had begun his preaching career here, and this is where almost all living Paulists had been ordained. It was a holy place imbued with tradition. It was filled with ghosts—friendly ghosts—and I felt humbled by the august company I was now keeping.

As we neared the sanctuary, I could feel the fear in my throat. "It's no laughing matter to fall into the hands of the living God," reverberated through my consciousness. But the terror was laced with wonder at what was happening to me. More than anything else, I could feel the Holy Spirit hovering over the place, getting ready to take hold of me, to use me for His purposes.

The ceremony of ordination was filled with beautiful symbols, four of which remain indelibly stamped on my consciousness.

To symbolize a new and deeper commitment on our part and a more radical taking possession of us on Jesus' part, we prostrated ourselves on the cold marble floor of the sanctuary while the choir chanted the litany of the saints over our heads.

—Lord, have mercy on us.
—Christ, hear us. Christ, graciously hear us.
—Holy Trinity, one God, have mercy on us.
—All you men and women, saints of God, make intercession for us.
—From anger and hatred, O Lord, deliver us.
—Through Thy coming, O Lord, deliver us.
—Lamb of God, who takes away the sins of the world, have mercy on us.

To symbolize the transmission of power and responsibility as well as the unbroken continuity with the apostles, the Cardinal placed his open hands on our heads. What he was doing was awesome, in a way, terrible, and his grave and solemn demeanor reflected it. God was seizing hold of me, pouring His light and life and love into me so that I could pour them into the lives of the people I would touch. I was being given a very serious mandate of service. I felt no charge of spiritual energy, but I knew my soul was being seared and that I would no longer be the same. "Thou art a priest forever according to the order of Melchizedek."

To symbolize our commitment to the Body of Christ, in the Eucharist and in the Church, our hands were anointed with oil and touched to the host and chalice.

To symbolize the passing on of the tradition and our initiation into a unique fraternity, the seventy or eighty priests who were present also imposed their hands on our heads.

After the ceremony, we went to the various side altars to bestow our first blessings. Very emotional, my father got there first. Very emotional, I blessed him, kissed and hugged him and then proceeded to do the same for my brothers and sister, my cousins and in-laws, aunts and uncles, friends and the people at large. It was as if I was scooping up grace from God and transmitting it to those I loved by making the sign of the cross over them and by putting my hands on their heads. It was a very happy day.

We were ordained on a Thursday. On Friday and Saturday, I said private Masses in the nun's chapel at St. Luke's parish in Glenside, a suburb of Philadelphia where my folks were now living. Each day, when I approached the consecration, I had an almost physical kind of reaction—a mixture of fear, terror, and awe—at the kind of intimacy with God in which I was now involved.

Sunday was the first solemn Mass. Three hundred and fifty of my friends and relatives crowded into the small Church of the Little Flower. Ben Hunt was the deacon. Gene Burke gave the sermon. Consecrating the bread and wine into the Body and Blood of Christ and then giving communion to my relatives and friends was a source of great joy to me, tempered only by the awareness that I was not doing so for my father.

At the reception afterward, he gave a welcoming talk. He said, "This is my beloved son in whom I am well pleased."

He also said it was the happiest day of his life.

Part Two

Building Speed

CHAPTER 5

PARISH PRIEST

If the seminary had isolated me from the world, denied me emotional communion with my fellow human beings, and distanced me from their problems and pains, worries and delights, leaving me in a state of emotional atrophy—a parched desert—then my ordination to the priesthood had just the opposite effect. It signaled my re-immersion in the world, a new and deeper involvement in the lives of other people, and a more complete sharing in the anguish and the ecstasies of being human.

The immediate experiences of reentry were rich and varied—painful experiences, delightful experiences, everything in between. Some were surface. But most were deep. And they all flooded in, irrigating the desert. I soaked them up. I reflected on them. I tried to assimilate them. But mostly I just delighted in them. People were good and I loved them. Some smelled and belched and did stupid things. But it made no difference. They were me and I was them and communion between us was flowing at riptide, and I rejoiced in its vitality. That flow was my life. It was our life. It opened out on God's life. And I gloried in it. I was coming alive in a new and fuller way, and I was so glad to be out of the seminary and part of the whole thing.

With classmate and good friend Bill Cantwell, I was assigned to Good Shepherd parish on the northern tip of Manhattan for that first summer; then, in September, to the Church of St. Paul the Apostle in Los Angeles. There I joined Fathers Joe Burns, the pastor, John King, and Ronnie Burt in serving the sixteen hundred families of the parish.

It did not take me long to settle into parish life. By and large the people were kind and gracious and went out of their way to make me feel at home. They called me Father, and on their lips the word conveyed not only respect but also affection. To be called Father by someone thirty or forty years older took some getting used to. I managed. It was humbling . . . and awesome.

For my parishioners a priest was a God symbol, a very weak and needy human sign of the Lord's presence to His people, a fragile and sin-prone sacrament of His love for them. Catholics are amazingly tolerant of the human shortcomings of their priests. Bad manners and bad sermons, drunkenness, money grubbing, even womanizing—they close their eyes and shrug their shoulders and tell their children, "Father is having a bad day." They do find pettiness hard to take—who doesn't?—but just two things they refuse to stomach in their priests: lying and arrogance, perhaps because both contradict so directly the nature of the God whose symbol the priests are.

The Church is a community of weak and struggling human beings and the parish is a family and I had a very special place in it. Mutual acceptance was presumed. So was mutual assistance. They could ask my help, and I was expected to come through for them. I could ask theirs, and they were expected to do the same for me. We belonged to each other. But that did not mean I could take them for granted. Nor they me. On one occasion I had to set limits.

The parish had two competing funeral directors. Shortly after my arrival, one of them took me aside and in very insistent language said, "When you are caring for a seriously ill person, tell the relatives to call me. Better yet," he said, a glint in his eye, "you call me."

I came home steamed. Joe Burns picked it up and asked me what was wrong. "You tell that son of a bitch," I said, "I work for God. Not for him."

I usually began the day with a half-hour meditation followed by Mass. In those preconciliar days, the Mass was in Latin and was offered with one's back to the people. It did not have the participatory and communal aspects of today's eucharistic liturgy. Yet the Mass was very important to the people of St. Paul's. Most came every Sunday. Some came daily. Why? Because the Mass was their way of tapping into the sacred, their way of giving themselves to God, and their way of receiving God's gift of Himself to them.

I first offered the bread and the wine—very earthy symbols of our own very earthy humanity—and then I transformed it into the body and blood of Christ. The symbolism was clear. God is present in the most mundane facets of our human situation. He is especially present when His people gather together to celebrate Jesus' gift of Himself. He is most fully present when they join Him in renewing and prolonging and extending that gift. When together we went to communion, we experienced something of what the word implies—union with God, union with each other, union with oneself. For the people of St. Paul's, the Mass was a communal meal, a love feast, a sacrifice, a making holy of creation, and a celebration of God's presence in the human. In sacramental form, in archetypal ritual, the whole fulfillment of human life, its meaning and purpose was made concrete before our eyes.

I have offered Mass almost every day for thirty-four years. When I first came to St. Paul's, I was warned it would become routine. It hasn't. It is the essential expression of who I am and what I want to be doing with my life. I know of nothing that so fully involves me, nothing in which I am so fully myself, nothing that on occasion gives me so much joy.

On Sundays, of course, there was a sermon, just about the most important thing a priest ever does. It is important because most people, when religious questions arise during the week, turn to the previous Sunday's sermon for answers—and for nourishment. A preacher's responsibility is a heavy one.

As a young priest I tried to take it seriously. Which meant I had to give serious thought to what I was going to talk about. I soon learned it was important to start this mulling process the previous Monday. That way it could work on my unconscious all week. I also had to pray about what I was going to say. And, of course, I had to do any research that was called for. Finally the material had to be organized, the right examples had to be found, and the talk had to be organized so as to build to a climax.

The people at St. Paul's were hungry for the Gospel. So I knew whatever I could give them would be appreciated. But they were also frank in giving feedback. They knew the real thing when they heard it and were not shy about letting me know when they thought I had missed.

In those early months at St. Paul's, I discovered the ham in myself. I discovered the delivering of a well-prepared sermon could be fun. But I also discovered its immediate preparation was seldom fun. It usually involved five or six hours of hard work.

Sometimes, when I was prepared and my words were linked to my prayer, a strange thing would happen when I preached. Out of the mysterious abyss in which we all live and move and have our being, the Word of God seemed to surface within me and take over, filling my soul, throwing sparks into my mind, energizing my heart. And once He did, He would reach through me, beyond me, to touch the people before me. And not only them, but the Word of God living in them. On these occasions, without my causing it or even reflecting on it at the time, and usually when I least expected it, His lightning would crackle on my lips and the fire of His love would melt the ice in my heart and somehow the circuit would be closed and the Word of God in me would touch the Word of God in them. A fire would begin to burn in that congregation, and the conflagration would spread and engulf all of us—priest and people—and we would soon be fused together into the one People of God on this earth.

This experience is not unique to me. Many other priests, ministers, and rabbis have told me they share it. (In an analogous way, so have a number of actors.) It is something we all cherish. Over the years I have found this kind of communion between preacher and people one of the transcendent joys of the priesthood.

As a celibate, I was, in a way, married to the people of St. Paul's, and so the experience of preaching for me was similar to that of a married man making love to his wife. He is moved by love and propelled by passion. He wants to give pleasure to his spouse. That's how he gets his pleasure. But he also wants to arouse and enkindle her, so that he can penetrate her and beget their child. In each case he is giving himself to his spouse and is trying to elicit a like response from her. At its best the process can be ecstatic. And always it is fruitful.

I soon found there was something paternal about preaching. Of its nature, it begot new life. People were reborn whenever the Word was authentically preached and heard and responded to by the Christian community. They came alive in a new and fuller way.

But, like the married man making love to his wife, neither the process nor the effects could be programmed. Sometimes, when I would leave the pulpit feeling I really did it—I held them, and they got it, they really understood, and they were moved, I could see it in their eyes—I would later discover I had not been very effective.

But on other occasions, when I tried my best but got mixed up on what I wanted to say—it just wouldn't come together—and I stumbled over my words and some of the people's minds wandered and they looked away or their eyes glazed over—those were the times, I discovered, when my words seemed to have had the greatest impact. That was the sermon, I sometimes found out afterward, that helped someone do what he had been trying to do for a long time—reconcile with a friend, break with a bad habit, make a commitment, open to God, get to confession. God continues to use the weak things of this world for His own purposes, and sometimes the weaker I am, the more powerful He is. Jesus continues to ride into Jerusalem on the back of a donkey.

What do people look for in a sermon? What is said, of course. But more than that. They look at the preacher, and they ask, "Does this man really believe? And if he does, what effect does that have on his life? Is he a stronger, more honest, more loving person as a result?" We feed off each other's faith. The members of a congregation seek to strengthen their own faith by nourishing themselves on the faith of the preacher. And the reverse is also true. The response of the people to the Word he preaches does great things for the faith of the one doing the preaching.

At St. Paul's I also spent four or five hours a week hearing confessions. As a penitent, I have always found confession a significant experience. As a priest-confessor, I found it even more so.

I guess there are people who go to confession to escape guilt, rationalize inauthentic life-styles, and prop up shaky egos. But I have run into very few. For most Catholics confession is a profound form of human communication. Why? Because it is more than human communication. And because it is, they step out of roles, drop defenses, go below personas, and reveal themselves not as they would like to be, not as they should be, but as they actually are. In confession Catholics wrestle with the naked truth in stark and brutal honesty. This means they bring into the light of consciousness and share with the priest the shadow side of their psyches—their hurts, angers, fears, weaknesses, and sins, what they have done and what they have failed to do. Not infrequently they tell the priest things they do not tell their wives, husbands, or therapists.

Sometimes I found this disquieting. It was as if I were swimming through a sewer. I was having dumped on me all the depravities of which people are capable. I never knew that human beings could foul up their lives and hurt each other in so many different ways. Nor did I have any idea of the intensity of loneliness, fear, guilt, and emptiness that afflicts so many of them. I was being asked to shoulder a great deal of pain. No fun.

But on a deeper level, I found hearing confessions an inspiring experience. What they shared with me may have been despicable. But they were anything but despicable. I was awed by the courage it took to bring the shadow side into the light, the honesty with which they faced their shortcomings, the faith with which they turned to God for healing, the trust with which they accepted His unconditional love.

At close range, I was seeing the Spirit of God act in human beings, and I was seeing the beautiful things human beings can do when they collaborate with Him. I was also seeing how powerfully healing Jesus' love is, what peace and joy it gives.

One penitent, whom I later discovered was a clown from a visiting circus, felt such joy after going to confession that he did handsprings right down the main aisle of the church. Two old ladies were sitting in the back of the church, waiting to go to confession. One nudged the other and said, "Go on, Mary Clair."

The other replied, "Nothing doing. Not when Father is giving penances like that."

The vulnerability my penitents shared with me was awesome. Why? Because it was no different from my own. They felt lonely. So did I. They were scared. So was I. They struggled to believe. I did the same. They felt guilty because they had sinned. So did I. They wondered how God could possibly love them. I did the same. Vulnerability is what we have in common. I saw myself in my penitents. They were me and I was them, and in the honest sharing of our vulnerability we experienced our common humanity and the unifying presence of God in us and between us.

Implicit in confession is a spiritual posture of submitting to God and accepting one's creaturehood. This can be a chastening experience. But it is also a healthy one. We are all tempted to play God, to buy into the illusion that we have no limits, that we are laws unto ourselves, that we can do anything. Confession shatters this illusion. It rubs our noses in the pain and guilt and fear inside us. Which is why we have difficulty doing it. It confronts us with the truth about ourselves: that we are frail and meandering creatures who forget so easily who we are and why we are here, that our limitations are built in, that we can become ourselves only by learning to live comfortably with them.

Confession confronts us with another truth—that, despite our failings, or perhaps because of them, we are unconditionally loved by God. Implicit in every confession is the unspoken question: "These are the terrible things I have done. Can God still love me?"

To which the Lord resolutely answers: "Of course I love you. Do you think those little sins of yours are big enough to block the flow of my love? No way. I have always loved you. I will always love you. Passionately."

These two truths—our limitations and our lovableness—are the bedrock of human integrity and the wellsprings of psychic health. Confession helps us assimilate them.

The people of St. Paul's were kind and generous and involved me in every phase of their lives. I rejoiced with them when their children were born and was happy soon afterward to baptize their babies. Sometimes the infants bawled their lungs out during the ceremony, and sometimes they slept right through. Either way, the happiness of the new mother and father was infectious, and I was delighted to be the occasion of their child's entering the family of God and sharing His life.

My biggest challenge and my most serious responsibility while I was at St. Paul's was the UCLA Medical Center, the three-hundred-bed teaching and research university hospital where I was the Catholic chaplain. As such I was responsible for the pastoral care of the Catholic patients and their families. It was my job to visit each of them, to let them know that someone cared, that counseling, confession, communion, and the sacrament of the sick were available if they so desired. Because at that time there were no regular Protestant or Jewish chaplains making rounds, I also tried to establish some kind of relationship with the patients who were not Catholic, so they would know they had a friend if they needed one.

I usually spent two full days a week going from room to room in the various wards. I tried to see everybody, but I kept antennae out for those in special need. The doctors and the nurses helped me spot them. With these people I would spend as much time as necessary.

Frequently they were in pain, and sometimes they were scared. Many had been abruptly removed from their homes, friends, and jobs. Gone were the usual concerns, activities, and distractions that filled their daily lives. Everything that was nonessential to their humanity was stripped away, and they were left simply with themselves—and with the basic dilemmas of the human situation: What is the meaning, the purpose, of this life of mine? What does it take to make it a success? Where am I going, and what do I need to do to get there? And what about death? Is it the end or the beginning? In a cancer ward, the net worth of one's portfolio is not terribly important. Nor is one's professional achievements, sexual prowess, or social status. Only one thing is important: What have I given to other people? And to God? Which, of course, amounts to the same thing.

On the treadmill that is modern life, there is not much time to think about these things. In a hospital the patients think of little else. And most of them seemed to want to explore these questions with someone whom they felt cared, whom they could trust, and who had some expertise. This is how I understood my job as a hospital chaplain.

I felt privileged to be invited in on this process, to be present as people went deep inside themselves, wrestled with these questions, and dealt with their need for God, sometimes for the first time in a long time. It was exciting to see them decide to open up to God's love and try to respond. It was also very satisfying to see the joy that lit up their faces when they succeeded.

One man in the cancer ward had worked for the Mafia for years. He was a miserable patient—uncooperative, mean-spirited, cantankerous, without any desire to live. He gave the nurses such a hard time they flipped to see who would take care of him. Whoever lost got the job.

We became friendly. I enjoyed listening to his stories about the jobs he had pulled. It was better than *The Godfather*. Once I asked him if he might like to go to confession and communion. He laughed nervously and said, "I've done too many things. Unforgivable things. God couldn't possibly love me."

I chuckled and said, "Who are you to put limits on God's love?" He shrugged, so I said, "You change your mind, you got a friend. OK?"

"OK," he said.

The weeks went by, and I stopped by regularly to see how he was doing and to hear another story. His condition was deteriorating.

At three-thirty one morning, my phone rang. It was the nurse from the hospital. "It's Joe," she said. "He's raising hell, waking up all the other patients, and he wants to see you right away."

"Now?" I gulped, looking at the clock and trying to evict the cobwebs from my brain.

"Now," she said, a note of pleading desperation in her voice.

"I'll be right up," I replied.

If I wasn't fully awake when I got to the hospital, I was by the time he had finished his confession.

I brought him Holy Communion the same morning.

The nurses noticed the difference in Joe. The bitterness drained out of him. So did the self-hatred. His joy in life returned. So did his desire to help other people.

The last time I saw Joe, he was tucking his roommate into bed. It was the last time, because eleven days after that early morning phone call, my gangster friend died. He went to the Lord a happy man.

But I do not want to give the impression that everybody exercised his freedom in the same way. Some said yes to God. Others said maybe or later or no.

One inactive Catholic woman with whom I had become friendly began to hemorrhage. I asked her if she wanted to receive the sacraments. She shook her head with a vehemence that surprised me.

My job, I felt, was to put the patients in an atmosphere where they could exercise their freedom. On occasion I tried to illumine their options. But I could not decide for them. Nor should I try.

I got splattered with a lot of blood in those days and held the hands of a goodly number of people as they breathed their last. Sometimes I was the one to tell the patient that he or she would be going to God in the very near future. At other times I was the one to tell the relatives. On occasion they asked, "Why? Why does God allow people to suffer this way?" I had no answer then. I have none now. I just try to surrender to the mystery of it all and help them do the same. In most cases, I have found, a glib answer does more harm than good. The best—and only—thing you can do is to be present to the people in their pain, love them, and support them as they wrestle with the mystery that is human life.

Sometimes it was heavy and my heart would break and I would need to go down to the obstetrics ward so that the new mothers could cheer me up and teach me about the joy of the Lord.

To be whole a priest must have an active prayer life, work in which he believes and at which he feels competent, and a support system—a network of open and accepting relationships with people with whom he can share his vulnerability and communicate freely and honestly; friends who love him, not as he should be, but as he actually is.

In my years as a Paulist, I have usually been able to find the makings of such a support system among the priests with whom I lived and worked. But this was not the case in Los Angeles in September 1956.

Part of the problem was me. Too often, in my insecurity, I played the role of super priest, the man with all the answers and none of the problems of other people. Who would want to get close to someone who acted as if he had it made, especially if the subtext of that person's persona was "why can't you do as much good as I do?" Compounding the problem was my enthusiasm. Enthusiasm is great for a day, but it does not wear well. Day in and day out, it can be hard to take. In those years I was sometimes hard to take.

Part of the problem, too, were the other priests. Except for one of the chaplains at UCLA who shared my love of ideas and with whom I had some excellent conversations, we did not have much in common. They were involved in their own work, were wrestling with their own problems, and seemed to have little psychic energy left over to invest in a relationship with me.

But the biggest problem, I think, was Joe Burns, the pastor and superior. A mercurial man whose moods swung wildly from intense inner conflict and depression to ebullient elation, his understanding of leadership was the impersonal, authoritarian, and macho model he had seen operating in the Marine Corps, in which he had served as a chaplain during the bloody battles on Guadalcanal in World War II.

The present constitution of the Paulist Fathers describes a superior as "a protector of the weak, a listener, a facilitator of community dialogue, an articulator of community consensus and an executor of the community's will." Not Joe Burns. He insisted on dominating every situation in which he found himself. This included the rectory dinner table. He did not listen. He talked and we listened. And he used the community meals to bawl us out. He was bright and articulate and knew our weak points and where we had made our mistakes and took great pleasure in pointing them out to whoever was present. It was great for digestion. Being the youngest, I was a regular target, and in my case he was most often quite accurate, which made the emotional mauling even worse. After a while I started to wonder where he got his information and how he had unearthed the specifics. One day he tried to pump me for information about one of the other curates, and then I knew he was also pumping them for information about me. Instinctively I recoiled and turned him off. I should also have told him off, but the newly ordained did not do that in those days. It was easy to figure out who had squealed. I stopped trusting him the same day.

Yet Joe Burns was also capable of great kindness. One year he discovered it was my birthday and insisted on taking me out to a fine restaurant for dinner. One Christmas afternoon he stayed home to play chess with John King, who was feeling lonely, rather than visit his friends, which would have been his preference. Many times he got out of a warm bed to dig somebody out of a bar and drive them home in the middle of the night because they were too drunk to drive themselves.

So what did I do for a support system? I reached out to the diocesan priests in the area, with whom I had much in common. And I developed homes away from home with three of the families in the parish. They gave me a lot of love and helped me through a tough and lonely time.

Joe Burns was convinced that the people of St. Paul's were too status-conscious, snobbish, and concerned with appearances, and that the best remedy for this situation was to assault their sensitivities on every possible occasion, including Sunday Mass. How much this judgment was conditioned by Joe's own sense of inferiority, I do not know. But I do know that with the parishioners he was frequently abrasive in manner, salty in language, cutting in repartee, and obscene in anecdote. Ten percent of the men in the parish loved it. The remainder of the men and all of the women were appalled. He outraged some and wounded others. John King, Ronnie Burt, and I had to work hard to contain the damage.

On the parish gossip circuit, Joe was soundly cussed out. Most everybody knew of his drinking problem. But despite his beet-red face, habitual shortness of breath, and protruding belly, most did not know he had an enlarged heart, high blood pressure, and water on the lungs. They also did not know he was struggling with another problem.

On the first Sunday after I arrived, Joe had broken ground for a new church. He had permission from Cardinal McIntyre to spend six hundred thousand dollars—three hundred thousand of which was in the bank, another three hundred thousand to be lent to the parish by the archdiocese. Now, in the spring of 1958, the church was nearing completion and Joe had gone over budget and spent more than nine hundred thousand dollars. He was regularly dunned by creditors for the money he owed and did not have. He was in a tough spot. He could not tell the Cardinal. If he did, the Paulists would have been thrown out of the diocese. In desperation he tried to borrow the difference from the Paulists. Wisely, they refused. Caught in the middle, the pressure built and his health deteriorated.

Before his heart gave out, he had the satisfaction of offering Mass in his new church. He also had the satisfaction of knowing that all those people who had criticized him so severely were now loud in their praise of the stunningly beautiful church he had built. He had no tact, but he did have exquisite taste.

One morning about five, his doctor called from the hospital to which he had been taken, to tell me he was sinking rapidly. I went at once. He seemed to be comatose, so I blessed him and gave him absolution. He opened his eyes and said, "Bud, will you please stop mumbling?" Then he lapsed into a coma.

That afternoon, as he lay dying, Father John Fitzgerald, who had recently lost the election for Superior General of the Paulists and who was now giving a mission at St. Paul's, was sitting by his bedside. One last time Joe opened his eyes and said, "Fitz, on the Fourth of July, at Hollypark, bet the fourth horse in the fourth race."

Those were Joe's last words. His heart gave out two hours later.

Fitz did place the bet. The horse came in, paying twenty-four dollars.

At the time I did not know how bad the financial situation was. But Joe had told Fitz, who moved into the vacuum and asked me to run the fund drive to raise the needed six hundred thousand dollars.

I agreed. Partially because I liked Fitz, partially because the situation was desperate and I liked being needed, but also, I think, to prove something to myself and other people. In the seminary I had always been called an impractical mystic. Was I? I did not think so. This was the chance I needed to prove just how practical I could be.

The previous summer, with the help of eight students from St. Patrick's seminary in Menlo Park, I had taken a census of the entire parish. We rang ten thousand doorbells and now knew who our parishioners were, where they lived, what they did for a living, and whether they were active or not.

I divided the parish into eight geographical zones, each of which had approximately two hundred families living in it. I appointed a chairman for each zone and helped each put together a team of twenty men who would be willing to contact ten of their neighbors. They were given pledge cards for each.

Fitz advised me to select the fifty people I thought could give the most and call upon them myself. In doing so, he also advised me to ask for three times as much as I thought I could get. "It flatters them," he said, "and raises their sights."

We held a pep rally for the workers. Fitz, who had now been named pastor, the lay chairman of the drive, and I spoke. The response was enthusiastic. We also wrote to all our parishioners asking them to be generous when they were called upon. And we preached three successive Sundays on the parish's need.

My first call was upon a rich and elderly dowager whose husband had been active in the parish but who had a reputation for being tightfisted. I asked Fitz what I should ask for. He said she was capable of giving ten thousand dollars but would probably give only five thousand. "So what should I ask for?" I repeated.

"Ask her for fifty thousand," he said. "Let's see what happens."

So I made the appointment, went to see her, and made my pitch.

"Mrs. Powell," I said, "The Paulist Fathers were very fond of your husband. He was a good friend of ours, and we would very much like him to have a memorial in our new church."

"Which memorial did you have in mind?" she asked.

"The baptistery," I replied.

"And how much would that be?" she asked.

"Only fifty thousand dollars," I answered.

In the gas station where I had worked, a customer who spent ten dollars was a high roller. In the seminary we were given no money at all, and since ordination I had been getting twenty dollars a month for spending money. So fifty thousand dollars was for me like a trillion—a sum so large it ceased to have any meaning.

"Fifty thousand dollars," she shrieked in horror. "I can't give you that. I'll . . . I'll only give you twenty-five thousand."

We were off and running. Fund-raising was no fun. It was not then and it is not now. But once you get beyond the feeling you are asking for yourself, once you realize you are asking for God and His people and are doing your prospective donors a favor by giving them this opportunity to participate, it becomes much easier.

In the weeks that followed, the men pounded the pavements, the people dug deep, and the pledges rolled in. Eight weeks later, we had five hundred and eighty-five thousand dollars in cash or pledges. We were out of trouble. Only then did John Fitzgerald tell the Cardinal what Joe Burns had done.

The fund drive was also part of my education. It taught me how profoundly generous the Catholic people are, how they will sacrifice their own comfort to feed the hungry, share the Gospel, or meet the needs of their parish.

One evening, midway through the fund drive, I took the visiting Cardinal McCann of South Africa out to dinner, in the course of which I complained about what fund-raising was doing to me. "I look at somebody now," I said, "and I no longer think 'Does this person love God?' but rather 'How much can he or she give to the drive?' "

"Do not fret, Father," he said. "You are multiplying the loaves and the fishes."

The fund drive also taught me something else: If something really needs to be done, and if I totally commit myself to getting it done, I can usually motivate enough other people to help me get it done. Mobilizing crusades is compatible to me.

This was a lesson that was to have ramifications in the years ahead.

CHAPTER 6

EVANGELIST

The church is dark, alive with shadows, the sanctuary lamp flickering off to one side. I try to pray, but I am restless, like a caged tiger before feeding time. I have dreamed of this night for years. And I have worked weeks to prepare for it—researching the course, publicizing the whole program. Adult education. In theology. What Jesus has to say about God, about the mystery that is human life, about why we are here, where we are going, and what we need to do to get there. But will anybody show up? In twenty-five minutes, I will know. All day the phone has been ringing with people asking for information. "Somebody must be interested," I say to myself. But how interested? Enough to give a night a week for three months? I wonder. "Do it bigger. Do it better," Dad had said. So I did. Six courses, one every weekday night, another on Saturday morning. Fitz had wondered whether it would work. I had assured him it would. "Adult education is big in Los Angeles, and the symptoms of spiritual hunger are everywhere." He had trusted me, said, "Go ahead, try it." But now I am not so sure. Have I overextended myself? What about organic growth, taking one step at a time? I try kneeling. "I want a success, Lord, but if you want a flop, it's OK with me." Too much energy. No place to go. I try sitting. Up straight. Deep breathing. A car shoots up the driveway into the parking lot. Then another. At least I'll have two people. "Lord, this is all in your hands. Send me the ones you want, as many or as few as you want." I can't sit still. Too much adrenaline. The church is deserted, so I get up and begin to walk up and down the main aisle. "Lord, they're gonna come looking for you, and all they're gonna find is me. I know you use the weak things of this world, but don't you think you're overdoing it a bit?" What have I gotten myself into? Talk about challenges. I'm not up to this. I look at my watch. Five more minutes. I could go down to the classroom now. That's where the action is. Greet the people. I say no. The co-instructors will greet the people. I know I give a better class, a better lecture, a better sermon, if I've had quiet time, prayer time beforehand. So, hands in my pockets, I continue to walk up and down the aisle of the deserted church. "Lord, I can't do this alone. Maybe you can do it through me. How about it? Please?"

Eight o'clock. I head for the classroom, feeling like a racehorse leaving the starting gate. At the registration desk, I catch the eyes of the head co-instructor. She gives me the thumbs-up sign. "Good group," she says. "Large and young." As I walk to the front of the brightly colored modernistic classroom, I can see that more than a hundred people have crowded in. I smile at them. They smile at me. We are checking each other out. Their faces are open, alive, expectant. They are looking for something. What? Can I give it to them?

The turnout is better than we had hoped, and I am delighted. Another three hundred people sign up for the five courses that follow. When we launch six more courses in January, the results are similar. In all more than a thousand people attended the Paulist Inquiry Classes from September 1958 through August of 1959. During the September 1959 through August 1960 school year, that number swelled to fifteen hundred, where it remained for each of the succeeding four years. From September 1958, when we started the Paulist Inquiry Classes, until August of 1964, when I turned over the directorship of the program to Father George St. Laurent, eighty-five hundred people had signed up for the classes.

Clearly we were touching a live nerve in the Los Angeles community. But who were these people? Why had they come? What were they looking for? Would we be able to meet their expectations?

Approximately fifty percent were Catholics, two thirds of whom were practicing. Of these most had accompanied a non-Catholic friend or relative to the classes. The remainder had come to brush up on their own faith. Of the nonpracticing Catholics, many were taking a fresh look at the Church. Some were in the process of working their way back to active participation in its life. Perhaps they had fallen in love and God was again a reality in their lives. Or they were now parents and needed to make decisions about the religious upbringing of their children. Or the American dream of affluence was not delivering the fulfillment it had promised.

Of those who were not Catholic, most said they believed in God. Many said they believed in Jesus. Some said they believed in some kind of church community. A very few said they believed in nothing. Yet for most, it would seem that God had not been a very important part of their lives until very recently.

A majority had some religion in their upbringing—usually Protestant church services and Sunday school. Most of the Protestants had not been active for a long time. But some were churchgoing Protestants who for one reason or another were looking around. A few were Jewish, some ethnically, others also religiously.

As I got to know these people well, I came to realize how belief and nonbelief are intertwined in all our lives. There is a believer in everyone—a side of us that says life is beautiful and full of meaning, that it is guided according to a purpose, that the deep reality that does the guiding is kind and loving. And there is a nonbeliever in all of us—a part that says that life is cruel and arbitrary, that it grinds us down in the process of going nowhere, that, at the deepest level of reality, there is nothing but a vacuum.

So those who deny the reality of God have a strain of belief in them. And those who affirm His reality and rejoice in it still have a strain of unbelief in them. We are all ambivalent, part believer, part unbeliever, possessed of faith, yet afflicted by doubt.

Paul Tillich, the great Lutheran theologian, goes one step further. Not only is the dialectic between faith and doubt inevitable, he says, but it is desirable. It throws off charges of spiritual energy that vivify the faith of the believer and propel his or her spiritual growth.

Working with the inquirers on an intimate level, I began to see something else: Few people lose their faith. Once they have communed with God and experienced His love, they are never the same. Such a person carries the memory of that experience inside. It does not evaporate. Nor does the faith that gave rise to it. As Mauriac said, "One is never cured of God when one has once known Him."

Theoretically it may be possible to kill one's faith, but that seldom happens. What does happen is the suppression of faith.

Why? Because it is associated with a great deal of hurt, disappointment, and frustration; or because it seems irrelevant, guilt-provoking, and at variance with the kind of life and the kind of values one has chosen. Instead of living for God, some people seek the meaning of their lives in money or pleasure or power or prestige or ego. These things become idols, the acquisition of which they hope will enable them to feel good about themselves. In such cases the faith of these people becomes the cause of so much tension and conflict because it is so contrary to the goals they have set for themselves that they are tempted to bar it from consciousness. They push it down into their unconscious, where it can no longer consciously motivate their behavior or give direction to their lives. They arrange things in such a way that their faith is bypassed and left to atrophy. But it never completely dies. It bounces around in their unconscious, sometimes peeping out at the strangest times. On occasion it may even burst into consciousness and scream, "Pay attention! You must pay attention to me!"

Such an experience may cause the apparent nonbeliever to renew the suppression. "Naughty child," they say with a slap. "Get back in there! Don't bother me!" Or it may cause them to reexamine nostalgically the faith of their past and even consider looking into those inquiry classes they have heard about.

So the real question for those in the inquiry classes was not "Do you believe?" but rather "What is shaping your life? What are you living for? Are you seeking your fulfillment in something higher or something lower?"

Some of the people who came to class said they were agnostic. At the deepest level, they felt unsure of the reality of God. Sometimes this was caused by a kind of spiritual insensitivity, which an overriding preoccupation with money, pleasure, and ego can produce. Sometimes it was caused by a reluctance to make the commitment that faith would demand of them. But sometimes it was caused by something very different: a sense of awe and wonder at the mystery of human life that was so intense it made one-dimensional conceptual systems, facile formulas, and glib explanations unacceptable. These people refused to empty the human situation of its transcendent dimension. They knew they could not put an ocean into a bucket and were not about to try. They called themselves agnostics, but they may have had a keener sense of God than they were aware of. No idols for them, thank you.

A small number of our inquirers said they were atheists. Some of these were university students who needed an unconventional label to pin upon themselves. They would attack during the question period and stimulate the entire class. This generated much emotional electricity, was sometimes great theater, and often created a marvelous teaching situation.

Others applied the label atheist to themselves for more serious reasons—sometimes because they did not want to be like the religious people they knew—but when I got to know them, I discovered they were not atheists in any sense in which I used the word. They were so wholeheartedly committed to the welfare of their families and to freedom, justice, and peace in the world, that I was able to understand the unselfishness of their commitment only in a transcendent context. Implicit in that commitment seemed to me some kind of religious faith. I think they were believers unaware of the fact.

I do think it is possible to be a real atheist, and I did meet some people in our classes who would have to be put in that category. They seemed to have no awareness of anything of value beyond themselves. Their commitments seemed devoid of any transcendent horizon. Frequently they had been badly hurt, sometimes by people who hypocritically called themselves believers. As a result they had pulled back into themselves. Concerned only with the immediate, they had closed out everything else. Yet they did come to class. Why? I do not know. I do know they did not come for an argument, so I tried to listen to their hurt and give them as much love as I could. They made me keenly aware of how wounding hypocrisy can be and how deceptive labels frequently are.

I have also met people who call themselves Christian, and who may be regular churchgoers, yet who in their personal and professional lives are so concerned with money and power and prestige and pleasure and their own egos that they are totally oblivious to the presence of God in themselves or in other people. Devoid of love, sensitivity, and joy, they effectively squeeze the reality of God out of their lives. They are practical atheists.

Some of our eighty-five hundred inquirers came alone. But most came with a friend, a husband or wife, a fiancé or fiancée. Why did they come? For eighty-five hundred different reasons. Each inquirer is unique, so his or her reason for investigating is going to be unique.

Ted Peterson was the toast of the surgical staff at the UCLA

Medical Center. A man of brilliant intellect and intense concentration, he had never lost a patient. When he operated, every facet of his being—his mind, his will, his iron nerves, and his perfectly coordinated fingers—was focused on the patient's well-being.

Idolized by the residents, adored by the nurses, revered by his patients, at thirty-five he was already internationally acclaimed.

Yet he was not a man you could get close to. As he explained to me later, "I had always gotten what I wanted, been able to do whatever I made up my mind to do. I really believed I could do anything. I did not need other people. I certainly did not need God. I was an arrogant son of a bitch."

Then Susan McGill, a lovely young mother with a defective heart, came in from Savannah for heart surgery. After a meticulous examination and a battery of tests, Ted thought they could operate. Susan was delighted. Ted called to reassure her husband, who was back in Savannah with the kids.

Ted was at his best as they neared the end of the procedure, completing the bypass and preparing to detach her from the heart-lung machine. But when they did so, for reasons no one could later understand, her heart did not respond by taking up the slack. Her pulse slowed, her blood pressure dropped. Cardiac output was much below normal. Ted ordered her heart injected with dopamine to stimulate it. That worked for a time. But only for a time. Ted ordered a double dose. She responded. But soon the heart was back to where it had been. They increased the backload of blood. It did not help. He hooked her back up to the heart-lung machine. Then slowly, patiently, he tried to wean her from it. It did not work. Ted remained cool and controlled on the outside. But inside he was becoming frantic. He tried everything he could, but her heart would not respond, and her condition continued to deteriorate. For four more desperate hours he did everything he knew. To no avail. After eight hours on the table, Susan McGill's heart gave out.

Ted was devastated. How could he explain this to her husband? What could they tell her children? He did the best he could. After talking to the husband on the phone, he kicked his foot through the partition in his office.

Exhausted, frustrated, and angry, he stopped at the beach on his way home. There he shook his fist at the stars and shouted, "How dare you? How dare you?" Ted had had a nominal religious upbringing but had not thought of God for years. Now he raged at Him. "I hate you. You hear? I hate you."

That night he cried in his wife's arms. She had not seen this side of him before. It was as if he were a little boy. "Was I crying for Susan, for her husband, for their kids—or was I crying for myself?" He said to me later, "I think I knew the omnipotent Ted Peterson was also dead."

Unable to sleep, Ted got up, put on his bathrobe, and went out onto his patio about 2 A.M. He just sat there for a long time. After a while he found himself praying—trying to draw into his emptiness the fullness of God.

Four weeks later he signed up for the inquiry classes.

For me as the priest teacher and for many of the inquirers, the classes and the private sessions that accompanied them were the beginning of a very special kind of relationship. It was an I-Thou friendship. But it was more than that. They were embarking on a once-in-a-lifetime journey and had invited me along as a privileged companion and guide. Many of them chose to share their hurts and fears and sins with me. I did the same with some of them. We entered each other's lives in a very special way, gave and received much from each other, and in a very real sense fell in love. In some cases we became a permanent part of each other's lives.

There was a sacramental dimension to this relationship. God was present in it. And He acted through it. Sometimes this relationship was the medium through which God spoke, the context in which His love was experienced and responded to.

This did not happen with everybody in class. It did not happen with everybody for whom the classes produced an awesome kind of spiritual growth. But it happened frequently enough for me to begin to appreciate its significance.

Not all of those who came the first night decided to take the whole course. Usually about two thirds persevered. I hated to see people drop off and sometimes wondered what I might be doing wrong.

Any sense of disappointment about the falloff was more than offset, however, by the excitement I felt at what was happening inside so many of those who remained.

I could tell Mary Jo Swenson was hurting when she came to inquiry class for the first time. I did not know why.

The first half of her life had been terrific, she was later to tell me. But then, fourteen years ago, her father left her mother, and that left a big hole in her life. She blamed herself. And when he did not come around much, when more often than not he forgot her birthday, she felt he did not care. She went a little wild after that. Gave her mother a difficult time. Didn't study. Got into shoplifting. And sleeping around.

"Why not?" she said to herself. "It doesn't mean much. Just like brushing your teeth."

At first it was the boys at school. But after a while, with the war on, it became the soldiers at the USO and then older men. "They had more money, could buy me better things," she explained.

Mary Jo loved the attention. She loved to turn the guys on, and she loved the nice things they gave her.

"Life was a drag," she told me. "So dull. So boring. But in bed, at the moment of climax, that's when I came alive. Then, and on the stage. I did two plays when I was in high school. I liked playing somebody else, and people really liked it when I did. I dreamed of being an actress. I got an agent, joined the union, went for auditions. But they didn't want me. Some people have it. Some don't. I didn't."

For a while after high school, she worked as a clerk and went to college at night. Then she quit college and took a job as a saleslady in a travel agency. She learned the business. And before long she was managing the agency for the guy who owned it. Then, last year, she bought it from him. Now, at twenty-eight, she had her own agency.

But still she didn't like herself. She felt she had nothing to offer anybody. Lately she had been sleeping with just one guy. But he was married.

She didn't like herself for that either.

Part of her was saying, "I've gotta have somebody to hold me, even if he does belong to somebody else." And part of her was saying, "I don't like what I'm doing. I don't want to live like this."

Then she started dreaming about his wife and kids.

That's when she decided to come to class.

She caught on quickly, had no trouble accepting what Jesus taught, and started going to Mass every week.

There were just two problem areas. The first was the most

fundamental. She had trouble believing God could love her, that He was, in fact, crazy about her. She struggled with that for a long time. The Good News was just a little too good for her to accept all at once.

We became friends. She liked talking to a man. Apparently she had had few serious conversations with the men in her life.

"You think God makes junk?" I asked her.

"But you know all the things I've done. The people I've hurt."

"So?" I said. "You're a piker compared to Mary Magdalene."

It took her a while to get used to the idea. Slowly she opened up and allowed God's love to come in.

Then she faced the other problem.

"You love this guy?" I asked.

"No," she said. "But I'm dependent on him. I'm afraid to be alone."

"But you're not alone."

"You say that," she exclaimed, "but I've gotta believe it." She paused, sighed, and said, "I guess I've been looking for love in the wrong place."

She did make the break. And she did come into the Church. And fifteen months after her baptism, I celebrated her marriage to a very loving man. They are very happy.

Many of the inquirers were like Mary Jo. During the inquiry course, they changed. They grew. They pushed back the horizon of their lives and explored facets of themselves that previously they did not even know existed. In the process, their lives began to make more sense. For the first time in their lives, they traveled deep within themselves, looked around, and more often than not liked what they saw. Taking charge of their lives, they broke free of those things that compromised their dignity and undercut their liberty. Possessing themselves, they began to give themselves. They exercised their freedom by reaching out in love to those around them.

Most important of all, they began to come to terms with the God who lived in their own depths and in the depths of the people around them. Sometimes they fought and argued with Him. Sometimes they pushed Him away. But God is not easily discouraged, and He would much rather be abused than ignored. These people were paying attention to Him. They were being present to Him. They were allowing Him to be present to them. In their own unique way, they were trying to communicate with Him.

Sometimes, but not always, the wrestling match with God culminated in the surrender we usually call conversion. This is the natural culmination of the whole process of spiritual growth and carries the inquirer onto a whole new spiritual plateau, enabling him or her to know and love in a deeper, fuller way.

Ron Ashton was like that. When I first met him, he was making a half-million dollars a year, but it was not enough. He felt empty and confused inside. An engineer and an entrepreneur, he had established one of the original small computer companies. It had prospered, but the price tag was terribly high: Month after grueling month, he worked sixteen-hour days.

It was not that he did not love his wife and three children. It was just that he got suckered in, and they got pushed aside. "You do what you have to do," he told himself.

His wife, Joanne, gritted her teeth and did the best she could. The kids were not so gracious. "Hey, Mom," said thirteen-year-old Billy, "who's this strange man you got hanging around the house?" Karen, his older sister, became sullen and resentful. It wasn't just the time. It was the attention. When Ron was home, he wasn't home. His mind was on the plant and their next project.

Then Jimmy, their seventeen-year-old, had too many beers and crashed his motorbike into the side of a neighbor's house.

While the doctors worked to save Jimmy's life—he had multiple skull fractures, several badly damaged vertebrae, and severe internal bleeding—Ron paced back and forth in the corridor outside. Suddenly, he realized, the company and its bottom line were not important. Only Jimmy's life was. Ron decided he had to make some changes in his life.

The boy did live. And Ron did make some changes. He turned over the operation of the company to other people. "From now on," he announced at dinner, "I'm concentrating on policy. Forty hours a week. No more." Joanne smiled. The kids clapped.

At forty-two, Ron was shifting direction. But he soon found out he could not do it in a vacuum.

Joanne was a Catholic. Ron noticed she had something he didn't. "Joanne goes through life on shock absorbers," he said. "I feel every bump."

When she told him of the classes, he agreed to give them a try. Yet he was very cautious. He had a deliberate and methodical mind, and his approach to God, while not antagonistic, was a skeptical one. Like the man from Missouri, he had to be shown. He had questions after each class and needed to make sure every step along the way had convincing arguments to support it. I enjoyed our conversations, and we became friends. Sometimes he wanted a kind of absolute certainty. I told him that came after the leap of faith, not before. "There's enough light for those who want to believe," I told him, quoting Pascal, "and enough darkness for those who don't."

He started to go to Mass with Joanne and the kids. He was still on the outside. But now, more and more, he wanted to be on the inside.

"I wanna believe," he told me. "I just don't."

"It's a gift," I told him. "Pray for it." He did. It didn't happen.

The course concluded. "I'm sorry," he said. "I want to. I just can't."

"Take your time," I said. "It'll happen when God wants it to happen. Not before."

About six months later it did happen. Nothing dramatic. Just one Sunday afternoon on a picnic with the kids, he was lying under a tree and the sun was glistening through the leaves and he was struck with how lovely it was and he found himself thanking God for having created such a beautiful universe. It was then that he realized he believed.

"Somehow God touched me," he told me. "He enabled me to see what before I couldn't see. Also to feel loved. I'm a very lucky man."

Ron was baptized three weeks later. Jimmy was his godfather.

There are as many different pathways to conversion as there are people journeying toward God. Yet each in his or her own unique way, at his or her own unique pace, seems to arrive at the same kind of experience. They begin to see into their lives and surroundings in a new and deeper way. Things that did not seem to fit together before now mesh into a harmonious whole. In God's light they see connections and discover meanings that previously had been elusive. They have started to look at reality through God's eyes, to put on the mind of Christ.

More than anything else, they become intensely aware of God's love. They open to it. They try to return it. Conversion always involves a kind of surrender, a turning of their lives over to God, giving Him complete freedom to work within them. As a result, the God who is the loving ground of their being surfaces within them. And He speaks His Word—who is Jesus—in them. Jesus in them becomes Lord, inasmuch as He takes over and begins to lead them to spiritual fulfillment. And He becomes Savior inasmuch as He heals their alienation and reconciles them to themselves, to other people, and to God. And that's not all. The Father and the Son who now live in them breathe forth their Spirit who is the Spirit of Love—and this Spirit draws them into the embrace of Father and Son. He also draws them into the life of the Church.

These new relationships cause new converts to come alive in a new and fuller way. They are born again. Their experience of life is transformed, and their psychic energies are redirected—from the surface to the depths, from the periphery to the center, from the outer to the inner, from the physical and sensate to the spiritual. Instead of being self-centered, they become God-centered.

Baptism—and the profession of faith that precedes it—is the sacramental expression of this radical turning from self to God. It involves a dying to greed, hedonism, and ego and a rising to a new fullness of life in Christ.

Running water is such a beautiful symbol of this kind of spiritual rebirth. There is something archetypal about it. Deep in my unconscious, I know that in the process of evolving, my prehuman forebears emerged from the seas, and I likewise know that for almost nine months, as I grew and developed, I was carried in a warm sack of water in my mother's womb. And I also know that, tense and fatigued, I can take a bath, shower, or swim and emerge feeling relaxed, refreshed, and reinvigorated.

But unlike the usually solitary bath, shower, and swim, baptism is a profoundly communal experience. It initiates me into the triune life of God and forges deep relationships with each member of the Trinity. It also initiates me into the Church, making me a full-fledged member of the family of God on this earth. The estrangement of life before conversion is replaced by the connectedness and belongingness of life after conversion. The tension and conflict of deciding to surrender is replaced by the peace and joy of having done so.

This is why converts are some of the happiest people I know.

During the six years I ran the inquiry class program, more than a thousand people entered the Church. Almost another thousand would have done so had it not been for their second or third marriages. Church law and pastoral practice were much more restrictive in those days than they are now. I very much regret having discouraged some of those beautiful people.

I loved teaching the classes. It was what I had always wanted to do. And I loved being part of the process by which these people came to God. At a crucial time in their lives, I was able to be there for them, and they invited me in and shared their fears, breakthroughs, and happiness with me.

Few experiences before or since have given me so much satisfaction—or joy.

CHAPTER 7

PRODUCER

As one series of inquiry classes followed another, a single question kept recurring to the media specialists promoting the classes: "If we are reaching fifteen hundred people a year this way," they asked, "how can we reach all five million people in Los Angeles?"

It was the right question at the right time. It forced us to broaden our horizons and think big.

Today the answer seems obvious, but in the spring of 1960 television was not as dominant an influence in American culture as it is now. Yet we were aware of TV's power, and so we began to talk seriously about televising the inquiry classes. Instead of asking people to come to us, TV would enable us to go to them, bringing the Gospel into their living rooms. Lost, we knew, would be the immediacy of the classroom experience and the sense of community that flows from it. Gained would be the large numbers we could reach in this way, many of whom would never think of enrolling in an inquiry class.

Joe Connelly, a parishioner and close friend, the creator and producer of "Leave It to Beaver," was active in these discussions. So was Jim Moser, another close friend and the creator and producer of "Medic." They knew drama. They knew network television. But they did not know how to secure local time. Through a mutual friend, we approached KTTV, one of the local independent stations. They had no time available. Without thinking it through, we went to KCOP, the least-watched independent station in Los Angeles, and offered to buy thirteen half hours. They turned us down. At this point, Joe Connelly sold two new comedy series to CBS. Riding high, he asked one of their top executives in New York to intercede for us with KNXT, the CBS-owned and -operated station in Los Angeles. This led to a meeting with its program director, Leon Drew, who liked our concept and agreed to make thirteen half hours available to us on a public-service basis.

On the least popular station in L.A., we had unsuccessfully tried to buy time. Now, on the most popular station in L.A., we were being given free time. God knew what He was doing even if we did not.

In offering to purchase time on KCOP, we had no idea of the implications of what we were doing. If they had accepted, we would have been venturing out on the slippery slope of financial dependency. Almost inevitably this would have led to on-the-air fund-raising. To succeed at this, we would have been tempted to shift the orientation of our program from the nonbelievers, who would be less inclined to contribute, to the believers, who would be more inclined to do so, and we would have subjected ourselves to almost irresistible pressures to truncate the Gospel, avoid the controversial, and tell people what they wanted to hear rather than what they needed to hear. As one of the contemporary televangelists put it, "Why should I say things that will alienate the customers?"

We were delighted with KNXT's offer and immediately accepted. I plunged into preparing the scripts. Almost weekly over the summer of 1960 I retreated to Joe Connelly's apartment at the Balboa Bay Club in Newport Beach to write without distraction, leaving after Mass on Tuesday morning and returning in time for class Wednesday night. Once I had completed a first draft, Joe and Jim Moser would go over the scripts, clarifying and punching them up. Only with tightly crafted scripts, they told me, could we be assured of a compelling program.

It was a rigorous process but also an exciting one. I was thrilled at the prospect of having a series. But I was also frightened. I think I sensed what was ahead, that my priesthood would be changed, that eventually I would be forced to give up many of the pastoral activities that I enjoyed so much.

I took my qualms to Bishop Raymond Lane, a foreign missionary who had been a prisoner of the Japanese during World War II and subsequently the Superior General of Maryknoll. He listened and understood. He suspected I was right about the price I would have to pay. But he said, "You cannot turn back. It is God who has brought you this far."

On one visit to KNXT I passed an intense young politician in the corridor who was struggling for the Democratic nomination for President of the United States. His name: John F. Kennedy.

Fitz was very pleased with the idea of the TV series. We made an appointment to tell Cardinal McIntyre what we planned and secure his approval. Fitz did most of the talking in the meeting that followed. He knew the Cardinal's twin enthusiasms—for St. Thomas Aquinas's natural law theory and for the teaching program of the Confraternity of Christian Doctrine—and so he presented the proposed TV series as an extension of the archdiocese's CCD to more widely communicate the principles of the natural law to the Los Angeles viewing public. The Cardinal responded positively to the idea and gave us his enthusiastic support.

In our original discussions with Leon Drew, we had talked about a Sunday afternoon time slot, but when it came time to make things final, he offered only Sunday morning at ten o'clock. This was unacceptable to us—since the available audience in the morning was only 25 percent of what it would be in the afternoon—and so an impasse developed. Finally, with the start of the series fast approaching, Joe Connelly tried unsuccessfully to get Leon Drew on the phone, then sent him an eloquently indignant telegram. In response, Leon called Joe and said, "Hey, I'm not a bad guy" . . . and offered a four-thirty time period. We accepted immediately.

Two weeks before the show's premiere, I again found myself in the Cardinal's office, this time alone, to explain to the diocesan consultors—twelve mostly crusty monsignors and Bishops Manning and Bell—what we intended to do. They listened intently, but the Cardinal did most of the talking after I had finished.

He objected to the proposed title of the series—"Facts on Faith"—and I agreed to come up with another. Thank God he did, because the result was "Insight," which conveyed so much better what the series would become. "Father, this script on happiness," the Cardinal continued, "it sounds like a Paulist Mission talk. I expected something out of St. Thomas."

"It's right out of the Prima Secundae, your Eminence," I replied, referring to a section of St. Thomas's *Summa Theologica.* The Cardinal missed the reference, but Bishop Manning did not. He had to struggle to suppress a chuckle.

"You say you plan a program on confession. I really don't think that's a good idea. People will laugh."

"For everyone that laughs, ten will want to go," I responded.

"Oh, Father," he said, "you are an enthusiast, and that's good in this kind of work. But I would like to see the script, and please do not be disappointed if I turn it down."

I did submit the script. He did turn it down. I was furious. That is the last script I ever submitted for ecclesiastical approval.

As the meeting in the Cardinal's office broke up, Bishop Manning came over to tell me I should not be discouraged. "It is a great idea," he said, "and will do much good." In his own oblique way, he was apologizing for the negativity and telling me to ignore the Cardinal. I tried.

Five days before we were scheduled to tape the first program, we went down to look at the set KNXT had built. It was medieval in feel, constricted and depressing. We complained vociferously. Several weeks before I had celebrated the wedding of an art director, Bill Malley, who quickly designed a new set—modern, cheerful, spacious—that KNXT agreed to build. I apologized to the head of KNXT's construction crew for the inconvenience we were causing. He shrugged it off, saying, "No problem. I figure God deserves the best, and you guys are just trying to get it for Him." This incident established an important precedent, for KNXT and for ourselves: We would not sacrifice quality for any reason whatsoever. At KNXT it also earned us the nickname "Ben Hur on Mondays."

Finally, with the scripts almost completed, the date of the first taping approached. Joe Connelly thought I should use contact lenses but changed his mind after looking at my face without glasses. We considered using a live class but rejected it as too contrived. We also considered using a TelePrompTer but rejected it as unnatural. So I set about memorizing the text—not too difficult when you have written it.

John Dugan, a Hollywood writer, Jim Moser, and my new assistant, Donna Wanland, helped me rehearse. I had a lot to learn about inflection and pacing.

The first program was called *A Tale of Two Testaments* and was about the Jewish experience of God. It also contained a ringing condemnation of anti-Semitism.

I did not think I would be nervous. I was wrong. As the countdown for the taping began, my body began to quiver and my kneecaps started to bounce around my upper legs. I prayed. I tried to turn everything over to God. I asked Him to use me.

"Ten . . . nine . . . eight . . . seven . . ." Director Jim Johnson's voice intoned over the PA. I started to wonder what the hell I had gotten myself into. But then the red light on the camera went on and I began to talk and my energy had someplace to go. I tried to remind myself that on the other side of that three-inch lens were thousands of people in their living rooms. I was their guest. They wanted to hear what I had to say. There were just two or three of them in each living room, so there was nothing to be afraid of. Just relax, make myself at home, and warmly, intimately, yet powerfully say what I had to say. It helped. I started to flow, and somehow I got through it. Afterward, in the postmortem, Jim and John and Donna thought it was good—a little too serious, perhaps, in need of some humor, of course, but basically OK.

I had peaked, putting out a great deal of energy. Now I subsided in exhaustion. I needed to unwind. That night Paulist Tom Comber and I went out for dinner and a movie.

The first taping was thirteen days before airdate. The second was six days before our premiere. After the second taping something was wrong, and I could not figure out what it was. Slowly I started to get a fix on it. I knew there were living, breathing human beings on the other side of that lens, but I had no experience of them, no sense of feedback from them, no feeling of emotional communion with them. I was putting out, but I was not getting anything back. I found that frustrating.

All of this changed with the airing of the first program. The reaction from the viewers was immediate and mostly positive. The parishioners liked it. So did my priest friends. But what moved me most were the telephone calls from Jewish viewers, some of whom were survivors of the Holocaust. The public acknowledgment of Christian sins against Jews, the condemnation of anti-Semitism as a contradiction of the Gospel, as well as the affirmation of the complementarity of the Old and New Testaments, came over to them as good news. One said, "This is new church doctrine. I never thought I would hear it. We are entering a new age."

He spoke prophetically. Five years later the essential content of my remarks, which simply reflected what Catholic theologians working in the field were saying, was made official church teaching in the Vatican Council's *Nostra Aetate,* which did indeed usher in a new age of Christian-Jewish relations.

The reaction of the viewers was very important to me psychologically. Now I knew I was being heard. People were listening, and they were responding. The circle of communication had been closed. This realization did much to give future programs a more relaxed, warm, and spontaneous tone.

As week followed week, we tried to add visual interest to the programs. Sometimes we illustrated the talks with contemporary photography and art masterpieces. On occasion we had actors deliver the statements of historical figures over the visuals. For one particularly abstract talk, a choreographer whom I had recently baptized brought his ballet students to the studio, and they danced and mimed the various stages in the search for God. We offered copies of each talk and averaged three hundred requests per program.

By the time the thirteen weeks were over and we had completed the series, we wondered if other cities in the country might not profit from what we had created. To find out, we transferred the videotapes to film and offered them gratis to any station in the country that would air them at a decent time. Don McGannon, the president of GROUP W, saw the audition and immediately committed his five stations. Within three months thirty other TV stations were also airing "Insight."

Once the series was produced and syndicated, we had time to reflect on the whole experience, and we came to two conclusions: First, television was worth every ounce of time and energy we could put into it; second, we needed to shift gears and take a new approach so as to tap the visual and emotional potential of television.

So we decided to do a second "Insight" series but to make significant changes in its content and format.

Jack Kennedy had just been inaugurated President of the United States. The cold war was at its height. The new FCC chairman, Newton B. Minow, was calling American TV a vast wasteland. Walter Lippmann was asking in *Life* magazine "What is America's national philosophy?" It is one thing to be against communism, he, in effect, was saying, but what are we for? What do we as a people believe in? What is America's philosophy of freedom?

This was an area of great intellectual interest to me. It was also an area in which the Church had much to say. Isaac Hecker, the founder of the Paulists, had written extensively on this theme.

So we decided to address these questions in a second "Insight" series, to explore in depth the connection between religious faith and human freedom, all in the light of the American experience. The best way to do this, we also decided, was to employ a documentary format, sometimes with animated sequences, sometimes with actors playing historical characters.

In the fall of 1961, I set about writing the new series, which premiered in January of 1962. With Gene Raymond playing William Brewster, we did one program on the early colonists' search for religious freedom. With Patrick McVey playing Thomas Jefferson, we analyzed the Declaration of Independence. With MacDonald Carey playing James Madison, we explored the Constitution and the Bill of Rights. With Eduardo Ciannelli playing Nietzsche and Everett Sloane playing Lenin, we did separate shows on the atheistic roots of both nazism and communism and looked at the connection between atheism and the human rights abuses of those regimes. We also created mini-dramas, so that we could interview a Hiroshima survivor played by Marvin Miller, a prisoner of the Chinese Communists played by Raymond Massey, and a victim of the gas chambers at Auschwitz played by Jane Wyman—all on the Job question: How can a loving God permit so many innocent people to suffer so terribly?

We found many people in the acting community—some of its bigger names and more talented performers—willing to volunteer their services. Initially we contacted them through mutual friends. As often happens, the most talented were usually the most cooperative. I remember with gratitude the self-effacing Raymond Massey coming over to me one day during a break in rehearsals to ask, "How does it sound? Am I doing justice to your words?"

I continued to host the series, building the bridges between the various segments, punching home the points, and providing the continuous personality that the audience would look for week after week. Some personality.

The reaction to the second series was better than the first. We were experimenting, feeling our way, trying things, some of which worked, some of which did not, learning as we went, trying not to make the same mistake twice. We tried hard to give our viewers the best show we could. I think they sensed this. They seemed to appreciate what we were doing and supported us all the way. The critics were kind. Our ratings were good. And what was true in Los Angeles was also true around the country. When syndicated, the second "Insight" series played on sixty-five stations.

Once we had finished the second series, we again took time to reflect on what we were doing. Should we try a third series? If so, should we retain the documentary format? Or should we try something else?

As the second series had unfolded, we found that more and more we were allowing people to tell their own stories. We did this because we had discovered that not only were the best actors in the world willing to help us, but that on their lips and in their faces stories of moral dilemmas and spiritual struggle made compelling television.

In retrospect the conclusion we were groping toward seems obvious, a happy confluence of the human psyche, the Christian religion, and the medium of television. After all, we are storytelling animals. It is how we make sense of our lives. Christianity and Judaism are both storytelling religions. Historically based, they chronicle the ups and downs of the human family's wrestling match with God. And television is preeminently a storytelling medium. It is what it does best. But what should have been obvious was not. Yet slowly, haltingly, we followed our instincts and finally embraced that to which we most fully resonated: a dramatic format. We opted for storytelling.

At this point, two men joined the "Insight" team who would be decisive in the years to come: John Furia, an up-and-coming writer, and Jack Shea, his best friend and an established director. Both were theologically sophisticated and were enthusiastic about our decision to adopt a dramatic format. Over the next ten years, they would spearhead the "Insight" production company, produce numerous series, mentor me in the ways of show business, and be my principal collaborators. They would also become two of my closest friends.

The decision to utilize a dramatic format confronted us with another question: Who would write the scripts for the new series? Up to this time, I had done all the writing. But I was more teacher than dramatist. So we decided to reach out to the writing community in Hollywood to see if they would help us with the third series. Initially only Dick Breen, John Dugan, Jim Moser,

Maurice Tombagel, and Liam O'Brien offered to do scripts. I was left with the remainder. But the decision to use professional writers was a harbinger of the future. After "Insight" III, almost all "Insight" episodes would be written by Hollywood pros, some of whom—William Peter Blatty, Michael Crichton, William McGivern, Carol Sobiesky, Rod Serling, Lan O'Kun, John Meredith Lucas, and Howard Fast—were among the most sought-after writers in Hollywood. By "Insight" IV I had shifted my energies to producing and would not return to serious dramatic writing for fifteen years. This decision assured us of top quality. It also involved me in the writing community and in the writing process in a new way. As a result I discovered this art form's tremendous potential for audience enrichment. I also made some of my best friends.

Seven of the thirteen episodes of "Insight" III were based on historical personages.

Dorothy Malone turned in a particularly stunning performance as Edith Stein, the Jewish nun who was killed at Auschwitz. She is a sensitive actress, and I still remember the radical change in her persona when she first put on the robes of a nun. She became luminous. That did not stop one of the cameramen from taking me aside between takes to whisper in my ear, "She's the sexiest-looking nun I've ever seen."

On shooting day Dorothy lost one of her contact lenses. We searched her dressing room. We scoured the studio. We even swept the floor of the stage. No luck. Then Dorothy found the missing lens—in her eye.

Ed Begley was compelling as a labor leader fighting for social justice. I'm sure this was Ed's way of saying "thank you" for the Oscar he had received two weeks before.

In one program we interviewed Marx, Lenin, and Stalin; in another, Popes Leo XIII, Pius X, and Pius XII. In between takes on the Pope show, Raymond Massey was seated between Leo Carroll and Gene Raymond, who were attired like him in white pontifical cassocks. With a quizzical look on his face, he looked at the other two actors and said, "Will the real Pope please stand up?"

All three actors jumped to attention.

Dan O'Herlihy played Klaus Von Stauffenberg, the German officer who, for reasons of conscience, led the July 20 plot to kill Hitler. This show explored the morality of tyrannicide, a particularly sensitive issue in some minds when it was aired, shortly after the assassination of Jack Kennedy.

Ricardo Montalban was moving as Abbe Pierre, the member of the French Assembly who befriended the homeless. Shortly before doing our show, he was asked in an interview what was his idea of a great Latin lover. "My father," he said, "was a great Latin lover. He was a virgin when he married. He made my mother deliriously happy for more than fifty years. That's my idea of a great Latin lover."

Ann Jillian portrayed Maria Goretti, the Italian teenager who was killed for resisting sexual abuse. Frank Gorshin was riveting as the murderer who was so moved by her deathbed forgiveness of him that he lost his bitterness, opened to God, and spent the remainder of his life serving people.

One of the principal financial backers of the rabidly anti-Communist John Birch Society saw this show in Los Angeles and was so upset at such evil being portrayed on a "Catholic" show that he tried to get the Cardinal to withdraw his permission. "If you show it," he said, "people will want to do it." Fortunately a priest friend headed him off.

In the third "Insight" series, we also created six fictional stories in which our characters wrestled with God—and with themselves—on the deepest level. We tried to make our viewers proud to be human beings. But we also looked for the moral dilemmas they faced. We sought out the hard edges and highlighted the value conflicts. "Guts Christianity" we called it.

When we made the decision to utilize a dramatic format, we did not realize all that was involved. (Thank God. If we had, we might not have gone ahead.) Good drama requires many hours of rehearsal. And it requires much camera time in the studio. The rehearsal time was not a problem. The actors were willing, and the inquiry classroom was available. But given Leon Drew's other commitments, more than four hours of camera time was a major problem for him.

As the weeks passed and one show followed another, we consistently went overtime. It was not that we did not try to stay on schedule. We simplified where we could. We tried to anticipate problems. Jim Johnson and Mike Cozzi, the KNXT directors, did all they could. But try as we might, we really needed eight full hours to make the kind of show we wanted. John Furia, Jack Shea, and I met with Leon Drew and pleaded for the extra time. He said his hands were tied. I appealed to his boss, Bob Wood, KNXT's general manager and later the president of the CBS network. "It is not a question of money," Bob said. "It's just that our broad programming responsibilities and limited studio facilities preclude giving any one program a full studio day." He was very nice but also very firm.

Looking for a way out of the impasse, and seizing on his statement that it was not a question of money, I said, "We have four shows left to shoot. One is already in rehearsal and is scheduled to be shot here on Monday. What would you think of giving us fifteen thousand dollars, and we will find another studio in which to shoot the other three?"

Bob blanched, then replied, "I am afraid that will not work. It's against CBS policy."

We were checkmated. Pushed to the wall, I begged and borrowed the needed money, and we moved over to Al Krivin's KTTV where we shot the remaining three shows.

I was sorry to leave KNXT. They had been very generous to us and it had been our home. But it was now clear we had outgrown its limitations and must go elsewhere if we were to continue to improve the quality of the show.

Many of the people at KNXT were also sorry to see us go, especially since, for a number of years, we continued to air the series on that station. Leon Drew was among these. With a chuckle he loved to tell the story of the young priest who had the gall to ask his boss for fifteen thousand dollars.

The audience response to our shift to storytelling was positive. People like people. They identify with the characters in a story, agonize over their decisions, look at reality through their eyes, and learn from their example.

We were involving our audiences more fully. But were we giving them as much? Were we, in particular, sharing the Christian Gospel with them? Were we helping them experience God's loving presence in the human? These were questions I kept asking myself. So did John Furia and Jack Shea. We knew "Insight" had to be a different kind of show, that if it entertained but did not enrich, it was failing in its purpose. But we were also coming to realize that drama, by its nature, is not a sermon. It can reveal meaning and give insight. It can challenge and inspire. But it cannot preach without violating its own nature. We were walking a narrow line. With few precedents to guide us, we were venturing out into a no-man's-land. We were attempting to explore that uncharted frontier where religion and drama come together.

As we reflected on the third series and began to plan the fourth, we decided not to hit our viewers over the head with the message, to trust them a little more, to give them more space in which to discover the truth for themselves.

Our experience at KTTV had been a happy one, so we decided to shoot the fourth series there. Without KNXT's directors to rely upon, we approached those of the entertainment community and asked them to donate their services. Their answer was a resounding yes. They displayed the same enthusiasm for the "Insight" idea and the same generosity as had the actors and writers. Within a very short time, some of Hollywood's best directors—Arthur Hiller, Buzz Kulik, Hal Cooper, Paul Stanley, Jay Sandrich, Marc Daniels, Ted Post, Dick Bennett, as well as Jack Shea—were directing "Insight" programs.

Up to this point, with the help of Father George St. Laurent, I had continued to run the inquiry class program and teach eight courses a year. Now John Fitzgerald, who had been elected Superior General, asked me to turn the inquiry class program over to George so that I could give full time to television.

"But I love teaching," I protested, "and I need the kind of rapport with people that the classes give me."

"I know," he replied, "but TV is very important, and the Church's presence in Hollywood will grow only if you work at it full-time."

Experience was to prove both of us right. I did need the classes and the emotional feedback they gave me. Yet concentrating all of my energies on TV did cause our impact there to grow.

I did as he asked. Late in 1964 he assigned Father Jack Mulhall to help me. Jack took over the distribution of "Insight" and vastly increased the number of stations carrying the series.

Television drama is a collaborative art form, the principal ingredients of which are acting, writing, and directing. Now we began to tap into the wealth of talent in these three segments of the entertainment community in Los Angeles, and I became deeply involved pastorally in the lives of many of its members. In a very real sense, I became their priest and they, whether Christian or Jewish, believers or unbelievers, became my parishioners.

What was there about the "Insight" idea that so attracted

these people and caused them to give their time and talent so generously?

Part of the reason was artistic. So much of American television, then and now, is so devoid of substance that these artists hungered for opportunities to exercise their art in a deep and meaningful way. "Insight" was one of the few opportunities available.

By 1965 the series had become the experimental theater of Hollywood television. We were exploring themes, staking out positions, experimenting with artistic forms, and utilizing dramatic devices that commercial programs could not risk. And we were showcasing new talent—usually writers and actors—giving exciting young artists their first real chance to show what they could do. All this captured the imagination of the industry. Most everyone wanted to be part of it. The Church was serving as the mother of the arts again.

Part of the reason for this generosity was also psychological. Most show business people are bright and sensitive, warm and loving. They enjoy their work and take great satisfaction in it. Yet the dynamics of show business keep them on a roller coaster, up and down, feast or famine. This does not help them feel secure. When they work they are well paid. But many of them spend weeks and weeks each year out of work. This aggravates their insecurity. They wait for the phone to ring, and when it does not they ask themselves "Why? What is wrong with me? Why am I not working?" The fact that there was little or no financial incentive to work on "Insight" was beside the point. Subject to these pressures, most people would prefer to work for nothing than not to work at all.

But the principal reason for their generosity was neither artistic nor psychological. It went deeper.

Like other human beings, artists need to give meaning to their lives. They need to actualize their potential and grow into the persons they are meant to be. They need to give themselves in love to their fellow human beings. And they need some reliable way of knowing that they are indeed doing these things, that they are good human beings, that they are living out their lives in the way they are supposed to. Transcendent affirmation is something they hunger for. The more consciously secular they are, the more unconsciously they seem to crave the affirmation of that which transcends the secular and comes from beyond the human. For those who worked on "Insight," my roman collar was a symbol of that transcendence.

Artists have no monopoly on these needs. At one time or another everyone seems to feel them. But I do think artists are especially in touch with these needs. Sometimes they almost seem to ache with them.

In my opinion most of the writers, actors, and directors who gravitated toward "Insight" did so as a way of meeting these needs. They are deep and loving people who saw in it a special way to give meaning to their lives, stretch their talents, and, most important of all, give themselves in love to their fellow human beings. The religious dimension of our operation was a reliable guarantee that what they were doing had transcendent value. It enabled them to feel good about themselves.

We also worked very hard to make "Insight" an enjoyable experience for those working on it. This involved us in community building in an intensive way. We tried to create an atmosphere where each person felt loved and where each would feel comfortable loving the others. This was not hard because show business people are bright and caring and easy to love.

Initially our cast and crew went to the neighboring restaurants for lunch and, when we went overtime, for dinner. But then we decided to bring the meals into the rehearsal hall, so that we could eat together. This did much to foster the relaxed atmosphere of loving community we sought. Often the shared food led to shared experiences and sometimes to shared lives.

I spent a lot of money for food in those days, and it was worth every cent of it.

We had religious reasons for wanting to create a loving community for our cast and crews. But there were also very practical reasons for doing so. In an atmosphere of love, people are not only happier but they do better work. This was most obviously true of the actors. Because they felt accepted and affirmed, they took chances and went deep within themselves, tapping into nuances of emotion that added texture, excitement, and color to their performances.

Initially the actors' agents tried to protect their clients from us. But all this changed once they were assured of our professionalism, saw how well their clients came off on "Insight," and heard how much they enjoyed the process.

In twenty-three years of making "Insight," I can count on one hand the number of times we had problems with actors' egos. I know of few actors I would not want to work with again. And the fact that so many of the actors chose to return year after year tells me they felt the same way.

Which is why, I guess, so many of the actors would accept the union minimum we paid them, endorse the check, donate it back, and then go on the "Merv Griffin" or "Tonight" shows to make jokes about it.

"I can't figure myself out," one said. "I have never worked so hard. I have never been paid so little. Yet I have never had so much fun. I don't know what's happening to me."

At its best our production company—cast and crew, artists and technicians—became a family, a closely knit team who shared a common goal and worked in close coordination with one another to achieve it. Each person was dependent on the others. Each felt needed. Each was expected to put out his or her very best. When everybody did and the goal was achieved, there was a great feeling of oneness, a kind of emotional high, a peak experience, a touch of magic. There is no business like show business.

We decided early in the history of "Insight" not to restrict our selection of writers, directors, and actors to Hollywood's "Vatican Circle" but to reach out to those who were Protestant or Jewish, agnostic or atheist. We wanted the best talents in the entertainment community, regardless of the religion they professed. As a result some of those working on the series were Catholic, a number practicing, most not. A smaller number were Protestant. But the vast majority were Jewish.

Ted Post was one of these. *The Cross of Russia,* which he directed for us, concerned itself with the discovery of the common ground between Roman Catholics and Russian Orthodox. While Ted and I rewrote the script in his dining room, his father-in-law was chanting the Torah in the living room.

Some of those working with us were deeply believing Jews who attended synagogue regularly. But most were highly secularized Jews who not infrequently were uncertain about the reality of God. Yet they were fiercely loyal to their Jewish identity and ethnic origins, even if they seldom, if ever, attended synagogue.

One famous Jewish director said to me: "I don't know about personal immortality. And I don't know about this God who seems to mean so much to you. But I do know about people. I know about discrimination and prejudice and injustice. I know about being turned down for a job because of the ethnic connotation of my name. And I know about being poor. Boy, do I know about being poor.

"Why am I working with you? Because you want the same things I do. Because maybe together we can build a world where there will be justice for everyone. It's the only chance we've got.

"Besides, for lunch, you serve the very best sandwiches."

All those working with us—Jews and Gentiles—were humanists. They believed in people, if not explicitly in God. Possessed of great good will and almost unlimited generosity, they had strong commitments and deep values. Yet few were active churchgoers. They were profoundly secular. This world was the only home they knew.

This decision to reach beyond the Vatican Circle propelled us into honest and profound dialogue with the secular and unchurched people with whom we were now collaborating. The common task to which we were all committed—making the most humanly enriching shows we could—involved exploring the nuances of the scripts we were shooting and the different sides of the issues we were raising. Such understanding was necessary if they were to do their jobs well. Without jeopardizing the quality of the shows, we could not turn off the unbelievers or refuse to hear them out. The least we could do was listen to their viewpoint, even if it was radically different from our own. They were happy to extend to us the same courtesy.

This did not mean we always came to see things in the same way. Often we did not. Abortion, the meaning of the sexual act, the uniqueness and totality of God's presence in Jesus, were areas of frequent disagreement. That did not make them—or us—bad persons. It simply meant we saw things differently. I had to respect their consciences. They had to respect mine. And together, despite our differences, we had to find a way to work together to enrich our audiences.

It sounds easy. It was not. The conversations were demanding and sometimes disconcerting. I pushed them and they pushed me.

"I'm surprised at you, Father Kieser." Monica was a brilliant writer and a radical feminist, her tone that of a scolding schoolmarm. "You want freedom for the people of Eastern Europe. You want freedom for the people of Central and South America. You want freedom for the black and brown people here in our own country. But you don't want freedom for the women of the world to control their own bodies and terminate a pregnancy if that's what they decide."

"Nonsense," I retorted. "Except for rape, if a woman is pregnant, it's because she chose to do those things that got her pregnant. A free person, a mature person, doesn't walk away from the consequences of her decisions. She faces them, lives with them."

"But you're a people person," she shot back. "What about the poor girl who gets carried away and can't possibly handle the baby?"

"I'll do everything I can to help her. But I can't forget the baby she is now carrying. That's human life, too."

"Who says?"

"The best evidence medical science can give us," I replied. "You recognize the sacredness of human life in the ghetto, in the barrio, on death row, in the Third World, in war zones. Why do you draw the line and refuse to recognize the sacredness of human life in the unborn?"

"Look," she retorted. "The woman has to decide. It's her body. Nobody can make that decision for her. Nobody. Freedom is the crucial thing. Nothing is as important as that."

"Nothing but life. You have to revere life before you can even talk about freedom."

"Do me a favor, will you?" There was a twinkle in her eye.

"Sure, what do you want?"

"Don't ask me to write a show about abortion. OK?"

After one of these particularly spirited confrontations, John Furia said, "It is getting harder and harder to save your soul these days."

The temptation was to back away, to break off dialogue, to try to escape its demands. I was tempted to escape in two different ways: worldliness, which would have meant abdicating my religious identity and jettisoning my religious values as I entered into this kind of dialogue with the secular world; or churchiness, which would have meant turning away from those with whom I disagreed, narrowing my vision, and restricting my caring to the members of my own church community. Continuing pastoral involvement with the people of St. Paul the Apostle parish, living with brother Paulists, and most important of all, the hour of contemplation each day, helped me resist the first. The secular people with whom I worked, upon whose generosity I depended and whom I had come to love, helped me resist the second. They made me painfully aware that billions of God's children live their entire lives without the spiritual consolations the members of the Church take for granted. In dialogue with them, I could hardly indulge in ecclesiastical narcissism or church navel-gazing.

My conversations with them launched a dialectic—the interaction of contraries—that threw off charges of spiritual energy that shattered my complacencies and challenged me to become more radically Christian. It also forced me to rethink the modes of religious communication, to take a new look at the relationship between religious language and religious reality, between God talk and that mysterious reality that transcends all language and every symbol, that renders speechless the wisest and most articulate of human beings. This dialogue had other benefits. It enabled me to see that it is possible in storytelling to help the viewer experience the reality of God without ever using the word, and conversely that it is also possible to use the name of God repeatedly yet not help the viewer to any experience of His reality. It was good for me. I like to think it was good for my collaborators. I know it was good for the shows we made together.

My conversations with these nonreligious yet deeply humanistic people clarified my own thinking about the role of the priest and of the Church in the secular world.

The priest is a transcendent symbol and must mirror the values of transcendence—integrity, love, joy—in his own life. He gains his credibility and earns his right to lead not by being brighter or more creative than his constituents but by being so totally committed to the service of people, so loving, so forgetful of himself—in a word, so Christ-like—that they want to see what he sees and be part of what he is trying to build. A tall order for any son of Adam, let alone this one.

The role of the Church in the world is to show forth in action God's love for people and so to gather together all those who care about people; to support them, and, if necessary, to lead them in their struggle to build a society that is characterized by peace and freedom, justice and human dignity. The Church's role, in short, is to involve itself fully in the humanistic coalition, to do all that it can to help humanely concerned people build a more humane world.

I remember shooting an episode of "Insight" V late one sweltering night in July 1965. After a particularly difficult take, the cast and crew poured out of the steamy stage in search of a breath of fresh air. Only the air was not fresh. It smelled. And the sky to the south was alive with flames. I hurried up to a stagehand who had switched his portable radio onto the police band. It spit staccato with desperate cries.

"What's happening?" I asked.

"Trouble in the black neighborhoods," he replied. "Burning, shooting, looting . . . one hell of a riot . . . in Watts." Armageddon had begun.

In September of 1965, with "Insight" V in the can, I left for Rome to cover the fourth session of the Vatican Council.

It was to turn my life upside down.

Part Three

Changing Pace

CHAPTER 8

VATICAN COUNCIL

When the history of the twentieth century is finally written, the Second Vatican Council will stand out as a watershed event of momentous significance, unleasing forces and setting directions that have already had—and will continue to have—a radical impact on both the secular and religious cultures of this century, affecting not only how the inhabitants of this planet organize their affairs and relate to each other but also how they feel about themselves, make sense of their lives, and open themselves to God. What has happened in Brazil, Chile, El Salvador, the Philippines, Korea, and Eastern Europe in the 1980s are only the most recent instances of its influence.

But in the summer of 1965, I knew none of this. I had rejoiced on January 25, 1959, when Pope John XXIII had surprised the world by calling a second Vatican Council to reform, renew, and update the Catholic Church. In his mind this was a necessary prelude to reunion with the Protestant and Orthodox communities, which, in its turn, was a necessary prelude to the more effective evangelization of the unbelieving world. Practical peasant that he was, John XXIII knew that he could not hope to accomplish either goal until he had put his own house in order.

I had watched in dismay as the Roman curia tried to sandbag him. Sometimes it seemed the old man was in retreat, as when he approved the deliberations of the synod of the diocese of Rome, which we had hoped would be a harbinger of what the Council might accomplish but which turned out to be regressive in the extreme; as when he approved a curial instruction making the teaching of theology in Latin mandatory. But he was saving his powder for the big ones, and every time they tried to thwart his plans, he moved up the starting date of the Council.

I read with enthusiasm Hans Küng's *The Council, Reform and Reunion*, but I did not then recognize it for what it was—the opening salvo of the ultimately successful attempt by the bishops and theologians of Western Europe to seize control of the Council from the curia and open it to the world.

I had been delighted by Pope John's opening address to the assembled bishops. It was optimistic in tone, visionary in scope, humanistic in concern, ecumenical in orientation, and pastoral in focus—everything it should have been. Hitting all the right notes, he told the bishops he had rejected the advice of those of his advisors whom he called "prophets of doom," and he asked them to trust in the Lord's providence and concentrate on the discovery, defense, and spread of the truth; to avoid any form of condemnation or rigidity; and to read "the signs of the times" by looking for God's will in the needs and aspirations of the world's peoples. He suggested the Council of Fathers distinguish between the substance of the Church's ancient doctrine and the way in which it is best lived out and presented, given the unique conditions of the latter part of the twentieth century. His objective was clear. He wanted the world's peoples to be lovingly served where they were, and he wanted the Gospel witnessed to in an authentically contemporary way. He called it *aggiornamento*, using the Italian word for modernization, updating.

It was a great speech. But then, in secret, behind closed doors, with the press excluded, the bishops began their deliberations. Catholics all over the world held their breath. And we prayed. In the words of Gus Weigel, the Jesuit ecumenist, we had great hopes but no expectations.

The periodic Vatican press releases told nothing of the drama unfolding inside St. Peter's. But fortunately—for the Church and for the world—there were leaks. One was a priest-journalist who used the pen name Xavier Rynne and wrote for *The New Yorker*. Another was Bob Kaiser, the Rome correspondent for *Time* magazine, whose network of sources included many influential bishops, theologians, curial officials, and Pope John himself. In *Time*, week after week, we were able to find out what was actually happening.

All of the preparatory schemas that the bishops were expected to rubber-stamp had been prepared by commissions dominated by the curia. One of the first to be presented was entitled "On Divine Revelation." Polemical in tone and subtly anti-Protestant in bias, it incorporated many of the more objectionable features of the traditional theology.

With the American bishops sitting on their hands, the German, French, Dutch, Belgian and Austrian bishops subjected it to withering, if erudite, attack. The curial bishops and the more conservative Italians and Spaniards rose to its defense. At issue was not only the document itself but the traditional way of understanding and communicating the message of Jesus. The debate was fierce, honest, and penetrating, but finally a consensus developed. By a margin of five to one, the document was rejected and sent back to its commission for total redrafting. No rubber-stamping for this Council, thank you. The forces favoring radical change in the Church had won a decisive victory.

Reading about this in Los Angeles, I should not have been surprised at the Church functioning in this way—look at the Acts of the Apostles—but I was. When Pope Paul VI, who succeeded to the papacy after the death of John XXIII, convened the second session of the Council and the press became more aggressive, I was delighted and became even more fascinated; partially, I guess, because it was a classic case of the good guys against the bad guys, and I knew whom I was rooting for. But on a much deeper level I was fascinated by the theological issues involved and began to sense that the Holy Spirit was indeed blowing up a storm, that what they were doing over there had tremendous relevance to what I was trying to do over here.

I was not totally dependent on the media for my information. One of my classmates—Tom Stransky—had joined the Roman curia and had been named to the great Cardinal Bea's Congregation for Promoting Christian Unity. He knew both Pope John and Pope Paul well, was part of the Council from the inside, and returned to the United States from time to time with glowing stories. And he was not the only Paulist so involved. During the first three sessions of the Council, at least a dozen other Paulists functioned as reporters or theological advisors to the bishops.

One of these was Ed Bader, who filled me with stories of the theological excitement of the conciliar process. As long as I was teaching the inquiry classes and producing "Insight," attending the Council was not an option for me. But once I was relieved of the inquiry classes, it became a realistic possibility. I began to think about it, and the more I did, the more I wanted to go. In the Church the Council was where the action was. It was on the cutting edge of history. I decided I wanted to be part of it. I talked it over with Fitz, and he encouraged me. In addition three Paulist friends—Tony Wilhelm, Wally Anthony, and Bob Quinn—were having similar thoughts. Finally we decided to meet in Rome, get a pensione together, and share the experience.

But it was not enough to take eight weeks off for this kind of self-enrichment. I felt I had to justify it, to myself, I guess, and to God, because nobody else was asking for any kind of justification. So with Jack Mulhall I created "Vatican Report," a weekly fifteen-minute radio show of commentary and interviews that I would record in Rome and ship back to him for distribution. For the eleven weeks of the fourth session, more than six hundred U.S. stations carried it.

But I did not go to Rome to do the radio show. I did the radio show because I had already decided to go to Rome and wanted an apostolic justification for doing so. The puritan ethic still had me in its grasp.

I was doing the right thing for the wrong reason, but as it turned out, "Vatican Report" did make a real contribution to the listening public's understanding of the Council, and it did give me access to the Council's best minds, whom I sought for interviews. So, despite the convolutions of my twisted psyche, God was at work.

The opening of the fourth session of the Council was great theater. Twenty-five hundred bishops—black, brown, yellow, white, representing every country on the face of the globe—decked out in all their episcopal finery—red robes, white robes, black robes—and seated comfortably in two long grandstands that faced each other and occupied most of the aula of St. Peter's; Pope Paul VI celebrating the opening Mass and preaching; the Protestant and Orthodox observers off to one side, the world's best theologians on the other; most of the stars—lay and clerical—of world Catholicism in attendance; the papal assistants, the Swiss guards, the rhythmic cadence of the Latin liturgy, the music, the incense; and an energy field of faith, love, and joy that would overload any Geiger counter.

I was deeply moved.

Yet if the opening session in the morning lifted me up, my dealings with the Vatican bureaucracy in the afternoon had the opposite effect. It rubbed my nose in the mud of our common humanity.

I had been named *Variety*'s Vatican correspondent. Because it was a show business paper, the Italian monsignor in charge did not want to issue me the tessera I needed to get into St. Peter's and attend the daily press briefing. It took a lot of pleading—and a carton of cigarettes—to convince him otherwise. And then he would only give me a one-time, one-week tessera. I was so furious I used Tom Stransky's curia typewriter to move back its expiration date. By the time it expired, the Swiss guards knew me, and I no longer had to show it.

In short order Tony, Wally, and I moved into the Pensione Baldoni, which was situated on the west bank of the Tiber, across from Castel San Angelo, just three minutes from the Via Conciliatione and ten minutes from St. Peter's. John Cogley, the religion editor of the *New York Times,* already lived there; and Teddy Cogley, Jim Forrest, the radical Catholic pacifist, and John Keating, the Paulist ecumenist, would soon join us. Our breakfast discussions were among the most exciting of the day.

Presided over by the ebullient Maria Baldoni, the pensione would be our home for the next eight weeks.

Life at the Council soon developed its own unique rhythm. I usually got up around six-thirty, prayed and meditated in one of the local churches, went back to the pensione for breakfast at eight, then to St. Peter's at nine for the morning session. Sometimes I listened to the speeches, but most often I walked the corridors behind the grandstands or settled down at the coffee bar to chat with whoever might have gathered there.

One morning I walked into a spirited discussion between a Spanish archbishop and an American scripture scholar. I knew them both. Archbishop Esprovisa was a genial man in his late fifties who smiled easily but who had been badly seared by the Spanish Civil War and as a result had a mind and a soul that were set in concrete. Freddie DeAngelo was a street kid from Brooklyn who had joined the Franciscans and done original research in Jerusalem. I had played basketball against him in Washington. Even then he had a mind that when meshed to his tongue functioned like a jackhammer. It cut through concrete.

"You Americans are possessed by this freedom thing," said the archbishop. "You act as if there's no difference between truth and error, between the teachings of the Church and heresy. In Spain we have a more orthodox view."

"In Spain you have Franco," cut in Freddie.

"God has revealed the truth," continued the archbishop, ignoring the previous remark. "And it has the right to be extolled and spread by every organ of society, including the state. Error is the cancer of society. It has no rights. It must be suppressed by every organ of society, including the state."

"You got it wrong, Pepe," Freddie exclaimed. "The truth doesn't have rights. People do. Even people who believe things that aren't true."

"Relativism. You're saying truth is relative. It doesn't make any difference whether you're a Christian or a Communist."

"I'm not saying that. You want to insert the politicians into the theological realm where they have no competence. Who are they to decide what's true and what's not?"

"They can always turn to the Church for guidance."

"I can't believe you, Pepe. You're living in the Middle Ages. Whether we like it or not, all the world isn't Catholic. Not even all of Spain. In case you haven't noticed."

"My point exactly. The Communists should be put in jail so they cannot sneak around and spread their pernicious poison."

"Let the Communists say what they want. We'll preach the Gospel. Let the other religions do the same. Then let the people decide where the truth is and what they want to do about it."

"The people need to be instructed. They aren't capable of deciding on their own."

"Of course they are. You seem to think you can march people into heaven at bayonet point."

Not all of the discussions at the coffee bar were so contentious. Some involved gossip. Some involved news of the latest political maneuvering. Most were leavened with humor. But all were driven by a single underlying question: What does it mean to be a Christian in the latter part of the twentieth century? This question seemed to top everyone's agenda.

Frequently I used the morning session to select and schedule my interviewees. Most often we would meet at Vatican Radio immediately after the session. On Friday mornings I wrote and recorded my commentary. Jack Mulhall did all the editing in the United States. Lunch was at one of the restaurants that dot the streets around St. Peter's, usually with someone I had met that morning. Sometimes I went home and grabbed a siesta but most often it was a rush to get to the English-language press session by three in the afternoon. Not infrequently these sessions crackled with controversy as the hard questions surfaced and the assembled reporters demanded answers. The press sessions were where the Church spoke to the world and the world talked back. I found the resulting dialectic exciting.

Sometimes in the late afternoon there were meetings of national groupings of bishops and sometimes there were talks by bishops or theologians. I remember one especially eloquent speech by Cardinal Alfrinck of the Netherlands. Said he, "The critics of the Dutch Church say we are anti-papal. That is not true. We have only the greatest reverence for the Holy Father. But sometimes they say we are anti-Roman. That is true. We don't like the way things are done in Rome. We don't like the fear, the rigidity, the arrogance."

Each evening many of the Americans and some of the English and Irish would meet at the Jesuit Generalate to celebrate Mass together. Dorothy Day—the founder of *The Catholic Worker*, mother of the Catholic peace movement, and friend of the poor—came regularly. One day Tony Wilhelm noticed she did not go to communion and asked her if something was wrong. She blushed and said, "I went this morning. I did not think I could get through the day without it."

Once, during the debate on the morality of nuclear arms, Dorothy disappeared for about ten days. When she returned we asked where she had been. Having lobbied all the bishops she could for the strongest possible condemnation, she had retired to a convent with a small group of similarly committed women for a total fast. They rejoined our community only after getting what they wanted. The Lord was not about to refuse those determined women.

Dinner was the leisurely meal of the day, and Tony, Wally, and I scheduled ours carefully. We wanted to touch souls with—and pick the brains of—the best English-speaking minds in the Church, so we made a list and systematically invited them out to dinner. Most were more than willing: Bishops Jim Shannon and Levin, theologians Hans Küng and Gregory Baum, scripture scholar Barnabas Ahern and liturgist Godfrey Diekmann, journalists Jim Sheerin and Frank Sheed, Protestant observers Albert Outler and George Lindbeck.

On most Sunday nights, we had dinner on the roof of the Paulist rectory in Rome, where many of the leaders of the American Church gathered for barbecued steaks, undiluted Scotch, and an evening of freewheeling discussion.

"Look," said Frank Curtis, a jowly, middle-aged theologian from Omaha with a pink face and a sports shirt to match, "you gotta judge a tree by its fruit. The birth control teaching is not fostering the values we intended."

"I'll tell you what it's fostering," said Jim McKeon, a young Jesuit with sandy hair and potbelly who taught high school. "The three A's."

"I do not understand," said Bishop Fred Williams, who had the habit of command and clipped speech of an NFL quarterback.

"Alienation, alcoholism, and adultery," replied McKeon.

"Oh," said the bishop. "Do you really think so?"

"I know so," said McKeon. "These bastards in the curia don't know what's going on."

"Which bastards in the curia?" asked the curia official with the smile and the Belgian accent.

"Not you, Franz," said the young priest. "You've been in a parish. You know where it's at. I mean those goddamned Italians. They see all these people flock into St. Peter's and they think everything is OK. I just hope the Communists win the next election. It would be the best thing that could happen. Purify the Italian Church."

"But," said Williams, his face starting to color, "there's the natural law. There is the way God wants the sexual act to be performed. Contraception is just not natural. It's a perversion."

"Who says?" said Curtis. "There's nothing in the Gospels about the natural law. That's something Aristotle dreamed up. It's an abstract intellectual construct that has no connection with reality."

"But if we change that," snapped the now bristling bishop, "people will begin to question the teaching authority of the Church. They'll just start doing whatever they feel like, indulge their appetites, live for pleasure. Marital fidelity will go. So will celibacy. Hedonism. Barbarism. We'll be back to the Dark Ages."

The bishop's quivering voice resonated with moral indignation. I watched the young priest, the jowly theologian, and the Belgian curial official look at each other, sigh, and drift toward other groups. I did the same. I had already learned nothing is worse than an indignant bishop.

Some nights about ten, we would drop into the common room of the Villanova House where, in bathrobe and slippers, a glass of Scotch in his hand, Jesuit John Courtney Murray, the greatest of the American theologians and the mind behind the declaration on religious liberty, would often be holding court. Many of the Chicago theologians also lived at Villanova and could usually fill us in on the latest news and rumors about the political machinations of the Council, frequently in vivid and profane Americanese. These machinations were often devious, sometimes nasty, always very human and alive. One night I asked myself the crucial question: Is the Lord present in all of this? Is this how the Holy Spirit works? After some little thought and prayer, I was led to give an affirmative answer to both questions. Yes, He is present; yes, this is how the Holy Spirit works, in and through the very grittiness of the human; yes, absolutely.

This kind of deep optimism—I might even say euphoria—permeated the entire conciliar community. There was a general awareness that what was happening had tremendous significance; that history was being made at the Council; that somehow, in His own mysterious ways, the Holy Spirit was guiding the whole process; and that, as a result, anything was possible. We also knew there would be plenty of surprises along the way.

The Council certainly called into existence a unique community. Never before, nor probably ever again, at least not in my lifetime, will so many spiritually gifted people be brought together in one place and engage each other in such intense dialogue for such a sustained period of time about matters of such tremendous importance.

It was the most intellectually stimulating, most spiritually enriching experience of my life.

It was certainly the most powerfully sustained experience of Christian community I have known.

Certain members of that community and moments in its life remain etched in my memory.

Mary Daly, the radical feminist, standing beside me in St. Peter's square on a Sunday afternoon as Pope Paul blessed the crowd and they responded with an enthusiastic "*Viva il Papa,*" whispering in my ear, "I won't be happy until they're shouting, '*Viva la Mamma.*' "

Harry McSorley, the Paulist theologian, after a couple of belts, leaning over the table and saying to me, "You know what the trouble is, Ellwood? The Reformation never got south of the Alps."

Paul VI being greeted with thunderous applause as he walked into St. Peter's after returning from New York City, where he had addressed the United Nations.

Mother Mary Luke Tobin of the Sisters of Loretto being hissed by Italian nuns when she walked into St. Peter's for the first time in a modern, short-skirted habit.

Cardinal Suenens, having given a talk on co-responsibility in the Church, stopping the chairman who had just opened the floor to questions, saying gently but quite firmly, "But I'm not here to answer questions. I'm here to listen."

Albert Outler, the Methodist theologian, saying with a twinkle in his eye, "The bishops have no idea what they are voting for. When they find out, they are going to have to learn to trust the Gospel—and those who believe in it—not to be swallowed up by the world."

Hans Küng, having been asked why he did not wear a roman collar, replying, "Because I'm not Roman. I'm Catholic."

The African bishop with a glint in his eye stopping me on the steps of St. Peter's and saying, "Wouldn't you like to come and work in my diocese?"

An American bishop, after counting sixteen Paulists at one of the Sunday dinners, turning to me and saying, "Who's minding the store?"

Douglas Steers, the Quaker observer, to my question "But can we trust nonviolence to keep the peace?" replying, "We will only know when we've tried it, won't we?"

Bishop Fulton J. Sheen, the hero of my adolescence, eating alone night after night in the dining room of the Hilton Hotel, seemingly out of it, a sad and melancholy figure. A potent reminder of the limitations of stardom.

Jim Sheerin, the wise and holy editor of *The Catholic World*, enjoying a delightful weekend with us at a Polish nuns' hostel on Capri.

At breakfast I challenged John Cogley about a piece he had written for the *New York Times* that said Paul VI was undoing the work of John XXIII.

"What would you do if you were in Paul's place?" I asked.

"About what he's doing," he answered.
"What would John be doing if he was still alive?" I persisted.
"Going crazy," John replied, only half in jest.

I went to the Council hoping for a significant experience. At some unconscious level, I knew I needed it; just how badly would not be clear for some time.

I had been a priest nine and a half years. The honeymoon was over. But I was happy and I enjoyed my work. I liked being a hospital chaplain. I liked hearing confessions and celebrating Mass and preaching. I liked teaching inquiry classes and making TV programs. And these things seemed to like me, because a great number of people gave me a great deal of affirmation, saying I had enriched their lives by doing these things.

In short the priesthood was working for me. But certain aspects of my present situation were not working. I missed parish life. I missed the emotional feedback that pastoral work gives. I missed the deep excitement of helping someone surrender to God. I missed that sense of communion one gets from an inquiry class.

Sometimes, with "Insight," I felt I was working in an emotional vacuum. I could not see the people I was serving, watch their eyes light up when I told them about Jesus, see their faces fill up when they started to experience God's love for the first time. Circumscribed by the technology I was using, I had little sense of communion with living, breathing human beings. On an emotional level, I seemed to be drying up. More and more I felt cut off and alone. Celibacy's price was becoming real to me. I was lonely.

Before going to Rome, I had met with Fitz and his council and told them I might not be able to continue working in TV. They understood and said the decision was my own. If I decided I needed a change, they would be happy to assign me to a more pastoral kind of work.

The other facet of my priesthood that was not working was intellectual. The brand of theology I had been given in the seminary—abstract, conceptual, cerebral—was proving itself more and more inadequate. The inquiry classes made me aware of this. But my work on "Insight"—trying to create stories that would reveal the meaning of human life and give viewers an experience of God's presence in the human—made it even more painfully evident. I needed a new way of understanding the Gospel, and I needed a new way to communicate it. But what? How?

These were the needs and the questions I took to Rome with me. I was thirty-six years old. I think I sensed that my midlife crisis was just over the horizon. And I lived in America. It was 1965. A President had been assassinated, a war was escalating, the demand for racial justice was intensifying, and a cultural revolution was about to break over our heads. I think I sensed that, too. I had been working at a rigorous pace since ordination. I needed time to reflect, to make sense of what I had experienced, to figure out where I wanted to go and how I might get there. I also needed time to listen to myself—and to God.

Rome gave me the leisure to do just that. It welcomed me to a loving community of faith, most of whose members were engaged in the same quest I was. From eight each morning until past midnight the next, we shared experiences, traded insights, told stories, made jokes, reflected and prayed together. The dialogue was nonstop, intense, and probing. It supplied the context in which I could ask: What does it mean to be a human being? A believer in God? A disciple of Jesus? A member of the Church? A priest, given the unique conditions of the contemporary world?

In such a Spirit-charged climate of dialogue, I learned more theology in eight weeks than I did in five years in the seminary. I was able to rethink on some radical level the answers to these fundamental questions.

But maybe rethink is not the right word, because what I came up with was not so much the result of a logical process of thought any more than it was the result of an intellectual comprehension of what my new mentors were telling me; but rather it was the result of moving into a new place in myself—a deeper, more centered place—and looking at myself, at other people, at God and Jesus and the Church and the world and my priesthood from there.

I used to think of myself as Aristotle's "rational animal," as the subject of Descartes's famous "I think. Therefore I am." I was a thinking animal. Thinking was the essential expression of my humanity. It was the root cause of my freedom and the foundation of my dignity. It made me like God.

In this perspective, thinking meant the rational activities of the conscious mind. Its language was the abstract concept and its mode of operation was syllogistic reasoning—the arrangement of concepts into propositions that could then be related to one another in a logical fashion so as to yield new propositions, the truth of which could be expressed with clarity and affirmed with certainty. The unconscious mind was not denied. It was ignored. Why? Because it was messy and hard to control. Its intuitive powers were left to atrophy.

The center of gravity in this perspective was an abstraction called Nature. It was a catchall for reality. Yet it was something out there, separate from me, objective. Nature was like a clock. It was perfectly designed. Everything had its place and its own proper function. There were rules governing everything. For the individual the most important thing was to find and occupy the niche you were supposed to fill in the organization of the whole, so that you could then carry out the functions and obey the laws that were proper to that place. In this way you would contribute to the well-being of the totality, perfect yourself, and maybe even save your soul.

For me the conscious mind was not only a fire tower from which I could view Nature and a computer for the storing, processing, and packaging of what I saw, but also a command center in which I decided how I wanted to respond to Nature and how I would impose my will upon it. Life was struggle. It was war. And in this war, certainty was very important. So was control. I had to be in charge at all times.

God, of course, was the author of Nature, the designer of the clock, the intelligence behind its order, the maker of its rules, the rewarder of those who followed them and the punisher of those who did not. He had made the clock, wound it up, and now He pretty much left it on its own. Distant and aloof, He transcended Nature. He was not very much a part of it. We knew about Him by studying what He had made. He was prime mover, first cause, the supreme analogue, an object, little more than an abstraction.

Jesus, however, was not an abstraction. He was real enough. God become man, the Word made flesh, the transcendent Creator getting involved, because we had screwed up the system by breaking the rules and only God could straighten out the mess we had made.

Jesus was God, which, despite what St. Paul and the early councils of the Church had to say, meant that He wasn't quite human. He was perfect. He had all the answers. He could do anything. He was not like you and me. He was superhuman.

The Church was His Kingdom. As such it was, like Him, perfect. Not that its members could not sin. They could and did —in spades. But that did not diminish the perfection of the Church. It was, after all, the Body of Christ. He was its head. He supplied its teachings and its marching orders, conveying both through the structure of authority that He had established—Pope, bishops, priests. When we listened to them, we heard the voice of Christ. When we did what they said, we fulfilled the will of Christ.

And then there were the sacraments—baptism, confession, communion, the others—visible symbols given the Church by Christ in order to communicate His grace. Their power to enliven spiritually was independent of the virtue of the one administering them, just about independent of the virtue of the one receiving them. Which is almost to say they worked automatically. Receiving them was like throwing an electric switch. A charge of spiritual energy immediately flowed into your soul.

There were definite psychological advantages in this way of understanding the Church: certainty, security, a kind of pride in being a Catholic. But it was easy to get carried away with this latter and begin to look down on those outside, as if Catholics had a monopoly on God. The poor Protestants and Jews. They don't have what we have. So many of them are so confused about what God wants. They will be lucky to squeak into heaven.

But if Protestantism was viewed with a degree of competitiveness, if the relationship between the two Christian communities was almost adversarial, the Catholic posture toward the unbelieving world was more negative still. The world was sneaky and seductive. If you got involved with it you'd get contaminated—or corrupted. So the best thing to do was stay away! The world was beyond redemption.

The Church served as a fortress to protect us from the corroding attacks of the secular world. In its maternal embrace, we were safe. Live its life and your salvation was assured.

As I read over this description of my religious universe prior to my moving to this new place in myself, I wonder if it isn't somewhat overblown, almost a caricature. Perhaps. I am not saying this was the whole picture. But this was part of it, and all of these elements were present in me—at least to a degree.

If this is where I started, where did I end up? Once I had made the transition and moved into this new place in myself, what did my religious universe look like? How did I experience myself, God, Jesus, the Church, and the world from this new vantage point?

The fact of the matter is this new place into which I had moved was located deep in my humanity, very near its center. To get there I had to let go of the order and security of my conscious mind and journey to a dark and scary place I knew nothing about.

What is this new place inside myself? The Bible calls it heart, the blacks call it soul, the psychologists call it the unconscious. It is wild and messy, disorganized and confusing, a jungle of conflicting emotions: some positive—love, peace, joy; some negative—fear, anger, doubt. Sometimes in this place I feel like a turbulent volcano. Like molten lava, currents of uncontrolled energy flow this way and that. I feel ready to explode. The anxieties—loneliness, guilt, meaninglessness—reside here. So do my other feelings.

In this place my mind is active, but now it is working in a new way. Gone is the cool objectivity and deliberate clarity of logical reasoning. In its place are the depth and immediacy of intuition. Gone, too, are the abstract concepts that served me so well when I lived in my head. They now seem flat and meaningless. In their place are images and symbols that are charged with intelligibility. They are my new language, and I think in them. They speak to me of reality. When I listen to them I not only know reality but I experience it. I penetrate its surface and enter into communion with its depths.

I try to sort things out in this new place, but that is not always possible. It takes me a while to get acclimated. Sometimes I don't feel comfortable, and sometimes I feel great pain. I don't like that. But there are things about this new place that I do like. I like to feel, to live passionately, to experience new things in new ways. I like to know in a multidimensional way. This place is real, and I like that. It is also alive and exciting. I like that, too. And it is me. Maybe not all of me. But a very important part. And so I decide to settle down and make myself at home.

Once I do I begin to realize how fragmented and incomplete and needy I am. But somehow that seems to be OK. I am held in existence by the Ground of my being. When I go deep within myself, I draw closer to Him. At special times, He seems to surface within me, to grasp hold of me, and if I give Him permission,

He will work within me, to heal my fragmentation, to empower me to love.

He is not only the Ground of my being, but He is the Ground of all being, Being Itself, the Epitome of Existence. His Being, of course, is good, and because goodness is diffusive of itself, God is love. Love is God's other name, the pulsating secret heart of all reality.

When I lived in my head, I was like a stargazer who on a crisp, cold, and cloudless night lies on his back on the desert floor and watches the stars sail through their orbits in perfect harmony. I get caught up in the wonder and the grandeur of it all, and I am filled with awe at the transcendent author of its order and beauty.

Now that I have taken up residence in my soul, I'm more like a surf-rider who balances himself precariously on the edge of a board that is perched on the crest of a breaking wave. God is immanent in the power of that wave, and I try to respond to the thrust of His love as He sweeps me forward in mysterious ways toward the shore of my growth and the fulfillment of His Kingdom.

But for this God requires my permission. He will not move without my free surrender. With eyes open, in full possession of myself, He wants me to let go of myself and turn myself over to Him in freedom. God is no rapist. He will not force His love upon me. He is not interested in any relationship that is not freely chosen.

The central challenge of my life—of every human life—is to open to that unconditional love of His; to accept it totally; to respond to it wholeheartedly; to do all I can to love Him as He loves me.

Jesus is the man who most fully did what I am trying to do, and so He occupies the central place in my religious universe. I say man because Jesus was a stranger to no facet of the human situation. Like us in all ways save sin, he knew birth and death, hunger and thirst, fatigue and temptation, pleasure and pain, love and loneliness, rejection and hate, effort and struggle, fear and failure, emptiness and defeat. Yet, in the midst of it all, His yes to the Father was absolutely complete, sovereignly free, unconditionally loving. In Him there was no holding back, no waxing and waning of His commitment. He gave the Father complete freedom to work within Him. As a result, the Father surfaced, permeating every fiber of His being. Jesus is the man in whom

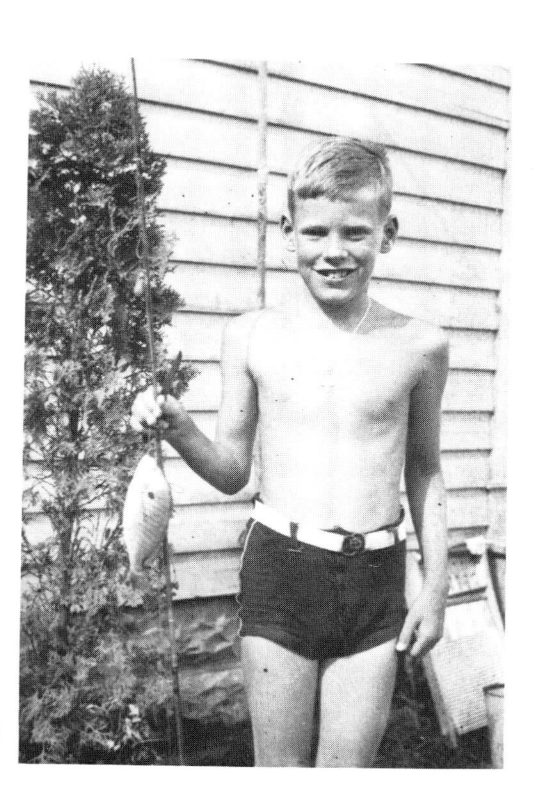

Ocean City, N.J., 1939:
A "sapling of a boy,"Kieser spent long and happy summer days on the Jersey shore.

"The emptiness of the desert sets the stage for an enrichment of spirit." So Father Kieser describes the time at the novitiate. Here he shares a few moments with his father, who struggled with his son's decision to become a priest.

May 3, 1956, at the Church of St. Paul the Apostle in New York City:
Kieser is ordained a priest by Francis Cardinal Spellman.

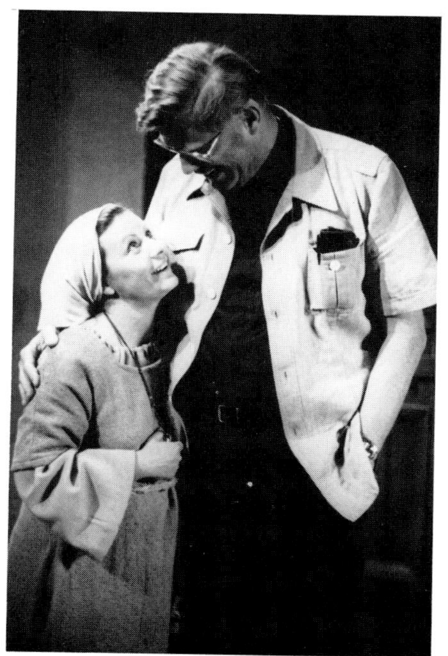

The earlier days of "Insight," the religious television series:
Father Kieser works with, clockwise from top, Jane Wyman, Patty Duke, and Edward Ciannelli.

1977:
Ed Asner, Father Kieser, Walter Matthau, and Carol Burnett on the "Insight" set.

Bob Newhart confers with Father Kieser in 1978 about the "Insight" production of *Packy*.

Flip Wilson, Martin Sheen, and Father Kieser on the "Insight" set in 1979. "The part of God can be attractive to actors," Kieser observes. Wilson and Sheen played the role on different "Insight" episodes.

Father Kieser speaks with Jack Klugman on the set of *Packy*. The program starred Klugman as a theatrical agent who believes his life has been worth nothing.

January, 1979, at the Taj Mahal in India:
On a sabbatical, Father Kieser gave workshops in India and Pakistan.

Father Kieser in Kenya in 1980:
He writes of the children faced with famine there: "Sometimes they would smile or even sing. But sometimes they cried, not a loud, lusty bellow like an American child, but a soft wail. I can still hear the wailing of those children."

Father Kieser went to Africa several times to get the word out about the famine, making trips there with John Amos, pictured here, LeVar Burton, Dick Van Patten, Patty Duke, and Cliff Robertson.

On the set of *The Day Everything Went Wrong*, in a 1983 comedy written by Kieser. From left to right, sitting: actors Robbie Rist, Florence Halop, Beverly Garland, Dick Van Patten, and Joel Higgins. Standing: Kieser and director Jay Sandrich.

Back to Africa:
Father Kieser and Ted Danson in Kenya, 1984, while shooting *We Are the Children*, an ABC movie of the week.

1988, Cuernavaca, Mexico:
On the set of *Romero*, Kieser shares a light moment with Raul Julia, whom he calls a "consummate professional" and who played the title role of the Salvadoran archbishop.

The Rev. Ellwood E. Kieser, C.S.P.:
"I have wrestled a lot with scripts and budgets, schedules and organizational tables. But I have always found it more challenging - as well as more difficult and satisfying - to wrestle with God and those I love on the deepest and most intimate of levels."

God is totally and uniquely present, the man whose humanity is alive with the presence of God, transparent to the Light and Life and Love of the Father. This means that Jesus is my point of contact with the Father, the human being in whom I can find the Father and through whom I can come to the Father. I go to the Father through Him. And the Father comes to me through Him. In Jesus, God and humankind are fused so He is the one mediator between God and the human family, a bridge on which the traffic flows in both directions.

He shows us what the Father is like and what we can become; the grandeur of the first, the possibilities of the second.

He also draws us into the Church, which is His body and the unique, if flawed, dwelling place for Him in space and time. The Church is a very human community that is afflicted by all the problems, shortcomings, stupidities, and sins of which human beings are capable. It is unique only because its members, in varying degrees, have heard and responded to the Good News. They recognize and celebrate what God has done for us in Jesus and what possibilities this opens up for all of us.

The Church is a community of equals, but it has a hierarchical structure—Pope, bishops, priests—to help it carry on its life. But this structure is subordinate to the community and exists to facilitate its dialogue; to serve, guide, unify, and nurture that community. The institution exists for the people, not the people for the institution. Which is just another way of saying the Pope works for us, not vice versa.

In Rome, during the Council, we really worked at communicating with each other—honestly, deeply, lovingly—and I began to see how crucial dialogue is to the life of the Church. I will go further. I think there was a direct connection between the Spirit-filled character of that conciliar community and the intense, prolonged, and faith-filled dialogue that characterized its life.

Isn't that the way it usually works? Whenever people really talk, God is present. When they don't—when they hold back in fear, play games, or go superficial, saying much, sharing little—God takes a vacation. It is as simple as that.

But the Church is healthy not only when its members communicate with one another, but also when, as a community, it opens itself to dialogue with the world.

The world is that portion of humanity that has yet to allow itself to be permeated by God. It is that portion of humanity that is untouched by God's love, sometimes because it consciously resists that love, sometimes through no fault of its own.

So the world lives outside of me. But it also lives inside of me, in that portion of myself that I have closed off from God, that I have held back and refused to surrender to Him. Church and world are intertwined in the heart of my ambivalent humanity.

Because of this, no believer can reject the world without also rejecting an important part of him/herself.

The world—inside me and outside me—can only be accepted and loved in all its fear, incompleteness, and frustration.

The world needs the Church to show it how to complete and fulfill itself in the embrace of the Father. And the Church needs the world to pull it outside itself, to challenge it and keep it poor and honest.

The Church-world dialectic is essential to the well-being of both parties.

My reflections on the Church-world relationship were considerably enriched by the eight days Tony, Wally, Bob, and I spent in Moscow, Zagorsk, Leningrad, and East Berlin during one of the recesses called during the latter part of the Council.

At that time the Soviet Union was officially an atheistic society. With systematic rigor, its institutions propounded the brotherhood of man while rejecting the fatherhood of God. Almost all the churches were closed, torn down, or transformed into museums. Most of the people we met had been required to take courses in atheism as part of their schooling. The scriptures could not be purchased, nor were they available in the libraries. In Moscow and Leningrad we celebrated Mass each morning in our hotel room, awed by the knowledge that ours was probably the only Mass to be celebrated that day in that city. Zagorsk—the ancient monastery town north of Moscow—was one of only two seminaries permitted to function in the entire Soviet Union. We attended an Orthodox service there. I was moved by the deep suffering etched on the faces of my fellow worshipers. They had kept the faith. They had paid the price. And it showed.

When the host was raised, we knelt, and our guide became very upset. We were putting her in an impossible position, she told us. In Leningrad she refused to take us to the Museum of Atheism, saying she found it very embarrassing. We went anyway.

I am glad we did. Housed in the Church of the Virgin built by the Russian people to celebrate their victory over Napoleon, the museum is comprised of floor after floor of exhibits. Only the first two exhibits present the philosophic case against the existence of God. The remaining exhibits, scores and scores of them, take the viewer through the last three thousand years, dramatizing every sin committed by religious people in recorded history. From human sacrifices to the Crusades, from the Inquisition to the Thirty Years' War, from the burning of witches in New England to fat monks stuffing themselves while poor Russian peasants starved on their doorstep, the subtext was: If this is what religious people do, what they believe cannot have any validity. Much of what was presented was fallacious. Almost all was in bad taste. Nevertheless, I found enough truth in it to make my visit there a searing experience. No wonder the Lord made the taking of His name in vain one of the Ten Commandments.

The party line in the Soviet Union was atheism. But were the Russian people buying it? They loved their country and its land. They were justly proud of the accomplishments of its people—in World War II, in the growth of their economy afterward, in their space program. But were they rejecting the faith that had permeated their history and their national consciousness for almost a thousand years? Were they buying the truncated state of consciousness, the single-dimensional view of reality preached by the leaders of their ruling party? I had real doubts at the time, doubts which subsequent events have confirmed.

I found the Russians a hard-working, patient, and lovable people despite the repressive system with which they had been saddled. I felt great respect and affection for them. I fantasized at the time about staying behind, learning the language, and working as a priest in Russia, building the Church from the ground up. I still have such fantasies. In 1965 I rejected these fantasies as unrealistic. In 1990, thanks to Mikhail Gorbachev, they do not seem quite so farfetched.

The Council launched a process that revolutionized the religious universe in which I lived. The transcendent God became immanent and involved, closer to me than I am to myself. The divine Jesus became very, very human, like me in all things save sin. The Church became not so much an institution as a people, a community of frail and flawed human beings who wrestle with God. The priest became not a spiritual superman, a member of a superior caste, but a man among men, yet set apart to be the servant of his brothers and sisters, a living symbol of God's love for all people. And the world became not something to be feared but something to be concerned about and feel loving compassion for. Its members hurt so badly and need so much that all who believe in God are called by Him to put themselves out to share themselves—and Him—with them.

Propelling these changes, but also, in a very real sense, being propelled by them, was a new reality in my interior life. Her name was Genevieve.

As the Council drew to a close, I was aware that I was once again deeply in love.

CHAPTER 9

GENEVIEVE

I did not meet Genevieve in Rome. I met her more than a year before, in August of 1964, at the retreat house run by her order. I had gone there to make my yearly retreat.

Hearing of my search for stories for "Insight," one of the sisters suggested I get together with their Sister Genevieve, who was doing doctoral work in American fiction at the University of California at Berkeley and would be stopping by the next afternoon for lunch.

"You may have something to give each other," she said. She had no idea how much.

So, with two of the other sisters, we arranged to have lunch the next day. Sister Genevieve was the last to arrive. I noticed she had the gait of a dancer, gliding as much as walking into the dining room. The lines of her blue-and-black traditional nun's habit converged on her face, which was not strikingly beautiful in any classic sense but was incandescent in a way that commanded my immediate attention. As the sisters got caught up on each other, I watched that intensely sensitive and intelligent face of hers go through a kaleidoscope of expressions, reflective and compassionate, serious and lighthearted, angry and joyous, impish and caring, sad and outrageous. I was fascinated by her.

The meal started at twelve-thirty. The other sisters excused themselves at one-thirty. The two of us continued to talk until almost four. She wanted to know about "Insight," about what I wanted to accomplish, why I wanted to accomplish it, and what the whole process did to me inside. The questions were penetrating and touched more than one live nerve. We talked about possible stories. Then she started to tell me about her experiences at

Berkeley, the people she had met, the philosophies and value systems they espoused, the conflicts and tensions that developed, the friendships that resulted and, throughout it all, where she was and what she was feeling.

I saw two things at once: Here could be a great story of the Church and the world in collision; and here was a woman with a genius for subjectivity, with a unique ability to articulate the most intense, personal, and complex of emotions—her own and those of other people.

I asked her to write the story. She declined, saying her dissertation did not leave her time for anything else. I reluctantly accepted that.

We continued to talk on an intensely personal level. There was electricity in the air, and it crackled between us. Some of the sparks were erotic, for she was compellingly feminine, pure anima, powerfully sexual. Some were intellectual, for in an existential manner she was brilliant, verbalizing things I had felt but never heard articulated before. Some were spiritual, for her soul was so alive and so close to the surface that you could almost touch it.

As we said good-bye, she smiled and said, "Let me think about it. Maybe I can find time to do that script after all."

I was deeply moved by the conversation and could pray about little else for the next twenty-four hours. She had pressed buttons in me that I did not know existed.

She did find time to write the script, but it was not very good —partially, I guess, because she was preoccupied with her dissertation; partially because her background and experience were literary rather than cinematic, the written word of the novel rather than the spoken word and video image of television; but primarily, I think, because the deepest and richest side of her personality is activated not by typewriter and paper, but by face-to-face contact in which the interpersonal magic of soul touching soul causes one person's emotions to trigger another person's emotions to flash point.

She spent the 1964–65 academic year at Berkeley, but she did come to Los Angeles at Easter, and we did get together to discuss the rewrite of the script. Only we did not spend much time on the script. Feeling pressure from her community to finish her graduate work, she was frantically preparing for her comprehensives and trying to finish her dissertation. She was discouraged and depressed and feeling a great deal of pain.

Suddenly her pain was my pain. I felt overwhelmed by it. I tried to give her as much support as I could. I also encouraged her to tap into God for the kind of support I frequently got from Him, but she said that did not seem to work well for her. I left the convent feeling great concern.

That spring, while she plugged away in Berkeley, we rewrote and, with Vera Miles in the title role, shot her story, which was now entitled *The World, the Campus and Sister Lucy Ann*. She was unable to come down for the shoot.

Sometime in July, trying to break out of a siege of personal loneliness, I called her in Berkeley, and we had a long and hilariously funny conversation. I told her I had decided to go to the Council. She was delighted, since she had been in Rome for the Council's third session and knew how exciting and enriching that experience could be. I asked her if there was any chance she could get to L.A. before I left. She said it was possible. I sent her the plane tickets the next day.

We had dinner at the convent where she was staying and I met some of her closest friends. Twenty-five years later I don't remember much else about that dinner. But I do remember the next conversation we had just before I left for Rome. It lasted for six hours, yet the time seemed like fifteen minutes. Communication was effortless. I did not have to reach for her. She did not have to reach for me. We were in the same place. I did not have to struggle to help her understand what I was talking about. She knew intuitively. Nor did she have to struggle to help me understand what she was saying. I, too, knew at once. It was a deep and joyful conversation that was full of the presence of God. I was not at all sure what was happening to me, but I knew I liked it.

I tried to put into words how I felt as I flew over the Atlantic. It was a very warm and affectionate letter, but it did not contain the three words that would have best summed up what I was feeling. I was not comfortable enough with my own emotions to say "I love you" first.

She said that and much more in the tape that arrived at my pensione shortly after I got to Rome. It was tender and loving. She said she had not intended what was happening, may not have even wanted it. But now that it was happening she was happy and grateful. My letters and her tapes zipped back and forth across the ocean, each one escalating the intensity of the relationship, each one picking up where the previous one had left off and taking us deeper into unexplored emotional territory.

I never thought I would be in love again. But here I was—passionately, intensely, gloriously in love. It scared me and it thrilled me. How it all fit together, how in particular it fit with my priesthood, I did not know.

I took it to prayer, and I said to God: "Here it is. Here she is. I give her to you. What do you want me to do? I'll give her up if that's what you want. Let me know. Please."

I made this same kind of prayer on a rather regular basis over the next two years. Always the answer coming back seemed to be: "I've given her to you for a reason. Take care of her. Love Me in her. Let Me love you through her."

Was this God's voice? Or the erotic yearnings of my own unconscious? Twenty-five years later, I still don't know. I like to think the first. But I am prepared to admit the second.

We had dinner together at her parents' home shortly after I returned from Rome. She had told me she would have significant news for me when I arrived. As soon as we had a private moment, she told me she had begun psychotherapy.

I was sobered to learn that she felt her problems were serious enough to require that kind of remedy. But I admired her courage in facing the situation and trying to do something about it.

She was finding therapy painful. She was not sure she should continue. She was not sure she could trust her therapist.

I read a book he had written, liked it, and told her she should try to trust him. It was the only way therapy could work, I said.

Later on I was to regret deeply giving her that piece of advice.

Genevieve was in the east the Christmas of 1965, but we arranged to meet at the retreat house shortly afterward. It was a glorious three days.

She would attend my Mass in the morning, and we would have breakfast together. She would spend the morning with the young nuns. I would read and pray. Then we would meet for lunch and spend the afternoon and evening together, sometimes walking the beach, at others times sitting and talking on the bank of a creek that runs through that area.

A lot had been happening to me—the conciliar experience, my love for her, my plans for "Insight"—and I needed to share these with her.

A lot had been happening to her—therapy, her love for me, her return to university teaching—and she needed to share these things with me.

I never thought I could take such great pleasure in simply talking with someone else. What we said to each other was important. But what underlay the words—the love, the emotional communion, the tuned-in-ness to each other—was even more important. I did not have to work at being totally present to her, nor did she have to work at being totally present to me. We just were. She shared herself with me. I shared myself with her—where we were, what we were feeling—without pretense or affectation, honestly, with complete trust and total candor. Neither of us wanted anything else. She was a deep pool into which I could plunge to refresh, energize, nourish, and nurture myself.

She once borrowed from Martin Buber's description of an I-Thou relationship to describe ours: two people standing opposite each other, open to each other, waiting on each other, saying an unconditional yes to each other. The walls between us were starting to dissolve. She was me and I was her. A kind of psychic fusion was taking place. In a note she wrote me on my birthday, she said, "Whatever the future holds for us—together or apart—we are part of one another."

These kinds of intensely personal conversations became the pattern for us over the next year and a half. Sometimes one of us would be traveling and we wouldn't see each other for a week or two. That did not seem to interrupt the emotional communion between us, since, in a real way, she now lived in me and I lived in her. Some kind of emotional osmosis had taken place. I talked to her inside myself and she talked to me inside herself. The conversations were ongoing, sometimes in words, sometimes wordlessly. When we were both in Los Angeles, we talked most every day on the phone. Two or three times a week, we would get together for several hours to talk, sometimes at the rectory or convent, at her office or mine, at the studio where I was shooting, or at the university where she was teaching. We were circumspect about our meetings, since a nun and priest spending so much time together was not socially acceptable, but our friends knew and, although they worried, they understood and affirmed. Her closest friend said to us, "I feel you two are very close, and you love each other very much. But I don't feel excluded. In fact, I feel included."

In these protracted conversations, we discovered we had a great deal in common. But we also discovered we were different in some very important ways.

She was highly subjective. What she was feeling, what those around her were feeling, these were paramount for her. They were the world in which she lived, the only one that seemed real to her. I was more objective, possibly too much so. I valued personal experience, but I knew I needed to situate my experiences in a larger context, in a world that existed whether I experienced it or not, that manifested certain qualities and obeyed certain laws whether I felt them or not.

More than anyone I have ever met, she lived totally in the present. The past and the future had importance for her only to the extent that they influenced her present. This left her without a sense of history, but it also enabled her to be totally present to whomever she was with and totally involved in whatever she was doing. I always had to situate myself in a time flow. I liked to reflect on the past and seek out its meaning. I liked to fantasize about the future and decide on its shape. Where I had been and where I wanted to go were important to my present. They helped me understand where I was at the moment.

Sexually there had been for her no masculine counterpart of Clair in my life—someone to help her get in touch with her sexuality and decide what she wanted to do with it. As a result of her therapy, she was now becoming convinced that her entrance into convent life, while motivated by deep spiritual experiences, may also have involved the repression rather than the sublimation of her sexual drives. In her late thirties, those mechanisms of repression seemed to be coming apart.

We were both caught up in the cultural revolution that characterized American society and the Catholic Church during the 1960s. The consensus that had characterized both society and Church was beginning to come undone. On every side authority, creed, and institutions were being challenged. Dogmas were suspect, certainties rejected, absolutes called into question, values rigorously scrutinized, and rules routinely broken. The sexual revolution was in full swing, and its initial message seemed to be: If it feels good, go with it.

Sometimes it seemed the foundations on which we had built our lives were collapsing beneath us.

The result of this for Genevieve, as for so many other Americans, was insecurity and confusion. She had been a dedicated and happy nun, secure in her commitment, certain in her faith. No longer. Everything seemed up for grabs. Nothing was certain. Her world was falling apart.

I found the turmoil confusing, but there were some things I was sure about—God, Jesus, the Church—and on these I tried to build my life. My experience of these realities gave me a psychic security—a sense of self—that unfortunately she did not seem to enjoy.

Religiously we were not in the same place. God was the most important reality in my life. I was ambivalent about a lot of things but not about Him. I loved her so much because in a unique way she enabled me to experience Him. I sensed God's presence in her. I felt God in myself when I loved her. And I experienced Him in the electricity that sang between us.

She elicited in me a desire she could not satisfy. Again and again my love for her drove me to prayer, to seek in contemplation the fulfillment that she made me want but that she on her own could not deliver.

Ours was a love in God, I told her.

That seemed to have no meaning for her. With tears of sadness in her eyes, she said the Gospels were nice stories, but they seemed unreal to her. So did God. I was the only God she knew, she seemed to be saying. She was ready to live for me.

I found that scary.

We talked a great deal about the central realities of Christianity: God, Jesus, the Church. She was not sure I was right, but she wasn't sure I was wrong either.

She was like the man in the Gospels who said to Jesus, "I believe, Lord. Help my unbelief." On some level she believed. On another level she did not. She was not unique in this respect. I was the same. We were different only in this: I chose to make the believing side of myself dominant, to use my unbelief to strengthen and fertilize my belief. She seemed unsure about what she wanted to do.

Were her faith difficulties connected to her sexual ones? I do not know. But I do know that when you repress any one facet of your humanity, you do violence to every other facet. Sexual repression not only inhibits your ability to relate to someone of the opposite sex. It also inhibits your ability to relate to God. In this respect it is much like inauthentic sexual activity. Both impede prayer. Both make spontaneous, joyful prayer impossible.

But now the pendulum was beginning to swing in the opposite direction. For the first time we began to be affectionate. But always within the limits that traditional Catholic morality set down for two unmarried people in love.

I did not like these limitations. Neither did she. But I could see no other way to be faithful to myself as a priest.

She kidded me about being her incorruptible one. We tried not to make things harder for each other than they had to be, but we did not always succeed.

On one occasion, with almost unbearable sadness in her voice, she said to one of the younger nuns, "He belongs to God." In her eyes it seemed to me, my belonging to God meant I could not belong to her in the way she wanted.

But neither of us was ready to face that.

Her therapy continued to be painful. She was being stripped of every defense and forced to confront head-on the nonbeing in her life. Sometimes it seemed she was caught in a whirlpool that was sucking her down and down into extinction.

Yet she would not give up. She was going to fight this battle through to its finish, no matter how great the pain.

I tried to give her as much love and support as I could. She was now my center of gravity. When she was up, I was up. And when she was down, I was down.

Sometimes I felt I was battling for the health of her mind; at other times, for the salvation of her soul. At times I felt I was carrying her on my back, and sometimes the weight was almost more than I could bear.

"I'm wearing you out," she said.

Somehow I had convinced myself that if I just loved her enough, she would be all right. She called me her knight in shining armor. But she recognized before I did the limitations of my love. "You can't save me," she said.

Once, quite desperate, I made a deal with God. I told Him, "If you'll make her well, if you'll keep her close to you, I'll give you anything. Anything. My job. My health. My career. My sanity. Anything."

When she found out—I could keep nothing from her—she was livid with anger. "Don't lay that on me," she said.

To better understand what she was going through, I attended

one of the marathon therapy sessions then in vogue—twenty-two straight hours—through a night and a whole day. When it was over I was tired but also exhilarated. I had enjoyed the interaction.

Only half in jest, she said, "It couldn't have done you any good."

In the summer of 1967, her order held its renewal chapter at the retreat house. I took some time off—to think, to pray, and to be with the sisters while they made the big decisions about the future of their order.

Genevieve was not elected a delegate. This hurt her. She was loved and respected by her peers, but I think they knew her commitment to the order was tenuous, and this was the reason she was passed over.

I found the chapter exciting. I also found the community life of the sisters profoundly Christian and deeply joyful.

Genevieve and I had been putting our love for each other into words for over twenty months. She had been in therapy for an equal length of time. While I was at the retreat house, I had a lot to think and pray about. We arranged to see each other regularly during the chapter.

With the chapter less than half over, she called to tell me she needed to see me right away. She had decided, she said, to ask for a dispensation from her vows. She was going to leave the convent.

On one level, I knew it was coming. On another, I did not want to face what in retrospect was inevitable. But now it was happening, and I had no choice but to deal with it.

When I asked her the reasons for her decision, she said the manner of living was no longer authentic for her. She did not feel comfortable with the role of a nun, and she did not want the restrictions. She also said she wanted to get married.

Partially to shield myself from the implications of this, partially in jest, I said, "Will you let me perform the ceremony?"

It was not what she wanted to hear.

The ball was now in my court, and I had some big decisions to make. Not that I had not already been wrestling with them. They were implicit in our love for each other from the beginning. But I had kept them on the back burner. I kept saying, "Later, I'll think about those things later." Or, "It won't come to that. I can have my cake and eat it too."

Now I could no longer shove these questions to the back of my consciousness. Nor could I delay facing them.

For several days after Genevieve told me of her decision, I talked to no one. The nuns thought I was in shock. Hour after hour, day after day, I walked the beach near the retreat house.

The ocean has always been a feminine God symbol for me—a God symbol because of its power, mystery, and purifying qualities; feminine because of its moodiness, playfulness, and caressing manner. I sought refuge in it now.

I should also have gone to a brother priest to talk through my dilemma and seek some perspective on it. But I knew of no one I felt could understand and affirm what I was going through. In 1967 priests and nuns just did not fall in love. I had tried once in confession to discuss my relationship with Genevieve and was cut off rather abruptly with a blanket condemnation. I was so stung that I made up my mind not to try that again. In retrospect I think there were plenty of priests who could have helped me at this time. I also think some of my lay friends could have done the same. But for some reason I felt I had to fight it through alone. Was this arrogance or guilt or the way God was leading me? I do not know.

So for weeks I dodged the breakers, the wind whipping through my hair and pulling at my jacket, the salt air filling my lungs, as I tried to sort things out. It seemed clear to me that my love for Genevieve was deep and real and authentic and that her feelings for me were similar. Our relationship was honest and caring. We respected each other. We enjoyed each other. We could really communicate. There was no doubt in my mind that we had the makings of a happy marriage.

Also, at this time in the life of the Church, priests could be dispensed from their vows, returned to the lay state, and allowed to marry with the blessing of the Church.

So there was no question about leaving the Church or breaking its laws if I was to decide to marry.

But there was also no question about the linkage between priesthood and celibacy in the discipline of the Church. It was a package deal: If you wanted the first, you bought the second. For better or for worse, that was (and is) a given in the situation.

I prayed. I told the Lord I would do whatever He wanted. I tried to mean that. I asked Him to let me know what that was.

It took a while. The more I prayed and tried to sift things out, the more it became clear that the essential question came down to identity. Who am I? Who is Bud Kieser? What is his unique essence? What activates and expresses that essence?

I knew enough psychology to know that identity flows from relationship; that we find out who we are by seeing ourselves in the eyes of that person who most loves us.

Genevieve had taught me a great deal about who I was. Our relationship had done much to help me explore that newly discovered place in myself that, as a result of the conciliar experience, I had so recently occupied. And it activated things in me I did not previously know existed.

Far from losing myself, in giving myself to her I was finding myself in a new and richer way. More than that, in the context of our love for each other I was coming alive and becoming myself in a new and deeper way. I got to know myself by letting her know me. I deepened my acceptance of myself by allowing her to accept me. And I was learning to love myself more fully by letting her love me.

But still, at the deepest, most radical level, she did not determine who I was. Only God could do that. My relationship with Him was the primordial and all-encompassing one in my life. It included in its embrace my relationship with Genevieve and all my other significant relationships. It alone was constitutive of my identity. It determined who I am. Which is just another way of saying my true self was (and is) to be the person God made me to be.

Who is Bud Kieser, I asked. He is that unique human being who in the pit of his being has been loved by God in a unique way, and who, from the pit of his being, has tried to accept that love and respond to it.

For me, that pit-of-the-being response involved priesthood. God had spoken in the depths of my soul, and He had invited me to be a priest. And I, wanting to respond to His love, accepted His invitation. I became a priest. It is my way of loving God. It is my way of serving Him in others. Priest is the essential expression of my relationship with God, and it is my essential way of relating to other people. It constitutes my identity. I am essentially priest. Priest is who I am.

Whether you root this in an indelible sacramental character imprinted on my soul at ordination, in the experience of rapport with God in prayer, or in what I was for other people and in how they responded to me, is not important for our present purposes. What is important is that by 1967, I was priest. That was my identity, who I was, a given.

Walking the surf, talking to the sea gulls, seeking my identity, I asked, "When do I feel most whole? Happiest? Most myself?" The answers always involved priestly functions. Many of my most unforgettable moments with Genevieve were priestly moments—moments of wonder, healing, risking, caring, and discovery.

Whichever way I turned, I was being faced with the same reality: Priest is who I am. I can only be myself if in some way I am living as a priest, relating as a priest, expressing myself as a priest. Apart from the priesthood, I could not be fully myself. I would be cut off from my deepest, realest, truest self. I would be alienated, unhappy.

In theory, of course, it is possible to separate priesthood and celibacy, and many people cogently argue the two should be separated. But in the real world of twentieth-century Roman Catholicism, the world in which Genevieve and I lived, it was not possible to separate the two. If I married Genevieve, I would give up the priesthood. If I decided to remain a priest, I could not marry Genevieve. It was that simple. The choices were stark and both carried price tags that seemed unacceptably harsh. I struggled with those price tags.

At each stage of the journey, I shared with Genevieve where I was and what I was beginning to see. She did not like the direction in which I was moving, for she was moving in the opposite direction.

Her dispensation came through. She bought new clothes, packed her things, and moved into an apartment in Hollywood. Sometimes I said Mass for her there.

On one occasion, to make sure I was aware of where she was and what she wanted, she put into words her desire to marry me. It was a difficult moment for both of us, and I know my response came off as a rejection. It hurt her. I now deeply regret the pain I caused.

I had not given her any indication in words that I might resign the priesthood, nor had that possibility really occupied my conscious mind for any length of time until she made her decision to leave the convent. But I am afraid my actions—and my physical and emotional responses across the whole spectrum of our relationship—were strongly suggesting that this was a real possibility. Deep within myself, on some unconscious level, I am sure I was considering it.

She must have sensed that. She always knew what was going on inside of me. Sometimes before I did.

But as the weeks passed and we continued to see each other and share our thoughts and feelings with each other, she could also sense that my decision was slowly making itself, that I was reaffirming rather than renouncing my priesthood.

She had trouble understanding my decision. Why are you doing this? How can you? These were the unspoken questions between us. She could not believe I was deciding as I was. And she had even more trouble accepting it.

That hurt me.

She continued to go for therapy. She got a job. She started to date. And then we faced another and equally agonizing decision. Welling up in each of us was a tremendous desire to consummate our relationship.

From her increasingly secular perspective, it seemed a reasonable thing to do. We obviously loved each other. This would significantly increase the likelihood that her first experience (and mine) would be a gentle and loving one. There certainly was plenty of chemistry between us. If I was not ready to marry her, why not the next best thing? Indeed, why not?

Because my perspective was not a secular one. Because I could see no way of separating the passion and pleasure of sex from its meaning. For me sex was something holy, a privileged form of communication. What it says was quite definite: I belong to you, only to you, forever. To engage in the sexual act and not mean what it said seemed to me a profound act of dishonesty, something that was incompatible with the kind of love I felt for her. I had never lied to Genevieve. I did not want to lie to her now. And so I did not want to say with my body what I did not mean with my heart and soul. And I could not with my mind, heart, and soul make a permanent and exclusive commitment of myself to her because I had already made a contrary one that I was not ready to renounce.

These are, I hope, the clear and convincing reasons why I pulled back from having an affair with Genevieve. But at the time, the situation did not seem clear, and I was not altogether sure what I was convinced of.

Physically, of course, I wanted to go ahead. I was revved up and raring to go. It would have been alleluia time. To have been able to express my love in that way, meeting her need and satisfying my desire, would have been fulfilling for me. And the experience of physical fusion to complement and express our spiritual fusion was compellingly attractive.

Yet I sensed the dishonesty involved. I was beginning to see that I could not hope to be faithful to Genevieve in the deepest and most radical sense—which means so much more than simply staying out of someone else's bed—if I was not first faithful to myself. And that, I now had to admit, meant being faithful to my priesthood and the celibacy that flowed from it.

And so I did the only thing I could do. I pulled back. She again felt rejected and hurt. That was not my intention. But it was the result of what I did. I am sorry about that, too.

The situation was hard on her ego and left both of us very frustrated sexually. This was nothing new for us. We had been living with a very high degree of frustration for months. But now it intensified.

In retrospect I do not think I was sufficiently sensitive to the tough position she was in. I was naive about the effects of what I was doing. For a long time, unconsciously but really, I had been sending mixed signals, part of me saying "come close," part saying "keep your distance." And now, without realizing it, I had put her in the position of seeming like the seductress of the knight in shining armor. Nothing could have been more unfair. Or further from the truth. I was no knight, and she was no seductress. This made her bitchy. She did not like herself when she was that way.

Nor was I admitting to myself how tense and frustrated I was. Sometimes I became irascible.

Fortunately I was continuing to spend the hour a day in prayer and meditation. That kept me in touch with my deepest self and with what was honest and what was not for me. It enabled me to tap into a source of power that helped me struggle for the kind of self-possession and self-discipline the situation required. It also helped transform a great portion of my erotic energies into spiritual ones. And at the deepest level, beneath all the tension and turmoil, it gave me a zone of peace and joy in which to live.

Without the hour of prayer and meditation each day, I do not think I could have gotten through this rather hellish period in my life.

But where did this leave Genevieve? Nowhere.

Very early in her therapy, her therapist—let's call him Harry—had suggested a degree of sex play to help her with her repressions. Almost all therapists would today consider this a serious breach of professional ethics. But in the 1960s such procedures were not uncommon. She went along. When she told me, I was furious. She decided to stop. But she was vulnerable. So was he. Once started, this kind of thing is difficult to keep in check. It became a problem that plagued her therapy.

By the summer of 1967, the problem became so serious that Harry arranged another therapist for her. But by the fall, they started seeing each other outside therapy, and it soon became very sexual. She hid none of it from me. I was enraged at what he was doing. Part was pure masculine jealousy. The subtext was "Take your hands off my woman." Of course, she was not my woman. I had no proprietary rights. But that is the way I felt just the same.

Part, too, was moral outrage. Not only was he being unfaithful to his wife—whom he professed to love—but he was betraying the trust I had asked Genevieve to place in him. It seemed to me he was using the residue of transference that can be a necessary and healthy part of the therapeutic process to exploit her vulnerability and impede her growth.

I was so furious that I began to spend my meditations thinking up ways to destroy him. In my eyes he became demonic—purely evil—and this caused the demonic to surface within me. I was filled with wild and uncontrolled energies that were bent on destruction. For the first and only time in my life, I gave serious thought to killing another human being.

Consumed by jealousy, filled with rage, choked with anger, I was afraid of what I might do. What was I to do? I had never met him. In my more rational moments, I knew he could not be as bad as I imagined him to be. So, to exorcise myself, I did the only thing I could do. I called him up and invited him to have dinner. He agreed, and we had a long and honest heart-to-heart talk.

I went to the dinner filled with hatred for him. I returned from the dinner with my hostility transformed into compassion. Like most of us, he was a weak, confused, and needy human being caught in a tough situation. On some level I liked him. I felt for him. I could see that he was bright. But I could also see that we did not see things the same way.

At Thanksgiving Genevieve told me he had left his wife and was filing for divorce. As soon as the final decree was granted, she and Harry planned to marry. In the meantime they were living together.

I was shattered.

I was shattered because this marked her definitive breach with the Church and seemingly with those values—love, fidelity, self-sacrifice, respect for the rights of others, honesty—that the Church had nurtured in us, and which I had always thought we had in common.

I was also shattered because I felt somehow responsible. If I had decided differently, would she be deciding differently?

She said she did not want to violate the values we both cherished, but she did not know what else she could do. Her own needs, her own right to fulfillment, had to be factored into the equation, she said.

She did say she would feel guilt for what she was doing to his wife for the rest of her life.

She also accused me of sending her to hell.

Christmas was sad that year. I was not in much of a mood to celebrate.

Genevieve called me on New Year's Eve to invite me to have dinner with her and Harry the next night. I was reluctant. But when she pleaded, I agreed. We met at the restaurant at 7 P.M. By two-thirty the next morning, we had adjourned to their apartment and were still going strong. They wanted to hear again the problems I had with the morality of what they were doing. We thrashed it out, point by point, but neither side moved any closer to the other.

For some reason Genevieve needed my approval for what she had decided to do. Harry wanted it, too. I could not give it to them. I could affirm her unconditionally. But I could not affirm the course she had chosen. To me it was both morally wrong and unworthy of her.

This hurt her, and her hurt transformed itself into fury as she lashed out at me like a mother tigress with bared teeth and slashing claws striking out at an assailant of her young. She said I had led her on. I had sought a relationship that implicitly promised what I had no intention of delivering. I had taken up so much of her time. I had deliberately frustrated her. I was anti-sex and anti-life. I was now trying to deprive her of her one chance for real happiness. She seemed to be trying to prove that she loved him more than she loved me.

It was mean and it was nasty and it left me in pieces. But there was love present, too. Once, Harry moved to the attack with a series of therapeutic questions. Genevieve knew where he was going, as did I, and called him off. "No, Harry. Don't."

It was the most painful night of my life.

I was so devastated that I walked around like a zombie for the next two weeks. I could hardly work.

But that night did have its positive side. Up until that point, I had always blamed Harry for what had been going on. He was the exploiter, the seducer. Genevieve was the innocent victim. Now I knew this was no longer the case. She was a full partner in what was happening. She was knowingly and willingly choosing the path she was taking.

Also, her attack on me—and on our relationship—caused something to snap within me. I had no desire to give love to someone who did not cherish it, so I let her go. I stopped clinging. I gave up the fight for her soul.

For the next ten years, we did not see much of each other. This was my choice rather than hers. I just did not want any more pain.

Genevieve and Harry did marry. They moved to the East Coast, where she now teaches English literature at an Ivy League school. They have two children. Despite the odds, the marriage has been a happy one. I am glad.

Inside me she continued to live—not as the sensitive, nurturing person I had loved for two and a half years, but as the snarling, biting, clawing tigress I had encountered New Year's night.

It is not healthy when an important member of one's inner community is that hurt, that angry, that at war with its fellow family members.

I was deeply wounded and was to remain so for several years. Her rejection of the Church and its values had become in my psyche a deep and personal rejection of me.

She, too, was deeply wounded. My pulling back from sexual intimacy and my refusal to approve of her marriage to Harry had come off as a searing personal rejection. And so I continued to live in her, not as the caring person she had cared so much about, but as a frowning, finger-shaking, vindictive father figure. He could not have been easy to live with either.

Sometime in 1972 I had a dream about Genevieve. She had died. The funeral was held in the auditorium of the university, where we had attended so many lectures and plays together. After the Mass the casket remained in the auditorium. I was deep into mourning. I looked around for some of her friends to mourn with. But they had all left. I was alone . . . and bereft. Then Gene Burke—who never liked Genevieve and never approved of our relationship—came up and said, "C'mon, Bud, let's play golf."

I did not have much trouble with the tigress after that.

I met Genevieve again at a Christmas party in 1977. I had gone to the party knowing she would be there. She had gone knowing I would be there. When I arrived the hostess, knowing of the relationship, said to me, "Genevieve's here. Do you want a drink?" I laughed, said no, caught Genevieve's eye, and suddenly there was no one else in the room for either of us.

We decided to have dinner. Driving to the restaurant, she made some caustic remarks about celibacy. I cut her off, saying she was an arrogant bitch who did not know what she was talking about. That seemed to clear the air. The rest of the evening was given over to soul talk. She wanted to know what my feelings were about our relationship and was relieved when I told her I felt my life was so much richer because of it. She also wanted to talk to me about where she was spiritually. She seemed accepting of my priesthood—something which was, of course, very important to me and which had not characterized our relationship for a long time.

"Do you feel loved by me?" I asked as I said good night.

"Yes," she said. "Thank you."

We have stayed in rather regular touch since then, usually having dinner together about once a year. The old conversational magic is still there. We can talk effortlessly for five or six hours on the deepest and most personal of levels.

Things have come together for her. She has not returned to the Church, but she remains the profoundly spiritual, deeply reflective, sensitively caring human being she has always been. She graciously gave me permission to include our story in this book.

I am no longer in love with her. She is no longer in love with me. We no longer need each other. But twenty-two years after that bloody New Year's night, we are still extremely important to each other. We love each other. We are part of each other.

Recently, musing with her, I asked why, after so many years, we were still so important to each other. Was it because we had entered each other's lives at such a crucial turning point? Or was it because, given our respective temperaments and spiritual dispositions, we had a dialectical relationship—man and woman, believer and skeptic, objective and subjective, historical and existential, rational and intuitive, healer and hurting person, ego and anima, Knight in Shining Armor and Lady Bountiful—that was archetypal and so possessed of rare energy and excitement?

She thought both of these played their part. "But the principal reason," she said, "is because we have always told each other the whole truth."

At the deepest of levels, Genevieve will always be the woman in my life.

She remains the most fascinating person I have ever met.

She is the person I can communicate with most deeply, most spontaneously, most joyfully.

As no one else, she has helped me experience the tenderness of God.

CHAPTER 10

AGGIORNAMENTO

When I returned from the Council in November of 1965, I hit the ground running.

In Rome I had had a powerful experience of Church. I had seen firsthand the presence of God in the life of His people, the freedom that is their birthright, the dialogue that is the essence of their life together.

Immersing myself in its life, I had moved into a new place in myself and had started to look at my life from a new vantage point. What I saw was promising. It was good news, and I was anxious to share it.

Like the new convert I was, I could not keep to myself what I had experienced. And the people of Los Angeles were ready to listen. The extensive media coverage of the Council had whetted their appetites. They wanted to know what the Council had been like from the inside and what it meant, in a practical way, for the Church in Los Angeles.

During the fall/winter semester of 1966, I gave a course for the priests and nuns of the Archdiocese of Los Angeles on the documents of Vatican II. More than five hundred attended these Friday afternoon lectures. I found this exciting, not only because of the quality and influence of my students, but also because its preparation forced me to mine the conciliar corpus for its lode-stones of theological gold.

The following year I gave a complementary course for the same group on the spirituality of Vatican II. The preparation for this second course involved not so much research on the conciliar documents as systematic and intensive reflection on the central realities of the Christian life as viewed from a conciliar perspective. This, too, was exciting, since it forced me to deepen my roots in the new place I had occupied within myself and push out from there, exploring the implications of the Council in an applied and practical way.

This had immediate significance for St. Paul the Apostle parish.

With the gentle and loving John Mitchell in the pastor's chair, we tried our best, through sermon, lecture, and discussion, to educate our people about the Council and to prepare them for the changes that were just around the corner. With some people we succeeded. With others we did not.

On the first Sunday of Advent 1965, we implemented the first of the liturgical changes. English replaced Latin in parts of the Mass. Over the next several years, one set of changes followed another, as, step by step, we put the entire Mass into English. The celebrant turned to face the people as portions of the Mass became dialogues between priest and people. Lay lectors read much of the scripture, and contemporary music was encouraged.

The purpose of the changes was to capture the essence of the ancient liturgical forms in a contemporary way, to help the people understand and respond to the Word of God as it was proclaimed to them in scripture and homily and to involve them in the Eucharist in such a way that they could participate in a communal manner.

The new liturgy demands much of the celebrant. For this some priests were prepared. Others were not. It took me a while to get used to it, but I came to love the new Mass. The most fulfilling half hour of the day became more fulfilling still.

It also took time for the laity to get acclimated. Much more was also demanded of them. But most, after a while, felt positive about the changes.

Most. Not all. Some reacted negatively to the very idea of change. They were used to the Latin Mass. It had worked well for them. They saw no reason to change it. A UCLA professor said to me, "It had not changed in fifteen hundred years. Now it has. I think I am losing my faith." Others complained about this or that change. "I come to church to talk to God," one man said to me, "not to shake hands with somebody I don't know and will never see again."

Some had justifiable complaints about the lack of poetry in the new liturgical forms, the quality of the folk music, the proclaiming skills of the lectors, or the mumbling and bumbling and fumbling of the priest, which were now so evident. "Pretty soon we'll be no different from the Protestants," one woman said to me. As if Protestant was a dirty word.

Underlying many of the complaints about the English Mass was an unspoken yet more serious one: a missed sense of mystery and transcendence.

Also unspoken, yet becoming all too evident, was something we should have been aware of but were not: Change is difficult for human beings, and change in the area of religion is the most difficult of all.

We listened to the complaints and tried to remedy those we could. We also saw that to impose changes on people who did not want them was counterproductive. So we arranged to have a variety of folk and Gregorian Masses, in English and in Latin, so that people could choose the form that worked best for them. "Squares have souls, too," one Paulist said.

Impeding the pace of renewal and encouraging those who wanted no change at all was James Cardinal McIntyre, the kind yet autocratic wielder of all authority and power in the Los Angeles archdiocese. Cardinal McIntyre was a New York stockbroker before he became a priest. He had voted with the arch-conservative minority against most of the conciliar documents because he liked the Church of his boyhood and saw no reason to change it. A simple, honest, straightforward man who was called the sixteenth-century fox by his more progressive priests, he tolerated the liturgical changes recommended by Rome and the U.S. Catholic bishops conference, but did not encourage them. He believed in his own authority and was not reluctant to exercise it. He chastised priests who preached against racial discrimination and the Vietnam War. He forbade the parish councils that enabled laypeople to participate in the decision-making of their parishes, and which were then beginning to become popular in other parts of the country. "Pray. Pay. Obey," was his idea of the laity's role. Priests' senates were also anathema to him. He hated any kind of controversy in the Church. "Why air our dirty linen in public?" he liked to say. When the Sisters of the Immaculate Heart tried to renew and modernize themselves, he fought them with every weapon at his disposal, including the revocation of their tax-exempt status. "Why don't they do as they are told?" was his general attitude toward women and young priests. A nun in dungarees was enough to give him apoplexy.

When scheduling "Insight," I would study his confirmation schedule, so I could run the more controversial shows when he was otherwise occupied.

Once he saw an "Insight" on the *Playboy* philosophy. He was offended by the graphic language and called my superior to complain. John Mitchell suggested I go down to see him.

"I know, Father," he said in greeting, "that you are a Paulist and are engaged in a national apostolate. But you make 'Insight' in my diocese, and you do air it here, and I don't think a Catholic program should contain that kind of language."

I could see there was a question underlying his remarks: Is this another rebellious young priest?

I was not, so I replied, "I'm sorry if the program offended you, your Eminence, but I was just trying to be honest to that subject matter. Besides, I don't intend to do another show on pornography."

"But, Father," he said, "you should do another show on pornography. But you shouldn't do it like that. I don't want that program rerun in my diocese."

"I won't rerun it here," I said.

"And I don't think you should run it any other place either."

"I won't rerun it here," I said, deciding to draw the line.

He let it drop. As we said good-bye, he remarked, "I think Loretta Young would have been much better than Vera Miles in the lead role."

Cardinal McIntyre's intransigence helped polarize the Catholic community in Los Angeles, and an underground church sprang up. We brought in progressive speakers from other parts of the country, tried to embarrass the Cardinal into allowing a priests' senate, did everything we could to shore up the beleaguered Immaculate Hearts, and celebrated underground Masses.

Today the liturgical form we used—everyone sitting around a table, just a stole for the priest, real sins being mentioned at the penitential rite, a dialogue homily, each person verbalizing his or her own intention at the prayer of the faithful, holding hands at the Lord's Prayer, an affectionate smooch at the kiss of peace, self-administered communion under both species—seems routine. And so like the Last Supper. But in those days it was bold and daring and so very exciting, partially, I guess, because it was against the rules. John and Ann Furia, Jack and Patt Shea, Judy Greening, and Sister Marjorie Sartoris were regular participants.

Although I considered myself a Vatican II Catholic, a progressive one at that, as the months passed and the polarization increased I was made increasingly uncomfortable, not only by the frightened traditionalists of the right who would call the chancery to complain about anything you said in your Sunday sermon they considered too avant-garde, but also by the strident and angry dogmatists of the left, who had black-and-white solutions for every problem, most of which seemed to have little connection with reality, and who seemed more concerned with confrontation than with dialogue.

It was a painful time in the Los Angeles Church, hardly a healthy atmosphere in which to exercise one's priesthood and minister to the people of God.

For some it was to prove lethal.

Since his ordination in 1957, Dennis Burke had been my closest friend, my brother in the traces of the Lord. He and Genevieve were my soulmates, the two people with whom I communicated most fully, the poles of my support system.

He and I shared our days off and frequently vacationed together, playing golf at Palm Desert, Carmel, or Newport. He was deeply pastoral, read widely, loved ideas. We talked incessantly about God, the Church, ourselves. From an old-line Los Angeles family, he was of Irish descent, which meant, he used to say, the faith comes with the genes. It also meant he had the kind of unconscious Eugene O'Neill made famous. He had a loving yet domineering father, which may explain why he had something of an authority problem. Once his Dad died, Dennis seemed to transfer his need for approval to the bishop of the diocese. He also found celibacy excruciatingly difficult.

In September 1964, after seven years as a parish priest in Glendale and Long Beach, where he taught at St. Anthony's High School, he got permission from Cardinal McIntyre to enter a doctoral program at the Catholic University of America. The Cardinal wanted him to get the degree in education. Dennis preferred to study theology. They compromised. He got it in religious education, taking most of his courses in the theology department and writing his dissertation on Henri de Lubac, the brilliant French theologian who was one of the fathers of Vatican II.

In 1964 the theology department at CU was filled with the

ferment of Vatican II. With Gene Burke, Charlie Curran, and Carl Peter lecturing, it had a decidedly progressive orientation. The student body, mostly priests, was even more liberal. Dennis loved CU, rejoiced in the ferment, imbibed the new ideas, bought into the new vision of the Church and its role in society. When he came home at Christmas or Easter or during summer vacation, he would regale me with stories of his teachers and fellow students. He also filled me with their ideas and insights. I did not then realize he was on a collision course with Cardinal McIntyre.

Returning from Catholic University in August of 1967 with his Ph.D., Dennis reported to the Cardinal for assignment. One possibility was a teaching post in the seminary. The Cardinal wanted to know where Dennis fit in the theological spectrum and if he agreed with his brother Gene, whose progressive views had been widely reported in the press. Dennis said he did. An argument followed. Bishops Timothy Manning and John Ward were drawn in. The argument became heated. Dennis hoped Bishop Manning, a family friend, would support him. He did not. When Bishop Ward defended the Cardinal's opposition to the Council, Dennis questioned his integrity. This infuriated the Cardinal, who threw Dennis out of his office. Shortly thereafter he was assigned to Our Lady of Lourdes parish in Northridge, with pastoral responsibility for the Catholic students at Cal State.

That lasted two weeks. Feeling rejected by those in authority, he was angry and resentful and left to take a post teaching theology at the University of San Francisco.

It was the beginning of the end.

The commitment of diocesan priests, unlike that of religious order ones, tends to take on a geographical focus. They do not commit so much to the People of God in general but to the People of God in Los Angeles or Detroit or Philadelphia or St. Louis. And the leadership of that Church, the bishop of that diocese, becomes, in a very special way, a God figure. So it was with Dennis. He had made a covenant with the Church in Los Angeles. Now he felt rejected by its leadership. That really hurt, and he was in San Francisco, apart from the ecclesiastical community to which he had committed himself, apart from his family and closest friends. He was very, very lonely. I tried to do what I could in the way of support, but I was four hundred miles away. The emotional underpinning of his priesthood began to give way.

He started to date—nothing serious at first, just somebody to have dinner with, talk to, share a laugh with.

The following summer, in August of 1968, Dennis, Gene, and I played golf together at Carmel and, on the way back, stopped at the Immaculate Heart Convent in San Jose to visit with Sister Margie Sartoris, who had been transferred there to work among the migrants. The attraction between Dennis and Margie was immediate and powerful. Gene noticed it. So did I.

He had, by this time, left USF and taken a job in personnel at a high-tech firm in Silicon Valley. He was feeling a great deal of anxiety and had begun psychotherapy. Part was the demands of a new job, but most was stress over his ambivalent situation. He came down with mononucleosis. Margie nursed him back to health. To those who knew them best, it was apparent that they were falling in love. Dennis told me he was thinking of getting married. His family was upset. Gene, in particular, was strongly opposed. So was I.

Part of my negative reaction was, I think, unselfish concern for the Church and the loss of a great priest. Part was concern for the two of them. Could Dennis be happy apart from the priesthood? If the priesthood was part of my identity, was it not also part of his? And if it was, could he be happy, within himself and with Margie, if he was not able to express that side of himself? "Business is fun," he once said to me, "but it is not as exciting as ideas, and ideas are not as exciting as salvation."

Margie was struggling with a similar dilemma. She sought a dispensation from her vows only after her mother died and the Immaculate Heart Sisters withdrew from canonical status.

But most of my negative reaction was rooted in self-concern. Genevieve was no longer an active part of my support system. Now it seemed Dennis was also pulling out. The two people who meant most to me, with whom I communicated most intimately, and to whom I most turned for understanding and support, were absenting themselves from my life. That hurt—a lot.

But if I am totally honest with myself, I must also admit that my negative reaction went even deeper. Dennis threatened me, and I threatened him. If he could marry, so could I. If I could rechoose the priesthood, so could he. We had so identified with each other that he was the Bud Kieser who could leave the priesthood and get married and I was the Dennis Burke who could rechoose the priesthood and remain celibate.

I thought I had made my decision in the context of my relationship with Genevieve, meaning the celibacy question was over and done with and I did not have to worry about that anymore. But reflecting on my experience with Dennis and Margie makes me realize how ambivalent that decision was, how these kinds of decisions always remain fragile. We work out our salvation in fear and trembling.

It was a strained and tortuous period in our friendship. I did not hide my negative feelings from either of them, which hurt both very deeply. When they finally did get married, I did not go to the wedding. That increased the hurt. I did not see how I could honestly celebrate it. All I could do was mourn—what had been and what would now be no more.

Over the years other close friends of mine—Tony Wilhelm, Charlie McCarthy, Terry Sweeney—have also withdrawn from the priesthood and married. Each caused me great sadness. But none rocked me like Dennis. His marriage to Margie left me feeling very fragile, very alone.

Which is just another way of saying I was beginning to feel an intense need for community.

I needed a network of open, trusting, affirming relationships, people with whom I could communicate honestly, share my vulnerability and be myself—who knew my faults and loved me anyway, who would always be there for me when I needed them.

At one level we are all alone, solitary creatures who inhabit a great silence that can be penetrated only by God. At another level we are all profoundly communal. "No man is an island," John Donne said, "entire of itself; every man is a piece of the continent, a part of the main."

Some people accept their need for community. Other people deny it. I took mine for granted.

I had grown up in a loving and supportive family. I had always been able to make friends. I had joined the Paulists, who had surrounded me with caring men of similar values and aspirations.

Sure I needed people, but I felt they would always be there for me when I needed them.

Now they were not, not in the way I needed them. Patt Shea, John Furia, and Sister Janet Harris sensed my pain and tried to be there for me. But still I ached with loneliness.

I read Paul Tillich, who said that loneliness, like the other anxieties of fear, guilt, and meaninglessness, is part of the human condition; that all anxiety has a providential role to play in our growth to full personhood; that it can play this role only if we face and assimilate it, allowing ourselves to feel its full force; that if we do, we can learn to transcend the anxiety and use it to enrich our lives significantly.

"The more non-being (anxiety) a being (the human person) can face and assimilate without being destroyed," Tillich had said, "the more alive that being becomes."

Instead of running from my loneliness, I tried to face it. On occasion, when I succeeded, I was able to ride the loneliness down into a very deep place within myself and use it as a springboard for contemplative prayer. But only on occasion.

It worked fine for a day or a week or even a month, but it was not, I soon realized, adequate for a lifetime. I was no rock. I needed friends. I needed soul talk. I needed to love—and be loved. I decided I had better find myself a community or build one, regardless of the price.

The Paulists were the natural place to start. I had many close friends in the society—Charlie McCarthy, Tony Wilhelm, Gene Burke, Bill Cantwell, John Carr, Kevin Lynch, Tom Comber—but none of them were in Los Angeles, and I have always found the telephone an inadequate vehicle for soul talk.

I shared religious and ministerial commitments with the men with whom I lived, but sometimes I seemed to share little else. I was a television producer. They were parish priests, university student chaplains, or traveling preachers. Our lives were very different. And more important, by background and temperament, they seemed uncomfortable with soul talk, with emotion, with the sharing of vulnerability I craved.

In retrospect I think I had unrealistic expectations. I also think they gave me what they could. They were caring people, and they met many of my needs. But they did not meet all of them. How could they? Genevieve had opened up whole new areas of my soul, areas that now needed to be irrigated, needs that no group of religious men could be expected to satisfy. She had so drawn me into the community life of the Sisters of her order—so free, joyful, and accepting, so comfortable with vulnerability, and so open about feelings—that they had become a second family for me, and their retreat house had become a second home. But when Genevieve left the order and she and I decided to go our separate ways, I pulled back from them. Too many of my nerves were exposed, and I was hurting too badly. For me, after a time, the retreat house became haunted by ghosts.

In search of community, I went to Esalen, and I took sensitivity training at Carl Rogers's Institute of the Person in La Jolla. The communication in these sessions was sometimes deep and honest, and these groups frequently became close. At the end of each day, we would gather in the backyard of the Catholic chaplain's house at the university for the Eucharist. These Masses were intense and full of feeling. But the emotional highs could not last.

These encounter groups and sensitivity sessions filled three days or a week. At their best they showed what communal life could be like. But they were no substitute for it.

I hungered for something more, something permanent and continuing.

I found it in the Jesu Caritas priests' fraternity. Rooted in the spirituality of Charles de Foucauld, the French playboy turned contemplative, the fraternity required a threefold commitment: to simplicity, if not poverty of life; to one hour of prayer a day; and to an all-day meeting once a month with the other members of one's fraternity. The central feature of this all-day meeting, besides the Eucharist, was the "review of life," which involved the sharing by each member of where he was, what he was struggling with, and how his ministry and prayer life were going.

When I joined Jesu Caritas in 1969, there were a dozen such fraternities in the Los Angeles area. Mine had seven other members, all diocesan priests. Each fraternity met once a month, and all of the fraternities got together for a three-day retreat during the week between Christmas and New Year's.

Jesu Caritas met a deep need in my life. As the months rolled by and one review of life followed another, I really got to know the other guys, and they really got to know me. Together we blew off steam, aired hurts, worked through problems, sorted out confusions, and made our decisions. As we did I felt accepted and affirmed by them, not because I was a well-known and apparently successful television producer, but simply and solely for who I was in all my screwed-up humanity. They rooted for me, for my spiritual growth, as I rooted for theirs. When I broke through to a new level of prayer or awareness, they were elated. When I stumbled and fell, abdicating my freedom, copping out, they were saddened. But always they were there, present to me, responsible for me, expecting me to be responsible to them.

In the review of life, each person was accepted, but his illusions and self-deceptions were not.

"You know, for eight years I break my butt for the guy," Al says. I can feel the pain in his voice. "Then I need some time off. So I take a leave of absence. What does the archbishop do? He cancels my health insurance. I tell you, I've been depressed all week."

"You know why?" Mark was usually the first one to jump in, most often with the nonthreatening question.

"It's like I no longer belong. Like I wasted my time."

"Were you working for him or for God?" You could always depend on Pat to cut through to the core of a problem.

"I don't think he knows the difference."

"Do you?" There was an immediacy in Mark's question.

But Pat jumped in before Al had a chance to answer it. "I think you're saying you need the old man's approval to feel good about yourself."

"That's not what I'm saying," Al snapped.

"That's exactly what you're saying," Pat shot back, "and I think it's time you grew out of that."

Absolute honesty—with oneself and with the group—was required in the review of life. The guys had a good ear for bullshit and would tolerate none of it. With them I could always be sure no one would tell me the lie I wanted to hear rather than the painful truth I needed to hear.

This became easier with the assimilation of a truth we discovered together. By providing a context in which we could share our vulnerability, Jesu Caritas enabled us to experience that vulnerability in a deeper and more honest way. Sound unattractive? It is. But it is also beneficial. Why? Because the experience of vulnerability, of being flawed, wounded, and broken, in pieces, incomplete and needy, scared and alone, opens us up to other people; vulnerability is, after all, what we have in common. It also opens us up to God, to whom we gravitate for healing, completion, and fulfillment. How can we hope to experience Jesus as healing Savior—let alone surrender our lives to Him—until we have first experienced our own need for healing and salvation?

In such an atmosphere, breakthroughs occurred on a regular

basis, and I watched in awe as, one after another, the guys made decisive progress in their search for intimacy with God.

Early in 1970 I had two dreams that, in retrospect, seem significant. In the first I was driving a car at high speed along a freeway when the steering mechanism jammed and the brakes gave out. Out of control, I careened from one side of the freeway to the other, smashing into one car after another. What was it saying; that I was a life out of control?

In the second there were no visuals. Just a Yahweh kind of voice that spoke from the deepest part of myself: "You will suffer a great deal until you learn certain things." The tone was authoritative. The subtext: You had better pay attention.

I told the guys at Jesu Caritas about the Yahweh dream. "What am I supposed to learn?" I asked. They had no ready answer. But that week, one of the guys—Don Kribs—called to tell me he thought I should consider psychotherapy. I was furious.

"I've got problems," I said, "but they are not that serious. I can work them out myself. Besides, I don't have the time. I don't have the money. But bottom line: I don't need it. You hear? I don't need it."

"Just thought I'd let you know what I think," he replied. "It was great for me. I think it would be great for you. Think about it. OK?"

I did think about it. I was upset. I was angry. "How dare he make such a suggestion. Who does he think he is?"

I was still steamed at the next review of life, so I said to the guys, "This son of a bitch thinks I should go into therapy. What do you think?" We discussed it at some length. Don gave the reasons he thought it would be helpful. I gave the reasons I did not think it necessary. The group kicked it around. Finally I said, "I want you guys to vote—therapy or no therapy. What does Jesus want me to do?" One guy abstained. The other six voted for therapy.

I was stuck.

In retrospect I think I reacted so negatively to the idea of therapy because it shattered my omnipotent self-image. On some level I still liked to feel I was totally together. I could surmount any challenge, solve any problem, resolve any dilemma. I needed people, of course, but not a therapist and certainly not therapy. That was for sick people, and I was not sick. I helped other people. I did not need to be helped. I was a healer who did not need to be healed.

Some time into therapy, I was sharing with the guys at Jesu Caritas my experience of therapy and noticed that one of them had a big smile on his face.

"What are you laughing at?" I said impatiently.

"I'm just happy," he said, "because super priest is dead."

But my negative reaction had another cause—a deeper, more significant one. I knew enough about therapy to know that it would entail a guided tour of my own unconscious. In 1970 my unconscious seemed dark and murky, the seat of turbulent and destructive energies that could hardly be controlled, a messy place filled with anxiety, like a lava-belching volcano, repulsive and dangerous. I had no desire to go down there. It would be like swimming in a cesspool. I might not like what I would find. What if I found out I did not want to be a priest or could not be celibate or, worst of all, did not believe? What would happen then? Better to keep the lid on. Better not to know.

I was frightened of my own unconscious. Which is just another way of saying I was frightened of the truth about myself. I had yet to make friends with all of reality, to learn to trust it.

That is why I reacted with such anger and defensiveness to the suggestion of therapy.

But now I was committed. So I set about selecting a therapist. I did not need a Catholic one. In fact, I did not want a Catholic. But I also did not want someone who would be hostile to the believing side of my psyche. That would make very difficult the kind of intimate trust I knew therapy demanded. I finally settled on John Cogswell, who came well recommended.

It was to prove a providential choice.

I was nervous as a cat during the first session. We talked face to face, but really that first hour was more like two wrestlers slowly circling each other, taking each other's measure. We both knew that for therapy to work this had to be a significant relationship. But neither of us knew whether such a relationship was possible, let alone desirable. Was this the kind of person I could trust to enter my psyche and take me on one of the most important journeys of my life? Did he have the balance and the sensitivity, the wisdom and the experience for the task? Could he understand me in my complexity? Would he respect my freedom and affirm my agenda, or would he try to impose his own? These were some of the questions that pulsated through my consciousness during that first session.

My immediate response to John was very positive. A round man with a balding head, he seemed in touch with himself and totally present to me. He was warm, earthy, and bright, at once understanding and full of feeling. Like your stereotypical Santa Claus, he had a twinkle in the eye and a laugh that came from the belly. I found in him none of the compulsive neediness or antiseptic cerebration I had encountered in other therapists. His general orientation was existential and Jungian, both of which I found simpatico.

At his suggestion I decided to go for therapy twice a week, which is what I did for most of the next two years.

After a month of talking face to face about where I was and what I was feeling, John suggested I lie down on the couch, so that I might surrender more easily to the gravitational pull of the depths, letting go of ego, of conscious mind, of conscious control, as I sank into my unconscious. Initially I found this frightening. It seemed so dark down there. But after a time, I got used to it.

Usually, after several moments of getting acclimated to my interior world, John would ask what I was aware of, where in my body I was feeling tension and discomfort. Allowing the tension into consciousness, immersing myself in it, I would often find it dissolving. And then I was freed to go deeper. Sometimes, on the trip down, I would meet people who were significant to me—Genevieve, Dennis, my father—and have a conversation with them. Sometimes I would run into currents of emotion—anger, joy, need, hurt. At other times erotic fantasies would fill my consciousness. Sometimes I would feel great loneliness or intense guilt or total futility or I would be very afraid. Fear seemed basic, and not infrequently it would raise up blocks to impede my passage. I knew I could not knock these blocks down or blast them out of the way. In the psyche, as in human relations, violence is counterproductive. But I could bring the light of consciousness to bear on them. Sometimes, when I did that, the block would melt. But on other occasions, it was better to make friends with the block and look at what was behind it. In this way, on more than one occasion, I was able to slip around behind it.

Often these emotional blocks were ways of shielding myself from some facet of reality I did not want to face; perhaps because it would disrupt my idea of myself or cause some other kind of anxiety.

Slowly, very slowly, I began to see that these blocks, defenses, and roles alienated me from my true self and consumed a great deal of energy; energy that I could have used to deal with the painful facet of reality or make the necessary changes in my self-image or assimilate the anxiety. I also learned that the truth, which is reality as grasped by consciousness, is my friend. It can be trusted unconditionally. Sometimes it causes pain and anxiety, but always it makes me more alive and freer, challenging me to grow and become my best self.

Therapy also made me intensely aware of my dreams, which often revealed much of what was going on in my unconscious. Most often the characters in my dreams were inhabitants of my unconscious, stars in my psychic constellation, members of that inner community that makes up my inner self. With John's help I learned to interpret my dreams and use them to enter unexplored regions of my unconscious. They also helped me get to know and accept the various members of my inner community.

Sometimes in therapy, I also played psychodrama. Moving from one chair to another, I would act out the part of Bud Kieser, Genevieve, Dennis, my Dad, as we tried to work out our mutual relationships.

"Why did you say those terrible things?" The empty chair was Genevieve's. John had told me to try to articulate where I still hurt. He was off to one side.

"What things?" I had slipped into her chair to speak for her.

"About deliberately leading you on. Taking so much of your time. Frustrating you." I was back in my own.

"That still bother you?"

"Yep."

"Why?"

"Because my love is special. I only give it when it's wanted. And that night you were saying you didn't want it. You didn't want me. That hurt. Plenty."

"I'm sorry about that. I wasn't rejecting you."

"So why did you say those things?"

"Not to hurt you."

"Why, then?"

"To get you off my back. Can't you see? I was fighting for my life. And you were suffocating me, making me feel guilty, sending me to hell."

"Hell is what I was trying to save you from."

"You believe in hell?"

"In the sense of fire and brimstone—no. In the sense of the absence of God, the freely chosen absence of God—yes. I believe we have the capacity to create that."

"I don't."

"Then why do you talk about it so much?"

"Because it scares me."

"How can something you don't believe in scare you?"

"Because I don't believe in it doesn't mean it doesn't exist. It just means I don't want it to be part of my consciousness."

"Why?"

"Why? I don't know why. Does there always have to be a why?"

As I explored my unconscious, got to know its inhabitants and tried to get them to relate to each other, John guided the process. He kept me pointed in the right direction. He affirmed, sustained, and encouraged me to go deep, be honest, include everyone and everything. He kept me moving ahead, and he would not allow me to escape, which, on more than one occasion, I felt like doing. But it was always clear that it was my trip, that what I was looking at was my unique unconscious, that any decisions I made in response to what I discovered were completely and exclusively my own, not his.

He made no attempt to interpret what I was seeing through the prism of his own set of dogmatic categories (as far as I know, he had none). Nor did he ever suggest a course of action beyond the process of therapy itself. His job was to help me discover the truth. It was my job, with the freedom the newly discovered truth gave me, to make the decisions.

Sometimes the therapeutic process was exciting, and I approached it with relish. More often it was just the opposite: hard work, boring, a crash course in original sin. Sometimes I felt like I needed a vacation from reality, that I could take no more pain, assimilate no more anxiety, eat no more blues. Enough is enough, I sometimes screamed to myself.

A great deal of garbage floats on the surface of the human unconscious. To get to the depths, you have to pass through the garbage. But once you do, you find pure gold underneath. By that

I mean that the deeper we penetrate the unconscious, the closer we get to God. For me, then and now, the essential meeting point with God is the depths of my own unconscious, that place in myself where I emerge from the Ground of my Being.

There were times in my therapy when the process became contemplative, when the couch occasioned experiences of close communion with God, when the attempt to illumine the unconscious with the light of consciousness became a luminous experience of Light surfacing within me yet coming from beyond me.

John enjoyed my erotic fantasies. He wept as I struggled with emotional blocks, wrestled with anxiety, and tried to navigate the straits of pain. And he responded with awe and envy to my spiritual experiences on his couch.

In the process of therapy, John and I became good friends. Sometimes he would share his spiritual aspirations and dilemmas with me. At one point we were spending as much time on where he was as we were on where I was. He was my therapist, and I was his priest. I noticed what was happening, told him it was fine with me, but also said I thought we should forget about his fee. He said he would think it over. The next session he told me he did not think it was a good idea. "OK," I said, "I'm quitting therapy."

I stayed away a month. But I soon realized I had started something I needed to finish. So I went back but only after we agreed on new ground rules: in his office the focus was on me; if he wanted to talk about himself, we went to the rectory.

As the process continued, I began to realize that I had so neglected the unconscious side of myself, the feeling, intuitive, compassionate, feminine, and aesthetic side that Jung calls the anima, that there was danger it might atrophy. I also realized that, in the name of self-discipline, I had sometimes suppressed important parts of myself and that the suppression was the cause of some of my compulsive work habits. I also realized how important it was to nurture and nourish this feeling side of myself; to listen to it, to allow it to fructify my consciousness. I also realized how important it is to keep conscious and unconscious minds in close communion.

In 1970 I made another important decision. I decided to go back to graduate school, to enter a doctoral program at the Graduate Theological Union in Berkeley.

Why, at forty-one years of age, at a time of great evangelical productivity, did I decide to do that? Very simply because I needed to.

Since returning from the Council in November of 1965, I had been teaching conciliar theology on a regular basis. I had been trying to incorporate its insights into my "Insight" shows. And I had involved myself in a pastoral way in the renewal and modernization of the Catholic community in Los Angeles.

But by 1969 I was aware that new questions were beginning to gnaw at me, as more and more intellectual lacunae began to appear.

The theology of the Vatican Council is essentially ecclesiastical. It concerns the nature of the Church, its role in the modern world. But what one thinks of the Church presupposes what one thinks of Jesus. And so, by 1970, I had a million questions about Christology, on the base of which ecclesiology is built. And about scripture, the source of our knowledge of Jesus.

The Council called for dialogue with the Protestants and Orthodox, and it recognized them as real ecclesial bodies, authentic Christian communities in whom Jesus lives and the Holy Spirit is active. In practical terms this meant that their theologians—men like Tillich and Barth, Niebuhr and Berdyaev—had much to teach me. But I had never studied them. I wanted to.

The Council called for an open response to the world and its needs. On a systematic basis, I had studied no sociology, political science, economics, or anthropology since undergraduate school at La Salle. I needed to.

Within myself I had decided on a new and more contemporary way of doing theology—moving from the abstract to the experiential, from an essentialist to an existentialist approach, from the static and conceptual to the dynamic and historical, from the construction of syllogisms to the interpretation of symbols, from the theology of the academy to the theology of the barrio. But I could not make this transition alone. I needed help.

I had left the seminary in 1956 with an overreaching world view that was consistent and integrated. It fit together and had an answer for most of life's big questions.

But by 1970, seeing how outmoded this synthesis was, I had left it behind. I had moved into a new place in myself and was looking at reality from a radically different vantage point. I had had profound experiences of the Gospel since ordination, experiences that had yielded great new insights into the meaning of

Christianity. But I needed to integrate these insights into a wholly new theological synthesis—an urgent need, yet no mean task.

In particular, for eight years I had been creating TV dramas with the hope of enriching my audiences in a Christian way. But what exactly does that mean? What is the connection between art and religion, aesthetics and Gospel, theater and theology, storytelling and evangelization, cinematic experience and the experience of God? I did not know. No book had been written on the subject. But much work had been done in the related disciplines. I needed a context to work out these interrelationships, to integrate them, to build a new synthesis, to formulate a theology of communication for myself.

There was no question of my leaving "Insight" and dedicating myself full-time to graduate studies. That was just not practical, given my situation. But a part-time program was practical, especially if the graduate school in question would consider my "Insight" activity as fieldwork.

But what kind of graduate school did I want? And what kind would want me?

I wanted an academic situation that was intellectually topflight, open and involved in the world; if not main line Protestant in sponsorship, at least with a full Protestant presence, with a faculty that brought the arts to bear on the study of theology.

For someone living and working in Los Angeles, there seemed just two possibilities: the Claremont School of Religion—about thirty miles east of the city—and the Graduate Theological Union in Berkeley.

I discussed my situation with Joe Hough, the dean at Claremont, whom I knew and liked and who would later hire me to teach at Claremont. I described the kind of program I was looking for. I wanted to reflect on the experience of living out the Gospel and build a new synthesis for myself, I told him, a synthesis that would include a theology of communication. I also told him I did not consider myself a scholar and had no desire to become one. I had in mind a dissertation that would include "Insight" episodes. He thought it a great program but said, "We should be ready for it. But we're not."

That left the Graduate Theological Union, a consortium of six Protestant theological schools and three Catholic ones that was affiliated with the University of California at Berkeley. I met with its dean, Joe Wohl, a Jesuit, who responded very favorably to my proposal. "It will fit in well with our new Theology and the Arts program," he said. "We need people like you, and we like interdisciplinary programs." He then suggested we adjourn to the tavern across the street to have a beer and work out the details. "We're ready for you," he said, "but are you ready for us? Are you ready to fly eight hundred miles a week to attend class? With your other responsibilities, are you ready to put in the kind of study time a program like this will require?"

I gulped and said yes.

It was an inspired decision, because GTU was to turn out to be everything I could have hoped—and more.

During the fall quarter, I would put on my brown suit and take the noon flight from Los Angeles to Oakland, rent a car, and drive to Berkeley in time for a two-thirty seminar. Afterward I would go to Newman Hall—the Catholic center at Cal run by the Paulists—for dinner and conversation. Back at GTU for another seminar at seven-thirty, I would return to Newman about ten, usually for a good bull session—the most interesting people frequented that common room—stay overnight, and be on the eight-fifteen plane back the next morning to be in my office by nine forty-five. Evenings and weekends, with a stolen afternoon here and there, I would do my studying. It was rigorous yet doable.

At GTU I affiliated myself with the Pacific School of Religion, an interdenominational Protestant college, and selected from its faculty Dr. Wayne Rood, a wise, earthy, and caring man who headed the Theology and the Arts program, to be chairman of my committee. He was also to become my mentor. During the winter quarter, I took theater and film courses at UCLA. This saved the long commute. I took no courses during the spring quarter, since I was shooting "Insight" then, but usually managed a tutorial or two over the summer.

Over the next two years I took courses on Jung, Buber, Erikson, Rahner, Schoonenberg, and Tillich. I also took courses on film aesthetics, contemporary theater, contemporary cinema, and contemporary sacramental theology. The professors were particularly generous with their time in tutoring me privately. The other students in the seminars were usually in their thirties—they had some real living under their belts—so there was plenty to reflect on. Kenan Osborn's classes on Paul Tillich produced discussions on salvation that remain with me still.

Once, while I was at GTU, I did "The David Frost Show." Appearing with me was an extremely attractive actress whom I had known from "Insight." The blouse she wore was abbreviated in the front and left little to the imagination. I guess she was a little embarrassed about it, because she told David that being on the show with me made her feel like a child who had been caught with her hand in the cookie jar.

Anyway, the interview went well, and a number of my classmates at GTU complimented me on what I had to say. But one of my teachers, atypical of the faculty as a whole, was upset. "You shouldn't do those shows. You give those people a dignity they don't deserve. That lady looked like a whore—I mean her boobs were hanging right out. I would have been very uncomfortable."

"The lady's no whore," I snapped back. "In fact, she's really quite nice. Why she dresses that way, I don't know. But she's gonna be on whether we like it or not, so why shouldn't I be on, too, talking about God?" He had no answer to that one.

At UCLA my teacher of contemporary cinema was Tom Peppard, a forty-nine-year-old, prematurely graying former Catholic with finely chiseled features who was now a Marxist and dogmatic Freudian. He assigned us a different picture to see each week, but all had the same theme—decadence. I challenged him on the one-sidedness of his selections, and he reacted sharply. "This is contemporary cinema," he said, "and contemporary means decadence. The modern world is rotten. It's shot full with death. You can't deny that."

In these discussions I noticed a strange dichotomy in the man, a brilliant and tightly controlled conscious mind, a wild and turbulent unconscious.

One day I lingered after class.

"Can I talk to you as a priest?" I asked.

"No," he answered definitively.

"As a brother then?"

"Oh, all right."

"Your mind is razor sharp, Tom. But below consciousness, I have the impression there's a lot going on. It keeps popping out. Every time it does, you panic and sprint away."

"So what are you saying, Father?" There was more than a touch of sarcasm in his voice.

"Just this. You might be pleasantly surprised at what's down there. Why not take a look?"

"I did that," he responded with a haunting sadness in his eyes. "Six years of analysis. I just can't take any more of that pain."

I backed off. No use pushing, I said to myself.

One day after class he called me over and thrust a paper bag into my hands. I could feel the cold steel of the automatic pistol inside.

"Please hold this for me," he said. "I'm . . . I'm afraid I might use it." He was hurting badly.

Weeks later he asked for the pistol back. I inquired how he was feeling, and he said much better. I returned the weapon.

After the course we drifted apart. I tried to keep in touch, but he always seemed too busy.

But I did hear how he died. He felt the beginnings of a heart attack, so he canceled his seminar. Instead of going to the emergency ward at the medical center, he put on his sweat suit and started to jog around the university track. The attack became massive before he covered the first quarter of a mile.

During my third year at GTU, I did a hundred-page essay on the theology of communication and defended it for my orals. Its basic premise was the presence of God in the depth of every human experience and the interchangeability of religious and human values. Also the human-enrichment potential of both TV and film. My dissertation was entitled "Cinema as Religious Experience" and included as examples five "Insight" episodes. Its basic premise was the intrapersonal nature of the cinematic experience and its capacity to elicit a surfacing of God within the viewer. Its defense was not as argumentative as my orals, and I was moved when the committee emerged from its meeting afterward to call me doctor. The Ph.D. was more important to me than I would have admitted.

At GTU I was to meet Mike Rhodes and Father Terry Sweeney, S.J., both of whom would come to work at Paulist Productions and make significant contributions in the years ahead. Both would also become close friends.

I graduated from GTU in June of 1973 and conducted a seminar for ministerial students that fall at Claremont. The following year I moved to UCLA and, for the next five years, taught philosophy in their adult education program. These were lecture series, and I sometimes had more than two hundred students. Many were teachers who were updating their credentials. Their experiences were deep and varied, and we had a lot to reflect on together. I loved teaching these courses. Working in the heart of the secular world, helping these very secular people grow and develop and become the human beings God wanted them to be, I felt most priest and most Paulist.

As I look over the years covered by this chapter—1965 to 1978—I notice a certain rhythm, an ebb and flow of my psychic energies, as, at times, I turned inward to enrich and fulfill myself (the Council, Jesu Caritas, therapy, GTU), and at other times turned outward to share what I had discovered with others. The 1973 to 1978 period was rich in this latter way.

The entire period was the best of times and the worst of times; a time of change, growth, and excitement and a time of confusion, pain, and turmoil; a time when I fell in love and a time when I painfully fell out of love; a time when I rechose the priesthood and a time when some of my best friends did not; a time when I experimented with different forms of community, found Jesu Caritas, underwent psychotherapy, completed a doctoral program at GTU, produced more than one hundred and fifty "Insights," and taught priests and nuns at Mt. St. Mary's, ministerial students at Claremont, and graduate students at UCLA.

In retrospect it is not difficult to understand why this was a great time and a miserable time.

The United States was caught up in a cultural revolution of rare magnitude, and I was plunked down in the middle of it. The immigrant Church of my boyhood collapsed as the Catholic Church in which I lived struggled to reform, renew, and modernize itself. In addition, these were the years in my life—ages thirty-six to forty-nine—when most men go through their midlife crisis. Did I think I would be any different?

No, it is not hard to understand why these years were the best of times and the worst of times.

I wouldn't have missed them for a million bucks.

But I would not repeat them for a million bucks either.

Part Four

Hitting Stride

CHAPTER 11

HUMANITAS PRIZE

"Look, Father, I know all about the needs of my viewers," said the program executive. I had gone to see him about improving "Insight" 's time slot. It was early 1972.

"But I can't do good until I'm doing well, and right now I'm not doing well."

It was as if he was telling me he had leprosy.

"You want me to be honest?" he went on. "You make a quality show. I'm proud to have it on my station. My kids watch it every week. But I can't put it on at night. Let's face it. Most people aren't interested in quality. By the time they plop down before the set at night they're tired. They don't want to think or feel. They just want to get away from it all. Massage their senses. Anesthetize their emotions. But stay away from their minds and hearts. No one ever went broke underestimating the taste and intelligence of the American people."

I started to argue but could tell he was not about to listen. I left his office steamed.

Maybe that is why I lost my cool two weeks later when I was doing the "Newsmakers" show on KNBC in Los Angeles, where "Insight" did have an evening time slot. I was in the hot seat and had three different interviewers coming at me at once.

"What's wrong with TV?" asked one.

"Why isn't it fulfilling its potential?" cut in another.

"The problem isn't the system," I shot back, the adrenaline flooding into my bloodstream. "It's the way the system is operated. By federal statute the stations are allowed to use the people's airwaves on condition they meet the needs of the people in their broadcast area. But in practice they consistently subordinate their viewers to their stockholders. Whether we like it or not, broadcasting in the United States is first and foremost a business and so its guiding principles are the bottom line, return on investment, and profits."

"There's nothing sinful about profits," interjected the third interviewer.

"Not if they're honestly come by," I replied. "But in TV, profits depend on ratings. The bigger the audience, the more the broadcaster makes. And so the overriding preoccupation of programmers is with what will appeal to the greatest number of people. What is the result? All too often programmers are more concerned with the numerical quantity of their audiences than they are with the humanistic quality of their programs. Ratings become the criterion by which everything else is judged."

"You feel strongly about this, don't you?"

"Damn right. Quality programs are turned down and sleaze is broadcast because someone thinks it might get a couple of extra rating points. The appeal is to the lowest common denominator, to the audience's baser instincts. Viewers are not treated as human beings who are cherished for their own sake, but they are pandered to as consumers who have value only because they can buy what the advertiser is selling."

The next morning John Zodrow, one of our best "Insight" writers, called to congratulate me on what I had said. "I'm glad you liked it," I replied. "But I've been kicking myself for getting carried away. I was too negative, and I never did get a chance to put the whole thing in a religious context."

"I disagree," John answered. "You were saying what needed to be said, and you were speaking for those who couldn't speak for themselves, and what you said was true. You weren't talking about Jesus. You were doing the Jesus thing, and that's even more important."

He gave me a lot to think about.

At this time I was trying to synthesize my theology of communication at GTU. I decided I had to start with the philosophic basics: A fulfilled person is an open, aware, free, creative, and loving center of life and activity. We are not born fulfilled persons. We become fulfilled persons through a long and arduous process of humanization. This process involves a search for the meaning of our lives. It also involves exercising our freedom to love, to see ourselves in our fellow human beings, to identify ourselves with them, to make their welfare our own. In this process we are not alone. God is intimately involved the whole way. He collaborates with us to move the process forward.

I then asked myself whether television's entertainment programs could contribute to this process. Specifically could its comedies and dramas facilitate its viewers' search for meaning, freedom, and love.

The more I reflected, the more I became convinced that they not only can do this, some of them actually do do this.

Good television comedy and drama are like any other art form. They compress reality and distill human life so as to reveal its meaning. They help their viewers grapple with the mystery they find inside themselves—the mystery that is human life—and extract some of its meaning.

No single program or series of programs can capture this mystery in its entirety. But each can chip away at the mystery and encapsulate some little piece of the truth about what it means to be a human being. These programs can throw sparks of light into the dark corners of our minds, helping us come up with our own answers to those questions with which we all struggle late at night. And when they do, they not only help us discover the meaning of our lives. They deepen and strengthen our freedom.

The more we know about reality and particularly about that special portion of reality that is ourselves, the freer we become and the more humanly enriching our decisions can be. And the most enriching of all human decisions is the decision to reach out with respect and compassion to our fellow human beings.

Television can help here by giving us an experience of our common humanity—at the deepest level, we are brothers and sisters of one another—so that we are motivated to share ourselves with those who are vastly different from ourselves in race, economic status, religious belief, and political persuasion. Which is just another way of saying that TV, at its best, can teach us how to love.

As I worked on my theology of communication at GTU, I continued to produce a new "Insight" series each year. By 1972 I had a television series that played on Sunday afternoons on a syndicated basis in most of the cities of the United States. Yet I dreamed of having a prime-time network series that would communicate the same Gospel insights and promote the same human values that "Insight" did, only to a much larger audience. Still my father's son, I wanted to do it bigger and better.

In mid-1972 there was an extended writers' strike that stopped production and in some cases forced the networks to run the same situation comedies three times in a twelve-month period. Not yet a member of the Writers Guild of America and so not yet thinking like a union man, this looked to me like a unique opportunity. I went to see one of CBS's senior programming executives and said to him, "I can give you first-run comedies that have bigger stars and will generate more laughs than any you now have. (No one has ever accused me of humility.) Why not run them this summer rather than your reruns?"

He looked at me and sighed. "It's a good idea. Someday perhaps we will be ready for it. But right now there's no way we'll put a religious show produced by a religious organization on in prime time. I'm sorry."

Walking out of his office, I knew my dream of having a prime-time series dealing with human values was not going to happen. We had to find some other way to communicate values to that huge prime-time audience. But how?

These were the early years of the classic character comedies—"The Mary Tyler Moore Show," "M*A*S*H," "All in the Family." They were highly popular. I watched them regularly. They were deliciously funny. But they were also insightful. They frequently explored moral dilemmas and said important things about what it means to be a human being. I would have been proud to have many of their scenes on "Insight."

If we could not have our own prime-time audience enrichment show, why not try to help the creators of these types of shows do their own audience enrichment shows better?

Indeed, why not? Because we would not then get the satisfaction of making the contribution ourselves? What does that have to do with anything? Maximizing the contribution is the important thing, not getting the satisfaction. Because they would then get the credit and we would not? That's a temptation faced by every do-gooder in a high-profile field. It must be firmly resisted. As Sam Rayburn once said, "There's no limit to the amount of good you can do if only you will let other people take the credit."

In those days, in Hollywood, there were a number of prizes to encourage the industry to pay attention to certain subjects. I remember in particular the Population Institute, which had been launched by the Methodist Church and which gave a monetary prize for shows that heightened public awareness of population problems. It seemed an approach worth considering.

In the spring of 1973, I developed another problem, a very practical one. For nine years Paulist Productions had been the rent-free guest of Bob and Lola Hanlon in their big castle on the beach in the Pacific Palisades. They lived on the third floor of the building, and we used the first two floors for our offices. Research, administration, production, and distribution all headquartered there. Now the Hanlons had decided to move to Palm Desert. They offered to sell us the building for eighty-five thousand dollars, a fraction of its market cost. I did not want to move, partially because I had no place else to go, partially because I loved the beach and swam every day. It was a good buy. There was just one problem. I did not have the eighty-five thousand dollars.

At this time I learned from Joe Hough, the dean at Claremont, that the Lilly Endowment, a multimillion-dollar Protestant foundation in Indianapolis, Indiana, was moderating its conservative policies and was opening up to Catholic requests. At his suggestion I called Fred Hofheinz, a former priest who had just joined their staff. I told Fred my problem and asked if Lilly might be interested. He said the Endowment had a strict policy against real estate grants. But he also said, "We really like what you do. We would look very kindly upon any project that would foster prime-time network programming that promotes human and Christian values. Come up with that kind of thing, and I can promise you a favorable hearing."

"Now," I said to myself after hanging up, "money isn't the problem. Creativity is. All we need is the right idea."

I decided to go for a swim. Two hundred yards offshore, the intuition hit. Why not create a prize for the writers of the entertainment community—a prize for writing network shows that communicate values and enrich their viewers? Not one prize but three prizes—one for half-hour shows, one for hour shows, one for ninety-minute and longer shows.

Why single out the writer? Because I had learned from "Insight" that everything depends on the script. The value orientation of a show, its depth and honesty, what it says about people, about the human situation, the meaning it sees in human life—all begin in the writer's mind, heart, and unconscious. In the beginning is the Word.

At that time less than a thousand men and women did more than 90 percent of the writing for prime-time American TV. Few politicians, preachers, or educators had their kind of moral influence. If we could just have an impact on these writers, help them do a more humanistic job, then we would be making a significant contribution. Instead of expending our powder criticizing American TV, we would be using it to elevate the moral tone of the creations of the most significant component of the most significant industry in the United States.

"Better to light one candle," says the old Chinese proverb, "than to curse the darkness."

I did not finish my swim. I was too excited. I called John Furia. He liked the idea. I called Jim Moser. He did, too. In the weeks that followed, we refined the idea. We decided to call it the Mahatma Gandhi Prize.

Once we had thought through all the implications, I called Fred Hofheinz and discussed the matter with him. His response was enthusiastic. "What do I do next?" I asked. "Discuss it with my boss," he said, "who will soon be coming to California."

So it was that Charles Williams, the head of the religious affairs department at Lilly, came to my office in January of 1974. His father had just died, and he was hurting. He was able to talk about it, and I told him I would pray for his dad. This seemed to mean a great deal to him. Jim Moser and I then presented the idea of the writers' prize. His response was immediate, positive, and profound. "In all my years with the Endowment," he was later to say, "only one other idea has aroused in me such a deep resonance." (It was for agricultural development in the famine-stricken Sahel.)

"It is the right idea at the right time," he also said. "But we need to move fast. I will return to Indianapolis tonight. Can you have a proposal on my desk in three days?"

I assured him I could.

In April of 1984, the Lilly Board approved an initial three-year grant of $180,000 for the writers' prize.

That's how the Humanitas Prize was born. But at this point it was still called the Mahatma Gandhi Prize.

Shortly after the grant was approved, I visited Indianapolis to meet the officers of the Endowment. Landrun Bolling, the president, was especially gracious.

"I love the idea of the prize," he said to me. "I have just one problem."

"What's that?" I asked.

"The name," he said. "I don't think most people know who Mahatma Gandhi was." (The movie had not as yet come out.)

I explained to him why we had chosen it. "Gandhi was a man of the spirit. He preached values. Yet he did so in an applied and practical manner. He was also a writer." I did not tell him that Gandhi had been a boyhood hero of mine.

I also listed the other names we had considered: "the Freedom Prize, the Humanitas Prize, the Liberty Prize, the Love Prize, the Light and Love Prize."

He said, "Why did you reject the Humanitas Prize idea?"

"Too Catholic," I replied.

"I wouldn't worry about that," he said. "Besides, it sounds Renaissance to me."

That's how the Humanitas Prize got its name.

At a press luncheon on June 25, 1974, we explained the purpose of the prize and spelled out the specifics:

"To the writer of the two-hour or longer program, which most fully projects human values and brings the insights of the Judaic-Christian vision of man to bear on our contemporary situation, this time next year we will be giving a prize of $25,000.

"To the writer of the best one-hour show, we will be giving a prize of $15,000.

"To the writer of the best one-half-hour show, we will be giving a prize of $10,000."

The reaction from the writing community was enthusiastic. "This is one of the most important things that has occurred in television in years," said Ray Bradbury. "It encourages me tremendously to know that there is a group that's willing to reward humanitarian values," remarked novelist James Houston. "You can't treat the audience like soil, in which you keep taking everything out and putting nothing back," commented writer-director John Korty. "The audience is malnourished. There's a great hunger for this kind of thing." Said screenwriter Leon Tokatyan, "From the beginning I never really wanted to do a story for the sake of doing a story. There has to be some celebration of man's higher capabilities—which is what this award is all about."

We were also deluged with questions. "What kind of values are you guys looking for? What makes a program humanizing? Dehumanizing? How can you tell the difference?" "I got a conscience. I know because it raises hell when I do something I shouldn't. And I got values. But they don't affect what I write. You saying they should?"

To answer these questions we put together a brochure, which we mailed to all the members of the Writers Guild. And to provide a forum for the exploration of value questions, we decided to institute a series of Humanitas seminars for members of the Writers Guild. Jim Brown conducted these seminars for the first two years, and I have done so since. We usually draw about twenty-five for these Saturday afternoon sessions.

Writers are deep and caring people, whose experiences are very rich. But in most cases, they have no categories to help them reflect on their experiences and no philosophic overview into which to fit them. The seminars helped meet this need. They also brought into existence a writers' community, a support system for those who care about values.

It was also necessary to work out the procedures by which the winning entries would be selected. We decided on a three-stage approach. Two members of the Humanitas staff would read every entry and select the ten to fifteen most humanizing programs in each category. The Humanitas Board of Directors—which included John Furia, Jim Moser, Arthur Hiller, Carol McKeand, Dan Tarradash, Liam O'Brien, and myself—would read these and select the three best in each category. These were then viewed by the Board of Directors and the Board of Trustees, a new group we formed to help with the judging. This latter group was composed of people with national reputations who had shown a serious commitment to human values. The first trustees were Eugene Carson Blake, Ray Bradbury, Charles Champlin, Helen Hayes, Vernon Jordon, Lawrence Laurent, John Macy, Donald McGannon, Budd Schulberg, Cicely Tyson, and Charles Williams.

For the first two years, with a great deal of help from Terry Sweeney, Jim Brown supervised the judging process. He also designed the Humanitas logo and the Lucite trophy. Since then Judy Greening, with much help from Judith Eagen, has done so. Judy is the executive director of the Human Family Educational and Cultural Institute, the new nonprofit corporation we established to administrate and award the prize.

I approached Stuart Schulberg, a good friend and the producer of the "Today" show, about interviewing the winning writers. He did not think his superiors would go for the idea, but he agreed to ask them. They did. As a result the Humanitas winners have been interviewed each year on the "Today" show. This has added to the prestige of the prize and increases the viewing public's awareness of what they have a right to expect from TV. We hope it also motivates them to support shows that enrich their viewers.

With all the nominees and the press in attendance, we announced the first Humanitas winners at the NBC studios in Burbank in June of 1975. The writer received the cash and the Lucite Humanitas trophy. The winning show's producer, director, story editor, network, studio, and production company also received the trophy.

In subsequent years we announced the winners at an awards luncheon that was held first at the Tail of the Cock restaurant in Beverly Hills, then at the Universal Sheraton, now at the Century Plaza.

These luncheons have become something unique in the entertainment industry, a time when an ordinarily cynical business becomes emotional, proud of what its best have accomplished. "It's encouraging for me, after fifteen years of struggle, to finally be rewarded for my stubbornness, for insisting that I write about things that matter," said Robert Eisele, a "Cagney & Lacey" writer. "It's rare in show business to feel such satisfaction from a piece of work and to experience the heartfelt appreciation of others," remarked John Markus of "The Cosby Show." "I look at Humanitas as a wonderful comfort," stated movie-of-the-week writer Clifford Campion. "Each year, when news of the participants is announced, I don't feel so lonely. It reminds me that out there, other men and women are working in their own gardens, sowing and reaping the very best they can through our medium." "It's nice to win a prize for being a person," declared comedy writer Earl Pomerantz.

The speeches are the most literate, and sometimes the most vulnerable, of the year. (Ray Bradbury's, Faye Kanin's, and Arthur Hiller's cling to memory.) And the energy field generated is so strong and so upbeat that everyone goes away glad to be alive and proud to be human. In a very real sense, these luncheons have become humanistic liturgies, celebrations of the transcendent beauty present in the most mundane of human creations.

Walking across the lobby of the Century Plaza on the way to one of these luncheons, I was stopped by a young man in his early twenties who asked, "Are you a real priest?"

"Yes," I replied. "Why do you ask?"

"I thought you might be an actor or something. Tell me about being a priest. How do you live? What do you do?"

Thinking I might have a vocation prospect on my hands, I said, "Well, the way of life comes down to poverty—we try to live simply, not be attached to things; chastity—we don't focus our love on one person but try to be open to whoever needs us most; and obedience—whenever we face a decision, we ask God to let us know what He wants us to do. As far as work is concerned, we try to make people feel loved by God. That's essentially what we do."

"That's very interesting," the young man said. "I'd like to think about that."

"Please do," I said to him, giving him my card. "If you ever want to talk, give me a ring."

We said good-bye, and I headed into the luncheon. About dessert time I felt a tap on the shoulder. It was the young man, who was our waiter.

"I've been thinking about what you said," he said.

"Good," I said, thinking the Holy Spirit had been working overtime. "Did you come to any conclusions?"

"Well," he said, sweeping his hand over the silver service and wine goblets of the very elegant luncheon, "if this is the poverty, I'd like to take a look at the chastity."

In some minds, the Humanitas Prize raised questions about our motivation. As I walked out after one luncheon, a balding, middle-aged reporter with a limp came alongside and asked, "Why are you doing this?"

"To help the entertainment industry do its job, which is to enrich the viewing public. To encourage the communication of human values through TV."

"I know that. I mean why are you doing this?"

"You mean me, Bud Kieser?"

"You and the other people running this thing."

"Well," I said, reaching inside myself for the most honest answer I could find. "I guess because we're trying to care about people."

"But why do you care about people?" he asked with a note of impatience in his voice.

"Because they're worth caring about. Because if we don't, maybe nobody else will. Because God's in them, and we can get to Him by serving them."

"Leave God out of it."

"How can I leave God out of it? He's the main reason I'm doing this."

"But I don't believe in God."

"That's your problem. Not mine," I said with more irritation than I intended.

"I don't get it. Either you people are crazy or you've got a selfish agenda hidden someplace."

He was shaking his head as he walked away.

I guess from a secular perspective—especially one afflicted by cynical ego-lock—what we were doing did seem absurd. Not only seem. From that perspective, it was absurd. But from a God-centered perspective, it made all the sense in the world.

I was beginning to see that an absurdly unselfish commitment to the service of other people is perhaps the only way to gain credibility with the dogmatically closed secular mind.

But the secular people were not the only ones who had difficulty understanding the Humanitas idea. In the late seventies, I was asked to give a workshop on the Humanitas Prize at the annual meeting of the World Association of Christian Communicators in Fort Lauderdale, Florida. Participating in equal numbers were main line Protestants, fundamentalists, and Catholics.

As I concluded my remarks, a middle-aged gentleman with a midwestern accent jumped up and said, "You believe in Jesus?" There was an edge to his voice as the audience squirmed in embarrassment.

"Of course," I said, trying to keep it light.

"You believe in the Bible?" he asked, trying not to sound pugnacious.

"Of course," I said, realizing what I was dealing with.

"You trying to evangelize?"

"Yes. I try to share the Good News that God is lovingly present in the Risen Jesus in everyone human, propelling them toward the full flowering of their humanity." That notion of evangelization seemed to sail right over his head.

"I've seen your shows. I don't hear you say much about Jesus. I listen to you talk about this prize of yours. You never mention Jesus."

"Look," I said. "There's three ways to evangelize. You can talk about Jesus. You can say what Jesus said. Or you can do what Jesus did. I'm trying to do what Jesus did."

"You don't sound like a preacher to me. You don't use biblical language."

"OK," I said, shifting gears. "With the Humanitas Prize, I like to think we're helping the blind see, the imprisoned go free, the poor have the good news preached to them."

"It's good to hear you quote the Bible," he said, softening just a bit. "But you still haven't told me why you don't talk about Jesus."

"For the same reason Jesus didn't always talk about his Father. Remember, He said, 'It's not he who says Master, Master who will enter the Kingdom of God. But he who does the will of my Father.' "

"And how do you understand the will of the Father?"

"The human growth, the human fulfillment of His children. He wants us to love each other."

"There you go again, confusing me. You talk about human values, not Christian ones. You talk about humanization, not evangelization. You talk about human fulfillment, not salvation. Somebody might get the idea you're a humanist."

"That's not a dirty word," I said. The audience chuckled. "Of course I'm a humanist. Proud of it. I'm a humanist precisely because I am a Christian. The Lord had to think rather highly of human nature to take one Himself. And because He did, the whole human situation is now alive with His presence. And because it is, I cannot separate human values from Christian ones, humanization from evangelization. For me they're all one. God wills our growth to fulfilled personhood. When we help that process along, we're evangelizing, whether we use the word or not."

"Now you're really confusing me," he said. But he was smiling. And so was the audience.

In 1975, 159 scripts were submitted for the Humanitas Prize; in 1976, 183 scripts; in 1977, 168 scripts; in 1978, 217 scripts; in 1979, 231 scripts; in 1980, 259 scripts. Since then it has remained in the 250 area for prime time. When we instituted two new prizes in 1985, for children's programming, an additional 100 scripts were submitted annually in this category. In 1979 the Humanitas Board decided to give a special nonmonetary Humanitas Prize for the documentary *The Fire Next Door.* This award is now given yearly at the Board's discretion.

As one year followed another, we noticed that many of the shows we considered the most humanistic were also the most popular, and we were led to conclude that entertainment and human enrichment are not only not incompatible, they complement and fulfill each other. An entertainment program that does not also enrich lacks substance. It is superficial and unsatisfying. And a show that attempts to be humanizing but is also dull is not really enriching anybody.

Look at the derivation of two words most often associated with entertainment: delight and enjoyment. Television delights when it throws light into the darkness that surrounds us, helping us to see who we are and what we're supposed to be doing with these lives of ours. It gives enjoyment when it occasions joy in its viewers, when it feeds and stretches their minds, frees their imagination to take a romp, stirs their hearts with challenge, and warms them with compassion.

The initial three-year grant from Lilly was for $180,000, which they supplemented with an additional $45,000 once we knew what the operating expenses would be. In 1977 they approved another three-year grant for $225,000. But in 1979, despite their great pride in the prize and what it had accomplished—the best thing we've done in years, one of their vice presidents told me—Bob Lynn, who replaced Charles Williams as the head of their religion division, sadly informed me they were unable to continue to fund us on a permanent basis and suggested we start exploring other sources of support. In 1980, to help us make the transition, they approved an additional $75,000 grant.

In 1977 Paulist Productions started producing the Family Specials—half-hour and hour dramas on the moral dilemmas of today's teenagers—for Capital Cities Broadcasting. As a result, I got to know their top executives—Tom Murphy, the chairman; Dan Burke, the president; and Joe Doughtery, the executive vice president—three shrewd businessmen who were also Irish Catholics with a strong sense of their obligations to the viewing public.

I heard from our liaison with them—Charlie Keller—that they

had a foundation, but I could not find out how big it was or what its giving pattern was. I discussed the matter with Joe Dougherty, who thought it worth a meeting with Dan Burke. At that meeting I presented the Humanitas concept and asked whether the Capital Cities Foundation might be interested in picking up where Lilly was leaving off. I also told him the prize was now too important in the entertainment community to be dependent on one man's ability to raise money. What was needed, I said, was a million-dollar endowment to make the prize a permanent part of American television. Bigger and better. Dan's response was positive. It presented a unique opportunity, he said, for independent broadcast groups like Capital Cities, Metromedia, Group W, RKO, Times Mirror, and Tribune, who were not always proud of what they were asked to broadcast, to influence the moral tone of their programming in a positive way. "What would you say if we tried to put together a coalition of these groups to fund the prize?" he asked.

"Great," I replied.

So it was that Tom Murphy, the chairman of Capital Cities Broadcasting, John Kluge, the chairman of Metromedia, and Dan Ritchie, the chairman of Group W, hosted a luncheon in New York City on June 17, 1980, for the chief executive officers of the twenty-five top broadcast groups in the country. I presented the Humanitas concept; David Seltzer, a two-time Humanitas winner, spoke of what the prize meant to the industry's writers; and the executives responded as we had hoped. After a persistent follow-up campaign by Joe Dougherty, we had the million dollars we needed.

Because we had been able to invest the money at higher-than-anticipated interest rates, in 1985 we were able to add two new Humanitas prizes of $10,000 apiece in the children's area: one for the most humanizing live-action program, a second for the best animated program. We singled out children's programming for special attention, since the need seemed so great and the audience so important.

In January 1989, the Humanitas Board celebrated the fifteenth birthday of the Humanitas Prize by making some important decisions:

1. To expand Humanitas's educational program to include:
   a) A ten-week course on values and entertainment writing;

b) A series of all-day workshops to be conducted by master writers on the same subject.

2. To facilitate the formation of writers' support groups and mentoring relationships for young writers.
3. To expand the size of the present prizes, so that they might keep pace with inflation.
4. To create two new Humanitas Prizes: one for PBS/cable, one for feature films.
5. To launch a fund-raising drive to add $4 million to the endowment, so as to finance this expansion.

Within twenty-four months, two thirds of this amount had been pledged by the production companies, studios, networks, and individuals who make up the entertainment community. Many of the entertainment community's most creative people—Marcy Carsey, Norman Lear, Grant Tinker, Gary David Goldberg, Alan Landsburg, Bob Daly, Lew Wasserman, Steve Bochco, David Jacobs, Barry Diller—committed sizable sums to this effort.

It seems clear that the industry is determined to help the industry fulfill its humanizing responsibilities to the viewing public. This is because as the years have passed and one television season has followed another, the Humanitas Prize has come to occupy a larger and larger place in the consciousness of the writing community in Hollywood. "What the Nobel Prize is to literature and the Pulitzer Prize is to journalism," Barbara Walters said on the "Today" show, "the Humanitas Prize has become for American television." To writers it says someone cares about human values. They care enough to put their bodies and their pocketbooks on the line to foster them. To them it also says communicating human values is what television writing is all about. Enriching the audience while entertaining it is the writers' job, the central purpose of their vocation. This is what gives meaning to their profession, and this is how they can judge their success or failure. "Humanitas has defined my identity," said David Seltzer. "It has told me what I am all about."

By defining the standard of excellence and the criteria of quality for the writers of the entertainment industry, the Humanitas Prize has made its most significant contribution. It has given the writing community an ideal to strive for and a goal to pursue.

Humanitas has also given me a great deal on a personal level.

By assuring that I read or view the best of American TV, the judging process has made me a serious student of the medium. It has made me aware of how good some American television is. It has also put me in the center of a coalition of humanistically concerned media people, and it has thrust me into a leadership position in the movement for human values on TV. This is what I had always said the Church should be doing—leading the humanistic coalition, being the mother of the arts again—so there was no way I could back off. This, in its turn, has brought me into a working relationship with some of the most creative minds and powerful executives in the industry. Not something I deserve, but something I enjoy nonetheless.

With "Insight," I was always asking people in the industry to join with me to give something special to the viewing public. They always responded generously. But sometimes I could sense the unspoken complaint, "Oh no. Not again."

With Humanitas, there was no such ambivalence. We were telling the industry's writers something they wanted to hear, and we were giving them something they were only too eager to receive. It is more blessed to give than to receive. It's also easier on the ego.

Humanitas is the best thing we have done in the entertainment industry. It has also given me the greatest satisfaction.

CHAPTER 12

INDIA

The beginning of 1978 was a bad time for me. For reasons that we will explore in the next chapter, it was becoming increasingly difficult to secure good time slots for "Insight." It was one thing to pour your creative energies into a show that was meeting a felt need and that many, many people would watch. But it was quite another thing to do so for a show the country's program directors could only find marginal time slots for.

In addition, in 1977, we had made a special "Insight." Called *This Side of Eden,* it was a comedy that looked in on Adam and Eve after Cain had killed Abel. Eve was so upset she did not want to sleep with Adam. God arrived to help them work through their problem. Delightfully funny, it was written by Lan O'Kun, directed by Jay Sandrich, and starred Carol Burnett, Walter Matthau, and Ed Asner. It turned out so beautifully that after we had edited it and put in the music, I took it to NBC to see if they wanted to run it as a prime-time commercial special. Their response was affirmative. I was delighted. Here at last was the precedent-setting network breakthrough I had dreamed of. I felt obliged to go back to all those involved in making it to secure their permission, since they had originally agreed to do a noncommercial syndicated show. I expected no problem. I was wrong. Most of those so involved were as enthusiastic as I was about the breakthrough. But not all. I tried to see those who withheld permission. One would not see me. I wrote to that person, giving my reasons for wanting to accept the NBC offer. Just after the first of the year 1978, I received a letter from that person's lawyer telling me the answer was *no,* the matter was closed, and I should desist from any further effort to contact his client. I was disappointed. So close. Yet so far away.

In addition I had worked hard to make Paulist Productions a loving community, in which everyone pulled together to enrich the viewing public. No community of human beings is ever perfect, and I do not think I expected the people at Paulist Productions to be so. But in 1978 we overdid the imperfect side a little bit. One individual with a strong financial orientation challenged my leadership of the company, calling me a not-so-benevolent dictator. I should have confronted him, telling him to buy in and accept my authority or get out, but I procrastinated, perhaps because I was afraid he might be right. As a result the wound festered. I nursed my resentments, and he continued his bad-mouthing as divisiveness in the company grew. Another individual whom I cared about entered into an affair with a married executive who did business with us. On one level it was none of my business. But it ate at me. And another individual, in our open group discussions, consistently made the company in general and my stewardship in particular the cause of her unhappiness. I knew why she was unhappy. I knew neither the company nor I had anything to do with it. But still it gnawed at me.

And in February my Dad died. Our relationship had grown over the years. He never did return to the Church, but somehow that did not seem terribly important anymore. I loved him. He loved me. He was proud of me. What more could a son ask?

In the last several years of his life, he suffered from Alzheimer's disease and needed to be put into a nursing home. It was a human warehouse, a storage facility for people waiting to die. I tried to visit him as often as I could, but I hated to see him there, hated to see this once proud man reduced to such helplessness. I prayed that the Lord would take him. But when the Lord finally did, I was rocked. I thought I was ready—he had certainly given me all he could—but I was not. It was like an amputation. A part of me had been severed. Part of my despondency was loss, part was a sense of my own mortality. Now I was leading the human procession. Now I was aware that I was moving inexorably toward my own grave.

I did not know whether I could give the sermon at his funeral without breaking emotionally. But I decided I had to try. What better way of saying good-bye, of saying I love you. I am glad I did.

Early in 1978 I came to another painful realization. I was going deaf. It was a slow process. For the longest time I had refused to admit it to myself. But after a while, there was no denying it. I went to Dr. Bill House. He ordered the tests. In the higher ranges (women's voices) I had lost close to 50 percent of my hearing. In the lower ranges (men's voices) the loss was not nearly so severe. I could hear. But I missed a great deal. Dr. House put me on sodium fluoride, which helped check any further deterioration.

I was not totally unprepared for the problem. My sister Shirley had previously lost 95 percent of her hearing. As teenagers we had both contracted pneumonia and been given sulfamyacin. It cured the pneumonia but did damage to our inner ears. This, combined with a hereditary weakness, was the cause of our problem.

I had watched in awe as Shirley struggled to adjust to her problem. Now I had to do the same with a lesser one. Blindness is tough because it isolates you from your physical surroundings. In a very real sense deafness is tougher, because it impedes communication and cuts you off from other people. Few things are worse than that.

All during 1978 I tried to cope. Late in the year, I got a single hearing aid. But I did not like it and seldom used it. I was used to doing what I wanted, when I wanted, in the way I wanted. Now I could not. I found the whole situation extremely frustrating.

My struggle with deafness, Dad's death, conflict and hurt at Paulist Productions, the failure to score the breakthrough at NBC with *This Side of Eden,* and the relegation of "Insight" to poor time slots—all took their toll. But I do not think these external frustrations would have gotten to me as they did if inside I had been in a good place. I was not. In retrospect I think I had allowed myself to desire too many things I did not really need, had become too preoccupied with professional success, was expecting too much of other people—as if my emotional needs were their responsibility rather than my own—and had become so concerned with my own fulfillment that I made it impossible. Frustration on the outside and narcissism on the inside are a dangerous combination. Mix in doubts about what one is doing and a desire for things not worth the desiring and you have a psychologically poisonous stew. I was in real trouble. My ebullience went first. Then my optimism. Next my sense of humor. My energy level dropped way down. I became despondent, tense, and strained. Most of the time, I was exhausted, depressed, emotionally drained. Prayer still nourished me on the inside. But I seemed unable to respond to pressures on the outside.

I was burning out.

A number of people saw me stagger and moved in to help. Once, on a business trip to New York, Paulists Kevin Lynch and Tom Comber took me out for dinner at a lovely Italian restaurant in lower Manhattan and told me what a great contribution I had made. Back in L.A. Mike Rhodes, after one particularly difficult meeting, put a hand on my shoulder and said, "I think it's time for you to go back to exploring the world."

I did have a dream about taking a trip—a long one—but dismissed it, saying, "Who would I go with?"

But then Joe Drown, a close friend, Insight Board member, and contributor, also sensed my situation and wrote me a letter saying he thought I might need something to look forward to and suggested I take a trip. In the letter was a check for three thousand dollars. I banked the check, not giving a trip serious consideration.

After wrapping up the shooting of "Insight" in June of 1978, I went to St. Andrew's, the Benedictine monastery in the high desert near Valermo, California, for a couple of days of prayer and quiet. While there I happened to have dinner with one of the monks, Father Eleutherius, who had been raised in Belgium, expelled from China, worked in India and Zaire, and now taught philosophy at Claremont. We got into an extended conversation about the Third World and his work in India. When I told him I had always wanted to go there, he said my Ph.D. and media experience would make me very attractive to the Indian Church. He suggested I write to Cardinal Picachy of Calcutta. For the first time, I started to give it serious thought.

I talked it over with John Carr, my wise old mentor from seminary days who was now the pastor of St. Paul's. He thought it a great idea and strongly encouraged me to go. I looked over my schedule and discovered a hole between the end of November and the end of January. I could go then without disrupting anything. I started to think about it. I prayed about it. And the more I did, the more I wanted to go.

Part was a desire to get away, far away from Paulist Productions and everything it represented. But part, also, was the long love affair I had had with the Third World in general and with India in particular.

In 1974 I had attended a nine-day workshop on catechetics, media, and economic development and had become friendly with Indian, African, and Filipino church leaders. In 1975 I had gone on a consulting job for the Jesuits in Colombia and Venezuela and had been seared by the poverty of the barrios in Bogotá, Medellín, and Caracas. I had long been haunted by the appalling statistics about malnourished children in the Third World, but now those statistics had human faces.

India had always held a special fascination for me. Part was Gunga Din and Rudyard Kipling, Gandhi and Francis Xavier. Part was Jack Bresnan, my best friend from La Salle, who over the years had told me so many stories about his work in India for the Ford Foundation. But part was also an intuition that India was not only exotic but uniquely spiritual, that at this time in my life it had something very special to give me.

I knew India would be a challenge. "You'll find it very depressing," everybody told me. But that was part of its attraction. How much non-being (destitution, misery, death) could I face and assimilate without being destroyed? I needed to find out. I was testing—and stretching—my limits.

Late in June I wrote to Cardinal Picachy, offering my services. Six weeks later I had a letter back from Packy McFarland, an American Jesuit, who was on the staff of the Indian Bishops' Conference, enthusiastically accepting my offer and offering to act as my host. He included a possible itinerary of workshops and lectures that would take us to eleven cities and as many towns and villages in all parts of India.

And so it was that late in November of 1978, I flew into Bombay. Packy was supposed to meet me. But the cable giving my flight number and time of arrival had not been delivered. No problem. It was dawn. I took the bus into the city, getting my first look on the way at the tired earth of India. It was as if the soil was drained, used up. At the terminal I was besieged by taxi drivers. They screamed at me, tugged at my clothes, and tried to grab my suitcase. They wanted my business in the worst sort of way. But none of them knew where Xavier College was.

I finally found one who did, but after getting settled at the faculty house, I was too excited and too filled with curiosity to sleep. Since Packy had yet to surface, I decided to do some exploring. I have usually found my first impressions of a new city/country/culture to be the most lasting ones, and this walk through downtown Bombay was no exception.

What most powerfully imprinted itself on my memory were the people of India, the teeming crowds of them, the sheer diversity of them. Black-skinned Caucasians, wheat-skinned Aryans, a European here and there, some who seemed a happy blending of all three. Village people just arrived in the big city, rolling up their mats and brushing the sleep from their eyes after a night on the sidewalk, starting to cook rice over a fire in a tin can or going off to a vacant lot to answer a call of nature, their only possessions the undyed clothes on their backs, the pot on the fire, and the rice they husbanded so carefully. City people, a little more affluent, perhaps more sophisticated, going about their business. The Moslem women, so covered in black that only the skin on their hands was visible; and their Hindu sisters, in a kaleidoscope of colored saris—that most becoming of feminine raiments—bright reds, deep greens, sunflower yellows, with what looked like chalk on their foreheads and gold ornaments in their noses, checking the ripeness of the produce stacked on carts that lined the streets or testing the texture of the cloth and trying its color against their complexions. The men, most in dhotis—a single sheetlike garment wrapped around their loins and sometimes drawn up over one shoulder—a lesser number in Nehru jackets, polyester or Western business suits. Some energetic, in a hurry, striding to get somewhere; others, more relaxed, sauntering along in no hurry to get anywhere. Nearly naked children darting through the crowd, chasing each other with yelps of joy. Tall erect Sikhs, with turbans and trimmed beards, from the Punjab. Shorter Tamils from the south of India. Scores of solitary people, sitting on their haunches, like so many birds in a tree, quietly contemplating the passing parade and peacefully communing with themselves. A circle of bearded old men locked in serious discussion, perhaps of the mystery of life and how to apply their wisdom to the problems of the world. Teenagers, giggling off in a corner. Worshipers crowding into temples and beginning to chant their mantras. Mothers waiting at the temple gate with their emaciated children in the hope of touching the heart of the devout or the conscience of some pink-skinned foreigner. A construction crew of bare-chested men and almost bare-chested women carrying bricks or wet cement on their backs up wooden foundations. Sweating, panting drivers trying to navigate their rickshaws through the maze of people. Cripples with contorted spines and spindly legs dragging themselves along on all fours. A leper with an ulcerous face and eaten-away hands. Merchants and customers haggling over prices at a fever pitch. A cacophony of sound assaulting the ears—the laughing, shouting, keening, whispering, screaming, arguing, gossiping of the human family, mixed in with the honking horns, blaring radios, and blasting stereos of their mechanical contrivances. India had yet to protect itself from noise pollution.

Over everything hung the aroma of dung fires. But also the smell of cooking food, incense, and urine.

In the midst of all the people, with pride of place, a plethora of cows, the sacred animals of the Hindus, their tawny hides stretched across protruding hips. Dogs, too, and water buffaloes to pull the carts.

On the surface, chaos—no one would ever accuse the Indians of being efficient—but a chaos that somehow seemed to function.

What struck me at once, what I found utterly compelling, was the sheer mass of compressed humanity: the energy field of the crowds, the press of bodies, the density of people, the power of them, the beauty of them, the vitality of them. Already I sensed the presence of a tremendous reality in them; a reality that was in them yet that came from beyond them, a reality that, gravity-like, drew me toward them—and itself.

India possesses the world's most cinematic culture, and I tried to open my senses and allow myself to soak it up as I made my way through the crowds and tried to commune with those beautiful people.

With my blond hair and pink face topping off a six-and-a-half-foot frame, I could hardly be inconspicuous. The beggars came after me, and so did the students who wanted to practice their English. At the temple they insisted on putting chalk on my forehead in return for the customary donation. I almost got run over by a cart pulled by a water buffalo, and its driver waved an apology to me. Our eyes met, and I felt a surge of spiritual energy pass between us.

Approaching overload after several hours, I returned to Xavier to find Packy McFarland waiting. A sixty-year-old, red-faced, beer-bellied Irishman from New Jersey, Packy had been sent to India by his Jesuit superiors at the conclusion of World War II to study theology. He fell in love with the country and its people and had spent the last thirty years working among them. Speaking Hindi and some Ho, he was a pastor in a village at the time of independence and saved scores of lives in the Hindu-Moslem bloodbath that followed. He had established the communications institute at Xavier College in Bombay and for years had headed up the media operations of the Indian bishops. Just recently he had turned that job over to a native Indian.

A rugged individualist of the old school, Packy was sandpaper on the outside—rough and abrasive—and jelly on the inside—sweet, warm, generous, and loving. I could tell we were going to get along.

After two lectures at the University of Bombay, we moved on to Pune, the site of Gandhi's imprisonment during World War II and a bustling university center. We lived at the Jesuit college, where I conducted a workshop for the students of the six or seven theological schools in the area. That first Sunday in India, to some of the most mystically exotic music I have ever heard, played on instruments I had previously neither seen nor heard, I celebrated Mass and preached for the Jesuit community—all from the lotus position.

Sunday afternoon, a red-bearded Jesuit seminarian from Rhodesia and I bicycled to a hostel for destitute and dying old men run by Mother Teresa's Missionaries of Charity. The sisters are dedicated to the service of the poorest of the poor and the inhabitants of this hostel certainly fell into that category. Most of them had nothing and nobody. Yet, as I made the rounds and he gave the sickest of the men a bath, I sensed a peace and serenity in the place that I soon discovered originated with the sisters. Most of them were middle-class girls who had taken vows of poverty, chastity, and obedience. Their lives were simple and unencumbered, rooted in the essentially human. Each sister had a rosary, a spare blue-and-white sari, socks, underwear, and one pair of tennis shoes. That was it. No other possessions. Their basic diet was a smelly kind of rice most Americans would consider inedible. They prayed. They lived in community, supporting each other. And they worked with the most wounded and rejected members of their society. That was their life.

They were not concerned about their own fulfillment. They were too busy worrying about the people with whom they worked, who needed them so badly. Yet I have seldom met such joyous and fulfilled human beings in my life.

On the way home, we stopped off to visit the large ashram run by Rajneesh, a guru who had a large following in the United States. There were few Indians in the ashram, but many Western Europeans and Americans, most of whom seemed restless and bored. I had a feeling of sexual satiation about the place, as if they were in sensory overload. Too much stimulation. Too much looking for fulfillment in the wrong place.

The contrast between the hostel and the ashram could not have been more striking.

The next day I visited another kind of ashram. Hindu in form, Christian in substance, it had been founded and was now run by a superbly educated British nun—Sister Janet—with the explicit purpose of exploring the common ground in life-style and meditation techniques between Hinduism and Christianity. Sister Janet was bright and articulate, with a deep mystical streak. She could also be very practical—she showed me how to eat rice with my fingers—and on occasion she could be tart-tongued. When asked if Mother Teresa was a saint, she replied, "My heavens, no."

In Goa, the former Portuguese colony that was first evangelized by St. Thomas the Apostle and is now 50 percent Christian, I was adopted by a retired Jesuit named Claude who took me to Xavier's tomb and to the ruins of St. Thomas's University, which was built by the Jesuits in the seventeenth century. At that time it seemed as though India would embrace Christianity. Its leadership was open and eager, and the people were flocking to be baptized. The moment of grace seemed at hand. But jealousy of the Jesuits and petty politics at the Vatican squandered the opportunity, and it was lost—perhaps forever. A tragedy of monumental proportions.

Claude and I attended a rally by an American evangelist who castigated his Indian listeners for what he called their all-consuming greed. His reading of Indian culture was a far cry from my own. When people are as poor as these Indians, I thought to myself, a little greed might do them good.

In Bangalore, at an ashram run by an Indian Redemptorist named Frankie, I gave a three-day workshop for local church personnel and attended a Mother of Consolation Novena that Frankie ran weekly. The latter, with its sentimental hymns, its unctuous preaching, and its articulation of things prayed for and received, reminded me of the Miraculous Medal Novenas of my boyhood, with two big differences: Almost half of those attending were under twenty-five, and 90 percent of the congregation was Hindu. The Mother of Jesus as a symbol of the feminine side of God, of God's warm responsiveness, unconditional love, and merciful compassion—Mary, in short, as a sacrament of God's tenderness—was very attractive to these young Hindus. As at the marriage feast of Cana, Mary was introducing people to her Son.

In Madras, where St. Thomas was beheaded, I did another workshop, visited with some of the thousands of squatters on the local beach, and ran into Mother Teresa's nuns again, most of them in their twenties, sometimes on bicycles, always working with the dregs of society, almost always with smiles on their faces.

By the time we reached Calcutta, it was the week before Christmas and no talks or workshops had been scheduled. Davida Coady, a medical doctor friend of mine who taught Third World medicine at UCLA, and who usually spent six months a year working without pay in one of the world's more hellish spots—Biafra, Ethiopia, El Salvador—was in Calcutta on holiday from a stint working with Concern in Bangladesh. (Concern is an Irish version of the Peace Corps.) We spent a delightful three days together touring the city and immersing ourselves in its life. She knew it well, having worked with Mother Teresa and for the UN during its successful campaign to eliminate smallpox.

At five one morning, Davida and I went to the mother-house of the Missionaries of Charity. I had met Mother Teresa in Los Angeles and Philadelphia, but this was the first time I had celebrated Mass and preached for her. The chapel was packed with two or three hundred sisters, most of them in their early twenties; so spiritually alive, so involved in the Mass. No vocation shortage in India. Certainly no shortage of applicants to the Missionaries of Charity. Why? Because joy is contagious. Everybody wants it. And because heroism attracts. Deep within everyone is that desire to go all the way, to give everything. I hope I gave something to the sisters, but the reality is they were giving my wilted spirit a lot more; just what I had not as yet figured out.

Walking out I noticed a sign under the crucifix. It said, "The miracle is not what we do. The miracle is the joy we feel when we do it."

We visited with Mother Teresa after Mass. Despite her international fame, I found her tranquil in her earthiness, comfortable with that peasant humanity of hers—a woman without illusions but with more than a little humor in her eyes. I was especially struck by her twisted, gnarled hands. I was also aware that while we were with her we seemed her only concern.

That afternoon we visited the home for the destitute and dying, the first of Mother Teresa's many establishments. While Davida looked in on the sickest of its inhabitants, I made the rounds, trying to be present to each person, helping each feel loved. One elderly Hindu gentleman, a former sergeant in the British army, told me his story. "I am all alone," he concluded. "I have nobody." Then he hesitated, looked upward, squeezed my hand, and said, "But I'm not really alone, am I?"

As Davida and I prepared to leave, the sister in charge came up to me and said, "Father, Jesus sent you."

"I hope so," I replied, a little taken aback.

"No, I mean it," she continued. "I was talking to Mother Teresa just this morning, and I told her I had no one to offer Mass for my people on Christmas morning, and she said, 'Do not fret. Jesus will send you someone.' And then you came."

It was three days before Christmas. I would have loved to have stayed to offer that Mass, especially since almost all the people in the home were Hindus and Moslems. But I was Packy's responsibility, and he had planned to return to the village three hundred miles north of Calcutta where he had been pastor thirty years before to celebrate Midnight Mass on Christmas Eve for his old parishioners. If I stayed behind, he would have felt he had to stay behind, and that would have broken his heart. The situation was made worse by my sense that the sister had had a bad day and desperately wanted me to offer that Mass. I was boxed. I tried to explain my predicament, but it only seemed to increase her dejection. I left feeling I had let her down.

The next morning Davida returned to Dacca and Packy and I took the 6 A.M. train for Jamshedpur, from which we went by Land-Rover to Chaibasa, where we were to spend Christmas. It was no longer a village but, with several thousand inhabitants, was more a town. All of the people in the vicinity were members of the Ho tribe, indigenous people whose way of life had not changed in two thousand years. Most of the Ho people could neither read nor write, and many hunted in the surrounding forests with bows and arrows. Like aborigines the world over, most of the Ho people are animists in religion. They worshiped God as

He is found in nature. Many identified God with nature and nature with God. Animism can be pantheistic. The Ho people are deeply spiritual and naturally contemplative. "We can't teach them a thing about prayer," the Jesuit novice master told me. "They are way ahead of us."

The Jesuits run a parish and a high school in Chaibasa. As a result the younger people were learning to read and write, and many families, at great personal cost, had become Christian. Like recent converts in other parts of the world, they had a keen sense of the holy and a great enthusiasm for their newfound faith.

Christmas Eve was memorable. The people had come in from the hills, some walking forty miles to get there. They were bedded down in the classrooms of the school, and in the early evening, when I went out to look around, they were cooking rice over great fires in the school yard. There was an air of quiet expectancy about the whole place. As midnight approached the people, attired in their finest, filled the church and began singing carols. The melodies I knew. The words I did not. The vibrations were joyously transcendent. Packy was principal celebrant at the Mass, and he had written out his sermon in Ho. I was the concelebrant and said the words of consecration in that language. Almost everyone went to communion, and afterward Packy and I held a statue of the baby Jesus out to the people as they came forward one by one to pay Him reverence. After Mass there was much merriment as the people exchanged greetings and danced to the rhythmic beat of drums. At six the next morning, the young people were still dancing.

Christmas morning Packy and I took a jeep about ten miles along a dirt path to a village with a dozen huts, where we again celebrated the Lord's birth with a Mass. The people were so grateful, they gave us a small bag of rice.

Christmas afternoon I was missing my friends in Los Angeles. So I wrote letters to John Carr, Patt Shea, and Joe Drown. That evening I joined the Jesuits for a dinner of chicken and rice.

The next day we took a bus to Ranchi, the capital of Bihar province and the home of a large Ho population. We stayed in the Jesuit residence at their college there. The previous four weeks had been one intense experience after another, so I was grateful we now had a few days of leisure time—to rest, to read a book on Hinduism, to reflect upon what I had seen, heard, and felt, and to begin to assimilate it.

To do this in dialogue with highly educated men who shared my values and faith commitment was a rare privilege. The Jesuit community in Ranchi was half-Indian, half-Belgian. All spoke English. Steeped in Indian culture, they knew their people well. As I shared my experiences with them, they helped me sharpen my perceptions and test their accuracy. They also helped me integrate them into my overall faith vision.

The Church in India is a droplet in a Hindu and Moslem sea. Only a minuscule percentage of the people are Christian. Yet the Indian Church is alive and respected. Through its educational institutions, it is making a very important contribution to the life of the Indian people. Its lay people, much more educated than the general population, are proud to be Catholic. They are involved in church activities and enjoy a collaborative relationship with the clergy. Vocations to the sisterhood and priesthood are numerous and of high quality. The Jesuits have as many men studying for the priesthood in India as they do in all the rest of the world combined.

Why the health of the Indian Church?

I think there are four reasons:

1. The Indian Church is rapidly shedding its European (and therefore colonial) image. Thanks to St. Thomas, the Malabar Christians, and the present predominance of native clergy, the Church is accurately seen to be indigenous to India.
2. The Indian Church is involved in the world. Ninety percent of the students in its educational institutions are non-Christian. Its contribution to the political life of India—even to its constitution—has been significant.
3. Like most everything else in India, the Church is poor. It is spared the distraction of material preoccupations.
4. Most important of all, its energies are focused on the essentials: bringing the Good News to those who have yet to hear it, and witnessing to God's love for all His people by educating the ignorant and feeding the hungry.

After New Delhi and Agra, we went on to Benares, the holy city of India, where swamis, gurus, and assorted holy men make up a significant percentage of the population. Everywhere you turned there were religious gatherings and processions. Sometimes the holy men painted their faces and lacerated their bodies. On occasion the devotion of the people approached frenzy.

I was fascinated by the cremation spots on the banks of the Ganges. The body would usually arrive with a procession of relatives. It was placed on a pile of wood, wax was poured on it, and then it was prayed over. Only then was the wood ignited and the body burned. A grisly sight, especially when the remaining bones were pushed into the river afterward.

Outside Benares I also visited the site of the Buddhist pentecost, the place where the closest disciples of Buddha had their illumination and began to spread his message. A Buddhist monastery marks the spot now, a place of prayer and peace that I enjoyed after the frantic religious activity of the city.

From that spot Buddhism spread to become the predominant religion in China, Japan, Tibet, Nepal, Korea, Thailand, Burma, Indochina, and Sri Lanka. But it never really took hold in the land of its birth.

Saying a grateful good-bye to Packy in Benares, I flew to Calcutta and on to Dacca in Bangladesh, where I was met by Davida Coady and Father Jack Finucane, the Holy Spirit priest who was the director of Concern in Dacca. Between planes in Calcutta, I discovered I still had about five dollars in Indian money, so I went outside and pressed it into the hands of a rickshaw driver. The look of surprise and happiness on his face remains with me still. I like to think that's what money is for—to make other people happy.

Bangladesh is one of the five poorest countries in the world—periodically flooded, with next to no resources, overpopulated—the unnatural product of the bitter hostility between Hindu and Moslem that has ravaged the subcontinent.

Concern had about twenty young people working in the refugee camps of flood victims. They took me to one of these, on an island outside of Dacca in the Ganges delta. The living conditions were appalling. Yet the people were striking, full of dignity and concern for each other. They had little, but what they had they shared. The smiles of some of the children would light up a coal bin at midnight. The Concern workers lived together in two houses and were great fun. Jack Finucane could not have been more hospitable. We became friends and would see each other again—in the United States and in Ethiopia. Concern also had a marvelous cook. Great for morale, Jack said. He was right, at least in my case.

I was now heading home, stopping in Bangkok and Hong Kong on the way. The Thai city had the beauty and serenity of a Buddhist culture, where many of the men spend a year or two in a monastery before starting their families and launching their careers. Hong Kong had the affluence, the bustling pace, and the good manners of Chinese doing good business around the Pacific. In Hong Kong I felt decompression, as if I had been swimming underwater for a long time and had now broken to the surface to breathe freely again. India had not been depressing. Far from it. But to switch metaphors, it was as though I had been carrying a heavy weight on my shoulders and someone had just lifted it off. I returned to Los Angeles in mid-January light in spirit.

The trip had been rigorous and demanding. I returned twenty pounds lighter, with a head full of impressions and a heart full of feelings. There was much to think about, reflect upon, assimilate. I did not as yet realize that I had gotten in India what I went for. More than that, I had gotten what I needed.

What was that? If I had been asked that question in 1979, I do not think I could have given an accurate answer. As I write this a decade later, I am still not sure I can give the whole answer. But I am willing to hazard an attempt.

Part has to do with those two great religious geniuses of India —Buddha and Mother Teresa. The Buddha's assertion that the pathway to spiritual fulfillment involves the renunciation not only of possessions, pleasure, and the ego itself but also the very desire for these things; and Mother Teresa's assertion that God lives in a special way in the poorest of the poor—these spiritual teachings strike American ears as strange, radical, revolutionary. Our whole way of life is predicated on the expansion and deepening of desire—whence our prosperity and inner emptiness—and we lionize the rich and the powerful and ignore the hungry and homeless on our own doorsteps.

But when viewed from an Indian perspective, through the eyes of 650 million impoverished people, these teachings do not seem strange at all. In fact, given the size of their population and the paucity of their resources, these insights seem more like an extension of common sense than anything revolutionary. This is not to minimize the genius of their articulators. These insights spring from profound spiritual intuitions. But they are completely of a piece with the fabric of Indian life and are the authentic response of these two sensitive and enlightened souls to it. Yet, if they arose quite naturally from Indian life, they remain universally true and relevant to American life.

Which is to say they had much to say to me.

From Buddha I learned to limit my desires. I did not cut back on my desire for God. (Although I had to be careful not to desire something I had created and labeled "God.") He is absolute, so I tried to desire Him absolutely. But I did cut back on my desire for everything but God. All else is relative and can be authentically desired only in a relative fashion. I began to see that not to desire something can be better than to have it. I also began to understand St. John of the Cross's cryptic statement, "If you would have everything, desire to have nothing."

This relativization of desire extended to the shows I would try to make about God. I wanted to produce good shows. I desired large audiences for them. I desired these things passionately and threw all my energies into their accomplishment. But still I needed to remember my identity was not dependent on them. Nor the meaning of my life. Nor my salvation.

Which is just another way of saying I needed to keep a sense of humor about them.

This cutting back on what I desired extended to my own fulfillment. Fulfillment is not a bad thing to desire, especially since God desires it, too. But the fact of the matter is you don't achieve it by desiring it. You don't find yourself by seeking yourself. You find yourself—and joy—by forgetting all about yourself in seeking the welfare of other people.

This limiting of desire also extended to what I expected from other people. I tried to be more realistic, to assume responsibility for my own needs, to treat as a gift whatever other people decided to give me. I had no right to make any demands.

So I became very discerning about what I desired. I had to be careful not to expect a created thing to fill the emptiness within me, for that is idolatry. Succumbing to it, I enter a world of illusion and become alienated. But once the idol shows me its clay feet, I am forced to let go of these desires. Once I do the illusions evaporate, and I am able to return to the real world. I find this process of disillusionment to be chastening, freeing, and integrating. It enables me to go deep into the center of myself and enter into a new and more vital relationship with the God who lives there.

This cutting back on desire—focusing on what is essential for a human being, pulling back from that which is not essential—was facilitated by what I learned from Mother Teresa. She helped me understand the tremendous reality I experienced in these impoverished yet beautiful people on that first walk through the streets of Bombay, an experience that was to be repeated with only slightly diminished intensity in every city we visited. God was there, the Realest of the Real, in them. There was no escaping that mysterious, transcendent presence.

In fact the compressed humanity of these lovely people, the density of God's presence in them, the God they caused to surface in me when I reached out in love to them—these were so real that everything else seemed unreal. So many of the concerns I invested such energy in seemed so insignificant by comparison. When a child is hungry or sick, nothing else is important but to get that child what it needs. Nothing. Not network time slots or laudatory reviews or the affirmation of my peers. Not my personal fulfillment or professional success or clerical celibacy or the ordination of women or the language of the liturgy. Nothing.

In the light of that experience, some of the dogmas of American life—that producing and consuming is what human life is all about, that happiness comes from things, that the good life means taking care of No. 1—were exposed as the lies they are. The poor shatter our illusions and help us see the truth—the truth that people are what's important, God in people, nothing else. Nothing. And this truth makes us free—free to give ourselves to the poor, free to dedicate our energies to their service, free to join them in their struggle for justice and dignity. And the fruits of that freedom—the unselfish gift, the wholehearted dedication, the self-sacrificing enlistment in the common struggle—break the stultifying grip of narcissism, propel us beyond our egos, and enable us to transcend ourselves.

The joy I so often found on the faces of Mother Teresa's nuns had such ego transcendence at its base.

All of this brought me back to the fact of tragedy. Pain, frustration, and defeat are part of human life; they cannot be escaped, yet authentically responded to, they can enrich it. It also brought me back to where I started: to the call of heroism, to the challenge of self-forgetfulness, to the realization that to live fully, I must be ready to die; to find myself, I have to be willing to give myself without counting the cost.

Did this mean leaving Los Angeles to set up shop in India? I did consider this option, and I did discuss it with one of the Jesuits in Ranchi, but I decided against it for the obvious reasons: India had no shortage of priests; I had no unique talent to contribute; I was steeped in American culture and spoke only English; to try to inculturate myself into India's culture and to learn its languages, at forty-nine (especially given my hearing problem), was just not practical.

Somewhere Gandhi said, "When facing a decision, ask yourself, 'What will be best for the poor?' "

The more I thought and prayed about it, the more I realized the best thing I could do for the world's poor was to return to Hollywood and be a voice for the voiceless Third World in the entertainment community. "Reverse mission," Maryknoll calls it.

Upon returning I decided to spend at least one month each year working in or for the Third World. This was for their sake. But it was also for my own. "The rich need the poor so badly," Mother Teresa says. "Where else can they find God?"

When my mother died, I inherited some money. When my father died, I inherited some more. Now I felt burdened by this money, as if it were weighing me down, complicating my life, distracting me from what is truly important. So I gave it away—to Mother Teresa, to the Hindu doctor with the clinic for destitute mothers outside of Calcutta, to Jack Finucane's Concern operation, and to a nun I had met trying to build a school in a Bogotá slum. Given the security a religious community affords its members, this involved no great sacrifice on my part. But it did give me a great sense of freedom and a measure of joy. And it did keep me in touch with that poor and hungry, insecure and needy man inside myself.

These six weeks in India involved a conversion experience for me; a radical change in my way of thinking and feeling.

I went to India an alienated and burned-out human being. I came back healed and energized, in love with those impoverished people and in love with the God to whom they were transparent. Those beautiful people gave me so much more than I could possibly give them.

I need to periodically touch base with people like them, to refresh myself with their richness. Sometimes I can do this in the course of my work in the Third World. Sometimes I do this by working at the Catholic Workers' soup kitchen on Los Angeles's skid row. A morning there giving out food to the homeless or washing their dishes is a great antidote for the illusions of Hollywood. For me it is a prescription for mental and spiritual health.

If I was involved in the education of seminarians—or raising teenagers, for that matter—I think I would try to incorporate field work with the poor into their training program. After several months with the poor, I don't think they would ever again be tempted to feel sorry for themselves.

India produced other changes in me, too. In the ten years since I have been there, I have come to cherish more fully my most significant relationships, those friends with whom I share my life and who share their lives with me. But I find myself less inclined to invest myself in those relationships that are superficial or in some way inauthentic. I am not very good at small talk these days.

I have also developed a great hunger for solitude, a need that takes me to a monastery for a mini-retreat five or six times a year. I still vacation on those islands in Lake George. If other Paulists are there, I am delighted. If there are not, and I am alone, I am equally happy. Sometimes I cannot tell the difference between vacation and retreat. I like to be alone. I like the freedom to go deep within myself. I like the space to listen to myself. I like the joy of silently communing with God.

This book arises from that space. So have the other things I have written since returning from India. From 1964 to 1978, I did little writing. Since 1979 I have done a great deal—dramatic scripts, magazine articles, and newspaper stories, now this book. I enjoy writing.

In late January, shortly after returning from India, I ran into Patt Shea in a corridor at CBS's TV City. To her "How are you," I answered, "Fine. I think things are starting to come together for me." The brightness of her smile and the warmth of her hug said, "Thank God. At last."

Those lovely brown-skinned people who had so little had given me so much.

CHAPTER 13

"INSIGHT," THE LATER YEARS

Every year, when we finished one "Insight" series and began work on another, I would wonder whether it was possible to come up with fresh ideas for the new shows. Yet somehow, each year, we seemed able to do just that. Between 1966 and 1983, we made a new "Insight" series each year, 179 episodes in all; some better than others, but most with a little piece of the truth about what it means to be a human being. It seems that an infinite idea —the Word of God—can have an infinite number of incarnations in story, and we were only beginning to scratch the surface.

Sometimes, in search of "Insight" ideas, I sought the help of groups I was working with in a different context. The groups varied—UCLA students, theologians, businessmen, nuns, social workers, military personnel, counselors, parishioners, psychologists, young priests—but the questions I put to them were the same: Where are people hurting? Where are the live nerves, the unfulfilled needs? What are the big problems, the unresolved issues? Who is making the precedent-setting, cutting-edge decisions? What does the Gospel have to say to people in this society? What do they need from the Church?

I was trying to work the no-man's-land between the past and the future, the frontier between the world and the Church, and needed all the assistance I could get.

And sometimes I needed to do more than listen. So, on occasion, I worked as an orderly on the fire department ambulance in Watts, picketed with Cesar Chavez and his United Farm Workers in the vineyards near Bakersfield and, much later, with the Franciscans at the nuclear test site in Nevada. I joined the Board of Directors of Center (an organization trying to use media to evangelize and promote economic development in the Third World) and the Board of Advisors for Beyond War, and flew to Japan to talk with the airmen at our bases there. And sometimes I went away for a weekend to a monastery and found deep within myself just the "Insight" idea I was looking for.

I developed a nose for theological dialectic, moral dilemmas, and value conflicts—the stuff of good drama. I kept jotting ideas down, so by the time I was ready to meet with writers to develop new scripts, I had a sizable list. Sometimes the idea was simply something that needed to be said, but more often it was a problem that needed to be addressed, an issue that needed to be explored, or an intriguing character in an intriguing situation.

As one "Insight" series followed another, we found that our shows fell into three general categories: God shows, which focused on the divine-human relationship; love shows, which focused on individuals relating to each other or to themselves; and justice shows, which focused on the problems of society.

Reverencing human life was the theme of these justice shows, and they ran the gamut of issues in this area: racial justice, Third World poverty, violence, substance abuse, the arms race, abortion, prison reform, capital punishment, ecology, the poor, the homeless, the retarded, and the aged.

I soon learned a good script comes from some deep place within the writer, a place that is deeper, less accessible, and more emotionally charged than the writer's conscious mind. My task as executive producer was to create an atmosphere in which the writer and I could find the theme, character, problem, or situation that would touch that place in the writer's unconscious, exciting his/her imagination and starting his/her creative juices flowing. I usually went to these story conferences with my list of ideas, and sometimes one of these would throw off the spark that would ignite the creative imagination of the writer. But sometimes the initiative was completely the writer's.

Some stories were deeply autobiographical: an affair; a nervous breakdown; therapy; difficulties with wife, husband, or kids; a suicide attempt in the family. I did not always inquire about the source. But usually it was not hard to figure out. Jim McGinn told the story of his reconciliation with his father. The old man saw it on the air and was so delighted Jim thinks it added a year to his life.

"We always went for reality," one writer said of our story

conferences. "I got thrown in jail. I did an 'Insight' on that. I spent time in a detoxification center. I did an 'Insight' on that. Then I had problems with my wife, so I did an 'Insight' on that. But I got a little worried when Kieser said, 'Jack, how about doing one on suicide?' "

With many writers these story conferences took on the character of the confessional. On both sides defenses were dropped and roles left behind as we shared ourselves with each other in an honest, deep, and vulnerable way. Such rapport is both satisfying and creative. Some of our most exciting and insightful shows arose from those kinds of conversations. So did some of my deepest friendships.

My job was to provide the stimulation so that the writer's imagination could take over. Like the playing of a child, which it closely resembles, the creative process cannot be programmed. Freedom and spontaneity are its essence. But it can be channeled, the imagination stretched, intuition nurtured. I tried to do that. I also learned to trust the process.

Some writers came back year after year. I like to think this was because they enjoyed the freedom we gave them, liked the way we treated them, and were proud of the shows we made of their scripts. Other writers did one or two shows and then moved on.

We were constantly on the lookout for new writers. Sometimes writers would call and volunteer their services or slip a possible script over the transom. At other times I would read a Humanitas script or see something on the air that I was particularly impressed with and seek out the writer.

What was I looking for? First, I wanted stories that explored themes that commercial television, for one reason or another, would not touch. If they would not—and it was important—we did. If they did, we would not. With the limited resources available to us, we tried to do only what we alone could do and did best.

Second, I wanted stories with characters my viewers could relate to and identify with, characters they could get inside of and feel compassion for. I prefer sympathetic heavies and flawed heroes.

Third, I wanted stories with honest conflicts. All good drama is dialectical. The interaction of contraries is the engine that drives a story. The more evenly matched the adversaries are, and the more uncertain the outcome, the more compelling is the drama.

Fourth, I looked for stories with forward movement. Something happens to the protagonist that propels him/her forward, compelling him/her to decide, giving him/her the opportunity to grow. I like stories that presuppose freedom, lift up the viewer, and make him/her proud to be a human being. If there are surprises along the way, so much the better.

Fifth, I wanted stories that would touch the archetypes and activate the unconscious of the viewer, giving him/her a depth experience. The deeper and more intense that experience, the more I liked it.

Sixth, I wanted shows that said something unique about the human situation; not in the sense of a verbal message or sermon, but in the sense of a different experience of or unique insight into what it means to be a human being. I was particularly interested in what we called "high Gospel density" shows—those that gave their viewers an intense experience of God's presence in the human situation, thrusting them forward to the fulfillment of their humanity.

We found the comedic approach especially suited for the God shows, since the interfacing of the divine and the human is so charged with incongruity, so full of surprises, and so prone to vulnerability that it quite naturally lends itself to comedy. God can be funny.

And the part of God can be very attractive to actors. Over the years, Bob Newhart, Ed Asner, Martin Sheen, Flip Wilson, Beau Bridges, Steve Landesberg, Lou Gossett, Keenan Wynn, Melinda Dillon, Julie Sommars, and Dick Van Patten played God for us. "Typecasting," one said to me. "I've been doing it all my life."

Gospel density was one criterion we used in deciding which shows to shoot. The other was "apostolic cost effectiveness": How much creative energy, moral capital (ability to motivate generosity), and money, we asked ourselves, do we need to expend to reach how many people how powerfully with the Gospel?

Money was always a problem with Insight. Even with so many people working so generously, we never had enough. This was because we had no sponsors, did not charge the stations that aired the series, and had a policy against soliciting donations on the air.

In the early seventies, we established a Board of Directors to help us with this problem. In the beginning the Insight Board was primarily an organization of wealthy, religiously motivated individuals who believed in "Insight" and were willing to contribute to its support. Membership on the Board increased their involvement and more often than not also increased the size of their contributions. However, as the years went on, more and more of Los Angeles's bright and aggressive young businessmen joined the Board. Unlike the fat cats, these Young Turks wanted to do more than contribute. They wanted to know all there was to know about Paulist Productions and, once they did, they wanted to help formulate its policies and participate in its management. Peter Mullin, Dick Ferry, Tom McCarthy, Dan Cathcart, Lou Castruccio, and John O'Keefe fell into this category. They came to care deeply about the company and made it their own.

Needless to say, I was delighted.

At one meeting, I gave a fiery speech, saying I was finding it very difficult to make the shows *and* raise the money. I suggested they assume complete responsibility for the financial side of our operation. They agreed. The discussion progressed. I could see a consensus developing in favor of a fund-raising benefit. I expressed my distaste. They ignored it. I said I did not feel comfortable charging people a hundred and twenty-five dollars for dinner when so many other people were going hungry. They ignored it. Finally, in exasperation, I said, "But I hate benefits." The chairman looked at me and asked, "Who is in charge of finances?"

"You people," I replied.

"Fine," the chairman said. "Let's have a benefit."

So we did. It was called "An Evening for Insight." Pam Mullin ran it. Six hundred people came. I gave a talk on what we were trying to accomplish. Bob Newhart entertained, telling the story of his first "Insight" rehearsal. "Father Kieser asked me to do it, so I thought it was going to be a very Catholic operation. Then I discovered the writer was Jewish. The director was Jewish. The other actors were Jewish. They aren't the chosen people for nothing. But I couldn't figure out how I fit in. Then I realized the part called for a nebbish, and there was no Jewish one available."

We made sixty thousand dollars on that first evening for "Insight." My opposition began to soften. Each year thereafter we had an "Insight" benefit. Bob Hope, Florence Henderson, Dionne Warwick, and Bobby Vinton were among those who entertained. Bob Hope defined a Paulist as a Jesuit who had signed with William Morris. Some years we made more than one hundred thousand dollars. I liked the money. I also liked this way of involving the business community.

By the mid-seventies, we had worked out a three-pronged strategy for the humanizing work of Paulist Productions:

1. With "Insight" (and whatever else we might produce), we tried to give the viewing public an experience of God's love operative in the human situation.
2. We sought to be a presence in the entertainment and broadcast industries for human and Christian values, helping them incorporate these values into their own programs.
3. We also tried to challenge these industries to be more responsive to the spiritual needs of their viewers, and we lobbied the FCC and the appropriate committees of Congress to make broadcast regulations more sensitive to these needs.

To understand how we became politically involved, you have to take a look at the policies and practices of American television stations from the late sixties onward.

Traditionally American television stations had been required to make sustaining time—e.g., free time, no commercials—available to the nonprofit organizations in their broadcast area as part of their obligation, in the words of the Communications Act, to program in the public's "interest, convenience and necessity." It was part of the price they paid for using the public's airwaves. But sometime in the late sixties, these regulations were changed, and no distinction was made between airtime that was donated to a local nonprofit organization and that which was sold to one of the televangelists.

This opened up a great opportunity for the TV preachers. All during the seventies they proliferated. By February of 1978, "Day of Discovery" had 193 stations; Rex Humbard, 191; Jerry Falwell, 189; Oral Roberts, 165; Jimmy Swaggart, 146; PTL, 137; and Robert Schuller, 109; compared to February of 1971 when "Day of Discovery" had 69 stations; Rex Humbard, 137; and Oral Roberts, 140. The others were not yet on the air.

All these evangelists purchased their airtime and asked for donations from their viewers to support their ministries.

These changes, which helped the televangelists, had a negative impact on programs that were supplied by local nonprofit groups and depended on sustaining time. To take just two examples, the Lutheran Church's "This Is the Life," syndicated and sustaining, dropped from 159 stations in 1971 to 70 in 1978. The same was true of "Insight." In 1970, 171 commercial stations carried "Insight," all on a sustaining basis. By 1978, despite aggressive promoting, that number had fallen to 101.

In the past the stations in many cities had made airtime available to the local diocese or council of churches which, in its turn, had asked us to supply "Insight" to fill it. By 1978 most of these time slots had evaporated. "Why should I give the time to you," one station manager said to me, "when I can sell it to the televangelists?" The fact that "Insight" was requested by the nonprofit groups in his local area, that it had a natural constituency there, a constituency that was a significant proportion of the total population, that it was ecumenical in outreach, aiming to enrich all the viewers and not just some of them, that it made no appeal for funds, was beside the point.

"I've got an obligation to my stockholders," one program director said to me. "They want a return on their investment. My job is to make it as big as possible. 'Insight' doesn't help me do that. That's why I can't give you a time slot."

I heard this again and again. But there were exceptions. In 1976 the general manager of KABC in Los Angeles agreed to run six "Insights" at seven-thirty at night. Lilly gave us money to promote these shows, and we did very well in the ratings. Using this as a precedent, we began to release our first-run "Insights" as Thanksgiving, Christmas, New Year's, Easter, Mother's Day, and Father's Day specials. For a number of years, the ABC-owned and -operated stations, Group W, and Metromedia ran "Insight" holiday specials in prime time. But these broadcast groups, with their fifteen stations, were not typical.

I analyzed the situation. I talked to other syndicators of sustaining shows. They were having the same problem. I talked to broadcaster friends in all parts of the country. "It's a new ball game," they said, "only the commercial pressures are more intense." I assured myself the problem was not "Insight" 's quality, nor the way our people were promoting it. The problem was the FCC, its rules, and what looked to us like an abdication of its responsibility to protect the common good.

Before these changes, the number of time slots filled by paid religious programs in the United States and those filled by sustaining programs were about equal. By 1978, after these changes had taken effect, 92 percent of the religious programming in the United States was paid; only 8 percent was sustaining.

The result was a severe imbalance in religious programming. The fundamentalists had no problem about buying airtime and raising money on the air. The main line Protestants and the Catholics did have a problem. They did not feel they should have to buy the airtime, and they did not like the idea of soliciting funds on the air. Besides, they had traditionally committed what money they had to education, worship, and the service of the needy and did not feel they should have to change these priorities in order to buy airtime. As a result programs that reflected a fundamentalist and pentecostal orientation come to dominate religious programming. The main line Protestants and the Catholics were denied access to their own airwaves.

At a broadcasters' meeting in 1977, I had met Dr. Everett Parker, the feisty and prophetic head of the communications office of the United Church of Christ. For years Ev had been a voice crying in the wilderness, denouncing the greed of broadcasters and the lack of affirmative action in the hiring practices of the nation's TV stations, filing against the licenses of those that acted irresponsibly. He was steeped in the Communications Act of 1934 and fearless in confronting those who violated either its letter or its spirit.

We liked each other. We also knew that each had something the other needed. He had the knowledge of broadcast law, the Protestant contacts, and the political savvy I lacked. I had the capacity to plug him into the Catholic community and help bring its clout to bear in Washington.

We decided to collaborate. He mentored me in communications law and politics. Together we decided to form a coalition of humanistically oriented, nonprofit organizations to petition the FCC to rescind its previous decision and reinstate its traditional policy of requiring stations to make sustaining time available to the nonprofit groups in their service area.

Specifically we called for the creation of a new program category called "Community Service," which we defined as "Any program (excluding sports) presented on a sustaining basis and supplied by or produced in conjunction with a nonprofit organization having significant membership in the service area." This category would include but not be limited to "entertainment programs not available on a commercial basis, such as opera, ballet, and serious drama." We also called for an expansion of the public affairs category to include "dramatizations when produced by or in conjunction with a nonprofit group and presented free of charge."

The original petitioners were the United States Catholic Conference, the National Council of Churches, the United Church of Christ, and UNDA, the Catholic broadcasters association. After the initial filing, we were joined by a host of other groups, including NAACP, NOW, the Urban League, the Population Institute, and Planned Parenthood.

A notice of inquiry for our petition, now called RM 2709, was approved by the FCC on October 5, 1978. Opinions were solicited from all quarters. As it made its way through the FCC system, I lobbied on its behalf with the commissioners, with the chairmen of the House and Senate subcommittees, and at the NAB. I testified before the House subcommittee. I also arranged, at Ev's suggestion, for church leaders to write to the Commission's chairman. I was surprised how influential a letter from a cardinal was.

It was futile. Our petition came before the Commission for a vote in September 25, 1980, and was decisively defeated. We asked them to reconsider. They refused on January 13, 1982. If we had submitted our proposal three years before, I was told, we would have won. But now the tide running in favor of deregulation was just too strong.

There seemed just one other tactic that might work, an unpalatable one: contesting the license renewal of stations that refused to make sustaining time available.

Shortly before our petition was voted down, I was informed that one of the network-owned and -operated stations in Los Angeles that had regularly made good time available to nonprofit groups was planning to do so no longer. In its license renewal application, it was significantly scaling back its commitments in the public service area. I went to see its general manager, whom I knew. He confirmed what I had heard. "Speaking for the Archdiocese of Los Angeles," I said, "I must tell you I would consider it irresponsible on my part to stand back and do nothing in this situation."

He looked at me long and hard. He knew I now had the legal expertise and advisors to file against him. He was trying to gauge whether I would do it. "You can't win," he said, knowing how the FCC had been handling these kinds of cases.

"I can't lose," I said, knowing the newspapers would make a big thing of it. I would be David. He would be Goliath. It would be embarrassing for him and for his station.

"I'm sorry you are taking this position," he said.

"What would you do in my position?" I asked.

"About what you're doing," he replied after a long pause. He called five days later to tell me their public service commitments would not be scaled back.

Could this be done in other cities, so that the broadcast community would get the message that the main line Protestant and Catholic communities would not stand by as they were stripped of the airtime they had traditionally been given? Everett Parker thought it was worth a try. I gave an impassioned speech at UNDA—the Catholic broadcasters' organization—challenging the communication directors of the various dioceses to take a strong stand, and I promised to assist them, to see they had the financial and legal help they needed if it became necessary to file.

I had no takers.

That was November 1981. We had lost at the FCC, and now it was clear the church militant was not about to be militant about this.

The handwriting was on the wall. "Insight" 's days were numbered.

We still had decent time slots in most of the major markets—nine out of the top ten. This was due to the tradition of responsible broadcasting that characterized the ABC-owned and -operated stations, Group W, and Metromedia. It was also due to my friendship with their presidents, Dick O'Leary, Bill Baker, and Al Krivin.

So we shot abbreviated series in 1981, 1982, and 1983. But securing good time slots for these shows was becoming difficult, almost impossible. Judith Eagen said she was banging her head against a brick wall. No longer could she get prime-time slots for the holiday specials. And then Dick O'Leary resigned and Al Krivin retired and their successors had none of the same enthusiasm for the kind of programming that "Insight" represented.

I discussed the situation with the Board. They were passionately committed to "Insight." They did not want to see it die. But they could see no way to reverse the trend.

Finally I made the decision alone. I had listened to advice from all quarters. Now I had to listen to myself. And to God. It boiled down to a question of stewardship, responsible stewardship. I had been given a life by God; a limited amount of time, talent, and energy. I had the capacity to motivate other people to commit their time, talent, and energy. How did God want me to invest these precious resources? What was the best way to maximize our contribution and build up God's Kingdom, fulfilling all those involved and enriching the viewing public?

I had poured twenty-three years of my life into "Insight." I was proud of it. It was the right idea at the right time, and it had made a significant contribution. But now there was an abundance of evidence indicating that time was over. "Insight" was no longer the best way to invest these resources. And so I decided to continue to distribute the series but to produce no new episodes. It was time to move on; not out of show business, but to different types of shows. Longer shows, hour and two-hour shows, network ones, commercial ones. It was time to go mainstream.

Terry Sweeney had long encouraged me to move in this direction. Now he told me he would be glad to help with any long forms I might come up with but that he was going to leave Paulist Productions to set up a Jesuit counterpart—Jesuit Media Associates. I understood his decision, but I was saddened by it. He had been a crucial member of our team and a great help with the creation and production of "Insight." He had also been a significant part of my personal support system—a confidant and almost a son—and I had hoped that one day he would take over Paulist Productions.

But it was time for him to move on, too. How far he would move—out of the Jesuits and into marriage—I did not then know.

We have remained close friends.

Some people thought I would be bereft without "Insight," depressed over its demise. I was not, perhaps because I had been feeling its death throes for so long. I did feel I had lost something—both a platform and a burden. I felt chastened by its termination. I needed to mourn. But I also felt freed: free to try new things, to experiment, to face new challenges.

Were the death throes also birth pangs?

I was excited by the possibility.

CHAPTER 14

FAMINE WATCH

"We've got a hell of a famine in the northwestern part of Kenya," Lynn Marshall, the communications director of Catholic Relief Services, barked into the phone from New York. "And a million and a half refugees from the civil war in Ethiopia have flocked into Somalia. They are hungry and they are homeless and we can't get any media attention. Can you help us?"

It was mid-September 1980.

"Like how?" I asked.

"Like last year in Cambodia. Rosalynn Carter and Joan Baez went over and created a media event, which focused world attention on the plight of the refugees. You know the rest. The world responded and hundreds of thousands of lives were saved. We need to do something like that. Would any of your actor friends be willing to go? Would you?"

"To do what?"

"Immerse yourselves in the situation. Talk with the officials of the government, church, and relief agencies on the spot. Return to the United States to do the news and talk shows, so as to educate the American people about the problem and mobilize support for its solution."

What do you say to that kind of invitation? On one level it had nothing to do with my work on "Insight" or the Humanitas Prize. But on another level, it had everything to do with them. I had not forgotten the poor people of India nor the commitment I had made to work on their behalf. I did not feel like cramming my six-foot-six frame into a seat made for a midget to fly halfway around the world, but that seemed an insignificant consideration when hundreds of thousands of people were hungry and homeless. How could I say no? The whole thing smelled of the Holy Spirit. Besides, I had never been to Africa, and this looked like a great adventure. So I said yes.

"Send me all the information you have," I told Lynn. "Let me check it out."

Was I testing and stretching myself again, seeing how much non-being I could face and assimilate without being destroyed, walking to the edge of the precipice of life so that the dragon of death could belch its acid in my face, opening me up to an influx of new life? I would not have said so at the time. But in retrospect, at some deep level, I think that is exactly what I was doing. I was opting to live on the frontier, push at the limits, and flirt with death, so as to become more fully alive.

I was committed. But I was of no value unless I could attract a star or two. I made a couple dozen calls to actor friends. Most were not available. In the minds of those who were, I soon found out, there was a huge difference between doing an "Insight" in Los Angeles and flying eleven thousand miles to immerse themselves in a famine.

"I don't think I could handle it," one said to me quite honestly.

"Scares the hell out of me," said another.

"I just wouldn't be comfortable with it," another said. (As if that had anything to do with anything.)

One actor agreed to go, but his wife protested so vehemently that he changed his mind. I called John Amos, the former Denver Bronco running back who had turned actor and played Kunta Kinte in *Roots.* He thanked me for the invitation and immediately said yes. I was delighted. I decided an actress would nicely round out the ensemble. An elderly star agreed to go. But when she asked for an assistant to take care of her wardrobe and wigs, I knew we were in trouble.

John and I decided to go alone. We got our shots, met Lynn in New York, and took the Pan Am flight for Dakar and Nairobi. From there we changed planes and flew on to Mogadishu, the capital of Somalia.

A poor and arid country hardly suited for agriculture, Somalia is about the size of Texas and borders on the Red Sea and the Indian Ocean in the horn of Africa. Most of its three and a half million people are nomads. All are Moslems. They live by grazing goats and camels on the barren plains. In 1980 their per capita yearly income was less than one hundred dollars.

At the time the Somalians were involved in a nasty little war with Ethiopia over a parcel of land called the Ogaden. For a while the Somalians were winning. But when the Ethiopians called in Russian and Cuban troops, the tides of battle began to shift. The Ethiopians retook the Ogaden and began to drive out its Somalian inhabitants, frequently killing their animals and sometimes poisoning their wells.

The result: a million and a half refugees poured into Somalia, 90 percent of whom were women and children. Their men were either dead or fighting with the guerrillas. Half of the refugees were absorbed by the Somali population. How I don't know. The other half—about three quarters of a million people—were crowded into refugee camps just east of the Ethiopian border.

We took a small plane to Lugh, a garrison town near the border, about three hundred miles west of Mogadishu. It was adjacent to six of the camps. Dropping out of the sky onto the tiny airstrip, we were met by a half-dozen soldiers, all with AK-47 automatic weapons.

We ate and slept in the courtyard of a hovel in Lugh, but almost all of our time was spent in the camps. Each contained close to twenty thousand people. They had constructed huts made out of bent branches and burlap to protect themselves from the wind, the equatorial sun, and the hundred-plus temperatures. Their diet was composed of cereals, vegetable oil, and powdered milk. Largely supplied by the governments of the United States and the Common Market countries and distributed by the Somalian government, it was terribly inadequate. When we were there, each person was getting less than one thousand calories a day, not nearly enough for human subsistence.

Everywhere we looked we saw evidence of hunger, if not starvation. The people were suffering from a kind of malnutrition that does not kill of itself but which so weakens the human body that it is powerless to throw off the most common diseases. The children were most susceptible. Forty percent of the kids who contracted measles died as a result. Diarrhea, so prevalent because of contaminated water, was also killing an appalling number. Forty-one percent of the families in the camps had already had a death. The situation was compounded by poor sanitation, a shortage of medical personnel, and, perhaps worst of all, the difficulty of isolating disease and so preventing an epidemic when people were so crowded together.

We met two French doctors and several Swedish relief workers who were struggling to improve the situation. A German engineering team had recently sunk a well that was producing clean water. And the ecumenical coalition we represented—Catholic Relief Services, Church World Service, and Lutheran World Relief—was concentrating its resources on improving sanitation and health care in the camps.

Some of my time in the camps was spent spotting for Mohinder Dhillon, our cameraman, trying to capture on film the plight of these lovely people. Some was spent directing John Amos as we recorded a series of thirty-second public service announcements for American TV. But in between times, I also tried to be present to the people, shaking hands, letting them know I cared, that I wanted to understand what they were going through, relating as best I could without being able to speak their language.

The kids were especially curious about this pink-skinned giant with the glasses and hearing aids. Sometimes, as I walked around, I had a dozen kids on each arm. On occasion I made a special friend who would ask for a present—not for money, but for a pen. More than anything else the kids wanted to read and write. In one hut the kids were using the Koran, written on wooden slats, as their basic text.

We went next to the Kakuma region of northwestern Kenya, where the situation was even worse. For centuries the Turkana tribe had lived there, grazing its cattle across the beautiful African prairie. The Turkanas are a nomadic people, warm and affectionate, many of whom have become Christian.

But in the eighteen months before we arrived, a terrible drought had struck. There had been no rain. The prairie had become a desert. First the grass died. Then the cattle died. And now the people were beginning to die. The situation was desperate.

We visited a Catholic mission in the area. It was run by two Irish priests—Niles and Desmond—who did a bang-up job. In the neighborhood of the mission, fourteen thousand people lived.

Thanks to food supplied by the American government and trucked in by Catholic Relief Services, the mission was feeding four thousand people a day. That is a lot of people, but the coin had a reverse side. The missionaries were forced to refuse the remaining ten thousand people. Why? Because they had no food to give them. That was bad enough. But what was worse was those ten thousand people had nowhere else to turn.

Because they had to choose, the missionaries decided to feed the most malnourished of the children. Sometimes they were able to feed the children and had to turn away their parents. That had to be difficult.

For some it was already too late. A starving adult is hard enough to take. But a starving child—I saw hundreds of them—that's too much. Their arms and legs were thin as pencils. No fannies. Just hanging skin. Their bellies were swollen as if, at three or four years old, they were nine months pregnant. Their skin pulled tight over their ribs, so that I could count every one. In some the lack of protein had given their hair a reddish hue and done permanent damage to their brains. Sometimes they would smile or even sing. But sometimes they cried, not a loud, lusty bellow like an American child, but a soft wail. I can still hear the wailing of those children.

When an American kid cries, the usual thing to do is to take him into your arms and give him a hug and tell him it's going to be all right. Those kids were so fragile I was afraid to take them in my arms for fear they would break.

Once, ready for a shot, I could not find John. Looking around I spotted him doubled up behind the jeep.

"Sorry," he said, tears coursing down his face, "I've . . . It's just too much."

I was having a difficult time with my own emotions.

What hit me most forcefully was the terrible reality of the situation. It was so real that everything else seemed unreal. The things we spend so much time worrying about—how we look, what other people think of us, what we have and what we don't—these things seemed so unimportant, so absolutely futile in the light of those starving people.

In the Gospels Jesus tells us He lives in a very special way in the hungry and thirsty, the naked and the homeless. I have always believed that. In India I had begun to experience it. But in Turkana I was blown apart by its reality. Those people were so real—God was so obviously present in them—that I felt like taking off my shoes and kneeling before them. Never before had I felt such reverence. I knew I was in the presence of the holy.

I wish I could describe what that experience was like. I cannot. Suffice it to say that it was both devastating and beautiful.

I also wish I could understand how it happened.

Was the stripped humanity of those endangered human beings more transparent and less opaque to the radiant light of the Lord's presence within it than is the humanity of those of us who have everything we need?

I do not know. But I do know of no other explanation for the meekness and dignity, the hospitality and joy we met everywhere we went.

Was the reality of their situation such that it made experiential the presence of the Realest of the Real?

I do not know. But I do know those kids took possession of my consciousness and have never let go.

Was our shock at seeing the fragility of their lives such that it pulled the scales from our eyes and enabled us to intuit the presence of Him who is the nonfragile Center and Ground of us all?

I don't know. But I do know God seemed so close in those people that I felt I could reach out and touch Him.

Was the love those beautiful people so joyfully gave me, and which I tried to reciprocate, the medium in which God showed Himself?

I do not know. But I do know on more than one occasion, I exchanged a look with one of those hungry people that released a charge of electricity between us. It was a touching of souls and much more.

Was my response to their catastrophic situation so overwhelming that it occasioned a surfacing of the Lord within me?

I do not know. But I do know it produced an earthquake inside, demolishing some long-standing emotional blocks. From the time of my mother's death to my immersion in the Turkana famine thirty-five years later, I did not cry. Not at the movies. Not when my father died. Not when things were at their worst with Genevieve. Not that I did not feel pain. I felt plenty of it. But I could not release the pain by crying. Not until October of 1980 and the Turkana famine in Kenya. Upon my return, I cried every day for ten days. I have cried regularly ever since.

I do not think I shall ever forget those swollen-bellied kids with the spindly legs.

Over the last thirty years, I have seldom missed my hour of meditation each day. I also need at least two weeks a year in a monastery. I do so because I cannot live without basking in the Lord's presence, walking in His light, tapping into His strength, soaking up His life, enjoying His love, and celebrating His joy.

But since India my most intense experiences of God's presence have not been on my knees in the chapel at St. Paul's, nor chanting the psalms with the monks at the Camaldolese Monastery at Big Sur, nor praying in the lotus position with the Cistercian sisters at their monastery at Whitethorn, nor celebrating Mass with the Pope at Dodger Stadium. My most shattering experiences of God's love have been in the slums of Djibouti, the barrios of San Salvador, the feeding stations of northwestern Kenya, the famine relief centers in Ethiopia, and the refugee camps of Somalia and Bangladesh. As nowhere else, I have found Him in the poor and the hungry, the naked and the homeless of the Third World.

Are these destitute people the eye of the needle through which this rich man must pass on his way into the Kingdom of God?

I suspect so.

John Amos and I returned to the United States late in October. The following Sunday, after the Masses, there was a carnival at St. Paul's. I went out to greet the people, as was my custom. I was unable to do it.

"This just doesn't seem real," I said to John Carr, the pastor. "I can't relate to it." Exhaustion, yes. Jet lag, of course. Culture shock, I'm sure. But more than that.

The following Friday John Amos and I did the "Today" show. He was eloquent. But what spoke most powerfully was the footage of those starving kids. Most of the viewing public had never before seen anything like it. It was the first inkling they had of the catastrophe. I appealed for funds. The response was immediate and generous.

I cried all the way back to the rectory. I had not been able to write the sermon I was to deliver at all the Masses the following Sunday. Now the dam broke, and it just poured out of me.

CBS's "Sixty Minutes" had decided to do a piece on our activities. They planned to shoot the sermon. Could I give it without crying? Did I want to break down on national television? I talked it over with John Carr and decided not to try to control it, to let happen whatever would happen.

"Sixty Minutes" did shoot the sermon. I did not break down,

but I came close. The people at St. Paul's responded with the biggest collection in their history.

Mike Wallace, who was to do our "Sixty Minutes" segment, was called away by the Iran hostage crisis, and the producers decided to shelve the story. We were disappointed.

In the following weeks, John and I did most of the talk shows —Merv Griffin, Mike Douglas, "Hour Magazine," Vidal Sassoon. On each we appealed for funds. Altogether more than a million dollars was donated to CRS and the other relief agencies. This was especially gratifying to us, because we knew how far a donated dollar went in that part of the world. It could feed a kid for a week.

Ten thousand members of the Turkana tribe died in the famine of 1980–1981, but one hundred and ninety thousand survived and are now living out their lives and grazing their cattle in that part of Kenya. I like to think John and I had something to do with that.

I do know that nothing I have ever done has given me so much joy.

CRS was also pleased with what we had done and asked me to put together another expedition the following October.

In October of 1981 there was no disaster of Somalian proportions, nor any famine of Turkana intensity. Just the chronic malnutrition and grinding destitution of the poorest of the world's poor, something we felt the American viewing public needed to be reminded of.

Patty Duke, of *The Miracle Worker*, who preferred to be called by her baptismal name Anna, and Dick Van Patten, of "Eight Is Enough," both old friends and frequent Insighters, decided to go, as did LeVar Burton of *Roots*. Jack Perkins, one of NBC's premier newsmen, came along with his crew so that they could do a segment for the new "NBC Magazine" show. Mike Rhodes volunteered his services as cameraman.

We traveled first to Nouakchott, the principal city of Mauritania in West Africa. In land mass this is a rather large country, two and a half times the size of California. But almost all of it is desert —the Sahara. There is no rain, few natural resources, and next to no arable land.

Traditionally the people of Mauritania had lived by grazing their goats and camels along the southern edge of the desert—

called the Sahel—where there was some grass and vegetation. But in recent years, for unknown reasons, the Sahara had been spreading southward. The grass and vegetation had died, and with it the herds and livelihood of the people.

What were these people to do? How were they to support themselves and feed their children?

What they had done was flock to Nouakchott where, without any available source of livelihood, they lived in tent cities, in squalor and destitution, barely subsisting on food donated by the American government.

Driving south of Nouakchott one day, the sound man noticed a nomad driving a camel across the desert. "Look at that fellow out there in the middle of nowhere," he said.

"To you it may be nowhere," Dick Van Patten replied, "but to him it's home."

We traveled next to Djibouti, a tiny former French colony sandwiched between Ethiopia and Somalia on the Red Sea and the Indian Ocean. A two-year drought and the civil war in Ethiopia had filled its refugee camps and urban slums with tens of thousands of people. They, too, had no means of feeding themselves—or their children.

In the Ali Sabiah camp there, I shook hands with a three-year-old boy who weighed fifteen pounds. I met another little girl who had hardly eaten in six months. She was literally skin and bones. She had just been brought in to the clinic, and the nurse was trying to feed her intravenously, but the only vein she could find large enough to receive the needle was in her scalp.

Immersion in such suffering was tough on all of us. "To take such a malnourished child in my arms, knowing that it would be dead within days, assaulted my maternal instincts," Anna said. "I felt like crying, but I could not let myself. Those beautiful people have such a sense of their own dignity that they would have been offended by my tears. Later, at night, I cried plenty."

From a distance the Balbala section of Djibouti looked like a garbage dump. When we got closer, we discovered it was home for thousands of human beings. Families of four, five, six, and seven lived in little tin shacks eight feet square.

As we walked through that slum, Anna looked up to heaven and in anguish said to me, "Why? Why does God allow this?"

After a moment I replied, "To challenge us to do something about it."

That was an answer. But it wasn't *the* answer, and I don't think it satisfied her. I know it did not satisfy me. Wrestling with this question, I found Ragamey's insight of greater help—that human suffering is not so much a problem requiring a solution as a mystery requiring a presence: the loving presence of God.

From Djibouti we continued on to Kenya. I wanted to see how the Turkana people were doing.

The answer: better, somewhat better. But not good. Not good at all.

Better because of the quantities of food that had been rushed in and because the relief efforts of CRS were now being supplemented by the International Red Cross.

Better, too, because there had been some rain; not much, but some, enough to raise sprouts of grass across the prairie. In some quarters there was evidence that the people were beginning to rebuild their herds.

Water was the big problem. The river was still absolutely dry.

I watched several women from the local village dig into the riverbed with their hands, going down five or six feet to get a bucket of water for drinking and cooking.

Some wells had been sunk. But not nearly enough.

As we drove over the countryside, we came across human skeleton after human skeleton. So many people were dying during the famine that there had been neither the time nor the energy to bury them all.

Mike Rhodes began to film the skeletons. "You're not going to shoot that," Anna protested to me.

"This is what we're trying to prevent, isn't it?" I answered.

"I guess so," she replied grimly.

On one level, the trip for me was like a journey through the bowels of hell. But on another level, it was also a foretaste of heaven.

Despite their need and destitution, the people in Mauritania, in Djibouti, and especially the Turkana of the Kakuma region in Kenya, were possessed of a kind of joy that seemed incomprehensible. That these people, suffering such deprivation, should exhibit such hospitality and joy is hard to comprehend. Why were they so happy? Did they know something we didn't? They were open and spontaneously friendly. They made us feel welcome. There seemed to be no loneliness, resentment, or hostility among them. They seemed to love one another. Certainly their sense of their own dignity was strong.

Returning to the mission one lunchtime after a morning in the villages, one of our team said, "I've seen more joy this morning than I have in ten years in Beverly Hills."

One night, about nine, we visited one of the villages where the people were singing and dancing.

It was a unique type of dance, with a high-jump in place as its most distinctive feature. At their invitation we joined in. Anna, Mike, and LeVar Burton picked it up quickly, but I had trouble mastering the rhythm and the right time to jump. The young women of the village giggled at my awkwardness.

In the midst of this, LeVar said to me, "This is outrageous."

"Outrageous good or outrageous bad?" I asked.

"Outrageous great," he replied.

They had no idea what they would eat the next day. Yet they were singing and dancing, with great smiles lighting up those beautiful black faces. A paradox. Yes. More than that. A mystery. I don't fully understand it.

Certainly their expectations were less than ours. This lowered their level of frustration and made them grateful for whatever they had.

They certainly were not hung up on *things.* They had so little. They looked for their happiness in nature and in each other, not in what they had or whom they were better than.

But I don't think that completely explained their joy.

I could only conclude that it flowed into them from beyond them.

Sometimes, early in the morning, I'd go over to the mission chapel to make my meditation and watch the people stop off for a morning visit with the Lord. For them a genuflection was more than a cursory nod in God's direction. It was a profound act of adoration. They prayed not just with their lips or their heads, but with their bodies, with their whole selves. Offering Mass with them was always a joyous occasion. They would laugh and clap and sing in celebration of the Lord's presence among them. They had a great sense of the sacred, an innate feeling for the transcendent.

We visited a center for malnourished children in Kakuma. It was feeding time, and one little girl with a very bad case of dysentery was able to eat her porridge. Yet within a very short time, the food had gone through her and she was sitting in a large pool of her own excrement. She started to cry. The black nun in charge picked her up by the shoulders and moved her to a dry spot. The child continued to cry. To comfort and cuddle her, the nun picked her up again, this time putting her arm under the child's bare, wet, and very dirty bottom.

I looked at Anna. Anna looked at me. "That's real Christianity," I said. She nodded.

Five minutes later I watched Anna do the same thing.

Physically the Turkana people were as poor as you can get. Yet spiritually it would seem they were rich. Very rich indeed. Their joy mystified me. I could understand it only as the radiance of the Lord's presence within them. Perhaps they have something to teach us about what it means to be a human being, about where human happiness is to be found.

Early in November we returned to the United States and did the various talk shows. Anna did the "Today" show and Dick "The Tonight Show." Jack Perkins's segment on "NBC Magazine" was masterful. It seemed our newly labeled "Voice for the Voiceless" program was beginning to have the desired effect.

In September of 1983, Lynn Marshall again called to tell me a very bad situation in Ethiopia was getting worse. In drought-ridden, war-stricken Tigre Province, a deadly famine loomed. I agreed to go. Lynn Redgrave offered to go with me. We began to clear our schedules and make the necessary emotional adjustments. We got our shots, visas, and plane tickets for a Tuesday departure. But on Friday afternoon, Lynn Marshall called to tell us their people in Addis Ababa were having trouble getting permission from the Ethiopian government for us to travel to Tigre.

"Why?" I asked in dismay.

"Your guess is as good as mine," he answered. "It could be a reluctance to admit the existence of the problem [nobody was using the word famine yet], the eruption of a major battle, the forcible conscription of young men into the army, or paranoia about Americans. We don't know."

Lynn Redgrave and I were left in limbo over the weekend. By Monday the trip was definitively scrubbed. It was futile to fly halfway around the world, CRS said, if we were not to be allowed to visit the most troubled areas. I was disappointed. So was Lynn.

She and her husband came by the office, and we mourned together.

At the time we did not know how tragic the aborted trip would turn out to be. If we had been allowed to visit and photograph the desperate plight of the people in Tigre, we would have been able to alert the world to the impending famine a full ten months before the word finally got out. Several hundred thousand lives might have been saved.

I think there is a very special place deep in hell for politicians who put power before people, especially when the victims of their arrogance are children who starve to death as a result.

The following September, at great expense, the Ethiopian government celebrated the tenth anniversary of its revolution. Only after it was over did they seem willing to deal with the catastrophe in their northern provinces. Shortly before the celebration, Mohinder Dhillon, my cameraman from Somalia and Turkana, got into Tigre and Wallo provinces and shot some of the first footage of the famine. It was subsequently aired around the world and in the United States by NBC.

The response from the world's peoples was immediate, and a massive relief effort was launched. CRS assumed responsibility for logistics—moving the donated food from the ports of Assab and Massawa to the relief centers, no small task in a country with few paved roads and only one railroad. They asked me to go over. I called Cliff Robertson in Tunisia and he decided to join me. So did L.A. businessman Dick Riordan. Mohinder met us in Addis Ababa.

Briefings by CRS and USAID (the United States Agency for International Development) personnel gave us the statistical overview. Of forty-two million Ethiopians, seven million were perilously close to starvation. In the last ten months, three hundred thousand people had died of malnutrition. In the next ten months, without immediate, massive, and continued help from the international community, many more times that number would likewise starve to death.

These statistics gave some idea of the problem's magnitude. But they did not prepare us for the devastating, yet somehow awe-inspiring, reality of the refugee camps.

We visited six of these feeding centers—Mariam Tesfai, Quiha, and Seharti-Wehareb in Tigre Province, near Mekele; and Korem, Harbu, and Bati in Wollo Province—all in the northern part of

Ethiopia, where the drought and the civil war had combined to intensify the lethal effects of the famine.

Flying into Mekele on a small plane gave us a good look at the ravages produced by the four-year-old drought. The mighty Wenchit River, which is one of the tributaries of the Blue Nile and used to be the width of a football field, had been reduced to a barely trickling stream. All of the smaller rivers and creeks had dried up. The mountains and hills were terraced for farming. But in the parched soil, nothing could grow. Around Mekele the terrain was like a moonscape. There were lots of rocks and clay, but no moisture; no vegetation—none.

Landing in Mekele, the capital of Tigre Province, we were confronted by another facet of Ethiopia's agony. Parked on the runway were close to a dozen Soviet attack helicopters. Off to the side was the carcass of a mortared DC-3. Less than a half mile from the airport, a large army camp was visible. And stationed on all the surrounding hills were scores of alert sentries, ready to meet any guerrilla attack, a precaution they felt necessary because the rebels controlled most of the countryside.

Six weeks before we visited them, two of the three refugee camps surrounding Mekele did not exist. Now the three camps contained almost fifty thousand people.

These people had streamed in out of the hills, deserting their villages, sometimes walking three or four days—drawn by reports of food. Some huddled together in large sheds with only a plastic roof to shelter them from the sun and wind. Others stayed in tents. Still others lived in the open, with only piled rocks to protect them from the icy wind. A recent cold snap brought pneumonia to a large number of the camps' inhabitants and dramatically, if temporarily, increased the death rate.

As soon as a family registered, the physical condition of its members was evaluated. The most malnourished children were put on an intensive feeding program. Others received supplementary rations. Some families were given a month's supply of food and sent back to their villages. This was because the camps were so crowded, sanitation so primitive, and health care so inadequate.

Despite this, in the Mekele camps, the famine somehow seemed under control. Food and medicine were streaming in via the nearby airfield, and the death rate had dropped to twenty a day—a significant improvement from just two weeks before. The kids were even going to school.

While we were in Mariam Tesfai (the name means "Mary, Help of Believers"), the chairman of Ethiopia's Communist Party and the head of its government—Lt. Gen. Mengistu Haile Mariam—came for a visit. His security guard was formidable. He gave no speeches. As far as I could see, he shook no hands. Nor did he smile. His bearing and manner seemed stereotypically military. He strutted around like a little Napoleon. I learned later his strange walk was due to the new elevator boots he was wearing. I don't think anyone would ever call him genial. Yet he came and, with television cameras whirring, he saw firsthand the desperate plight of his starving people, and his presence (he visited another camp—Bati—two days later) symbolized the commitment of his government to work at long last with the international community and the relief agencies to alleviate the famine.

The Mengistu government had helped cause the famine by its artificial depression of food prices, its expenditure of the country's meager resources on armaments rather than agricultural development, its favoring of urban over rural populations, its forced collectivization of farming, and its policy of confiscating the land of those who produced more than they consumed, thus discouraging the building up of food reserves. But now the officials of the United States government and those of the relief agencies were unanimous in testifying to the practical sincerity of the government's commitment, although it was always subordinated to the prosecution of the war. (Shortly before we arrived, Mengistu had refused a food truce to allow supplies to enter the rebel-held areas.)

We traveled next to Korem, a feeding center and refugee camp high in the mountains above Alamata. The situation there was quite desperate. They needed fifty tons of food each day to feed their forty thousand people. They averaged ten. Most of the people were emaciated. Many could not walk. A quarter were without shelter. The impressive young doctors and nurses from the French organization Médecins Sans Frontières, who worked without electricity (the camp had no generator) in the three huge sheds housing the sickest people, were fighting against impossible odds. They were saving many lives. But they were also losing 101 people a day. We visited the tent morgue at eleven in the morning. Already thirty-five people had died of hunger-related maladies.

In Korem we also saw the government's relocation program in action. Seven hundred people a day were moved from the camp via truck and plane to areas in southern and western Ethiopia that were not drought-afflicted. Only the healthiest, the poorest, and the youngest families were selected. The government claimed the program was completely voluntary. Critics wondered how free was the choice of people so hungry. Or how prepared to receive them the communities into which they moved were. Or how pure the government's motives were. Wasn't this a way to deprive the guerrillas of their manpower pool?

In an orphanage near Korem, which was run by Save the Children and cared for 8,300 children, I walked into a huge shed where a thousand youngsters were sitting. As soon as they saw my white face, they started to clap their hands and chant, "*ferenje, ferenje,*" which means "foreigner, foreigner." They did so, not with the pejorative overtones so often associated with that word, but with joy, affection, and gratitude. For them "foreigner" meant help. It meant food. And that's what these people needed more than anything else.

We went next to Harbu, a refugee camp twenty-five miles south of Kampulcha, which was run by Concern under the leadership of my friend from Bangladesh, Father Jack Finucane. Its team—which was composed of a doctor, several nurses, a nutritionist, a mechanic, and a social worker, all under thirty-five—collaborated with several times as many Ethiopians to operate the camp. It was a tough job.

Because so many of its 12,500 people were malnourished, disease was rampant at Harbu. When we visited it, there were five hundred cases of measles, widespread dysentery, more than a few cases of hepatitis, jaundice, malaria, at least one case of leprosy, and a fever of unknown origin. They were losing thirty-five to forty people each day.

I tried to comfort a young mother who had already lost her husband and now lost her only child. How much, I asked myself, could one person be asked to take? I felt helpless as another woman whose teenage son had died was so overcome by grief that she danced around his lifeless body.

At the end of the day, the Concern team gathered around the dinner table in the simple, overcrowded house they occupied on the outskirts of the camp, and together we shared the Word of God, the Body of Christ, and more than a few laughs over a supper of potatoes and cabbage.

The next day we drove to Bati, which was the most desolate and desperate of the camps. It did not have Harbu's disease problem. The dedicated Red Cross personnel were working hard to prevent that. But everywhere we looked—there were seventeen thousand people in Bati—we saw emaciated, exhausted, almost unconscious human beings who had just dragged themselves in off the desert. They had deserted their villages, trekking across the barren countryside in a desperate search for food, with only the ragged clothes on their backs to shield them from the equatorial sun and the piercingly cold wind, in the process burning up the protein in the muscles of their arms and legs until there was nothing left. Many collapsed quietly and died on the way. Those who did reach the camp were not just hungry. They were starving. And they had been starving for a long time. Some were so weak they collapsed at the entrance to the camp, unable to seek out the limited amount of food that was now within reach.

When we were in Bati, there were twenty-eight grave diggers and only three doctors. The daily death toll was over a hundred. Sometimes people died before they had a chance to be registered. Many died and were buried without ever having their names written down.

As I write this six years later, the agony of their faces still haunts my memory.

Some of them died before my eyes.

If unconsciously I had come to Ethiopia in search of a dying that would make me more alive, I think at Bati I may have gotten more than I bargained for.

In Korem, Harbu, and Bati, as in other parts of Ethiopia, the famine was out of control.

Usually, at night, our team would gather over supper to talk about the day, share experiences, and ventilate emotions. There were plenty of laughs, but most of the humor was of the gallows variety.

Except for Mohinder and our interpreter, we were all Americans, and Cliff Robertson and I were the only members of the team to have previously been involved in a famine. (Cliff had been in Biafra.)

All of us found the experience devastating. To move among

people who had been stripped of everything, who suffered such total want and destitution, was searing for the soul. I am not sure any of us will ever forget some of the things we saw. Nor will any of us ever again be quite the same.

In such a situation, a number of our group went into emotional overload. This should not have surprised me. I had done the same on previous occasions. Different members of our team reacted in different ways.

One got away from the supper table as quickly as he could. He spent every free moment playing chess with a computer. He didn't want to have to think about what he had seen.

Another became irrationally angry—he couldn't say why—and dumped his rage on whoever was handy.

Still another found the camps so hard to take that he collapsed inside, almost traumatized. Emotionally he simply closed up, turned off, and shut down. Unable to function, he spent the last four days sitting in the hotel lobby smoking his pipe.

One member of our team sailed through the experience with little outward show of emotion. But he had migraine headaches for the first eleven days he was back. His repressed emotions were taking their revenge.

Our Ethiopian interpreter, who was from an affluent family in another part of the country, became profoundly depressed. For reasons she couldn't quite articulate, she blamed herself for the catastrophe and felt great guilt.

To no small extent, I believe these negative reactions were due to the shock of having been plunged for the first time into a disaster of this magnitude and intensity.

Yet many of the relief workers in the camps had backgrounds not unlike those of our team. They were Americans or Europeans. They, too, were college-educated and middle class. They also had found their first experience of the camps devastating. But now, weeks or months later, they had worked things through and were coping. Better than that, they were not only meeting the needs of the desperate Ethiopians with efficiency and humor, but they were finding the whole experience an enriching one.

I asked a Concern nurse at Harbu why she did what she did. Matter of factly, she answered, "Because I love these people. They give me so much."

"Like what?" I asked.

"Like their friendliness and joy."

"In a place like this?"

"Oh goodness yes," she replied.

The serenity and lack of self-dramatization with which she talked of her motivation assured me of her sincerity.

Our conversation helped me sort out my own feelings. I kept reaching for an idea or image or symbol that would help me make some sense of what I had been seeing and hearing. So many of my immediate emotional associations were those of the Holocaust—the skeletal figures with skin stretched tight over bodies without flesh, the protruding ribs, the large and extended eyes, the close-cropped hair, the rows of corpses, the frightened faces of those about to be packed into vehicles for transportation into the unknown. Parts of Ethiopia in 1984 were like Auschwitz in 1944.

Like the Holocaust, the disaster in Ethiopia was bound to stir strong emotion, some of which would be negative. That human beings should suffer from malnutrition is wrong. It's not what God had in mind for His favorite creatures. That children should starve to death is even worse. It's intolerable. I know of few things more evil. And so we react with outrage and indignation and feel compelled to rear up on our hind legs and say a passionate NO to it. The reverse side of the NO is the wholehearted commitment to do whatever is necessary, at whatever personal cost, to see that no human being, let alone any child, ever goes hungry again. Such a response is obviously healthy and authentic.

But when my anger becomes diverted and looks around in desperation for someone to shift responsibility to, to lay blame on, to dump upon and condemn, then it's neither healthy nor authentic. It's simply a form of self-righteousness.

When I do this, what am I really doing? I am taking the revulsion that I authentically feel at the situation (and perhaps also at myself) and projecting it outward onto the first credible scapegoat. As I rant and rave in condemning that person, I can feel so good about myself. With smug satisfaction I can say, "At least I am not like him."

In Caracas, Medellín, and Bogotá in 1975, I had gotten sucked into this kind of thing. In Ethiopia in 1984, I was not about to make that mistake again.

Anger is a terrible waste of energy in a disaster situation, to say the least.

The same can be said of guilt.

By the standards of the Third World, most Americans would

have to be classified as rich. That's no reason to feel guilty. It's not our fault there's been a drought in Ethiopia. We did not create the civil war. The policies of the Ethiopian government that helped cause this famine were their doing, not ours.

So any guilt Americans might have felt about the famine in Ethiopia was largely without basis. It was neurotic rather than authentic guilt, for there is no sin in being rich as there is no sin in being poor. But there's a terribly great sin in having more than you need and not sharing with those who have less than they need.

But that's the rub. Such destitution, given the solidarity of the human family, calls for generosity and self-sacrifice. But there is a part of each of us that does not like that. We say to ourselves, "Don't get carried away. Gotta take care of Number One." We prefer to feel guilty. In fact, by a perverse form of spiritual masochism, we enjoy feeling guilty. It gives us all the excuse we need to sit on our fannies and do nothing. "Poor little me," we say. "These people have it so bad and I have it so good. They make me feel so terrible."

Guilt may make us feel terrible, but it doesn't cause us to change our affluent life-style. Nor does it cause us to open our purse strings in any meaningful way. Nor does it motivate us to become politically active at home. Guilt paralyzes us. We stay locked behind the four walls of our own egos, caught up in a narcissistic embrace with ourselves. Neurotic guilt is nothing but a subtle form of self-indulgence.

By the time I got to Ethiopia, I knew how futile—and ultimately self-serving—anger and guilt are. How then was I to respond to this situation? What was I supposed to do? After I had informed myself about the situation, captured on film both the beauty and the desperation of the people, and given away all the granola bars my pockets could hold, what was I left with? The nitty-gritty demands of presence, that's what. How could I let these needy and destitute people know I cared? How could I understand where they were and what they were going through? How could I get inside their pain and feel with them in their need and destitution?

Is authentic presence even possible? Can a middle-class American who has never known real physical deprivation in his life enter into the pain and share the feelings of those who are starving to death? If it is possible, what does it demand? In the camps I wrestled with these questions. Finally I began to see that the only way I could be present to people who had been stripped of everything but the very essence of their own naked humanity was to let go of everything of my own so that I could enter into the essence of my own naked humanity and so relate to them from there, as one stripped human being to another. This meant washing the glue off my fingers and clinging to nothing: not to my ego or reputation or relationships or accomplishments or personas or possessions or dreams or secret agendas. It meant I had to let go of everything that might give me security or separate me from the center of myself. I found that scary. But I also found it exhilarating. Scary because it involved a radical experience of my own fragility, of my own precarious hold on life. Exhilarating because it put me in touch with my own deep need for that which is not fragile and precarious. It released energies of need and desire that could carry me into the arms of God.

Of all Third World peoples, the Ethiopians are my favorites. Their granitelike courage in the face of disaster, their ability to affirm their dignity in an appallingly dehumanizing situation, their tenacious loyalty to their families, their profound faith in a God of Love, even when His creation has shown them nothing but cruelty, the joy they radiated and the hospitality they showed me, combine to make them very special. The fact that we shared such a terrible time together make them part of me at a profound level. The Ethiopian people are indeed the meek who someday, somehow, some way, will inherit the earth.

Our farewells were difficult. But for their sake as well as our own, Cliff and I needed to return to America. I was awash in emotion on the flight to Rome, my eyes trickling with tears. Cliff noticed. He put a hand on my shoulder. It said, "I know what you're going through." I needed that. We were met by CBS News. The next morning Cliff was on the "CBS Morning News" with our footage. That night I was on the "CBS Evening News" with our footage. The same night it also played on the "ABC Evening News." In the days ahead, singly or together, we did the "Today" show, Merv Griffin, Phil Donahue, and "Hour Magazine." We told the story as best we could. But what spoke most powerfully were the images of those beautiful but very hungry human beings.

Back in Los Angeles, thanks to Bill Baker and Dick Hirsch, I collaborated with Group W to make a documentary—*Ethiopia,*

Land of Hunger, Land of Hope—which was broadcast across the country. I did articles for the *Los Angeles Times* and *America* magazine. I also preached on the famine at all the Masses at St. Paul's and, later, at St. Monica's, Corpus Christi, and St. Bede's parishes in Los Angeles. These parish appeals netted $170,000.

What Cliff and I did was a small part of an avalanche of publicity generated by the famine. It was voted the number-one news story of 1984. More to the point, the media coverage had the effect we hoped. In the fifteen months that followed the news of the famine, the government of the United States sent 644,000 tons of food to the beleaguered Ethiopians. In addition, the American people donated more than a quarter of a billion dollars to the private relief agencies working in the area—Catholic Relief Services, Lutheran World Relief, Church World Services, Save the Children, World Vision, Red Cross, and UNICEF. The peoples of Canada, Australia, Japan and of the European Economic Community responded with similar generosity.

These donated funds were expended to buy and transport food for the hungry Ethiopians and to help them provide for themselves in the future. The old adage remains true: "Give a man a fish and he will be hungry again tomorrow. Teach him how to fish and he will never be hungry again." The money was spent for immediate famine relief and for long-range agricultural development. Both are of crucial importance.

Hundreds of thousands of Ethiopians starved to death in the famine of 1984–85. But millions of people who might have starved to death were saved by the most massive relief effort of its kind ever attempted by the world's peoples.

Cliff and I were privileged to have been a small part of that.

Little did I know when I left Addis Ababa in December of 1984 that nineteen months later I would be back in Ethiopia, hoping to shoot an ABC movie of the week there.

Part Five

Second Wind

CHAPTER 15

GOING MAINSTREAM

It is always easier to move on, to let go of a situation that has been good, if you have a reasonable expectation that the situation into which you are moving will be even better.

It was that way with "Insight." It had been great. But it was over, and now it was time to move on. To what? I hoped to the mainstream of American broadcasting—to producing for the networks, to specials, movies of the week, mini-series, to hour and half-hour series; in short, to commercial programming. (Only later would we begin to dream of entering the still more exclusive world of feature film production.)

This was an area into which religious production companies had not ventured before. Was that a reason not to try it? I did not think so. Could it be done successfully? That was a more difficult question. My advisors were divided. Network programming was a highly competitive field. We would be playing in the big leagues and competing with the best. What chance of securing network commitments did we have? Nobody would hazard a guess. Would our religious motivation and the value-oriented type of programming we wanted to do help or hinder us? Nobody seemed to know. Implicit was another question: Did we have something the networks needed? If so, what was it? Nobody had an answer to that one either. Was the commercial agenda of the networks—selling viewers to advertisers, the more the better—incompatible with the type of audience-enrichment programming we wanted to do? And on a more personal level, was it possible to operate in this highly charged secular media world without compromising our religious values?

For better or for worse, when we made the decision to go

mainstream, I was not aware of all the ramifications. "God is merciful not to show us the future," Gene Burke used to say. "If He did, we might not sail into it so blissfully."

I sailed in, excited by the prospect of programming for the networks. Part was the religious challenge involved—to function as a priest in the heart of the secular, to operate on the cutting edge of value transmission in our increasingly media-saturated society, to work at establishing a Gospel presence in this most powerful organ of popular culture. Part of my excitement at going mainstream was more mundane. Network programming guaranteed huge audiences. It meant synchronized promotion on a single night. It also meant I no longer had to raise money to produce my shows, nor did I have to ask people to work for union minimum. With the budget supplied by the network, I would be able to pay the cast and crew their going rates. Nothing wrong with that.

I was only dimly aware that these attractions had their price: buying into the networks' commercial agenda, which tends to make the size of the audience more important than the quality of the show, and so doing those things that are guaranteed to deliver a huge number of viewers. This means selecting high-concept stories and big stars. High-concept stories mean those that can be reduced to a single short clause of sufficient emotional impact to make the reader of *TV Guide* want to tune in. Big stars mean those who may or may not be superlative actors but whom a large portion of the viewing public know and like.

Programming for the networks also means surrendering a high degree of artistic control over the programs you make. The network retains final approval of the writer, script, director, cast, location, and fine cut. Whoever pays the piper calls the tune. Sometimes this works to the producer's advantage. If the network executive is creative and shares the vision of the producer, director, writer, and actors, he or she can add a valuable ingredient to the creative process. If the executive does not, the effect can be the very opposite.

My enthusiasm for network production was also based on the relationships I had with a number of the top executives at the networks. I knew they were quality human beings who shared my humanistic orientation and cared about the moral health of their audiences. My enthusiasm was also based on my own experience in the commercial arena with the Capital Cities Family Specials.

Over the years I had gotten to know Joe Dougherty, the executive vice president of Capital Cities, a former professional basketball player, and a fellow Philadelphian. He had helped me place "Insight" on his stations. Late in July of 1976, during a visit to his New York office, he told me his superiors at Cap Cities—Tom Murphy and Dan Burke—were interested in doing some audience-enrichment programming.

"What kind?" I asked, intrigued.

"Whatever is needed," he said.

"On what basis?"

"We're not interested in making a lot of money, but we don't want to lose a whole lot either."

"Why do you want to do it?" I probed.

"We've been doing pretty well. We feel we owe the viewing public something. We don't want to just take, take, take. Like the farmer with his soil, we feel we should plow something back." He paused, then asked: "Would you be interested in exploring the possibility of collaborating?"

"Yes, definitely," I said with a gleam in my eye.

"I thought you'd say that," he said. "The guy we've asked to head this up is Charlie Keller. I'll have him come see you."

"Fine," I said.

"There's just one problem."

"What's that?"

"He went to St. Joe's, too. We used to kill you guys from La Salle."

Charlie did come to visit. We liked each other at once. Like Joe, he was Jesuit-educated and a devout Catholic. He screened our Bloomin' Human film series, which were ten-minute value education films we had made for the public school classroom. Aimed at the primary grades, financed by the Lilly Endowment, produced by Mike Rhodes and Terry Sweeney, and directed by Mike, they were filled with Christian values but contained no obvious religious teachings or God talk.

This combination appealed to Charlie, as did the artistic quality and dramatic impact of the films.

Together we launched a research project, which revealed that teenagers were not only a very needy portion of the American population, especially in the area of moral values, but were also a segment of the viewing public that was largely ignored by the nation's TV programmers. Why not do a series of dramatic specials on the moral dilemmas of teenagers? Indeed, why not?

Charlie presented the concept to his superiors. They liked the idea and gave the go-ahead. That's how the Family Specials were born.

Sister Helen Weber, who had been our values education specialist on the Bloomin' Human series, conducted focus groups for teenagers. What did they want? Where were they hurting? What were the questions they asked, the problems they faced, the dilemmas they wrestled with? How could we help them integrate those fragile identities of theirs?

The search for identity—Who am I?—or, more exactly, Who do I want to be? seemed the key to unlocking the teenage psyche. Identity was the magnet that drew all other teenage concerns, like iron filings, to itself, revealing their meaning and laying bare their underlying dynamism. How to know, accept, possess, and give oneself; how to relate to one's parents, peers, and possible sexual partners; and the values one needs to navigate the turbulent rapids of the adolescent years and put together the teenage identity—these were the areas into which we ventured as we sought to select the themes we would explore and the manner in which we would explore them in the four half-hour shows Cap Cities had decided to finance and distribute each year.

In consultation with Charlie Keller, we decided to do the first shows on sexual responsibility, teenage alcoholism, death, and the meaning of success. In the years ahead, we would also do shows on friendship, suicide, violence, divorce, peer pressure, lying, communication, sexual maturity, personal growth, pregnancy, self-affirmation, heroism, drugs, career choice, teenage and parental unemployment, courage, reckless driving, honesty, cheating, hope, fidelity, compassion, and egotism.

Mike Rhodes produced all of the Family Specials. Sometimes he was joined in this task by Terry Sweeney, Judy Greening, Marina Angelini, or Lewis Abel. Developing a genius for eliciting exceptional performances from teenage actors, Mike did almost all of the directing.

The Family Specials concept elicited the same kind of generous support from the acting community that had powered "Insight" over the years. Many young actors found the Family Specials good launching pads for their careers. Emilio Estevez, Joan

Chen, Judge Reinhold, Meg Tilly, Laura Dern, and Charlie Sheen did Family Specials.

Sometimes on the Family Specials, as on "Insight," we went down to the wire on casting.

Jack Shea liked to tell a story of my praying, "Lord, we are so glad you are helping us make this show. It is Your show, and we could not possibly make it without You. You give us the scripts, the budget, the director, the actors. But Lord, do You always have to wait until the last minute?"

With that, God leans over and says:

"Father, that's show biz."

Our financial relationship with Cap Cities was a simple one. They paid the production costs, sold the commercials, and placed the series on the country's TV stations, after which we promoted the shows together. Paulist Productions retained the school and international TV rights.

They made no money on the series. Neither did we. But that's not why either of us was making it.

Cap Cities had theme, script, cast, and fine cut approval. Charlie Keller shared our vision and was easy to work with. We seldom ran into crunch situations except in the script area. Here I sometimes found him exceptionally cautious, and some spirited arguments ensued. In retrospect, he was right some of the time and, in my opinion, he was wrong some of the time, but the process pushed us to the limit and generated better scripts and so better shows, which is what we all wanted.

The Family Specials were syndicated to individual stations rather than placed on a network.

Bill Mulvey was the Cap Cities executive responsible for station placement. He did an exceptional job. Clearances for the first series (four first runs and two reruns) averaged 87 percent of the country, with an average 8.8 rating (over seven million viewers per run). The following year we went over 90 percent in clearances. The time slots were usually prime-time access—between six and eight in the evening. In 1981 the highest-rated syndicated special in the country was a Family Special, and in the following year, six of the top twenty rated syndicated specials were also. These statistics encouraged us to think that humanizing shows—those that explored moral dilemmas and said something important about what it means to be a human being—could pull competitive audiences in the marketplace.

The critics were also kind. The Associated Press, UPI, the *New York Times*, the *Christian Science Monitor*, the *Los Angeles Times*, and *Variety* consistently gave us good notices, and the series won the Ohio State, Gabriel, and ACT (Action for Children's Television) awards.

In 1980 Jim McGinn wrote *The Girl on the Edge of Town*, an exceptionally good Family Special on teenage pregnancy. I liked it. So did Charlie Keller. There was just one problem. It was long —almost an hour in length—and I did not see how we could cut it. I asked Charlie if he would consider making it an hour. He said no, it just would not fit. While we were arguing this out, I had a meeting with the head of children's programming at CBS on another project, and he asked what else I was working on. I told him about *The Girl on the Edge of Town*, and he asked to read it. He, too, loved it and said he was ready to make a deal to film it for one of his after-school specials. When I told Charlie about this, he was upset. Cap Cities had paid for the script and owned all the rights. He did not want to let it go. After considerable soul-searching, the Cap Cities people decided they could break the mold and release an hour program after all. Starring Sherry Hursey, Patty Duke, and Billy Greenbush, it turned out to be the most highly rated Family Special we ever made. The critics also loved it, except those at the *New York Times*, the *Philadelphia Inquirer*, and one Miami paper, who savaged us, apparently because the heroine in the show decided to have rather than abort her baby.

The success of *The Girl on the Edge of Town* opened Cap Cities to the potential of hour specials. We made two others—*High Powder*, on drug abuse, and *The Juggler of Notre Dame*, a modern version of the medieval legend, which was released as a Christmas special.

Casting the lead in Lan O'Kun's *Juggler* script presented a special problem. We needed an actor who could juggle or a juggler who could act—a tough combination, even in Hollywood. We finally settled on Carl Carlson, one of the country's best jugglers, who had considerable acting experience. Mike Rhodes worked his magic, and Carl turned in an excellent performance. Merlin Olsen, Melinda Dillon, and Patrick Collins joined him to make it a tremendously moving show.

Shot in and around the old mission at San Juan Capistrano, it is one of my favorites; partially, I guess, because it enabled me to pay my dues to Jesus's Mother. It has become a Christmas classic, playing every year since its premiere in 1983. So many people have been touched so deeply by that show that they write in to tell us it brought tears of joy to their eyes.

The television academy named *The Juggler of Notre Dame* the "outstanding achievement in religious programming" in 1983 and gave it an Emmy.

In 1984 Charlie Keller came to me with a new idea. Instead of making a value-oriented teenage anthology in which each show had a different locale and a new cast of characters, why not make a teenage series on values in which the locale and the characters would be the same episode after episode? This would enable our viewers to know and love our central cast, which would, in its turn, bring them back to us time after time. Because of the production efficiencies involved, it would also have obvious economic advantages.

We liked the challenge he had thrown at us. We started to brainstorm and came up with "Buchanan High," whose main characters would be a strong-willed female high school newspaper editor and her laid-back male staff photographer. The newspaper office would be the central set from which our characters would radiate out into the school and neighborhood.

Charlie bought the concept, and with Sherry Hursey and Ike Eisenmann in the leads, we shot four episodes of "Buchanan High." Station reaction to the new concept was excellent, and clearances left nothing to be desired. The new series looked like it would have a bright future. But in March of 1985, Cap Cities decided to buy ABC. As a consequence they were barred by federal law from making or distributing syndicated programming. This is the way the Cap Cities Family Specials and "Buchanan High" died. Not with a bang. Not with a whimper either. But with a stroke of the pen and the merger of two of America's communications giants.

The success of *The Juggler of Notre Dame* as a Christmas special caused us to look for something comparable for Easter. "The Other Wiseman," a short story written by the turn-of-the-century Presbyterian minister Henry Van Dyke, was an obvious possibility. It tells the story of a fictional wise man who spent his whole life looking for Jesus, only to miss him at each step along the way because he had stopped to help someone in need. Finally, on the first Easter morning, broken in body and despairing in spirit, his money gone, the wise man is dragging himself outside of Jerusalem on his way back to Persia when the Risen Jesus appears to him. He is delighted to see the Lord but confesses to having nothing to give him.

"You have already given it to me," Jesus replies.

"I don't understand," the feeble wise man confesses.

"I was hungry," Jesus responds, "and you gave me food; thirsty and you gave me drink; homeless and you took me in; a prisoner and you came to visit me."

"But when?" stammered the wise man.

"Whenever you did it for the least of my brothers, you did it for me," Jesus answers.

The wise man dies, happy in the realization that he has fulfilled his quest.

I had first heard the story from Sister Grace Menton, my eighth-grade teacher at Melrose Academy. It captured my imagination then. It still held it now. I loved it, perhaps because it was mythic and conveyed so powerfully what I consider the heart of the Christian Gospel. I made up my mind to do whatever I could to get it made.

I presented the concept to Charlie Keller. He liked the idea but did not feel he could justify another hour special. Looking for another outlet, I presented the idea to several friends at advertising agencies. They did not think they could sell it either. Their clients were more interested in two-hour movies of the week, they said, than in hour specials.

So even before the demise of "Insight," I set about developing concepts for movies of the week. A two-hour special based on the life of Mother Teresa seemed a distinct possibility. There was plenty of drama—not only Mother Teresa's interaction with the poor and destitute and her struggle to establish the Order, but also the radical change she made in her own life. Until well into her forties, she was a conventional nun. A midlife crisis saint, I called her.

Jim McGinn, the Bristol-Myers representative on the West Coast, one of our most prolific "Insight" and Family Special writers, and a member of our Board of Directors, thought his company would be enthusiastic about sponsoring such a movie.

I had met Mother Teresa in Los Angeles and had seen her

again in Calcutta. I thought I would have no trouble getting her permission. I was wrong.

I wrote to her. I received no answer. I asked Cardinal Manning to write to her. He did not get an answer either. I called her in Calcutta. She said she had been terribly busy but would get back to me soon. She didn't. Finally I called Eileen Egan, a mutual friend, to intercede for me. Eileen called Mother Teresa and got an answer, but it was not the one I wanted.

"Would you shoot such a picture in India?" Eileen wanted to know.

"I would try to," I responded.

"Would you use real lepers?"

"I certainly would want to."

"But you would use an actress to play Mother Teresa?"

"Of course. How else can you make a drama?"

"How about making a documentary?" she asked. "Mother would be glad to help you with that."

In retrospect, Mother Teresa's negative response to a TV drama based on her life is not difficult to understand. At that time the only movies she had seen had been the sentimental and escapist romances of the Indian cinema. She could see no evangelical possibilities in them.

I also suspect she was concerned with the way we would present her. Saints are detached from many things, but not from their public image.

Nor should they be.

Dorothy Day took a similar tact. "Wait until I'm dead," she said.

Yet with "The Other Wiseman" on the back burner, I remained intrigued with heroes—with stories that would make their viewers proud to be human beings—and so we developed the concept for a series of two-hour TV movies on contemporary heroes—Klaus Von Stauffenberg, Antonia Brenner, Cesar Chavez, Lech Walesa, Helen Caldicott, and Dag Hammarskjöld—to which we gave the generic title of "Courageous People." Jim McGinn helped with the research and was enthusiastic about the concept. He thought his superiors at Bristol-Myers might be interested in these, too.

So it was that in June of 1983 I found myself in the New York offices of Marvin Koslow, Jim's boss and the head of advertising at Bristol-Myers. I had carefully prepared my presentation of "Courageous People," and Marvin listened with considerable interest. "I like the idea," he said, after pondering a bit, "but it doesn't work for us because we do not have enough products to fill up the advertising slots on a two-hour special. What do you have in the hour form? That's what we're looking for."

I gulped and pulled "The Other Wiseman" off the back burner. "That's a good story," Marvin said after I had finished, with just a touch of a tear in his eye. "A damn good story. Can you get me a concept piece within a week?"

We had the concept piece on his desk within four days, and within two weeks we had a commitment from Bristol-Myers to finance the script. To avoid any possibility of conflict of interest, Jim McGinn did not feel he should write it, so I selected another of our "Insight" writers, one of the best. He labored long and hard during August of 1983 and had a first draft on my desk by Labor Day. I made some suggestions for the rewrite, but I was still not satisfied with what resulted. So I did a version of my own and submitted that to Bristol-Myers. They rejected it, and the project seemed dead in the water.

I talked the situation over with Jim McGinn, and he said Bristol-Myers still liked the concept but was not about to put up the money for another script. I debated within myself whether Paulist Productions should do it. It seemed too good an opportunity to let die, so I decided to take the risk.

Looking around for another writer, I settled upon Tom Fontana, a playwright and one of the producers and principal writers of "St. Elsewhere," whom I had gotten to know through Humanitas. He, too, had heard the story as a boy and been captivated by it. The Holy Spirit seemed to be working overtime. Tom was delighted to be asked to do the script, cleared the project with his superiors, and agreed to work weekends and nights on it. He also came up with the theatrical device—an everyman servant for the wise man—that the first script had lacked, and which was needed to make the story work. By October 15 I had a first draft, and by November 1 I had a script I was delighted with. I submitted the script, now entitled *The Fourth Wiseman,* to Bristol-Myers, and they shared my enthusiasm. Together we met with the ABC people in charge of specials—John Hamlin and Luana Newman. I told them the story. They liked it. They read the script. They liked it even better. ABC agreed to make a prime-time hour available. Bristol-Myers agreed to purchase the time and supply the production budget. Paulist Productions agreed to produce the program. Nobody doubted Mike Rhodes was the right man to direct it. But we needed to agree about cast. I drew up a list for the top two roles. Martin Sheen headed my list for the wise man, partially because he was such a superb actor, partially because he was such a good friend who believed so fully in what we were trying to accomplish. Alan Arkin headed my list for his everyman servant, because he had the depth, range, and comedic sense the part required. Bristol-Myers and ABC approved both, with some backups in each case. We contacted Arkin. He committed himself at once. We contacted Sheen. He could not get free for the four weeks we needed to rehearse and shoot. We went to the backups. They weren't available. I drew up a new list. Only a few were acceptable to both Bristol-Myers and ABC, and they were not available either. We had hoped to air the special at Easter of 1984, but now we were running out of time. Finally Bristol-Myers withdrew its commitment. Marvin very wisely did not want to compromise quality by putting us in a time crunch.

It looked like "The Other Wiseman" was once again dead. So close to a network breakthrough, yet so far away.

Fortunately, through Jim McGinn's gentle advocacy, we were able to resurrect the project in June of 1984. Marvin Koslow agreed that if we could get Martin Sheen and Alan Arkin, he would renew his commitment. ABC did likewise. Again Alan committed, and finally Martin was able to get loose for the week of rehearsal and the three weeks of shooting we would need in late October and November.

The signals were once again flashing green.

Mike Rhodes began preproduction just after Labor Day. With Lewis Abel's help, he was able to assemble a superb free-lance crew. We found an old mansion in East Hollywood that looked like a magi's palace. We decided to use the unusual rock formations near Vasquez in the Antelope Valley for the leper colony and to build the Bethlehem and Jerusalem streets at the Paramount Ranch in Malibu. The desert scenes would be shot in Death Valley. Paramount Pictures agreed to lend us their biblical props and sets, and Sun Classics, which was going out of business, agreed to sell us their entire stock of biblical costumes for five thousand dollars.

While Mike and Lewis worked at preproduction, I concentrated on the cast, setting Eileen Brennan, Richard Libertini,

Ralph Bellamy, Lance Kerwin, Jerry Houser, Sydney Penny, and Charlie Sheen to round out the superlative ensemble.

The filming was scheduled to begin with an all-night shoot at the magi's palace on Friday, October 26, 1984. The previous Wednesday, we launched the production with a Mass and a party to which the cast and the crew brought their families. More than one hundred and fifty people attended. The Mass was an important part of the mix, I felt, so as to make it clear to everyone what we were doing and why we were doing it. We were making a show about God. We were making it for God. But it was also important, I told them in the homily, to make it *with* God, to invite Him in on the creative process, to tap into His creative energies. It was also important, I said, to ask Him to help us transcend our egos and love each other as we made the show, despite the inevitable and intense pressures of the production.

At Vasquez Rocks, at Death Valley, and at Paramount Ranch (where we used the well top in the Bethlehem square as an altar), we also celebrated Mass together. The Jews, the Protestants, the unaffiliated, as well as the Catholics, participated. It made for a different type of production experience.

Mike was well prepared and had plenty of support, so, despite the magnitude of the shoot, it went smoothly. We got our extras from the local parishes, Hasidic boys with the paeot down the sides of their faces from a local orthodox synagogue, and an Israeli dance troupe for our harvest festival scene from a nearby temple. The only time we could shoot this scene was on a Friday night. They hesitated to commit themselves because it was their Sabbath. But they talked it over and decided this was indeed God's work, so they decided to go ahead. We were grateful.

Midway through the shoot, with the strain of the production becoming intense, several of the actors, all of whom were being paid the same—union minimum—began to give Jim McGinn a tough time, saying he had used me to get them to work below their going rate and thus secure for Bristol-Myers a cheaper than usual show. This was both untrue and unfair. I got wind of it and decided I ought to confront the problem head-on. I assembled the actors and explained to them that the show was my idea; I had talked Bristol-Myers into it; they had given me the budget I had requested; from an advertising standpoint, a biblical show was not as good a buy for them as a contemporary one; and they were doing this for the same reason we all were: to give the American viewing public an Easter present, to say something important to them about the meaning and purpose of human life. I also told them I thought they had been doing an excellent job under difficult circumstances and that I appreciated it more than I could tell them. They asked questions about the dollars involved and seemed satisfied by my answers. As a result, their anger subsided, they apologized to Jim, and went back to the superlative performances they had been giving.

We completed *The Fourth Wiseman* on the eighteen-day schedule we had planned and, while I went off to Ethiopia, Mike plunged into the editing. By the time I returned in the second week of December, he had a rough cut for me to look at. I saw two things at once: With exquisite performances, superb photography, marvelous production values, and a story that worked, we had the makings of an excellent show; and we were very long and would have to make significant cuts. Here I made a serious mistake. I felt ABC should be part of the decision-making process about what should be cut, so, in response to their frequent requests, I screened the rough cut for them. The people from the specials department who saw it were accustomed to looking at taped variety shows and so were unimpressed with the film rough cut we showed them; so unimpressed that they formed a negative view of the whole project. This was to hurt us later.

We made the cuts, completed the edit, added the sound effects, recorded the music, did the color corrections, and screened the completed show for our Board of Directors and their guests. Their response was enthusiastic. With an exultant gleam in his eyes, Peter Mullin came up to me afterward and said, "We've got a hit."

We were happy with what we had made. But what would the critics think? And more important, how would the viewing public respond?

Airdate was set for March 30, the Saturday night before Palm Sunday. Bristol-Myers hired the public relations firm of Gail Cottman Associates to promote the picture. It was a felicitous choice. Gail loved the picture, was bright and aggressive, and knew how to get results. I found her a delight to work with. She did a series of two- and three-minute video segments for transmission via satellite to the local TV stations around the country for insertion in their newscasts. With Martin Sheen and Alan Arkin off on other projects and so unavailable, I did most of the interviews. "Sixty Minutes" did a segment in which Morley Safer contrasted our approach to evangelization with Jimmy Swaggart's. The televangelist and I did the "CBS Morning News" together. AP and UPI both did stories, and Gail had me travel to Washington, D.C., Philadelphia, New York, Boston, Detroit, and Chicago for both press and TV interviews. And I did more than forty-five press interviews by phone. The uniqueness of the event—it was the first time a priest had produced a commercial, dramatic program in network prime time—was the angle taken by most of the reporters. *Advertising* magazine did an in-depth feature on me personally and carried my picture on their front cover. You can imagine what the priests at the dinner table did with that one.

Because of the negative impression they had formed of the project, ABC did not do as much promotion as we had hoped. This especially hurt us in the "on the air" department. Elsewhere Gail was able to take up the slack, and ABC did supply tapes of the show to the nation's TV critics. Their reaction was better than we could have hoped. *People* magazine called it "a small and charming tale that relies more on storytelling than sermonizing." "An inspired fable," said the *New York Times*. "The plot is simple, the imagery vivid, and the intended lessons blazingly clear. The message is timeless." The *Detroit News* said "it has all the earmarks of a television classic, one of those shows that keep coming back for encores around the Christmas holidays." The *L.A. Times*, *TV Guide*, and the *Philadelphia Inquirer* were also enthusiastic, as were scores of other papers across the country. Bristol-Myers said they had never seen such an avalanche of favorable publicity. ABC was so impressed that their executive in charge wrote Jim McGinn and me letters apologizing for misjudging the program and for the lack of promotional support they had given it.

I watched the program with Jim and Patty McGinn at their home in the Pacific Palisades, awed by the realization that millions of other Americans were also watching it at the same time.

Marvin Koslow called me the following Monday to tell me how happy Bristol-Myers was with the whole project. "Twenty million Americans were given something very special last Saturday night," he said, "and we were very proud to be part of it."

The Fourth Wiseman made me something of a mini-celebrity. I had had personal exposure before but nothing as concentrated or as widespread as this. Part of me enjoyed the celebrity role. Everybody knew who I was. Everybody seemed interested in what I had to say. Most everybody wanted to be my friend. Who wouldn't like that? Suddenly, if only for one brief period, I had a high-profile national platform from which to communicate the Gospel. Nothing wrong with that either. But part of me recognized how dangerous fame can be, how seductively deadly it can become. I found myself basking in what others were saying about me, reading stories three and four times. I began to allow my idea of myself to be formed by what others said about me, instead of taking it from my own experience of myself as weak and needy, wounded and flawed. None too soon I realized I was in danger of entering a world of illusion, a sure recipe for spiritual and psychological disaster. Fame is like a narcotic. It can take us away from the loneliness, fear, guilt, and emptiness; in a word, from the non-being that is so much a part of the human situation and so necessary an experience if we are to remain rooted in the real world and achieve psychic health.

It can also split apart a tight team in which everybody subordinates their individual interests and works for the good of the whole. It can make its members suspicious and jealous of each other.

This experience gave me some understanding of and sympathy for the problems of superstardom, whether athletic, political, ecclesiastical, journalistic, or cinematic. It also made me aware that if sometime in the future I have to act again in a high-profile way, I must never, under any conditions, allow this to separate me from my teammates or from the non-being within myself. To lose that, I now know, is to lose myself—and God—and that is entirely too high a price to pay.

CHAPTER 16

WE ARE THE CHILDREN

I returned from Ethiopia in December of 1984 torn up by the question: How can an American middle-class psyche cope with the kind of horror in which I had been immersed? I needed the answer for myself. I was still trying to make sense of what I had seen on the most basic of levels. But the more I thought about the famine, the more I also saw it had the makings of a compelling movie of the week. Certainly it was high-concept. Television, magazines, and newspapers had deluged the American public with vivid pictures of the famine. Most people had been seared by those images and many had, as a result, made an emotional investment in the welfare of those hungry children. Such a motion picture would also be rich in Gospel implications, not only because it was about the poor and the hungry but because life in a refugee camp, I was beginning to see, left an American with only three options: get out, go crazy, or reach for God as you let yourself be stripped of everything. I was especially taken with the dramatic possibilities of the stripping process, possibly because I was caught up in something of a stripping process of my own.

This was not the first time I had tried to create a movie of the week. "Courageous People" was in that genre. And even before *The Fourth Wiseman* had given us the network breakthrough we sought and established our credibility as prime-time producers, we had taken the first steps toward placing movies of the week on the networks.

Christine Foster, a former Immaculate Heart nun who was the executive in charge of MOWs for Columbia Pictures, was my mentor. "It's a tough and competitive game," she said. "You've got to pitch twenty ideas to get one script commitment, and you have to prepare five scripts for every production commitment you're going to get. No fun." She also tried to give me some idea of network thinking, what they were looking for, what they considered commercial. "There's no absolute incompatibility between your agenda and theirs," she said, "but you're going to have to look very hard for the areas of overlap."

Through Christine, "Insight," and Humanitas, I was able to form collaborative relationships with the principal players at the networks. All were intrigued by the possibility of our producing for them. On a rather regular basis, I began to discuss movie of the week ideas with them. Initially I did not fully understand their agenda, and so my early pitches were wide of the mark. But as time went on and the dialogue deepened, I began to come up with ideas that they liked a lot.

In the spring of 1982, CBS's Greg Maday called to say that the Oscar-winning Jon Voight was ready to do his first television movie and that he wanted to play a priest.

"Would Paulist Productions be interested," he asked, "in collaborating with Jon's production company to create such a movie?"

"We would," I replied.

Greg committed CBS to a script deal.

In June of 1983, I pitched the Dorothy Day story to NBC's Karen Danaher. She liked it and got us a script commitment.

In January of 1984, I pitched ABC's Lou Ehrlict a concept that blossomed into "DMZ," an idea for an hour television series. He committed to a two-hour pilot script and turned it over to Ann Daniels and Jordon Kerner.

In the spring of 1985, CBS's Peter Frankovich told me he wanted to do a terrorism story and suggested I submit some ideas. I did. The result was a script commitment for *Pressure Point.*

All of these projects were stillborn. One out of five, Christine had said. I liked the script we prepared for Jon Voight, but neither CBS nor Jon's producer did, so they turned it down. Karen Danaher left NBC to head up Don Ohlmeyer's TV operation, so Dorothy Day was left without a friend in court and was rejected. Jordon Kerner loved our "DMZ" script and was ready to make it, but when he left to become an independent producer (Lou Ehrlict and Ann Daniels had already left) his successor at ABC rejected it.

The executive to whom Peter Frankovich assigned *Pressure*

Point loved the script we had developed. But when Peter was shifted to mini-series and the executive was fired, the project got caught in the cross fire. It, too, was rejected.

We Are the Children was to have a happier fate.

Skiing with my sister and her family at Tahoe after Christmas in 1984, I started to outline a story set in the Ethiopian famine. By mid-January my mind was racing, my creative juices were flowing, and the characters in the story were starting to come alive. I presented the concept to Eileen Berg at ABC who liked it but made certain suggestions. I rethought the story accordingly. The main character became Annie Keats, an idealistic yet unbelieving twenty-seven-year-old American doctor who volunteers for a three-month stint at a mission clinic in Ethiopia. Never having known real pain or deprivation, Annie looks at life through rose-colored glasses. There is no problem she cannot solve, no challenge she is not equal to. All you need is intelligence, goodwill, and lots of hard work, she told herself. Shortly after arriving in Ethiopia in September of 1984, she finds herself engulfed by the famine. The heart of the drama is her struggle to deal with it.

She has little difficulty letting go of the physical comforts to which she is accustomed. But letting go of her morally superior and supremely competent self-image is something else again. By the end of the story, Annie has grown up and learned to live in the real world of pain and need and insoluble problems. She had wanted to give so much to the poor Ethiopians. Now she realizes they have so much more to give to her.

In late February I presented the recast story to Eileen with a seven-page treatment that delineated the concept, depicted Annie's character, and described the stages in her emotional arc as she struggles to cope with the famine. Eileen liked the changes and promised to present it to her boss. I held my breath.

In late March she called.

"I have good news and I have bad news," she said. "The good news is you have a script commitment if you can find a writer we can agree on." I breathed a prayer of thanksgiving. "The bad news is," she went on, "I am leaving this department and moving over to ABC Circle Films to become a producer."

"Here we go again," I sighed to myself.

I drew up a list of writers I thought would be good for the project. Most were not available. ABC suggested Michael DeGuzman. I read three of his screenplays and liked them. We had lunch together, and I liked him even more. He read my treatment and looked at the footage we had shot in Ethiopia and was intrigued. We decided to work together on the project.

Twice a week during the latter part of May and the first part of June, we spent the afternoon talking through the story, the situation, the characters and their evolving relationships. Mike decided he wanted to add an Ethiopian woman—Amassa—to the ensemble of supporting characters. She joined Duffy, the cynical American reporter who becomes Annie's love interest; Kebret, the guerrilla leader; Brenda, the American nun; and Emmanuel, the Ethiopian priest—the last two of whom work with Annie at the mission. In the process, Mike drew up a detailed outline of the story, which we presented to ABC in the latter part of June. They liked it and gave us the green light to proceed to screenplay.

For the next six weeks, Mike worked alone. By the first part of August, he gave me a first draft. I made some suggestions, he incorporated them, and our story was starting to take shape. A couple more polishes, and I was happy with it. We submitted it to ABC early in October. We then had to work our way through the layers of personnel whose approval we needed to get a production OK. Our liaison, Eileen's replacement, liked the script but wanted to give the nun a problem—temper, drinking, something. Her boss had more serious problems.

"There's too much talk about God in this script," he said. "This isn't 'Insight.' It's not a religious show. It's prime-time network television."

"Look," I shot back, "this is a spiritual growth story, the story of a girl who becomes a woman by dealing with an impossible situation."

"Can't she do that without God?" he asked.

"In Ethiopia most people don't," I said.

"I don't want God in the story," he shouted.

"Are you telling me," I asked, "you feel you have the right to exclude from your prime-time programming the beliefs and values of 95 percent of the American people?"

"You say 95 percent," he retorted. "The people I go around with don't believe in God."

He was right. Most of the unmarried professionals in their early thirties who live in Beverly Hills do not profess any religious faith. At least they don't express it by serving the poor or going to church. But fortunately they are not typical of the country. Nor of those working in the feeding centers of Ethiopia.

Some of his other script suggestions were good ones, and we tried to implement them. In our next meeting, he said the religious dimension of the story no longer bothered him. By December we had a script everybody was happy with. But that did not mean a green light for production. It simply meant we had completed the rewrite process.

In January we were informed that the president of ABC Entertainment had read the script and thought it was all right. Not great, just all right. I was beginning to feel their fear. They sincerely wanted to do something about starving people. I had no doubt about the genuineness of their humanistic impulses. But they were very afraid of the price they might be asked to pay for having followed those impulses. At the heart of their dilemma was the very real question: How much painful reality will the American viewing public support in an entertainment medium? Wrestling with the dilemma, the executive in charge told me this kind of program would pull the needed ratings only if it could be billed as a major TV event. And a TV event meant not only a major star or two, but a superstar.

I was given a list of eight actors who fit this category—Sally Field, Jane Fonda, Meryl Streep, Ann-Margret, Tom Selleck, Jeff Bridges, Mel Gibson, and Ted Danson—and told that if I could secure any one of them, ABC would authorize the shoot. I gulped and said, "You guys are expecting a miracle."

"That's why we've got you," the executive said with a smile.

I agreed to give it a try.

I liked Sally in the role. She was not twenty-seven years old but had a girlishness about her, a vulnerability that made her right. Her people read the script but passed, saying it was not what she was looking for. Jane's people thought she was too old. Meryl's agent said they were not interested in TV, and Ann-Margret was not available. Nor was Tom Selleck or Mel Gibson. That left Jeff and Ted. I had given Jeff his first acting job on "Insight" fifteen years before and knew he was passionate about the hunger problem, and so I thought I had a chance. He read it but was unenthusiastic about the part and had severe scheduling problems.

That left Ted Danson. I called his agent, and she said he was not available. I broke down the script and concluded that we could shoot all of his scenes in two weeks. Through a mutual friend, I checked out his schedule and found a two-week window between a movie of the week commitment and his return to "Cheers." I called back his agent. She became impatient. "Father Kieser," she shouted into the phone, "you're not hearing me. He's not available. You got it? Not available."

My back was now against the wall. I decided to do what you are not supposed to do: go over the head of an agent and approach the client directly. So I asked the mutual friend to give me Ted's home number. He did not feel right about that, but he did give me the home number of Ted's partner, Dan Fauci.

When I told Dan the situation, he said, "There's no way Ted Danson will turn down a script about hungry children. Get it to me and I'll have him read it." Ted read and liked the script. He, Dan, and Ted's wife, Casey, stopped by the office the next day to tell me why he couldn't do it.

"Look," he said, "I'm starting my own production company. This doesn't fit. I usually get leads. This isn't. The schedule is tight, almost impossible. I don't see how I can make it work."

I showed them some of the pictures we had taken in Ethiopia. Casey devoured the pictures of the kids.

"Here's the situation, Ted," I said. "With you the picture will be made. Without you, it won't. It's as simple as that. When again will you have the opportunity to do a picture that will actually save lives?"

I was playing hardball. He knew it. So did I. "Explain that to me," Ted said.

I did, telling him about the continuing problem, not only in Ethiopia but in Mozambique and the Sudan, about the lack of political will in this country, about compassion fatigue.

"I'll let you know tomorrow," he said as he walked out. He did. It was affirmative. ABC could not believe it. We had the picture.

I let Ted tell his agent.

I now brought John Furia aboard as supervising producer with Mike Rhodes and Lewis Abel as producers. Together we tried to figure out how to make the best possible picture within the confines of Ted's two-week window.

One option was to build the mission compound in the Mojave Desert—the terrain was not dissimilar to Ethiopia's—and use as extras some of the ten thousand Ethiopian refugees in Los Angeles, many of whom were looking for work. By intercutting this footage with second-unit shooting in Africa, we felt we could make a good picture. But somehow it seemed a cheat. The terrain might look the same. But the people would not. They had the high cheekbones but not the angular, hungry look. Too many of them had been eating at McDonald's.

The only alternative was to go for broke and shoot the entire picture in Africa. This would require Ted to work fourteen straight days, flying three and filming eleven. That was asking a lot. I hesitated to ask, but when I did, he immediately agreed.

Weeks later he was to publicly thank me, saying his trip to Africa was the most rewarding experience of his life.

But where in Africa should we shoot? Ethiopia was the obvious first choice. My friends in the American Red Cross checked with their friends in the Ethiopian Red Cross, and there seemed to be no problem. In fact the Ethiopian Red Cross offered to sponsor the project and be our liaison with the Ethiopian government. It seemed too good to be true. It was.

Mike Rhodes flew off to Ethiopia to begin the preparations.

John Furia and I concentrated on rounding out the American cast and selecting the right director.

The role of Annie was the crucial one. It was her story, and whoever played her would make or break the movie. ABC did not like most of the suggestions we came up with, one of whom was Ally Sheedy. They were afraid she was too young. I saw everything she had made and concluded this should not be a major problem. I also met with her and saw how deeply she understood the transition Annie goes through and how passionate she was about the Third World. I decided to recommend her wholeheartedly. ABC said yes.

ABC also approved Judith Ivey, our first choice for Brenda, the American nun. She read the script and immediately agreed to play it.

The other actors we would get in England or Africa.

We still did not have a director, probably the most important single ingredient in the making of a movie.

I submitted a list to ABC. They rejected most of them. Those they approved were not available. I submitted another list. They approved even fewer, none of whom were available. They gave me a list of people they liked. I was not enthusiastic about any of them. It seemed we were at an impasse and the precious days of preparation were scooting by.

I decided to recommend Mike Rhodes. He had not done a two-hour movie of the week before. But he had lived and shot in the Third World, knew how to relate to its people, had made some superlative hour shows for the various network series, and had a special talent at eliciting exceptional performances from actors. I made up my mind to fight for him.

I did not have to. ABC decided to trust John Furia and me and gave their approval. I called Mike in Addis Ababa to give him the good news. I also called the actors' agents to fill them in.

Two days later John Furia and I flew off to Ethiopia to finalize the arrangement with the Ethiopian government and to look over the locations that Mike had selected. Up until this point, neither the Ethiopian government nor the Ethiopian Red Cross had asked to see the script. The morning of our arrival, they did. That night I had dinner with the head of the Ethiopian Red Cross, who thought things would go smoothly. After dinner an official of the government asked to see me.

"Would you be willing," he asked, "to delete the section of the script where the heroine is captured by the guerrillas and to remove any mention of them in the other parts of the story?"

As politely as I could, I tried to explain how impossible that would be, since the civil war was one of the principal causes of the famine, and Annie's experiences in captivity were essential steps in her spiritual growth.

At that time I did not know the Ethiopian government, in all its official pronouncements, denied the very existence of the guerrillas.

The official nodded at my answer and excused himself. The next morning we were informed that our case had gone as high as the country's vice president, that permission for the shoot had been refused, and that the government was being gracious enough to allow us to leave the country. Thanks a lot.

We took the next plane for Nairobi, where Mohinder Dhillon met us at the airport, submitted our script to the Kenyan government, and got permission for us to film in that country. For several days we flew by small plane from one mission to another in the northern part of Kenya until we found Korr, a small town in the Kaisuti Desert where the terrain and the racial mix of the people are like those in Ethiopia.

Then the bombshell hit. Exhausted, I went to bed early one night in Nairobi and was awakened by a phone call from Los Angeles. The actors and their agents had gotten together and decided they would not do the picture with a director who had not done a movie of the week before. "We have nothing against Mike Rhodes," they said. "We just want a more experienced director."

That night in my hotel room I turned to John Furia and said, "What is He doing to us?"

As upset as I, he replied, "I don't know. I just don't know."

By long-distance telephone I tried to reason with the actors and their agents. They were adamant. I decided to fly home at once to try to turn them around. I spent ten days trying. It was futile. They had careers and followings they were just not willing to entrust to a director who did not have years and years of experience.

Meanwhile, as one anguished day followed another, we were losing the time we needed to properly prepare the shoot.

Finally, in desperation, I threw in the towel and agreed to hire another director. Mike was very disappointed, but, transcending his ego, agreed to stay on and produce the movie.

Ally Sheedy's agent suggested Bob Young. I looked at his films and liked them. A documentarian who had lived and shot in Africa, I could see he had a unique ability to communicate with actors. Ted Danson liked him, too, and ABC gave their approval. I approached him. He was interested, he said. He read the script overnight. A deeply religious man in an unconventional way, he understood it intuitively. He had just one problem. He was not sure he could extricate himself from his present commitments. He anguished almost a week about doing so. We were down to the wire.

I can still remember the Sunday morning near the end of that week. I stopped by his house at 9 A.M. He was still in bed when I arrived, but we talked for an hour, after which I ran off to celebrate the ten-thirty Mass. At the end of Mass, I told the people of my problem and asked them to pray for Bob, that he might say yes. At twelve-thirty I was back at Bob's, and we continued to talk about the project. In the course of this conversation I told him I had four hundred and fifty people praying for him. He gulped and said, "What is this—pray or play?"

The following day, Bob committed. Having lost almost three

weeks of preparation, we were at last back on track. He spent the next day working with Mike DeGuzman on the script and the three following days rehearsing with Ally and Ted. Then, with Mike Rhodes, he flew off to join Lewis Abel in Kenya. We had a short three weeks to prepare the shoot.

John Furia and I stayed behind in Los Angeles to finish the casting, assemble the crew, and negotiate the license fee with ABC. I thought our problems were over. I did not know they were just beginning.

The negotiations took longer than we expected, and ABC was less generous than we had hoped, but finally we were able to make a deal with which everybody was satisfied. For economic reasons, John decided on a British crew. He hired—let us call him —Jim Stafford to put it together. A Welshman, Jim came highly recommended. Nobody knew that a picture in which he had recently invested a great deal of his own time, money, and dreams had just collapsed, and he was a bitterly unhappy man.

In Kenya Bob Young and Mike Rhodes, with Lewis Abel's help, were finalizing the locations. The mission compound would be built at Korr, a small village in the Kaisuti Desert, 280 miles north of Nairobi, with a mission, a school, and two cooperative Indian priests. We would shoot there for the last eighteen days. The first four days would be spent at Marsabit, a town with a game lodge and other accoutrements of civilization on a plateau that jutted up from the desert floor in the most northern part of Kenya.

Shortly thereafter Jim Stafford, accompanied by the key members of the crew, arrived in Nairobi and immediately clashed with Mike Rhodes and Lewis Abel. Jim did not want to take orders from them, especially in front of his British compatriots. Part of this was age. They were younger. Part of it seemed to be a very wounded self-image that had been rubbed raw by his recent disappointments. Part, too, was his serious misreading of them. Their dialogical management style, openness to advice, and general vulnerability seemed to him to be incompetence. "Fucked amateurs," he called them more than once.

Nothing could have been further from the truth.

Back in L.A., I was only distantly aware of the seriousness of the problem, and so I responded favorably when Jim—and the accountant he had hired—requested authorization to sign checks. "If we can't trust them, we shouldn't have hired them," John

Furia said in recommending it. I went along. It was a mistake. It gave Jim entirely too much power. Later on it allowed him to forget who was boss and take the show hostage.

Meanwhile we got some other bad news. John Furia had gone to the doctor because he had been feeling washed out. The diagnosis: mononucleosis.

We talked it over. "No show is worth jeopardizing your health for," I told him. He agreed but thought he could return to Kenya for the shoot if he was careful and paced himself. I said OK.

Bob Young, seeing the locations and the tribal people, decided he wanted to shift the emphasis of the picture from what he construed to be a white people's story with a black people's background to a story of white and black people reaching out to each other across the racial and ethnic divide. He also wanted to make some significant script changes. I liked his idea of whites and blacks connecting, but the proposed script changes made me uneasy, partially because we were so close to start date, partially because with Bob in Nairobi there was no way to involve ABC in the decision-making process. In addition John Furia and Michael DeGuzman were opposed to them. I decided to move up my departure and fly at once to Nairobi to discuss them with Bob. I should have asked Michael DeGuzman to come with me.

Bob and I spent six hours discussing the script on the day I arrived, but we came to no meeting of the minds. Finally, with the shooting date approaching and the crew clamoring for direction, I yielded. There seemed nothing else to do.

The cast and crew were aware of the script differences between Bob and me. They were also aware of the rancorous personal conflict between Jim Stafford on one hand and Mike and Lewis on the other. By this time, I suspect, I was also considered one of the rank amateurs, the object of Jim's scorn. I should have confronted him up front and made it clear that he reported to Mike and Lewis, who reported to John Furia, who reported to me; but I was so afraid of a delay that I put it off and allowed the lines of authority to become muddied. This was confusing for the crew, and it put Mike in an impossible position. It was a hell of a way to begin a shoot.

I suggested we have a Mass at Marsabit Lodge the night before we were to begin. "The crew's already overextended," I was told, "maybe later." Again I yielded. I should have gone ahead with the Mass for whoever chose to attend. Not having it allowed the basic religious motivation for making the picture to be obscured in the minds of too many people. It also deprived us of an influx of love energy that we would desperately need in the weeks ahead.

At Marsabit we lived in a lovely game lodge that is situated on the banks of a lake in a forest that is populated by antelope, baboon, lion, and elephant. The four days we were scheduled to shoot there became five, but I was happy with the quality of what we were getting. The British crew was hardworking and solidly professional. They were still playing catch-up, but morale was reasonably good. Ally, Ted, and Judith had fallen in love with the people, the terrain, and the animals and were turning in quality performances.

In Korr, where we moved next, the living conditions were more primitive. Each of us had our own small tent, pitched on the desert floor. Every ten tents had a latrine and every four a shower, into the top of which a bucket of warm water could be poured. At one end of our tent city was the kitchen and mess hall for the food, which was quite adequate. At the other end was the airstrip. Nairobi was an hour and a half away by small plane, twenty hours by truck. The closest phone was sixty miles away. We did have a shortwave radio, which occasionally worked well enough to enable us to communicate with our production office in Nairobi.

Ten thousand people of the Rendille and Samburu tribes lived in the villages that were scattered about Korr. They are a warm and hospitable people who live by grazing their camels, goats, and cattle between the highlands where there is vegetation and Lake Turkana—eighty miles away—where there is water. Their way of life is not unlike Abraham's of forty centuries before.

We fell in love with them.

The mission compound had been constructed about a mile from our living area. It was composed of a church, school, three houses, and a warehouse. It was there we shot each day. The equatorial sun was brutal, and the temperatures frequently approached 105. The wind was incessant, sometimes whipping the red sand into mini-tornadoes. Bob Young's gray beard took on a decidedly reddish hue, as did my blond hair.

On one shooting day, the roof of the warehouse was lifted ten feet into the air by one of these small tornadoes and dropped back down atop a hundred extras. Fortunately no one was seriously hurt.

There was no wild game in the area and next to no vegetation; only an occasional acacia tree. We had none of the usual problems with dysentery. Not even germs could live in the Kaisuti Desert.

At first our people were captured by the romance of the desert —so inhospitable to physical life, yet so supportive of the life of the spirit; and by its inhabitants—so poor on the outside, so rich on the inside. Ally said her first hours at Korr were the most fulfilling of her entire life.

But as one day followed another, the romance began to fade. Part was fatigue. The crew insisted on working seven days a week. "What's there to do here?" they asked. "We'd rather take our days off in Nairobi." I foolishly went along.

By the second week, Korr had become a drag; and by the third and last week, all of us were dying to get out of the place.

Contributing to the malaise was the continuing rancor between Jim and the coterie with which he had surrounded himself and Mike, Lewis, and me. The situation deteriorated further when John Furia's mononucleosis flared, and he was forced to go home. Jim moved into the power vacuum created by his absence. For the sake of the show, Mike decided not to contest his running of the crew. He would concentrate his energies on organizing the Rendille and Samburu tribespeople, hundreds of whom were working for us every day as extras. I focused my energies on Bob Young and the actors.

Late one night, after the actors and I had gone to bed, Jim got drunk and got into a shouting match with Lewis. As a result he told the crew not to show up for work the next morning. Two hours after the original call, the associate producer talked him into relenting. But you can imagine what that did to the emotional peaking of the actors. "I don't understand," Ally said, "how people can worry about these things when children are starving."

That afternoon Jim Stafford gave me an ultimatum: get rid of Lewis or he would quit and take the crew with him. I refused to send Lewis home but asked Jim as a personal favor not to carry out his threat. Two days later he apparently decided to go ahead with it, changing his mind only at the last minute. Why did he pull back? I was not able to find out. Perhaps he took a poll. I was reliably informed that only six persons of the sixty-person crew would have gone with him. But even those six would have cost us a couple of shooting days that I could not afford.

The morning after the ultimatum, I wore a reddish cross about my neck to the location.

"What's that?" Jim asked.

"That's my exorcism cross," I answered.

He didn't get it.

That night I dreamed the small plane in which Jim was flying crashed. As I awakened, I was aware that part of me was mourning his death and part was saying, "Served the bastard right."

I think there is a direct correlation between the amount of love the members of a production team share with each other, the enthusiasm they feel for the picture they are making, and the quality of the performances delivered by its actors.

By the time of the mutiny threat, Ted Danson had returned to Los Angeles to resume the shooting of "Cheers." Ally and Judith behaved like troopers and made the best of a very difficult situation. So did Khadijan Ali Ahmed, the lovely Somalian woman whom everybody called Lam Lam and who played Amassa, the Ethiopian woman who became Annie's Ethiopian sister. Zia Mohyeddin, who played the mission priest, did the same. Both turned in exemplary performances.

I think Bob Young had a lot to do with containing the negative vibes. His creative energy, enthusiasm for the project, and unselfish concern for the cast and crew were exceptional. He kept everybody's spirits up.

We became very close in the course of the shoot.

Jim Stafford was not the only problem person at Korr. At three o'clock one morning, one of the night guards forced his way into Lam Lam's tent and tried to rape her. Fortunately I got there in time. He was arrested and taken to Nairobi. Lam Lam handled it very well. Father Murphy never told me it would be like this.

Nor did he tell me that with 90 percent of the picture in the can, the head of the local police would point his automatic rifle at me and say, "Father Kieser, I have orders to shut you down."

I did not know whether he was serious or not, so I said, "Joseph, don't you know it's a sin to point a gun at a priest?"

He didn't laugh.

"Father Kieser, I have orders to shut you down—now!"

He meant business.

It seems the Ethiopian government found out we were shooting in Kenya and lodged a strong protest with the Kenyan government. Closing us down was their way of placating their northern neighbor.

We flew immediately to Nairobi, met with the officials involved, and finally, after two protracted meetings and a lot of promises, got the order of closure lifted.

Another near disaster. Even so, it cost us a full shooting day.

Over the years I have learned to enjoy the filmmaking process. Making motion pictures can be fun. But the making of *We Are the Children* was no fun. Never before had I lost control of a shoot. The uncertainty about what Jim Stafford would do next, the calculated rudeness of his coterie of people, the hurt in Mike's eyes at my failure to protect him, combined with the difficulties inherent in a Third World shoot made it the most unpleasant experience of my professional life. If my first and most important responsibility as a priest is to build a loving community, I had failed miserably.

I knew about taking one day at a time. Some days I couldn't do that. I had to take one hour at a time. The hospitality of the two local priests, the friendship of Bob Young and the lighting crew—I ate with them most nights—and the hour of prayer a day got me through it. It was months before I could forgive Jim Stafford.

Not that there were not bright spots. Ally and Judith got especially close to the local children and bought bright clothes for some of them. The mission school was overcrowded and needed four additional classrooms. At five thousand dollars apiece, Ted and Dan financed one, Ally and Bob another, Paulist Productions a third, and when I got back and told Christine Foster about it, she put together a group of her friends to pay for the fourth. I remember the people of Korr with great fondness. They were desperately poor and many were acutely hungry. The money we paid them was not only very welcome but also badly needed. Most of the people had never worked for wages before. Their situation confronted us with a strange irony. We were making a film about starving people in the midst of a people who did not themselves have enough to eat. Yet their poverty did not diminish the warmth of their hospitality nor the depth of their joy. Like the Ethiopians with Annie, they had much to teach us about what's really important and where human happiness is to be found.

An additional irony: We were making a picture about a person being stripped, and in the process Mike, Lewis, and I were undergoing a kind of stripping of our own.

Finally we completed the picture. In order to decompress, Bob Young and Charles Stewart, the cameraman, decided to take a couple of camels and hike across the desert to Lake Turkana. Mike decided to go scuba diving at Mombasa. Battered and bruised in spirit, I just wanted to get home.

During October and the early part of November, under Bob Young's supervision, Arthur Coburn and Eddie Beyer edited the picture. Initially the executives at ABC were enthusiastic. (They were not the same ones we had developed the story with. During the course of the preparation and shooting of the picture, we had had three different immediate liaisons and two different heads of that department.) They had seen the dailies and were high on the project.

Planning a big promotional campaign, ABC had elicited strong interest from *TV Guide* in a cover story. It was all very encouraging. But Ally was too busy—or too bruised—to meet with the *TV Guide* reporter, and the opportunity evaporated. It was downhill from there.

In mid-November we showed the first cut to the ABC executives. They were horrified. "It is too painful to watch," they said. "The American people, after a hard day's work, do not want to look at a lot of emaciated black aborigines in strange clothes. We thought this was a love story," they demanded.

"The love story's there," we said, "but so is the story of the famine and the story of the heroine's spiritual struggle."

"We're not interested in those," one shot back. "We only want the love story." It was a long and painful meeting. I knew and liked the executive who was doing most of the talking. I could not believe some of the things he was saying.

The next day he called to apologize for the wild talk. The subtext was, "I'm sorry to hit you like this, but you've got to listen. My bosses think the picture has to be completely reedited. You've got to make changes, big changes. Play up the love story. Play up the stars. Get rid of all those hungry black faces. And get rid of that praying scene at the end."

I told him I wasn't going to do that.

He said they weren't going to air it as it was.

We were at an impasse.

In retrospect the problem was the unresolved original ambivalence. We were committed to showing the reality of the famine. We were betting the American people were mature enough to deal with it. They disagreed. "They can't take that much reality," our liaison said. "They'll flip the dial by the millions."

Finally he calmed down. So did I. We started to look for the middle ground. John Furia agreed to do a cut, giving them as much as we could without compromising the story we wanted to tell or the values we wanted to communicate. Bob Young was not unhappy with the result. Neither was Michael DeGuzman. The praying scene where Annie finally lets go of her illusions and surrenders herself to the deep mystery of life stayed in, somewhat abridged. The show was not as strong or as smooth as Bob, Mike, and I had wanted. But from a Third World perspective, it was stronger and more realistic than anything any network had ever run before. In retrospect it took courage for ABC to do what it did.

We Are the Children ran on ABC from 9 to 11 P.M. on March 16, 1987. The ratings were disappointing. The reviews were mixed, more negative than positive. The critics liked Judith Ivey and Lam Lam. Ally and Ted took their lumps. Watching it with the other priests at the rectory, I was struck by the contrast between the stark realism of the show and the blatantly illusionary tone of the commercials it carried.

Brandon Tartikoff, the president of NBC Entertainment, saw it and walked into an NBC staff meeting at Burbank the next day to ask, "How did we let that one get away?"

Genevieve called it "a courageous near miss."

At lunch with the new head of the movie of the week department at ABC some time afterward, I expressed my disappointment at the ratings. He said, "You shouldn't feel bad. You did as well as many of our other Monday night movies."

Looking at *We Are the Children* now, I see where it could have been better. I see some of the compromises we made. I see the scenes that work very well and those that don't work nearly so well. But I also see the inner dynamism of Annie's spiritual struggle. And I see the awesome beauty—the sheer reality—of those hungry black Africans, and I say, "It was worth it. I'm glad I made that."

CHAPTER 17

ROMERO

There is one great advantage in making as many mistakes as we did on *We Are the Children.* On your next film you know what *not* to do.

There is also some advantage in having as much bad luck as we did on *We Are the Children.* By the law of averages, you are bound to do better the next time around.

If *We Are the Children* was the wrong way to make a movie, I think our next film—*Romero*—was the right way to make one.

Murphy and his law had a field day on *We Are the Children.* He took a vacation on *Romero.*

We put people into the key spots we knew we could trust. We took plenty of time to prepare. And we had some excellent luck with people, situations, and places. But what happened with *Romero* went beyond good luck. I like to think it was the Lord's hand, making happen what He wanted to happen, in the way He wanted it to happen.

After it was mostly over and we had locked the fine cut in November of 1988, I went for a week's retreat to Our Lady of the Redwoods Monastery at Whitethorn, California. There I ran into Sister Godelieve, whose first question was, "Well, how did it go? *Romero*, I mean. How did it turn out?"

"Very well," I answered. "Better than we could have hoped. Certainly better than we deserved."

"I knew it," she replied, with a gleam in her eyes. "I've been praying for it every day since you were here last."

She prayed. The other sisters at Whitethorn prayed. The school kids at St. Paul's prayed. The Paulists in Westwood prayed. The families of the cast and crew prayed. And their prayers had their effect. They enabled their authors to tap into that infinite energy field of love that is God and to direct a potent flow of spiritual energy toward all those involved in the making of *Romero,* lighting up their minds, warming their hearts, guiding their decisions, making nimble their fingers and agile their feet.

We worked our tails off making *Romero.* But we also had some special help at some special times, which may explain why it is such a special movie.

Archbishop Oscar Romero, the embattled champion of the poor and defender of human rights in El Salvador, was shot while saying Mass on March 24, 1980. Four days later writer John Sacret Young sent me a newspaper clipping and a note saying, "This could make a fascinating movie of the week." John had won the two-hour Humanitas Prize in 1978 for his "Special Olympics." At the time I had been struck by his statement that his life had been changed by his work with the retarded children. I was also impressed when I learned he gave away most of the prize money.

The Romero idea intrigued me, so I called to see if John was interested in writing it. "I would be," he said, "if my plate was not so full."

I found another excellent writer who was interested and through Terry Sweeney I discovered a Jesuit—Jim Brockman—who was doing a book on Romero. In early 1982 we arranged for Jim to fly out from New York, and Terry, the writer, and I spent two days talking through the Romero story. Jim left a typed copy of his manuscript with us, and I remember crying as I read the last ten pages. "This is really Gospel," I said to myself.

The writer did a six-page concept piece, and we took the story to each of the three networks. All turned it down. "Too depressing," one said.

"No love interest," said another, as if a relationship with God was not a love interest.

"Too controversial," said the third. "I'd have to be crazy."

There seemed no way over, under, or around the wall the networks had constructed, so I started to think of making "Romero" a feature film.

At this time I met Mona Moore, who was helping Transworld International move into the feature film business. Terry and I presented the story to her, and she was captivated. She took it to her boss, and he approved it. Mona had questions about our writer, but still it looked very good. Then Transworld decided it did not want to go into the movie business after all, and the whole thing collapsed. We were back to square one.

I applied to the Catholic Communications Campaign for enough money to finance the script. They were interested but had trouble with the treatment's approach. They wanted me to get another writer. I talked it over with the writer involved, and he agreed to withdraw. "Do what you have to do," he said.

By this time I had decided I did not want a Catholic to write it. The best life of a saint I had seen, *A Man for All Seasons,* had been written by Robert Bolt, a self-styled agnostic. The best life of Christ I had seen, *The Gospel According to St. Matthew,* had been written and directed by a Marxist, Pier Pasolini. Neither was reverent. Both were slightly skeptical in tone. Yet both were more theatrically moving and religiously powerful as a result.

At this point I went back to John Sacret Young to see if he might be able to do the script. We decided to get together to talk about it. That produced a dialogue, which culminated in a close friendship . . . and a commitment to do the script.

John had an unconventional approach to the world of the spirit and a love-hate relationship with the Catholic Church. An Episcopalian by background, he had majored in religious studies at Princeton. Looking like the linebacker he once was, he liked to bait me, playing skeptic and cynic; but in talking to him, I got the feeling that was a cover for something much deeper. He snorted at the externals of religion but constantly wrestled with its inner core.

In retrospect I think he was the perfect writer for *Romero.* But I did not know that when I hired him. The Lord knew what He was doing, even if I didn't.

We decided to go down to El Salvador to research the story. Jim Brockman gave us a list of people to see, and the local CRS people offered to set up our appointments, extend hospitality, and translate for us.

We planned our trip to coincide with the Pope's visit to San Salvador because we knew the religious life of the people would peak at that time, and because certain people we needed to see would be in the capital for the Pope's arrival. We also chose that time because the influx of journalists would make it safer. We arranged to get press credentials.

In San Salvador we spent time with those who had been closest to Romero—the family to whose home he went to relax, the nuns at the hospital where he lived, and the six priests who were his closest collaborators and formed his brain trust.

From these sessions we got the portrait of a mouse of a man, a deeply flawed, traditional churchman, rigid, frightened, and neurotic, who, by all normal standards, should not have been named the archbishop of San Salvador; a man whom few of his priests wanted and more than a few detested; yet who, when he was appointed, was transformed by the responsibilities and grace of office into a fierce tiger of a man—rooted, centered, whole, and healthy—who became joyfully luminous in his defense of the poor and courageously defiant in his denunciation of the oligarchs who exploited them and the military who terrorized them.

John and I went to El Salvador knowing we had a good story, but after talking to those six priests, we knew we had a great story. Theologically it was of high Gospel density, the story of a weak and wounded man who is dragged kicking and screaming into heroism but who finally lets go and surrenders his life to God and lets God act in him and speak through him. He had been threatened with death many times. He knew if he continued to speak out, the threats would be carried out. He was frightened. He did not want to die. So he thought it out and he prayed it through. In the end he decided he had to go ahead. The rest is history.

And such homilies. Reading them now, I find myself saying yes, yes, yes, as I do with no other contemporary writer. For me, they are pure Gospel, the inspired words of a transparent and transcendent man.

No wonder the hard-bitten, cynical reporters with whom we were living at the Camino Real Hotel spoke of him in a tone of voice—reverence is the only word I know of to describe it—they used for no one else.

In our sessions with Romero's friends, and later with his enemies, I usually took the initiative, asked the questions, and drew the person out. John preferred to lie back, sensitize himself to the emotional nuances, and take notes. "I try to be a blotter," he said, "open, receptive, soaking everything up."

In our session with the present archbishop, Riviera y Damas, I asked him how he felt when he, the obviously better-qualified man, had been passed over and Romero was named the new archbishop of San Salvador.

"I was upset," he said, "for about half an hour. But then, you know, I calmed down and said, 'It must be God's will. I will support him.' Just before he was killed," the archbishop went on with a sad twinkle in his eyes, "Archbishop Romero told me I was his best friend."

After the interview, outside the archbishop's office, the Salvadoran priest who was translating for us turned to me and said, "Romero told a lot of people he was their best friend."

Not that all the priests of El Salvador were impressive. One monsignor we talked to seemed to have succumbed to the pressures and taken the easy way out. A vacuum of a man, he made a lot of noise in his emptiness, all of it bitterly critical of Romero. When he entered the room where we saw him, something seemed to leave. When he left, that something—the freedom to breathe, to laugh, to live—came back.

"A sad guy," John said compassionately.

"A son of a bitch," I said noncompassionately.

Flying back to Los Angeles, John and I had a great deal to think about: not only what we were going to do about what we had seen and heard, but also how we were going to tell Romero's story. That its central thrust was the transition from mouse to tiger, from everyman to hero, from coward to reluctant martyr, was clear. But beyond that we were groping.

This process took John the better part of a year. Only then could he begin the script. I tried to accelerate the process. He did not want to be pushed. With a fierce integrity about him, he marches to his own drummer and allows nothing to interfere. This is his great strength—as a person and as a writer—but I sometimes found him exasperating to work with. He can be so intent on marching to his drummer that he forgets that you have to march to yours.

His scripts reflect his integrity. The choices he makes are never the obvious, easy, or safe ones. He leaps. He stretches. He takes chances. The results can be exciting—or opaque.

He once told me he was no smarter than anyone else (I don't believe that), just more persistent in rewriting, rewriting, rewriting—combing, he calls it—until he gets it just right. This means his scripts are always good—very good, but also late—very late.

John and I went to El Salvador in March of 1983. It was April of 1985 before I had a first draft of the script.

It was worth waiting for. I loved it.

But I did have some suggestions. (What are producers for, anyway?) He incorporated them. By the fall of 1985, I had a script I could take to the studios and show to directors. It had all the dramatic elements I could have wanted: a topical and suspenseful story that was full of surprises, yet which also had humanity and humor, a life-and-death premise, profound conflict, archetypal depth, an emerging hero the audience could identify with and root for. In addition the story said important things about the meaning of human life and the capacity of each person, no matter how flawed, to make a difference. Deeply theological without ever being preachy, it was a statement of Christian hope, an affirmation of the power of God's grace to transform a man, an experience of Good News. What more could I want?

I took it to Bob Daly, an old friend who was now chairman of the board of Warner Bros. "Would they be interested in financing it?" I asked.

"We finance few features," he replied. "It's a good story, a very good script. Get a good filmmaker committed, and we might have something to talk about."

I took it to David Puttnam, another friend who had become the chief executive officer at Columbia. He loved the idea but thought the script needed work. "But that's not my real problem," he said. "My real problem is it's too close to *The Mission.* If I hadn't made that, I'd love to develop it with you."

So, while I waited for ABC to make up its mind about *We Are the Children,* I made a list of the world's top thirty dramatic directors and sent it out to those who seemed possible. Some responded favorably. Larry Kasdan *(The Big Chill)* called it "a quality script—powerful story"; Roland Joffe *(The Mission)* "a very good script"; George Roy Hill *(The Sting)* "a magnificently written script"; but no one would commit to shoot it. Milos Forman *(Amadeus, One Flew Over the Cuckoo's Nest)* called it "a powerful story, yet too foreign to everything I know." John Huston said that if he were younger, he would do it. Lindsay Anderson *(The Whales of August)* said much the same thing.

Martin Scorsese read the script, and we had lunch afterward. "This movie must be made," he said. "The script needs work, but they all do." He was ready to give it serious consideration, he said, but only after *The Last Temptation of Christ.* Consideration then, but not a commitment now. For a producer with a passion to make a picture, that was not good enough.

I kept our board apprised of what I was doing. I gave them copies of the script at the October 1985 board meeting. Their initial reaction was skeptical. "Another Kieser brainchild," was the subtext, "only this one's very radical *and* very expensive." At this point they were disposed to go ahead only if someone else was prepared to put up the money. At the January meeting, they set up a special committee to look into the various ways *Romero* might be financed. To its June meeting, the special committee invited Kerry McCluggage, a senior executive at Universal Pictures, and Larry Mortorff, a former ICM agent and now an independent producer. Both praised the script and the project. Both stated unequivocally the project was commercially viable. Rick Guerin, Peter Mullin, Dick Ferry, and George Fritzinger peppered them with hard questions, and the dialogue ricocheted from one corner of the meeting room to the other like a championship racquetball game. But the questioners got their answers, the skeptics were convinced, and the special committee voted unanimously to recommend *Romero*'s production. As one special committee member after another chronicled the change in his thinking, the board the next day caught fire and voted unanimously to make *Romero*.

Was their enthusiasm based on the high Gospel density of the picture or on the commercial viability of the project? I do not know. Probably some combination of the two.

At that same meeting Rick Guerin, a financial wizard whose mind processes figures faster than most computers, was elected chairman of the board. Through his involvement in the special committee and his own adventures in the entertainment community, he had caught the *Romero* bug and become passionate about getting the picture made. By the September meeting, he promised to present a plan to secure the three million dollars needed to make the picture.

He did. It was a two-track plan. The first track was to continue aggressively to seek commercial financing. The second was to secure the three million dollars from three sources: one million from the endowment, which the board had put together for Paulist Productions; one million from foundations across the country, which I undertook to raise; and the third million from the board, either in the form of donation or investment. When it came crunch time, most of our board members preferred to donate, compressing three years' worth of donations into the single year of 1986, when the charity deduction was worth more to them.

Larry Mortorff had now joined the board, and from the fall of 1986 through the following spring we presented the project to all the major studios. None was interested. "Too risky," they said. We did have serious interest from a number of private investors. They were ready to put up 50 percent of the budget, but only on terms Rick, Larry, and I considered unacceptable. They wanted us to do all the work, take all the risks, and add their overhead and the salaries of their people to our budget. They also wanted to recoup their investment first and get a disproportionate share of the profits if there were any. Like frightened leeches they lay in wait for the long-shot winner, hoping to hitch a ride—and secure a percentage—as it headed for the homestretch.

I found the world of motion picture financing big on promises and short on follow-through. So many of the people in it seemed to be living in a world of illusion. So much of what they told me had no connection with reality. I think they actually believed what they said, but in retrospect I can see there was no way they could have done what they promised.

As the months passed, the board became more and more enthusiastic about *Romero.* The road they traveled to this increased commitment was not without its bumps. One member refused to read Brockman's book, saying it might force him to change his thinking about El Salvador, and he did not want to do that. Another read the book and the script and said, "I have no doubt he is a saint. But the story is implicitly critical of American foreign policy (Ronald Reagan's), and I do not want to be part of that. I will continue to give you money. But you are to use it for operating expenses, not, under any conditions, for *Romero.*" The fact that the Catholic Communications Campaign—the media financing arm of the American Catholic bishops—committed an additional $188,000 (they had already given $50,000 for research and script), and that their Latin American Secretariat had added $50,000 more, helped with the board's commitment. So did $100,000 from the Paulists and a $100,000 interest-free loan from the Raskob Foundation.

Finally, in June of 1987, at Rick's and Larry's urging, the board voted to increase the endowment's share of the budget to two million dollars. With the million we had already raised, we had the three million we needed to make the picture.

But we still did not have a director. The word was now out in Hollywood, and many directors came to us, wanting to do the project. But none of them had what we felt the project required.

In July of 1987, Dick Pearse, a friend of John Sacret Young's and a quality director *(Heartland, Country)*, read and liked the script but thought it needed to be recast—moving it away from the docudrama toward the mythic, sacrificing some of the facts so as to get more fully at the inner truth of Romero.

I had heard this criticism before and could see the validity of it. Dick offered to work with John on the rewrite. John agreed. The presumption was that Dick would then direct the picture. During August they worked long and hard on rewriting the script. I liked the direction in which they were moving.

In mid-September, with half of the rewrite in hand, Dick and I flew to New York to read an actor. While Dick observed, I read opposite the actor; only Dick's attention shifted from the actor to me, as he became aware that the words in the script meant more to me than they did to him. We talked afterward about our differing approaches to the story. It soon became clear that a clash of ideas, a conflict of values, had more dramatic appeal for me than it did for him. He became concerned that he could not give me the kind of film I wanted; so concerned that he decided to withdraw from the project. Sadly I accepted his withdrawal.

Almost immediately another American director surfaced. He loved the script and had very impressive credentials. But he wanted more money than we could pay.

I was back to square one. But not really. The changes in the script that Dick Pearse initiated were major improvements. They gave it new depth and nuance.

Sister Godelieve was getting through.

In my continuing search for the right director, I called Cary Brokaw, a friend who was the president of Avenue Entertainment. He highly recommended John Duigan, an Australian. Over the years I had been very impressed by the caliber of Australia's directors—Peter Weir, Hugh Hudson, Bruce Beresford and Fred Schepisi—and so I looked at two of John Duigan's films with great interest. I liked both. Yet in each case, I found the male lead lacked soul and emotional resonance. Was this the actor's doing or the director's?

When John Duigan came to Los Angeles in November of 1987, we arranged to have breakfast. In his late thirties, he had a presence about him that struck me at once. From a room full of leading men, you would immediately select him to play Hamlet. Educated in England as well as Australia, he had worked as an actor before becoming a director. With a master's degree in philosophy, he had a predilection for metaphysics and a moral passion about Latin America. He loved the script and understood the delicate shadings of Romero's character and the tortuous transition he goes through. "Where are you theologically?" I asked.

"I guess you would say I'm a pantheist," he answered. "I find all of reality energizing."

"I find all of reality energizing, too," I replied, laughing, "but I don't consider myself a pantheist."

We were off and running on the first of many metaphysical conversations we would have in the months ahead.

"This is a very human story," I said, "but it is also highly theological, and its setting is Catholic. Does that bother you?"

"It's about freedom and human dignity, isn't it?" he replied, shrugging. "You blokes have no monopoly on that. If we succeed, we may just turn out a born-again humanist or two."

I told him the kind of money I could pay. No problem. Money was not a high priority for him.

I told him how I function as a producer. "I'm hands on," I said. "I won't tell you how to direct the picture. But I do want to stay in dialogue with you the whole way." No problem.

I also told him about the problem I had with the two pictures of his I had seen. I told him I wanted to see his most recent picture—*The Year My Voice Broke*—to assure myself of his ability to elicit "soul" performances.

Four days later I saw and loved *The Year My Voice Broke.* No lack of soul in that one. The deal was consummated the same day.

We had our director.

When I hired John Duigan, I knew he was a good director. I would not know how very good until several months later.

In mid-January John Duigan returned to Los Angeles, and we plunged into completing the script, casting and preproduction. It was so good to have a go picture at last.

John Sacret Young took John Duigan's concerns and incorporated them into yet another revision of the script.

The decisions apropos casting were more difficult. Everything depended on who would play Romero. Even before John Duigan came aboard, I had done considerable thinking about this. It was a great part—better than any most superstars are offered in their lifetimes—but it was also difficult; very, very difficult.

At first I was thinking of American actors like Robert De Niro, Al Pacino, or Alan Arkin. But then we turned to the British and gave serious consideration to Albert Finney, David Suchet, and Bob Hoskins, the last two of whom physically resembled Romero. But as the dialogue progressed, we zeroed in on two American actors with Hispanic backgrounds: Raul Julia and Ed Olmos. Both read the script, loved the part, and wanted to play it. John Duigan and I agonized over the decision. We looked at most everything both men had done. Both were consummate actors. Both had the star quality, the magnetism necessary to carry a picture. Both had an abundance of Latin soul, the mixture of spirituality and compassion needed in anyone playing Romero. Raul was the more accomplished actor, with what seemed like a broader range. He tended to be laconic, but so much was going on behind those eyes of his. He was also tall and good-looking, qualities Romero lacked. Eddie was shorter, less handsome, more physically akin to Romero. He had an engine that made him dynamic. It was a tough choice. But finally we made it. We chose Raul.

It was an inspired decision. When we made it, we did not know Raul had been brought up in the Church, that he was a man of deep faith, that he was Jesuit-educated and theologically sophisticated. We also did not know (although maybe we should have guessed) that the role would activate archetypal depths in him, tapping into currents of emotion that had been left untouched by his other roles.

In the course of the shoot, Raul and I talked theology incessantly. We became good friends.

To play Rutillo Grande, Romero's Jesuit mentor, whose murder, more than any other single incident, propelled the change in Romero, we chose Richard Jordan, an Insighter, brilliant, unpredictable, a rainbow of colors. It was off-center casting and worked out exceptionally well. For the oligarch widow whom Romero befriended, we chose Ana Alicia, and for the two radical young priests, Tony Plana and Alejandro Bracho. Eddie Villez, Tony Perez, Robert Viharo, Lucy Reina, Al Ruscio, Hal Gould, and Harold Canon-Lopez rounded out the cast. Not a weak performer among them.

In the latter part of January, I ran into Mike Rhodes. He had immersed himself in free-lance directing since *We Are the Children,* and I had seen little of him. Only half-seriously, I said, "You want to produce *Romero?*"

"I might," he said with a twinkle in his eye. I had originally planned on a Mexican supervising producer to deal with the unions and the government down there and to take the gringo curse off us. But the prospect of working again with Mike seemed almost too good to be true.

Within three days we cut a deal and he was aboard.

The prayers were having their effect.

Mike and I had been working together on and off since 1972. A Yale undergraduate with a master's degree in film from Southern Cal and another in theology from GTU, he was raised a Lutheran but worshiped as a Presbyterian. Over the years I had watched him develop a style of working and living that sometimes made me impatient but more often filled me with awe. He seems to sense the soul in other people and will allow nothing—not that other person's ego, not his own—to keep him from connecting with it. Not that he doesn't have a good, strong ego. He does; but he does not live in it. Like most of us, he has his limitations. But unlike most of us, he is comfortable with them. Both as a director and a producer, he is consistently open and vulnerable, admitting his own mistakes, affirming the best in his adversary. Perhaps adversary is not the right word. For him, even the toughest, most confrontive situation is not a contest, an "us guys" against "you guys" thing. It's more "Let's look this thing over together and see what's best and fairest for everybody." Mike trusts the truth to speak, and he is ready to adjust his own position if that should be called for. Which doesn't make Mike a patsy. No one has ever bamboozled him, manipulated him, or gotten away with lying to him. He can confront. I have seen him break off negotiations, and he has fired his share of people.

Because he is so open, everyone knows where he stands. There is no need for games. And I always know the company's welfare, and my own, are just as important to Mike as his own. Loyalty is his other name.

We had made more than a hundred TV dramas together. *We Are the Children* was the only bad experience we had had. I think one reason we were so glad to be back in harness together was the desire to expel the poisonous vibes of that wrenching experience.

In 1987 Panama, Costa Rica, Brazil, and Colombia had approached us about shooting *Romero* in their countries. But none of them could offer what Mexico had: film crews of the highest professional caliber, a population of the same racial stock as El Salvador, a dollar-peso exchange rate that made the economics very attractive, a wide variety of locations, and proximity to Los Angeles and New York. For these reasons we opted for Mexico. Cinematografia, the film office of the Mexican government, approved the script and authorized the shooting of *Romero* in their country.

Late in January Mike went off to Mexico to explore possible core locations—Veracruz, Oaxaca, or Cuernavaca, while John Duigan, Roger Ford, our newly arrived Australian scenic designer, and I went off to El Salvador to look over the places where the events in the script actually took place.

We caught up with Mike in Mexico City, where we met with the officials of the actors' and technicians' unions and looked over the locations in the Cuernavaca area. At Mike's recommendation, we decided to shoot in Cuernavaca because of its climate, the variety of its locations, the quality of its accommodations, its proximity to Mexico City, and its excellent film office run by Luciana Cabarga. While in Mexico City, John and I also read more than sixty actors, some of whom were quite exceptional.

Returning to Los Angeles, Mike drew up a budget, which John and I went over carefully and were able to trim somewhat. At John's request we also decided to use Australians with whom he had worked before in certain key positions—director of photography, sound, lighting, and editor. Paul Weber, the deacon who is general manager of Paulist Productions, volunteered to serve as production accountant. The core team was starting to take shape. We completed the script, wrapped up the casting, and drew up a tentative schedule. We decided on an eight-week shoot, to begin about May 2, with an eight-week preparation period. While John immersed himself in the script, blocking the scenes and planning his shots, I hired a tutor and started to learn Spanish.

Mike and John returned to Mexico in March. By the time I went down in April, two significant problems had arisen.

The first was with the Catholic diocese of Cuernavaca. We needed the use of the Church's buildings in the worst sort of way. Yet their pastors were reluctant to commit them. Why? With some reason, they felt the Bishop of Cuernavaca was unenthusiastic about our project. My archbishop, Roger Mahoney, an ardent supporter, had already written to Bishop Cervantes, telling him of the film and asking for his support. Apparently that had not made much of an impression.

With Luciana Cabarga I went to see Bishop Cervantes the morning after I arrived. A rotund man with protruding lips and the muscle tone of a baby hippo, he was cordial and candid. "Why have you chosen to make this picture in Cuernavaca?" he asked.

Possibly he was afraid, I was later to be informed, that we had come because of his immensely popular yet very radical predecessor, Mendez Arceo, from whose shadow he was trying to escape.

"Because it looks like San Salvador," I said, "because it is close to Mexico City without its smog and congestion, and because you have such an efficient film office." Luciana beamed.

"All well and good," the bishop continued. "But let's get to the real issue." He paused to select his words carefully. "Is this picture going to be a platform for radical liberation theology?"

The priest doing the translating winced in embarrassment. I knew where the bishop was coming from. I also knew that any kind of discussion of liberation theology would be like venturing onto a mine field. I decided not to answer his question directly.

"Look, Bishop, I'm not doing a theological dissertation. I'm telling the story of a saint, a man of God, a man of the Gospel, a man of prayer, a man of the Church, a man of tremendous loyalty to the Holy Father."

As the words were translated, I could see the bishop sigh in relief. "What do you want, Father?" he asked. "We'll give you anything we can."

That afternoon we picked up a letter of approval instructing the priests and nuns of the diocese to give us whatever we needed.

The second problem was with the Mexican military. For our shoot we needed two tanks or armored cars, three or four jeeps, and enough automatic weapons for several hundred uniformed extras, some of which would have to be able to fire blanks. Luciana did not think there would be any problem.

Mike went through channels. He did things as he was told to do them. He submitted the script. For the longest time, we got no response. Then we got a turndown. We were then told to go see a retired army general who could arrange these kinds of things. Mike and I went to see him. He was so drunk when we arrived that he could hardly walk. But his mind was lucid. He could get us everything we needed, he said, including conscripts to play the extras and a helicopter or two if that would help. In return we had to make a $35,000 donation to the old soldiers' home and pay him $1000 a week and an assistant $500 a week for the eight weeks of the shoot for their supervising services.

I did not like the smell of the whole thing, especially after I learned that the contribution to the old soldiers' home was most likely a bribe—*mordida.* But we had little room to maneuver. We made hurried inquiries about Panama, Costa Rica, and Nicaragua, but they were not at all encouraging. To move at this point would have cost us at least 15 percent of our total budget.

Mike told the general to see what he could do. Two days later, very drunk again, he got back to us, saying the situation was more complex than he had imagined. It would take more money, and there would have to be script changes. Mike met with a colonel at the department of defense, so that we could nail down what they were talking about in the script area. It turned out the script changes they wanted were largely cosmetic. We felt we could live with them. Then the whole thing blew up in our faces. The Mexican military at the highest level, we were informed, had decided our picture should not be made. At the very least, it should not be made in Mexico. Why? Because it portrayed the Salvadoran military in an unflattering light. The military went to Cinematografia, the civilian bureau that had already given us permission to shoot, and tried to get them to revoke their permission. Cinematografia refused, telling the military to mind their own business. They had given permission, and they were not about to revoke it. Things became very tense. We were caught in the middle of a turf war. We pushed back our start date. Then Mike worked his magic. The Mexican military still refused to help us. But they agreed not to hinder or harass us either. We had to improvise quickly. We brought in the uniforms from Los Angeles. There we also found a warehouse full of toy automatic weapons that looked so authentic they were not allowed to be sold. We bought three hundred of them cheaply. We hired the SWAT squad of Morelos State to handle the real guns and fire the blanks. Roger Ford designed two armored personnel carriers, which we built out of steel plates bolted onto wooden frames attached to Ford chassis. When they were given a coat of camouflage paint, no one could tell they were not the real thing.

We also hired the son of the general as life insurance.

At long last, we could get under way.

One of the reasons I had studied Spanish was to be able to celebrate Mass and preach for our cast and crew. Already sensing that this was going to be a very different kind of shoot, the Mexicans, the Australians, and the Americans turned out en masse on the Saturday evening before we were to begin for the first of four Masses and fiestas. The Australians and Americans sang "The Battle Hymn of the Republic" and "Blowin' in the Wind," and the Mexicans sang "De Colores" and "Allegro." Roberto Muñoz, the head of the technicians union, and Luciana Cabarga read the scriptures in Spanish, and Ana Alicia and John Duigan read them in English. Paul Weber read the Gospel in Spanish, and I did so in English. I had written out my homily and had it translated into Spanish so I could give it in both languages. Raul Julia also led the prayer of the faithful in both languages.

At the offertory, each person was invited to bring to the altar a symbol of his or her craft, that it might be blessed and consecrated along with the bread and wine. John Sacret Young brought the script; John Duigan, his viewfinder; Mike Rhodes, his schedules; Paul Weber, his account books; the cinematographer, his light meter; the lighting man, a bulb; the sound man, a roll of tape; the makeup people, their paint and rouge.

Afterward we had a great party, with tacos and enchiladas, hot dogs and hamburgers and plenty of dancing.

If the Mass is, as Albert Outler once said, the miracle that makes strangers friends, then that first Mass not only made everyone aware of the transcendent importance of what we were doing —let's make a film worthy of the man, I had suggested in the homily—but it transformed three very different ethnic groups into a single family.

That word family means something special to the Mexicans. It means love and loyalty, acceptance and sharing. It means they are ready to die for each other. That night, primarily as a result of the Mass, they took us into their family. The embraces at the kiss of peace in the Mass—as well as the shared Eucharist—were symbols of the deep bonding that was taking place. We were no longer strangers. We were friends. No longer adversaries, we were collaborators. No longer gringos, we were brothers.

Romero became their film. They bought in, and they committed themselves to do everything in their power to make it the very best film they could. They recognized Romero as one of their own. They were delighted to collaborate with us to bring his story to the world. Not once over eight weeks, despite some very long hours and some very frustrating situations, did I see a flagging of that enthusiasm or a lessening of that commitment. In the course of doing their job, the crew did not walk. They ran, and they did so joyfully. They knew this was an uncommon film worth all they could give—and more.

Prior to the beginning of the shoot, we rehearsed for two full weeks. This gave John Duigan, John Sacret Young (now functioning as executive producer), and me time to explore with the actors in a leisurely fashion the characters they were playing and the significance of each scene. The leisure meant the actors' unconsciouses could be open and receptive, so that the emotional marinating process—so crucial to an actor's creativity—could begin. It also meant we had time to experiment and make last-minute script adjustments. The rehearsal period also enabled us to spot a mistake we had made in casting. We were able to remedy it before it hurt the picture.

The shoot itself went well. A natural leader and a take-charge kind of director, John Duigan was meticulously prepared and knew what he wanted and how to get it. Considerate of his crew and sensitive to his cast, he had the respect of both. He was very serious; so serious that sometimes I tried to break the tension by telling him funnies. He had the good grace to laugh. We had no trouble staying in communication.

My job was to see that John had everything he needed, keep an objective eye on performances, and help everybody in the cast and crew feel valued. That was not hard. They were.

Alan Arkin once told me no human being should have the kind of power an actor has once shooting begins. This is because everything depends on the actors. The director, the producer, the crew, can do nothing without them. Actors have great power. But they also have the pressure of acting, which is among the most intense and demanding of professions. Stories of vain, arrogant, and narcissistic actors abound in Hollywood. Fortunately on *Romero* we had few such problems.

Raul Julia took a little while to get his bearings with John and me. I think he needed to feel secure that we knew what we were doing. We also needed to feel secure that he knew what he was doing. The fact of the matter is, he did.

A consummate professional, Raul deeply immersed himself in the role. He insisted that I get him the tapes that Romero dictated at the end of each day and which formed his diary, and also the tapes of his homilies. He listened to them, not just for their content, but for their emotional tone. "I'm searching for the essence of the man," he said. He was not just playing Oscar Romero. In a way he became Oscar Romero. All during the shoot, I found him reading St. John of the Cross, the great Spanish mystic. He had carefully calibrated Romero's emotional arc—from mouse to tiger—thinking through each stage and working out the particular gestures, inflections, and mannerisms needed to communicate what Romero was feeling at that particular time. On more than one occasion, I was surprised how deeply Raul had penetrated Romero's character and how fully he understood it.

Sometimes Raul and I battled over what he should wear. Romero, in many ways, was a traditional cleric, so most often he wore a cassock. I preferred a simple and unadorned one. Raul preferred one that was more flamboyant and ornate. He said I was too liberal and did not understand the Latin temperament. I called him an ecclesiastical peacock. Looking at the picture now, I find it a good balance between the two.

We found some exquisitely picturesque locations in Cuernavaca and Cuautla. One I will never forget: the local garbage and trash dump. Acres and acres of it. Some burning. Some rotting. Teeming with flies. A stench that assaulted the nostrils while smoke scarred the eyes. The particular section where we worked was filled with hospital dressings, some pus-filled, some blood-soaked. An appallingly unhealthy environment. Yet there were families living there, children playing there.

We hired them as extras and shot three compelling scenes in the dump.

Three times a week, we would gather to watch the dailies at the Gaby house where eight of us lived. By the third week, a consensus was developing that we had a special film on our hands—Raul's performance, those of Richard Jordan, Ana Alicia, Tony Plana, and the others, the locations and camerawork, the faces of the extras, and the production values all contributed to this realization. And the more we realized this, the harder we worked to make it better still.

On one occasion Raul looked at a particular take and said to John, "That's good. Why did you ask me to do it again?" Then he saw the next take and said, "I'm glad you did. That's better."

Sometimes, looking at the dailies, the cast and crew would

applaud a particular performance, set design, or feat of camerawork.

It was that kind of shoot. People loved each other. They loved what they were doing and what they were making. They loved the man the picture was about, and they loved what his life said about our lives on this planet. They recognized it for what it is: Good News.

Not a bad way to make a movie.

The reporters coming down from Los Angeles commented on the positive energy field. Ana Alicia, needing to go up to Los Angeles on business, came back two days early. She did not want to be away from it all. "This shoot has changed my life," she said.

Finally we got our last shot, the movie was wrapped, several of the production assistants were dunked, and we had the last of our four Masses and a wrap party together. We sent buses to Mexico City because so many of the families and friends of the cast and crew wanted to come. Three hundred and fifty people attended. At the end of the Mass, I thanked everybody for all they had done and threw the floor open. John Duigan, Mike Rhodes, and Raul Julia spoke, saying they were glad the movie was done, but they were so very sorry to be leaving all the new friends they had made. And then people started popping up from the congregation.

"I've been making pictures for twenty-five years," one crewman said. "I hope to make them for another twenty-five. But I never expect another one like this. This was the finest. Because you all are the finest."

The leader of the Salvadoran band that had played for the Mass and would play for the dance declared, "I wish to thank all of you in the name of my countrymen. You have brought justice and freedom a little bit closer."

The location photographer, a Lutheran, said, "I remember Jesus saying He would be with two or three who had gotten together in His name. Well, we're more than two or three and we are Mexicans and Americans and Australians and we're here in His name and He's right here with us and I will never forget any of you."

Raul, who had not been an active Catholic for years, went to confession near the end of the shoot, and I gave him communion at this final Mass, something that made me almost as happy as it did him.

"I always believed in God," he said. "My problem was the Church. I thought it dragged people down. Now I saw it lifted them up. I wanted to be part of that."

We edited for two months in Mexico and for two more in Los Angeles. Under John Duigan's supervision, Franz Vandenberg and Margaret Sixel did the editing with some crucial help, once we got to Los Angeles, from George Folsey and Malcolm Campbell.

The editing process was not without its tensions. Once, while John Duigan was still working on his director's cut, I made some suggestions, and he exploded. "You push, push, push. You never give up. You say you're a priest. You think you stand between God and the people. Like you have a monopoly on wisdom. Let me tell you, you're not the only one who cares about this picture. Nor the only one with a stake in it."

I was really surprised, because this was out of character for John and in no way typical of the kind of relationship we had. I did not know how to respond, so I said nothing. But two days later I did. "John, about what you said Tuesday night. Your theology of the priesthood is antiquated. I obviously have no monopoly on wisdom. But I was wise enough to hire you."

We chuckled about the incident afterward. He said it was caused by editing-room claustrophobia. He also said I should be sure to use it in this book.

"You gonna get the last word?" he asked quizzically.

"Of course," I said, "it's my book." He laughed uproariously. So did I.

We completed the picture by the end of January 1989 and immediately scheduled screenings for each of the major studios with the hope that one of them would decide to distribute it. All liked the picture. None was ready to distribute it. Two came close —Warner's, which declined, one of its top executives told me, only because they had recently bought Lorimar and had a surplus of product; and MGM, which decided against it only because they had already committed to *A Dry White Season,* which they considered a similar kind of picture.

Five independent distributors made offers on the picture and a committee of the board, now functioning under Lou Castruccio's leadership, decided on Four Seasons, a new company run by Peter Myers, the former head of distribution at 20th Century-Fox. It was a good choice.

We premiered in New York City on August 25 and in Los Angeles and twenty other large cities on September 8, with a rollout that finally carried the picture to more than three hundred cities and towns in the United States. The premieres were preceded by an avalanche of feature stories on TV and in the press, some on Raul, others on Ana Alicia or me. The U.S. reviews were mixed—two thirds favorable, one third unfavorable. Some critics seemed to have more of a problem with the Catholic auspices of the picture—or with the Church itself—than they did with the picture. The reviews in Canada, Australia, Mexico, Brazil, and Korea were much more universally favorable. So was the reaction of the religious press, both Catholic and Protestant.

Domestic box office, which reached $1,882,268, was respectable for this type of picture but hardly overwhelming. Internationally *Romero* played in most of the countries of the world, doing quite well in Korea, Panama, Canada, and Germany, rather well in Australia and Mexico, and just fair in Spain, England, and Brazil.

But if the American critics were not as universally enthusiastic and the U.S. box office not as large as we had hoped, the videocassette sales and the television exposure in the United States more than made up for the shortfall.

Vidmark sold more than sixty thousand cassettes of *Romero,* almost all of which went to video stores. For the first nine weeks after its release, *Romero* averaged 2.6 rentals per cassette per week, which kept it on the top fifty chart. After that it began to taper off.

CBS's Peter Tortoricci decided to include the picture in his Tuesday night movie lineup, where it ran on April 16, 1991. Bob Turner's Orbis has contracted for the subsequent TV syndication rights, which involve twelve runs over nine years.

Our exposure via cassette and television has been and will be mammoth, and the income from these two areas will put *Romero* in the black. This has allowed us to plan the production of a second feature film—on Dorothy Day.

But neither the size of the TV and cassette audiences nor the recouping of our investment is what pleases me most about *Romero.*

What sticks with me, what warms my heart, is the reaction of audiences to the picture.

I traveled with the picture, promoting it, to nine cities in the

United States; to Montreal and Toronto in Canada; to Sydney, Melbourne, and Perth in Australia; and to Havana in Cuba. In all these places, I tried to get a sense of the audience's reaction. The audiences varied: college students, clergy, congressmen and their staffs, members of the FMLN, socialites, show business people, the general theater-going public.

Romero's closest friends saw it on cassette in San Salvador. "You really captured him," said one. "For a while I thought Oscar was alive again," said another. "The picture is so true to my uncle's spirit," said Romero's niece. "So accurate about the way it was," said his grandnephew. "I was so afraid of what you would do to my friend," said the head of the Episcopalian Church's human rights commission in San Salvador at the time. "I have to tell you I am delighted. You were completely faithful to the man, his experience, and the situation in El Salvador."

At the Motion Picture Academy in Los Angeles, spontaneous applause broke out four times during the screening. But most often, at the end of the picture, there was not applause but a stunned silence. People did not stir during the credits. Nor did they talk to each other on the way out. They were having a depth experience and did not want to break the spell.

Afterward many people needed to be alone. But then, after a time, they wanted to talk—about what they were feeling, about what Romero meant to them, about what God was doing in their lives.

Several couples told me they talked all night after seeing it.

Other people said it was the most powerful cinematic experience of their lives.

Others that it occasioned an experience of God.

What more could a priest-producer want?

I think *Romero* is the most important picture I have made. I also like to think it is the best. Oscar Romero was a great man. He deserves a great film. Many, many people reached deep within themselves and worked hard to give it to him.

And we had some extraordinary help.

Romero is indeed the film the Lord has made.

CHAPTER 18

DOROTHY DAY

Dorothy Day was a feisty, street smart, combative, yet compassionate American Mother Teresa who will one day be canonized by the Church but whose past included a socialist interlude, several affairs and an abortion.

Born into a dysfunctional family in Brooklyn in 1897, Dorothy grew up in Chicago and attended the University of Illinois where she lost what religious faith she had and gravitated to the far left of the political spectrum. Bored, she moved to the Greenwich Village section of New York City which, in the late teens and early twenties, was much like America's campuses in the sixties—idealistic, hedonistic and turbulent. There she expressed her ongoing love of the poor by working for socialist newspapers. She also joined the literary circle of Eugene O'Neill, Hart Crane, Floyd Dell, Allen Tate and Mike Gold.

She had an affair with Lionel Moise, a drinking buddy of Ernest Hemingway's. When she told him she was pregnant, he told her to get an abortion or he would leave her. She complied but he left her anyway.

Hitting bottom, she went to Europe, wrote an autobiographical novel, then returned to New York where she lived in solitude on the beach at Staten Island. There she was befriended by a nun and entered into a common law relationship with an anarchist—Forster Batterham. They had a child, a daughter whom they named Tamar.

Rejoicing in this new love—and in the child—she turned to God in gratitude. Forster balked at this. When she decided to have Tamar baptized and become a Catholic herself, he left for good.

Dorothy now had to try to put together her lifelong love of the poor with her new faith. The result was the Catholic Worker movement which she founded with Peter Maurin in New York City in 1933 at the height of the great depression. To this day, Catholic Workers are still feeding the hungry, clothing the naked and sheltering the homeless in almost a hundred American cities. Fifteen years after Dorothy's death in 1980, her newspaper—The Catholic Worker—continues to apply to contemporary life the movement's basic evangelical platform: voluntary poverty, community prayer, nonviolence, social justice and, most important of all, direct, hands on, person to person service of the poor. A daily communicant, Dorothy lived these values to a heroic degree for the last fifty years of her life. She was a thorn in the flesh of both the Church and the government, allowing neither to forget the needs of the poor or the power of love to resolve conflict without violence.

As I mentioned earlier, I became friends with Dorothy Day at the Vatican Council in 1965 and asked her permission in 1978 to tell her story in a network movie of the week. She told me rather brusquely, "Wait until I'm dead." So I did. In 1983, as I also mentioned earlier, I presented the idea to NBC's Karen Danaher and secured a script commitment from her. But to my intense disappointment, the script Dick Fielder and I prepared was turned down by Karen's superiors and I moved on to other things.

In the spring of 1990, with "Romero" fully promoted, I began to look for a new focus for my energies and my thoughts returned to Dorothy and her story. Could it work as a feature film? Did it have the unique combination of audience appeal and Gospel density that is necessary? I began to think and pray about this. So did other members of Paulist Pictures' Board and staff.

Theatrically, the story had everything: a protagonist in whom the audience could find themselves and for whom they could root; a heroine whose roller coaster spiritual adventures were charged with emotional excitement and a trajectory of breakthrough spiritual growth that would thrill an audience, give them hope and make them proud to share the same planet with a person like Dorothy Day. It also had a constellation of dilemmas—confronted and overcome—that reads like a compendium of the live nerves of the contemporary American psyche: tension between sexuality and commitment, between child and career, between taking care of one's own and taking care of the poor and homeless; the hunger for transcendent meaning and connectedness, for a personal center and ground, for God and personal fulfillment; the scars left by an alcoholic parent; the shortcomings of the institutional church; what to do about the arms race, societal injustice and the violence that flows from it; plus feminism, abortion and single motherhood.

Theologically, the story also had everything—a spiritual journey which begins in Dorothy's confused self indulgence but which flowers not only into self discipline, self acceptance and self giving, but also into a joyous ego transcendence that enables Dorothy to forget all about herself in reaching out to God as He lives in the poor; a role model of contemporary Christian heroism that reveals not only what God is like, but also what He can do in a human life when given half a chance; a clarion call to viewers to respond to God's challenge, and to involve themselves in the transformation of human society so that it might become more responsive to the needs of its less fortunate members.

The more I thought about it, the more I became convinced the Dorothy Day story was possessed of what we call high Gospel Density. The story could give its viewers an intense and powerful experience of God's presence in the human situation, propelling them to the full flowering of their own humanity. I also thought that it had the theatricality to attract a sizable audience, that we had a reasonable chance to recoup its production costs, that businesswise it made sense.

I brought the decision to the Lord in prayer. What did He want? I was aware that the clock was ticking, that at sixty-one, I had a limited amount of time and energy left. How did He want me to invest them? I told Him to let me know what He wanted, that whatever it was was all right with me. I tried to mean that. I also tried to be authentically open, to really listen. And the answer seemed to come: go for it. Was that the voice of the Lord or the sublimated yearnings of my own ego? I do not know. Probably some combination of the two.

The priests with whom I live kid me about confusing God's will with my own. They say I use prayer to give God His marching orders. I hope they are wrong. But I am not sure they are. Over the years, I have become increasingly aware of the temptation to take God's name in vain, to use His name—and the generosity it can elicit—to get what I want. Was I doing that here?

I also took the decision to Dorothy Day in prayer. What did *she* want? Her response was less than enthusiastic. "I'd rather you spend the money on the poor," she seemed to be saying.

Was this an authentic expression of her desire? Or a projection of my own qualms of conscience about spending so much donated money on a movie when so many people, in this country and in the Third World, were in such desperate need? I don't have the answer to that question either.

I struggled with my ambivalence. I tried to sift things out. I listened for the voice of the Lord in the midst of it all. Slowly, at times painfully, the clouds began to lift and I began to see what I was supposed to do. I was to make the picture. But then a new set of questions crowded in on me. Would the Board agree? Could we secure the necessary funding? Who would we ask to write the script? To direct the picture? To play Dorothy?

I could feel the picture taking possession of me. The main character—and her story—were resonating deep within me. They were activating things inside of me that I did not even know were there. I was becoming passionate about telling Dorothy's story. Part of me loved that. But part of me hated it. Why? Because I sensed the price it would demand of me.

I did not know the half of it.

I discussed the project with the leading members of the Board. They felt "Romero" had been a resounding success and favored a two-track strategy: the aggressive pursuit of Movie of the Week commitments from the networks *and* the ongoing yet highly selective production of feature films.

Armed with their support, I presented the concept to the full Board at their June, 1990 meeting. The discussion was freewheeling and spirited. They saw the Gospel dimension of the story. But they were uncertain about the financial feasibility of the undertaking. Could this be a popular picture, recouping its production costs? They were not sure. Part of their hesitation was due to the doldrums into which the American economy had slipped. The expansive "the sky's the limit" economic binge of the eighties was over and the American economy was left with a hangover. It was facing fierce foreign competition and was being forced to downsize. In addition, the Los Angeles real estate market had collapsed, seriously hurting many of our potential contributors. Caution was the prevailing mood in the business community. As a result, the Board decided they did not want to risk the company's future by borrowing the bulk of the picture's productions costs as we had done previously on "Romero." They preferred to raise the entire production budget. But was that possible, given the flagging economy? No one was sure but the Board was ready to give it a try. After much discussion, the Board voted unanimously to proceed with the project, approving the expenditure of the money needed for the script. Under John O'Keefe's and Tom Grojean's leadership, they also formed a committee to draw up a plan to raise the whole budget and approved the rolling over for the Dorothy Day project of the million dollars we had raised for, and recouped from "Romero." This was the beginning of the idea of a revolving capital fund to spin off one picture after another without having to resort to fundraising between each one.

In the months that followed, Bill Finnegan and I did some hard thinking about where best to shoot the picture. New York City was too expensive. Poland seemed a possibility. So did Canada. But after two trips to the former and intensive investigation of the latter, we decided to shoot it in Los Angeles where we could live at home, be with our friends, and have access to the best acting community and production houses in the world.

This decision enabled us to put together a budget for the picture. We estimated we would need $4,163,000 to make it, a 20% increase over "Romero," due to inflation and the difference between American and Mexican wages. This in turn enabled the development committee to set a goal of $3,163,000, draw up a prospectus and begin to put together a prospect list. To expand our base, we decided to hold a series of cocktail parties in the various affluent sections of Los Angeles. Jane Ackerman organized these and they proved to be productive. We also approached all the major Catholic foundations in the United States as well as the bishops' media funding agency, the Catholic Communication Campaign. Buoyed by the success of "Romero," almost all responded with generous enthusiasm. On a one-to-one basis, I also contacted the more affluent members of the Board and asked them to make pace-setting, five-year pledges, significantly increasing what they had given to "Romero." Again, I got a favorable response.

Cardinal Roger Mahony agreed to write to a number of wealthy individuals and foundations in the Los Angeles area. And Cardinal John O'Connor, in whose New York Archdiocese Dorothy Day had lived and worked and who is promoting her canonization, invited some of his wealthier constituents to a breakfast so that I could present the project and solicit their support. At the end of my presentation, a well-heeled, yet extremely conservative gentleman rose and said, "You say she's a saint. Not my kind of saint, I'll tell you that. She's been in my house a number of times and she was always angry. Saints aren't angry. Mother Teresa rides in my private jet and she doesn't get angry. That's my kind of saint, not Dorothy Day."

I did not get any help from him. Nor from a number of other people, some of whom are my friends, who found Dorothy too confrontational and left of center. "She was a troublemaker," said one, "always agitating for this or that." Dorothy's pacifism, her abortion, her picketing with Cesar Chavez and his United Farm Workers bothered others. We were turned down many times. But there were bright spots—and providential moments.

After I presented the project to a large Catholic foundation in Philadelphia, its president asked, "And how much money would you like us to give, Father?"

"Do you think you could consider a hundred thousand dollars?" I replied.

"Oh, heavens, no!" she answered. She took the project to her Board and two of its members had serious reservations. At the request of the president, I returned to Philadelphia to meet with them. After an hour of dialogue, their reservations seemed to dissolve. At its end, one of them asked, "And how much are you asking from this Foundation?"

I replied, "Do you think you could consider $25,000 a year, for each of the next five years?" He was noncommittal.

I called the president the day after the full Board met on our request. "How did we do?" I asked.

"The letter is in the mail, but I think you will be pleased," she said.

"Can you tell me how much they approved?" I continued.

"Two hundred and fifty thousand dollars," she replied.

I was afraid my hearing aid was playing tricks on me, but the next day the letter arrived confirming the phone conversation.

The Holy Spirit had struck again.

We were off and running. But then, three million dollars is a lot of money and we were not at all sure it could be done. I tried to see at least five prospects a week, accompanied, if possible, by a Board member who knew the person. We operated on the premise that you can eat an elephant if you cut him up into enough pieces. Over the next four years, we cut that three-million-dollar elephant into a great number of pieces, and we were turned down frequently, but finally, because of the generosity of our prospects, and the persistence of our committee, we went over the top. We had the budget we needed to make the picture. But that is getting ahead of our story.

After the Board's decision to proceed with the project, I approached an old friend who has since become one of the country's top TV writers and asked him if he would be interested in writing the script. He knew of Dorothy, loved her and everything she stood for, and agreed immediately. I secured for him the necessary research materials and we talked through the project. Four months later, he sent me the first half of the script. I felt it was wide of the mark. We talked at great length and finally he decided to withdraw from the project. "We both love Dorothy Day," he said, "but I'm afraid we're in love with different women."

We have remained close friends, working together on other projects.

Back to square one. I called John Sacret Young, who had done such a superlative job on the Romero script. He said that he was overwhelmed with his China Beach TV series, but that he had on his staff a writer whom he thought a major talent and who had exactly the right background.

Four days later, John Wells and I had dinner. The son of a socially progressive Episcopalian priest, John had done more than his share of hurting, deepened his faith as a result and had acquired from his father a degree of theological sophistication rare in Hollywood. He also had acquired the requisite literary and dramatic skills. A graduate of Carnegie Mellon, he had, before joining the writing staff of China Beach, managed several little theaters and done some production consulting for Paramount Pictures. After finishing the Dorothy Day script, he would become the driving force behind E.R., the hit TV show of the 1994–95 season.

We met at a restaurant in nearby Westwood and hit it off immediately. John has an outgoing personality which does not obscure but rather expresses a deep interiority. I could see at once that he is extremely bright, intensely caring and radiates a bubbly joy that I found quite attractive. He knew of Dorothy Day and was very interested in telling her story. I told him I was most interested in dramatizing Dorothy's spiritual journey and thought we should concentrate on the period between 1917 and 1937, from Dorothy's twentieth to her fortieth years, because that was the period in which she faced the great crises of her life and made the decisions which shaped all else. John agreed.

We also talked about the religious themes of Dorothy's odyssey and agreed they should be explored in the movie: the incompleteness of human life without God; the unique presence of God in the poor and needy; the fulfillment to be found in serving Him in them; the power of love to resolve conflict without violence.

The more we talked, the more I could sense John's passion about the project. Yet he did have a problem and also several questions. The problem: as executive producer, he was deeply involved in and contractually committed to the production of China Beach and would have little time to devote to the Dorothy Day script until that year's season was complete in March. Could I live with that? I gulped. This meant a five-month delay. "Do you intend to do China Beach next year?" I asked. "No," he replied quite firmly. "OK," I said, "I'll live with the delay."

"How offended," he wanted to know, getting to the first of his questions, "would Dorothy's constituency in the Church be if we honestly portrayed her failings? And how candid are you willing to be?" "Completely," I answered. "I have no doubt Dorothy is a saint, but she made a lot of mistakes and we would betray her if we were less than honest about them. If her devotees have a problem with that, then that's their problem, not ours."

"And how honest are you willing to be," he went on, taking a deep breath, "about Dorothy's criticism of the institutional Church? Won't you jeopardize your own constituency there?"

"My constituency may be more mature than you think," I answered, "but let me worry about them. Dorothy was prophetic. She said things people did not want to hear. But those things are true and they need to be said. The whole Church needs to hear them. So does the world. Our job is to help them do just that." John breathed a sigh of relief. "One other thing," John said. "Dorothy's life is incredibly rich, religiously *and* theatrically. We're going to have to compress a lot, rearrange some things. Are you ready for that?" "Of course," I answered. "We're allowed theatrical license with the facts. But I would like to be rigorously faithful to the heart of her experience, to her truth. Do you have any problem with that?" "Not at all," he replied. "That's why we're doing this, isn't it?"

That was the beginning of the Dorothy Day script. It was also the beginning of a rich friendship.

It was not, however, a script—or a friendship—that progressed without glitches along the way. I immediately secured for John as much reading material as I could: Dorothy's three autobiographies, her autobiographical novel and the best of the books written about her. By March 1991 he had completed the China Beach season but was so exhausted that we agreed he would take a month off to recover his energies. By early May, he had hired a researcher and was plowing his way through the written material. Early in June we set out on a research trip to the East Coast, visiting in Plattsburg, New York, Tessa Day, Dorothy's sister-in-law; in Newport, Rhode Island, Tamar Hennessy, Dorothy's daughter, and Ada Bethune, an old friend of Dorothy's and one of the Catholic Worker's earliest cartoonists; and in New York City, Eileen Egan, probably Dorothy's closest friend (they went around the world together) and a former editor of the Catholic Worker. Most of the buildings where Dorothy lived and worked are still standing and Eileen took us to them all. She also gave us crucial insights into Dorothy's psyche. This was invaluable. Not only did this enable John to get a clearer fix on Dorothy as a person, but it also enabled him to situate her in her milieu, to write scenes with the geography clearly fixed in his imagination. I could see the wheels of creativity beginning to spin in John's head. He said he was nearing the point where he could begin writing. I was delighted.

After the research trip, John returned to Los Angeles and I took a couple of weeks off at Lake George. I called John shortly after I returned to see how he was progressing. "I have bad news for you," he said. I braced myself. "China Beach has just been renewed and John Sacret Young was desperate for help and I agreed to executive produce again. I feel I owe it to him. But I know this has to be disappointing for you. I can work nights and weekends on Dorothy Day, or would you prefer to find another writer?" It was disappointing. More than that. It was exasperating and infuriating. But I did not want to go with another writer. By this time I was convinced John was the right man for the job. So I decided to wait the eight months.

When John had completed the year's order of China Beach in March of 1992, despite being exhausted he plunged immediately into writing the Dorothy Day script, as he had promised. By mid May he had completed a first draft, which he gave to his secretary to be typed. Immediately, he got on a plane for a four-week mountain climbing excursion in the Himalayas.

I read the script and despite patches of brilliance found it not to my liking. I gave it to several of my most trusted advisors. They also responded negatively. What was I to do? Start over with another writer? I decided to stick with John. I wrote him an eighteen page, single spaced memo, delineating what I liked and what I didn't like about the script. I knew the memo would pain him. I did not want to do that. But I also knew I owed him—and Dorothy—the truth, so that we could get the best possible script. But when should I send the memo? If I sent it at once, it would ruin his vacation. But if I held it until he returned, he would have little chance to assimilate it. I decided to send it to him just before his return, so he could think about it on the plane ride home.

It says something very good about John that he did not at that point walk away from the whole project. We met just after his return and went over my criticisms in detail. He agreed with some but not all of them. Since China Beach had now been canceled and John was rested and had the next several months more or less free, we decided to work very closely together over the summer so that hopefully, by fall, we would have a script we both could be happy with. I went through the script and marked the scenes that I felt should be retained, and those that should be rewritten or discarded. Together we decided the screenplay should have four major sections: Dorothy's bohemian life in Greenwich Village; her retreat to Staten Island, relationship with Forster Batterham, Tamar's birth and her conversion; the return to New York City, the establishment and growth of the Catholic Worker; Dorothy's dark night of the soul as she pays the price for the lifestyle she has chosen. And together we did a scene breakdown, a section at a time. We also discussed the orientation of the important scenes, and on occasion John asked me to give him patches of dialogue for the more theological sections. It was a strategy that worked—but only because John was totally dedicated to the project and brought to the task his considerable resources of mind, heart and imagination. It also worked because John never let his ego get in the way of improving the script. We argued a lot but it was never a case of my way versus his way. It was always a case of what was truest to Dorothy's experience and most enthralling for the audience. This was collaboration at its most creative.

By September, we had a script I felt was close. By November, after some intensive rewriting, we had one I felt I could take to directors and actresses with pride.

It had taken us two long years to get there. But it was worth it.

Producing a movie is not a terribly complicated process. You select a great writer and work with him or her until you have a great script. You select a great director and together you select a couple of great actors. These three ingredients—the writer, the director, the actors—are central to every movie. Get great ones and you have a chance for a great movie. Fail to get greatness in any one category and you will end up with a mediocre movie. It sounds very simple and on one level it is. But the decision-making process by which you select the writer, the director and the actors is anything but simple. And the process by which you contact those you select and secure their involvement is more complicated still, especially when you do not have the prestige of a major studio behind you and can only offer guild minimum as compensation. (In 1995, guild minimum for a feature film was $54,266 for the writer, $123,097 for the director, and $1752 a week for each of the actors, plus pension and health insurance.)

At Paulist Productions, we have always worked on the premise that the Lord deserves the best and it was our job to get it for Him.

We felt we had been true to this mandate in the script department. We now turned our attention to securing a great director. Since Dorothy Day's story had strong feminist undertones, we decided to seek a woman director. In Hollywood, unlike acting and writing, directing has been a masculine province, but in recent years a number of talented women have broken through the gender barrier and made some first class pictures. During the winter of 1993, usually working through their agents, we approached: Randa Haines, Penny Marshall, Martha Coolidge, and Mary Agnes Donoghue. Later we approached Gillian Armstrong and Diane Keaton. All were either not available or did not think the material was suitable for them. "I'm best at relationships stories," said one, apparently not putting Dorothy's rapport with God into that category.

So I turned to male directors. After reading the script, one old friend said, "I like it but not enough to spend eight months of my life on it." Another, Ed Zwick, liked it but was preparing to shoot "Legends of the Fall." "You know," he said, "I have worked on "Thirty something" with a young director whom I consider brilliant. He has already won a couple of Emmys and a DGA award and is looking for a feature. I'd send him the script if I were you." So I did. He loved it, saying on the phone, "I have never been religious but I have always envied people who could get in touch with the transcendent and Dorothy went one step further: she was able to *commit* to the transcendent. I am fascinated by that." We had lunch. I liked him. He was bright and creative and open to dialogue. I felt I could work happily and productively with him. I also checked him out. He had worked for Bill Finnegan and Kerry McCluggage, two of my principal advisors in this area, and they also gave him high marks. I decided to go with him. I set up a meeting with John Wells, so the director could give us his ideas for polishing the script. They were good ones and John incorporated them into a new version. In that meeting he also committed to direct "Dorothy Day."

By this time, I had drawn up a list of possible actresses to play Dorothy. It included, among others, many of the top stars in the twenty-five to thirty-five age range: Michele Pfeiffer, Geena Davis, Jodie Foster, Sarah Jessica Parker, Meg Ryan, Debra Winger, Robin Wright, Julia Ormond, Holly Hunter, Mary Stuart Masterson and Emma Thompson. "Name recognition—marquis value—is crucial for this kind of picture," my advisors told me. "It is the only sure way to get people into the theaters."

Those on my list were, of course, major stars and their agents would not ask them to read a script unless a definite offer accompanied it. Which means you can only send it to one actress at a time. And you never know how long it will take them to read it. Some read it in a week. Others took a month or longer. I am not sure some read it at all.

During the summer and fall of 1993 and into the winter of 1994, using an order that the director and I had drawn up, we continued this agonizing process. I asked the priests in the rectory, the kids in the school and the sisters at Whitethorn to pray that we would find just the right person. It did not seem the Lord was listening. The partner of one major star called the script extraordinary, but too close to a story they were developing for their own production company. Another said she liked the script, but not enough to cut her going rate of pay by 95%. Two other actresses responded enthusiastically to the script and set up meetings to discuss it, then canceled at the last minute. Two others committed to play the part, one after two meetings to discuss it, then backed off when it was time to sign a contract and set dates. For one reason or another, the others also passed.

Like the director, I found this process very painful. I knew if I could sit down with some of these actresses, I could motivate them to involve themselves. Or at least find out why they chose not to do so. But the system does not give you that opportunity. Actresses have agents to protect them from producers like me. But sometimes they protect them too well. And, on more than one occasion, I suspected the agents were not discussing the project with their clients or even giving the script to them to read. I found this exasperating and all the while the clock continued to tick and I wondered if the Lord wanted me to spend what little time and energy I had left knocking my head against a stone wall, stomaching one rejection after another, in this most volatile and frustrating of businesses. I also wondered if Dorothy Day was sabotaging me.

I tried to understand what was happening. It was a great part, the kind most actresses say they would give their eye teeth to play. The script was first class. There was a consensus about that. Why then were these actresses (and their agents) not grabbing it? Was it the money? Or the lack of backing by a major studio? Or the fact that our director had not done a feature film before? Was it because, in militantly liberal Hollywood, Dorothy was not politically correct? She did regret her abortion and she did become a Catholic—two no-nos in the dogmatically secular decalogue. Or, on a much more profound level, was it because playing a character like Dorothy Day involved a journey into uncharted territory, a descent into mysterious depths, to do what Dorothy had done—wrestle with God, enter into communion with Him—all in all an awesome experience of the holy, the kind of thing that would be frightening for any sensitive person and absolutely intimidating for many. I did not know then, nor do I know now the answer to these questions. But I did know the clock kept ticking, the sand kept streaming through the hourglass, and I had no lead actress.

In January of 1993, while I was still seeking a director, I read in the *New York Times* an interview with Moira Kelly who played Charlie Chaplin's wife in Richard Attenborough's film on the great comedian. It talked about her staunch Catholicism and quoted her as saying she had always wanted to play Joan of Arc. Here is an actress, I thought to myself, whose heroic archetype is close to the surface, something we needed in the Dorothy Day part. But I dismissed her as a possibility because she was at the time only twenty-four.

But that was early in 1993 and it was now well into 1994. If she was not now twenty-six, she had to be very close to it. That meant she was within the age range. Her name kept coming up at casting meetings. The director was enthusiastic about her, saying she had not as yet broken through as a major star, but had the presence and the magnetism that would almost certainly enable her to do so. I decided to check her out. I looked at "Chaplin" again. I also looked at "Twin Peaks," "Daybreak" and "Cutting Edge." I liked what I saw. So did Paulist Production's core staff. Moira did have a presence, a buoyant integrity and a quality of intelligent innocence that seemed just right for "Dorothy Day." I sent her the script. Her agent called ten days later. "She likes it," he said. "What's our next step?"

Three days later Moira came to my office for lunch. In the interim, I contacted the Board. Some knew and liked Moira, but were not enthusiastic about going with a less than major star, saying it made recouping our investment much more difficult. But others said the decision was mine and they would back me whichever way I decided to go. "Follow your gut," one said incisively.

I prayed up a storm before the lunch. I did not want to make an impulsive decision born of my impatience to get the project moving. I knew this decision was a make or break one, for the actress who played Dorothy would be in every scene and had to carry the whole picture. Everything depended on her.

Moira brought her best friend—Dara Kelly (no relation)—to the lunch, perhaps to check me out as I was checking her out.

We talked about two and a half hours, some of the time about show business, Paulist Pictures, her career and the Dorothy Day role, but mostly it was soul talk, about what we believed and how we experienced God and how we tried to live out our faith in Him. I could see that her faith was at the center of her life—a fierce faith, passionate and ready for battle, that permeated her entire life. And because it did, she radiated a kind of exuberant Irish vitality that was magnetic. I could also see that she was bright—very bright—and that she, like Dorothy, marched to her own drummer, regardless of what other people might think. I could also see that she was passionate about the part, a delightful change after all the ambivalence I had been encountering. We touched souls during the lunch. There was no ambivalence in my gut about what I should do. I offered her the part. She accepted.

At last, all the lights were flashing green. That night I phoned the sisters at Whitethorn and asked them to join me in saying "Thank You."

But then disaster struck. I called the director to let him know Moira was aboard. He was pleased in a rather subdued sort of way. We talked about shooting dates and when we would begin preparing the picture. He said he would have to look at his schedule. We also talked about casting the other roles. Raul Julia had aleady committed to play Eugene O'Neill, Melinda Dillon to play Sister Aloysius and Martin Sheen had sent word he would like to play Peter Maurin, Dorothy's mentor in the early days of the Catholic Worker.

I called the director several days later, hoping to lock in some kind of schedule. He was evasive, saying he had to resolve a couple of things before he could set anything in concrete. I should have confronted him on his ambivalence, but I did not want to face it. Four days later he called to say he had to withdraw from the project; that his wife had had a baby; that they needed to buy a house; that he was being offered several jobs that would pay many times what ours would pay; that he was overcome with guilt at having to do this, but that he felt he had no choice. I could not contest his reasons. I could see he had made up his mind. I could also see he was drenched in guilt. I had no desire to increase it. So I accepted his withdrawal without protest.

But I was devastated.

"What are you doing to me?" I bellowed at the Lord that night. "I've had it. You treat your friends like dirt. This is it. The end. Kaput. Make your own picture. Or get somebody else to do it. I can't take any more."

By the next morning, I was no longer angry. Just depressed. What did I do now? I could walk away from the project. But not without leaving in the lurch all those I had asked to involve themselves: John Wells, Moira Kelly, the contributors, the Board, the core staff at Paulist Productions who, although always supportive, were chomping at the bit. Besides, I did not want to quit. I loved the woman. I wanted to tell her story. But how?

I told Moira. She was disappointed. Two days later she called back. "What would you think of Richard Attenborough?" she asked. "Great," I replied. He had directed "Gandhi," my favorite picture of all time. "But do you think he would be interested?" "He might," she replied. "I'll ask him to read it."

She did. He loved it. Convinced the Holy Spirit had struck again, I flew at once to Chicago, where he was shooting a picture, to discuss the project with him. We met in his hotel suite. During the initial pleasantries, I could tell he was taking my measure as I was taking his. I liked him at once and he seemed to reciprocate. An actor turned director, Sir Richard has a Santa Claus persona. Yet, beneath the hearty laugh, the twinkling eyes and the English charm, I sensed a penetrating mind of considerable erudition and a heart of acute spiritual sensitivity. We talked about Dorothy Day, about her spiritual journey, about the challenges of communicating it. His enthusiasm was very evident. He loved the complexity of Dorothy's character, the subtlety of John's writing—and the humor in the script. Having directed Moira in Chaplin, I asked him if he thought she could carry the picture? "Indubitably," he answered. "This will stretch her as nothing else has, but she's up to it, believe me."

"This is a religious odyssey story," I went on, "with all kinds of theological implications. Are you comfortable in that area?"

"Well," he replied, "I'm not a practicing Christian."

"Well, I am," I answered. "Do you think that could pose a problem?"

"What a charming answer," he said, "I can't imagine our having a problem."

We talked about organizing the shoot, about the personnel we would use, and about the budget. I said I thought there were two possible ways to go: the way we had gone with "Romero," asking most everybody to work for guild minimum and soliciting generosity from every possible quarter. The other way was the studio route with a budget that would allow us to go first cabin and pay everyone their going rate.

Sir Richard said that ten or twenty years ago he would have been happy to take the first route, but at seventy-three (he also was aware of his ticking clock and there was even less time on his than on mine), he only wanted to make pictures that would be seen all over the world and only a major studio could guarantee that. He estimated he would need seventeen to eighteen million dollars to make the picture.

"Do you think we can get that kind of money from a major studio?"

I asked. "Not in England," he replied. "But maybe in America." We called his American agent from the suite and the agent said he thought it was doable. I agreed to return to Los Angeles and work with the agent to approach all the major studios. I spent the summer of 1994 doing so. All turned us down. "Dickie makes great pictures," one executive told me, "but as often as not they do not make money and that, unfortunately, is the name of the game for us." I was shattered.

Since the Los Angeles riots of 1992 I had moved my Sunday Mass and preaching to a black parish in South Central Los Angeles. Moira frequently joined me in my celebrating there, and sometimes we would have brunch afterwards. We had become fast friends. She too was disappointed that it was not going to work with Sir Richard. "Maybe I'm not ready to play Dorothy Day yet," she mused one Sunday. "Or maybe you're not ready to produce a picture on her yet." That jolted me. Out of the mouths of babes and sucklings comes wisdom.

I decided I had to intensify the praying. The kids in the school were now back from summer vacation and I asked them to pray I would find the right director. I got the priests in the rectory to do the same. Likewise the sisters at Whitethorn. But still I had no director. I asked Oscar Romero for help. I asked deceased Paulist buddies Jim Gollner and John Carroll to help. And I decided to have it out with Dorothy Day.

"Are you working against me?" I demanded.

"You should spend the money on the poor," she replied.

"That's what I'm doing. Helping the spiritually poor—those who are confused and mixed up and empty inside. I think this movie can help them discover the meaning of their lives. Give them some idea what God is like and what they can become," I shot back.

"I'm talking about the physically poor," she retorted.

"But I didn't raise the money for the physically poor. I raised it to make this movie. I can't just spend it any way I want."

"You could feed and clothe and house a lot of people with that budget of yours."

"If we succeed, this movie will open the eyes of millions of people to the beauty and dignity of the poor. Think of all the people it will motivate to reach out to help them, and the hope it will give to women who have had abortions and don't think they can be forgiven."

"Words, words, words. You *hope* your movie will do those things. I *know* what that money could do."

"Look, Dorothy," I said finally in exasperation. "You've got to face something. I'm going to make this movie. If you continue to work against me, it will be a turkey. If you help me, it can be a great picture and do a lot of good for a lot of people. Now what do you want?"

She looked deep into my eyes, took a long breath and said, "OK, I'll help you."

She did.

During September and October of 1994, I approached eight more directors. One hated the script. Three liked the script but had contrary commitments. Two said they wanted to direct it, but backed off when it came time to set dates.

The board was getting impatient. The subtext was: all this talk and still no picture. Some of the contributors were wondering out loud what I had done with their money. Moira's agent was telling her he did not think it would ever happen. And their impatience was nothing compared to mine.

"Have you thought of Mike Rhodes?" Patt Shea asked when I ran into her at a broadcasters meeting. "He's working for Walter Coblenz and doing a great job."

I had thought of Mike Rhodes. We had worked happily together for sixteen years at Paulist Productions and he was something of a son to me. After "Romero," he had launched out on his own and became one of the industry's hottest Movie of the Week directors. He was now anxious to make the transition to feature films and had, through his agent, let me know he very much wanted to direct "Dorothy Day."

When Mike worked at Paulist Productions he tended to be a "soft" director. We always loved his characters and his stories had a great deal of heart, but there was not much sharp conflict. I felt that the Dorothy Day story had to be gritty, that the conflict had to be raw and her pain palpable, so I didn't feel he had the right sensibility to direct it. What I was not considering was the growing he had done—theatrically and personally—since leaving Paulist Productions. I got an inkling of this when I took some of his MOW's home the following weekend.

I decided to call Walter Coblenz, an old friend. He was glowing in his praise of Mike. I told him my concern. He dismissed it, saying, "My story is as hard edged as TV gets and Mike is doing just fine with it." I did some further checking. Kerry McCluggage gave Mike high marks, but another of my advisors was strongly opposed, saying Mike lacked subtlety. I decided to take a day to think and pray about it. I knew Mike would give it everything he had. I knew we worked well together. I knew he was excellent with actors and this was preeminently a performance piece. A devout Presbyterian, I also knew he would help me build the loving community I feel so important for a successful shoot. I could sense I was getting close to a decision to go with Mike. I put in a call to the advisor who was so opposed, to give him an opportunity to talk me out of it. When he took his time calling me back, I made my decision. I found Mike in a motel in Seattle where he was directing Walter's Movie of the Week and asked him to direct Dorothy Day. I could feel the emotion in his voice as he said he would be pleased to do so. "Thank you, Lord," was the subtext. I should have been saying the same thing because in the months that followed I was to see that Mike Rhodes had exactly the right combination of qualities to direct Dorothy Day.

Dorothy had not been working against me. With both Mike and Moira, she—and the Lord—had simply been protecting me from my own mistakes, making sure that I ended up with exactly the right people to make the picture we all wanted.

We were now off and running. The months—years really—of debilitating waiting were over. My adrenaline started to flow. Mike and I decided to begin preproduction right after the first of the year 1995 and to start principal photography early in March. While he finished his picture, I started to assemble the production team. Our core staff at Paulist Productions—Paulists Greg Apparcel and Mark Villano, Jesuit Chris Donahue and my assistant, Jane Paulson—helped with this. In short order, we hired a production manager and co-producer (Peter Burrell), a cinematographer (Mike Fash), a scenic designer (Chuck Rosen), a production coordinator (Trish Riordan), a casting director (Caro Jones), a location manager (Paul Brinkman), an assistant director (Carl Ludwig) and an accountant (Tom Kenniston). Greg volunteered to be general manager of the office during the shoot and, with his encyclopedic knowledge of actors, to join Judy Greening in assisting Caro Jones with the casting. Mark volunteered to recruit extras, no mean task since we needed so many. Chris Donahue joined Peter Burrell as co-producer and post production supervisor, and Jane Paulson would run my office and handle the press.

In the weeks that followed we rounded out our cast, hammered out a budget, set our locations, worked out a schedule and hired the remainder of the crew.

We set Boyd Kestner and Lenny Von Dohlen as Dorothy's lovers, Heather Graham as Maggie, Dorothy's best friend, James Lancaster as Eugene O'Neill (we lost Raul Julia to a stroke in October 1994), Paul Liebek as Mike Gold, Allyce Beasley as a Catholic Worker, Heather Camille as Dorothy's daughter, Tamar, Tracey Walter as a derelict turned Catholic Worker and Brian Keith as the Archbishop of New York.

Getting the budget in line proved to be a herculean task. It was an ambitious picture. Richard Attenborough's estimate of eighteen million was conservative. My advisors said more like twenty. We had to find New York in Los Angeles. We had an abundance of exterior street scenes with milling crowds. And most difficult of all, it was a period piece, requiring the unique costumes, hairdos, props, sets and cars of the late teens, twenties and thirties. Not an easy proposition. Nor an inexpensive one.

But we found many generous people in Hollywood who believed in what we were trying to do. Over the years we had made a lot of friends, and I have no compunction about cashing in my chits and asking people to be generous. I begged a lot. Our people haggled a lot. As a result, Warner Brothers offered their costume department and prop house to us without cost. Fox lent us sets. Paramount let us use their standing New York streets at a considerable discount. Deluxe film lab did our developing and printing without charge. Fuji gave us a considerable discount on the film stock. We were able to rent the camera and lights for a fraction of their usual cost. We joked about multiplying the loaves and fishes, about turning water into wine, but there was an element of truth in it. I asked my department heads for a zero based budget. Having already stretched their dollars, they smiled and gave me one with a certain comfort level built in. I argued and cajoled and tried to cut away the fat and finally we settled on a budget of $4,302,000—more than I had planned but something I could live with.

In the early stages of Dorothy Day, I had to be the engine driving the whole process. Now the picture took on a momentum of its own and I had only to steer it, to make sure it was staying on track and moving in the right direction.

We began rehearsals early in March. Moira, Mike and I had already gone through the script, delineating Dorothy's character arc, scene by scene. I was beginning to see the depth and breadth of Moira's emotional range, and the texture, the color, the nuances and the abundance of luminous energy she would bring to the role. I was delighted.

Early in March, we also held our final production meeting, with all department heads and most of the crew in attendance. As I did also on the first day of rehearsals, I tried to set the tone of the shoot by sketching out for them the importance of the picture and its underlying religious themes. I told them I thought it deserved all the energy and creativity we could give it. Then, with Mike taking over, we went through the script, scene by scene, letting each person know what would be expected of him or her and where and when it would be expected.

There would be no unresolved questions on this shoot. Thanks to Peter Burrell and Chris Donahue, we were meticulously prepared.

We began shooting on Tuesday, March 14. The previous Saturday night, we held a Mass and a launch party for the cast, crew and their families. Most everyone came. It was a great way to start a picture.

At the homily of the Mass, I told everybody present I had reason to believe the next eight weeks could be among the most memorable of our professional lives, that the film we were about to shoot could be something of which we would always be proud. It was, I said, a film *about* God. I hoped, I also said, that we would make it *for* God. And *with* God. That in the process of making this film, we would tap into the Lord's creativity and avail ourselves of His love energy, so that together we could love each other and commit ourselves unselfishly to making the very best film we could.

At the offertory of the Mass, each person brought a symbol of his or her craft and laid it on the altar to be offered to God with the bread and wine.

It was a lovely celebration, joyous but serious. I think people realized this was something special, a once in a lifetime experience, and that God was involved in a unique way. In addition, after Mass, people who had been strangers began to talk, eat and laugh together. The connecting, the bonding had begun.

As a producer, I have always felt my job was to hire the very best people, get them what they needed and then get out of their way so that they could maximize their creativity and make the very best picture they could. I tried to do this now. This did not preclude keeping an objective eye on performances, being the final decision-maker on editing and any significant departures from script or budget, and staying in dialogue with the director, seeing that he had everything he needed.

Not surprisingly, the first ten days were difficult as our bodies adapted to the grueling schedule and each person struggled to find his or her own rhythm. Additionally the members of the various teams (a film crew is a collection of interlocking three- to five-person teams, e.g., camera, lighting, sound, set design, props, wardrobe, construction, etc.) had to seek out the best way to interface with their teammates and their colleagues on the other teams. This entailed some trial and error. And there were, of course, the inevitable tensions between what we wanted and what we could afford, between the creative people who wanted to make the picture as big as possible and the money people who were responsible for keeping it on budget. But after the first two weeks we seemed to hit our stride, almost everyone found their rhythm and with few exceptions people were working efficiently and happily with one another.

The first week was especially difficult for me. Lurking in the dark recesses of my mind, only barely conscious, was a gnawing fear. Had I raised this money, recruited this talent and mobilized this army to now march it off a cliff, in the process squandering the generosity of so many people, and making a picture that would be unworthy of the woman it was about and an embarrassment to all those connected to it? In my darkest dreams, I heard a cacophony of angry, incredulous and painfilled voices: Dorothy's: "What did you do to me?" The donors: "I sacrificed for *that*?" My spiritually hungry viewers: "This is Good News?" Not at all conducive to serenity.

Were these fears irrational? Not completely. Filmmaking is not an exact science. Even the best producers turn out poor pictures. Why is that? Because filmmaking arises from the interfacing of the unconscious minds of scores of people, minds that can be nurtured and cultivated but never manipulated or programmed with any degree of certainty. Which is simply to say that filmmaking is a dicey business and every movie is a crap shoot. All you can do is fight for the best possible odds and then turn the whole thing over to the Lord.

My fears on the Dorothy Day shoot began to dissolve after I watched the dailies from the first week's shoot. Not only the quality of the performances but also the overall look of the picture—which meant, in particular, Mike Fash's photography and lighting and Chuck Rosen's sets—convinced me we had the makings of something special. At that point, I knew all this energy and time and money and effort and talent were not being expended in vain. So I began to relax and enjoy the shoot.

As a priest producer, I felt my job was to be the visible, if flawed symbol of God's presence on the set and involvement with the shoot, keeping everyone focused on our goal—the spiritual enrichment of our viewers—and seeing that everyone, especially Mike and Moira, felt supported. I also tried to be available to anyone who wanted to talk about their relationship with God.

Mike was a delight to work with. I marveled at his boundless energy, his sensitivity to the subtle nuances of the script, his exquisite use of images to convey emotion, his concern for the "little people" on his set, his ability to communicate with his cast and crew. But most of all, I was awed by Mike's ability to concentrate totally on the task at hand while staying open to dialogue. Ongoing dialogue with his actors, his cinematographer, his assistant director and his producer is at the heart of Mike's style of directing. As Moira said, "He's the best."

Moira was also a delight to work with. A tomboy when around the crew, a Mafia gun moll when clowning with Martin Sheen, an Irish charmer when meeting with the public, an articulate and theologically perceptive interpreter of the Dorothy Day story when doing an interview—Moira is a disciplined professional with an emotional range and depth surprising in someone so young. (She was just twenty-seven when we shot the picture.) She has an uncanny ability, even in the midst of a crowd, to close her eyes and go deep within herself in order to play in her head the scene she is about to shoot—as well as those that come immediately before and after—so that she can get in touch with just the right emotions. I never saw her miss an emotional beat. I never saw her deliver a line that did not come from deep inside her. In many ways she is like Dorothy Day—intelligent, feisty, tough, fiercely independent *and* faith-filled. I have no doubt her portrayal of Dorothy Day arose from that place deep within herself where she too wrestles with God.

"She's so good," said John Wells after seeing some of the dailies, "there is a danger she will blow everybody else off the screen."

I think Moira Kelly will be a major star. I hope this picture will enable her to break through into that exclusive company. I also pray she may resist its temptations and remain the centered, rooted, faith-filled and delightful human being she was on this shoot.

Along with many other people, she and Mike were the Lord's—and perhaps Dorothy's—gift to me on this picture.

They made my job so much easier.

She was the perfect person to play Dorothy Day.

He was the perfect person to direct "Dorothy Day."

There was a reason for all those rejections.

The Lord knew what He was doing even if I didn't.

Deo Gratias.

After thirty-five, twelve-hour shooting days, and a succession of locations that involved several warehouses and an old firehouse in the center of Los Angeles, the Franciscan stage, the Disney Ranch, Oxnard, Broad Beach and the Lincoln Heights jail, we finished "Dorothy Day" a day ahead of schedule and under budget on May 1 and celebrated with a wrap Mass and party on May 3. We had conspired and haggled and fought and loved and created and struggled and sweated and argued and laughed and prayed together for seven long weeks. We had given it our best and we felt good about the result. We also felt good about each other. There is a unique kind of camaraderie that develops on a film shoot. You become very close. More than that, you become part of one another. At the opening Mass, I had asked them to love each other. They had done so—and me—and I, them. I shall never forget so many of those beautiful people.

I write this at Lake George in mid July, 1995. Mike Rhodes is putting the finishing touches on the editing with Geoff Rowlands, and Bill Conti is hard at work composing the music. After we finish mixing the picture in September, we will begin showing it to distributors. We do not know how they will react. We do not know what the critics will say. Nor how the theatergoing public will respond. We don't know either whether we will recoup our donors' money, so we can roll it over toward our next two projects—a series of two hour films for cable on the characters of the New Testament and a seven hour PBS historical series for the millennium on how the world's various ethnic groups came to faith in Jesus, how they experienced Him in their prayer, conceptualized Him in their theology, imaged Him in their art and expressed their faith in Him in their liturgies, both official and folk.

We hope the response is positive. We are proud of the film we have made. We feel good about the way we worked together in the process of making it. The rest we leave in the hands of the Lord. As is obvious from the foregoing, He has been intimately involved all along the way. He too has an investment. As does Dorothy Day. We do not think either of them will desert us now. And we take comfort from the words of Jacques Maritain that began this book: "The important thing is not success. The important thing is to be in history, bearing the witness."

Part Six

Over the Shoulder

CHAPTER 19

THE JOURNEY

I push down the accelerator and speed down the interstate toward my sixty-seventh birthday, squinting into the rearview mirror and wondering where I have been, what I have done with my life, and what it has meant.

I climb a hill and can look out over the expanse of road I've covered through the valley below. The light is good, so I can see not only each phase of my journey as one segment has flowed into the next, but I can also get some perspective on the whole. What is this journey we call human life? What, in particular, has my journey meant? Where have I been going? How do the various stages of my life fit together? Where do I go from here?

For each of us, I think, life is a journey into the world of other people, in the hope of penetrating their depths and tapping their richness, so that we can touch the ultimate reality that resides within them. And for all of us, life is also a journey into ourselves —from the surface to the depths, from the periphery to the center —in the hope of passing through that center and coming to the God who lives on the other side.

If we progress on this journey, we move from existing to living, from illusion to reality, from fear to love, from isolation to community, from vegetation to contemplation, from manipulating the truth to surrendering to it, from self-absorption to God intoxication.

Whether we look at the journey as an objective movement outward from the self to the world or whether we look at it as a subjective movement inward to the center and depths of the self, the destination is the same. All of us, whether we realize it or not, whether we intend it or not, travel in the hope of finding God. He is the final destination of every human life.

Forty-seven years later, the central intuition of that freshman-year term paper—that we need God, that everything we do is a reaching for Him, that He alone can satisfy the ravenous desires within us—has proven itself to be right on target. We hunger for God. We can be happy and fulfilled only when our emptiness is filled full with Him.

As I look over my life, I see I have reached for God in many ways. I have looked for Him in nature—in the redwood forests at Whitethorn, the rock-strewn seascapes at Big Sur, the waterfalls at Yosemite, the regal peaks of the Grand Tetons, the desolation of Death Valley, the rippling savannahs of Kenya, the majesty of the Himalayas, the exquisite islands of the blue Aegean, the fjords of the Dalmatian Coast of Yugoslavia, the pine-studded islands of Lake George, the sunsets over the Pacific through the windows of my office on the coast highway. All have spilled the beauty and the radiance of the Lord through my eyes and into my heart, healing and nurturing me.

I have sought God in study—not only in scripture and theology, but also in philosophy because it probes the heart of being and the ramifications of existence; in psychology, social analysis, and history because human nature is a mirror in which the face of God is reflected; and in literature, whether fiction, drama, poetry, or biography, because these literary forms explore the mystery of human life and frequently penetrate to its transcendent base.

I have detected the luminosity of God in painting and sculpture, the melodious harmony of His grace-filled movements in ballet, the emanations of His being in music and His proclivity for compassion and surprise in the movies I have watched.

I have known Him in the breaking of the bread in the Eucharist and in the smiles of the people to whom I have given communion. I have sensed the stirrings of His life in the pouring of the waters of baptism, and I have heard Him sigh with relief as I said the words of absolution. I have felt the surge of His Word as I tried to articulate it in lecture, seminar, or sermon.

I have seen flashes of His light in story conference after story conference when, after long hours of seemingly futile effort, we finally break through and discover how to make a story work.

I have noticed the heat of His passion fill the face of an actor when a role slips into place and he or she catches fire.

And I have detected His fingerprints all over a show like *Romero.* He wasn't going to let us screw it up, no matter what.

I have been bumping into God all my life. Even when things went bad, when I staggered in confusion, ached with loneliness, reeled in pain, He was there. Earthquakes come and earthquakes go, but the God who is the ground of my being remains firm under my feet.

Even when I have wanted to, I have not been able to get away from Him. He's in the students I teach, the patients I visit, the famine victims I succor, the priests with whom I live, the writers, directors, and actors with whom I work, and the viewers whom we try to serve.

He has nurtured me through the families of which I have been a part—the Kiesers, the Paulists, the Hobergs. He has given Himself to me through the communities to which I have belonged—the priests in Westwood, Jesu Caritas, the team at Paulist Productions. He has shown me His face in the women I have loved, especially Clair and Genevieve. He has sustained and supported me through those very close friends who for decades have been a part of my life—Jack Bresnan, Patt Shea, John Furia, Liz Bugental, Dennis Burke, Irene Fugazy, Bill Cantwell, Don Kribs, Lan & Barbara O'Kun, Judy Greening, Terry Sweeney, Miles O'Brien Riley, and Jim Moser. I have felt His caring in those who have mentored me and in those I have mentored. As we have shared ourselves with each other, He has shared Himself with us.

God has not touched me in a vacuum. I have felt His breath in the down and dirty, thrashing about, give and take, stagger and swagger, exciting and exhausting process of trying to live out a human life lovingly. I do not think I am unique in this respect. For all of us, the journey to God passes through the heartland of our humanity. There is no shortcutting the human. We will find Him in other people, in ourselves, and in the very imperfect love that joins us together, or we won't find Him at all.

Even the approach to God that is prayer takes place in and through the human. At its most intense, it involves a descent into the depths of our humanity and a taking up of residence at its center.

I spent the four-day New Year's holiday of 1978 at the Camaldolese Monastery at Big Sur. Perched on the side of a mountain five hundred feet above the rock-strewn Pacific, the monastery is a contemplative's paradise. On some days you can look down on the blue-green sea and watch the white-foamed breakers smash against the rocky coastline a half mile below. On other days the ocean is shrouded in fog and, with a dark blue sky as a backdrop, you can peer down on the layers of mist and watch the sun burn them away.

During this mini-retreat, something significant was to happen inside of me.

It had been exactly ten years since that pain-filled New Year's night when Genevieve and I had decided to go our separate ways. It had been just ten days since that Christmas party at which Genevieve and I had reconnected and begun the process of our reconciliation. I arrived at the monastery singing inside, so happy to be in touch with her again; happy, too, to feel myself affirmed as a priest by her.

In between my dinner with Genevieve and my arrival at the monastery were the excitement and joy of Christmas in the parish and four days of good skiing with my sister and her family—the Hobergs—at Squaw Valley. I am not a great skier. But I love the sport. It always touches things deep within me. Part is primitive, the pitting of man against mountain. Part is the freedom of letting go, surrendering to a natural force and hurtling downhill at colossal speed, the wind tearing at my face. Part, too, is aesthetic: the view from the summit over the rocks and smaller hills to the frozen lake below, as I pause for a breath at the top before launching out; the snow glistening off the pine trees with the crystal-clear sky in the background as I zoom past; the ballet-like grace of the other skiers as they glide down the slope ahead of me. There is an exhilaration about skiing that is almost ecstatic.

Over the years I have found skiing a great launchpad for contemplation, which is why I usually try to find time for a short retreat at a monastery afterward. So it was at New Year's 1978.

As I began the retreat, I was aware that I was in a good place, physically relaxed, emotionally free and flowing. Genevieve was part of this. So was the skiing. But neither could completely explain what was to follow.

I had hardly begun to pray and meditate before I realized things were different within me. It soon became apparent that I had dropped down into a new and deeper place and that different things were going on inside me. Just what, I did not know. This was nothing new. Like the ocean with the fog, my wrestling match with God is often murky. I guess this should not surprise me. God is mystery, so there is no way I can comprehend Him. Full of surprises, He never does what I expect. And He is not the only mystery involved. The deeper reaches of my humanity—those layers of my soul where I struggle with God—are usually fogged in. Who can fully fathom the depths of his or her own soul? I know I can't.

At the very beginning of this retreat, I was confronted by these interlocking mysteries, and so I did what I usually do in this kind of situation. I tried to go with the experience, responding to what God was doing inside me in as honest and loving a way as I could. After a while I also tried to explore the new place in which I found myself. In this regard, I began to reach for symbols that could help me understand where I was and what was going on. One symbol that helped then, as it had helped before and has helped since, is the center of myself.

This center is like the hub of a wheel, the place into which, like spokes, all the various facets of my being converge.

It is a fire tower. I can look out through 360 degrees of glass to see everything that is going on around me.

It is a communications and command center from which I can initiate and coordinate what I decide to do. I am wired to every part of my being.

And it is like a cozy den. God often lives there, and I am whole and comfortable whenever I am there communing with Him.

Sometimes in those days I lived in this center, but sometimes I was alienated and did not. On previous retreats my first task had always been to get myself into this center so that I could look over my life and commune with God from there. At times this was easy—a simple matter of surrendering to the gravitational pull of the depths. At other times it was not. On this retreat, as I sat in the monks' octagon-shaped, wood-paneled chapel with the Blessed Sacrament off to one side, the dynamic was different. It seemed as if I did not need to struggle to get into the center of myself. I was already there.

On past retreats, upon arriving in the center of myself, I had usually walked around the circle of windows in my psyche and looked over the shaded contours of my life from there—at the people I was connected to and how I might improve my relationship with them, at my work as I tried to evaluate what I was doing and how I was doing it, and at my own relationship with God as I asked how I might make that better, too.

But on this retreat, I had no interest in the windows. I felt drawn to the room itself and to something that I had previously ignored. In the center of the room was a trapdoor. I guess it had always been there, but I had not noticed it before. Now I was fascinated by it. I pulled up the lid and looked in. It was completely dark down there. But there was a ladder. Where did it go? What was down there? And where was God? Was He down there? I had to find out. So I went through the trapdoor and down the ladder, and pretty soon I was surrounded by sheer blackness. But I kept going. Down. Down. Lower and lower. And then suddenly there was no more ladder and I was free-falling through space and I was surrounded by blackness and I should have been frightened but somehow I was not and I kept going deeper and deeper into this blackness that was the cellar of myself. And now the blackness had sides and it was a tunnel—a sometimes horizontal, sometimes vertical mine shaft, which twisted and turned as it went deeper and deeper into the heart of reality, getting closer and closer to that frontier region where the human and divine came together, where being and Being touched, where I emerged from God.

How did I know these things? How, in particular, did I know that God was at the end of the tunnel? I certainly didn't see Him. I didn't see anything. Yet I knew He was there. Did I feel it? Sense it? Intuit it? I didn't know how I knew it, but I did. This is why I pushed ahead. I needed to get to Him. I wanted to get to Him. I was propelled forward by the anticipation of getting to Him.

But as I moved down this tunnel, I found it becoming more and more narrow. A tight squeeze if ever there was one. Not only could I take none of my friends with me. I couldn't take anything else either. Not a grip or an attaché case. Not even a cassette player. Nothing. To traverse this tunnel, which stretched out beneath the center of my center and which was becoming so narrow that it resembled the eye of a needle, I had to leave behind not only the people I loved, the activities I enjoyed, the things that gave me pleasure; but I had to leave behind the desire for these things, the need for them, all reliance on them.

And I had to leave behind my reputation, any status or talents I had, my dreams and ambitions, too: the pictures I wanted to make, the places I wanted to visit, the things I still wanted to do. Nor could I take with me the psychic patterns I had developed over the years to facilitate my functioning: the defenses I employed, the roles I played, the categories I used to process reality, the images of myself I had created, both real and illusionary. They all had to be jettisoned. Especially the illusion of being better than other people. Moving through the tunnel meant traveling light in body and in spirit, no baggage of any kind. If that wasn't bad enough, I soon saw I had to leave my ego behind. Imagine that. I spend the first forty years of my life making it big and strong. The last twenty I spend experiencing its limitations and trimming it back. Now in the tunnel the walls were closing in, and I realized it had to go. Too big. Too heavy. Everything had to be stripped away, left behind. Everything. Even the shirt on my back. No clinging. None at all. Wash the glue off my fingers. Let everything slip away. Let the memory of it go. Let the desire for it go.

But what's left? What could I take through the eye of the needle? Just me. My naked humanity. The essence of myself. What's real. The stripped-down truth. Nothing else. No lies. No illusions. Nothing. We are naked when we emerge from the birth canal as babies. We are naked when we are reborn as adults, and all of us go stark naked into the presence of God.

The further I went, the tighter the squeeze. I thought I had left everything behind. But then I found I hadn't. I had been clinging to some things without even realizing it. So I allowed these things to be peeled away, too. It was a continuing process, and it never seemed complete.

The walls were narrow and the squeeze was tight and I should be feeling claustrophobic but I wasn't, perhaps because there was ground under my feet and I could move ahead under my own power. But then, suddenly, the tunnel opened out on the side of a mountain and a blast of arctic air hit me in the face and I could go forward no longer. Above and before me was a starless sky on a crisp, cold winter night. Below me was a sheer drop into black nothingness.

So that's what God is like. A light so bright that it seems darkness to my eyes. A plenitude so full nothing my mind can manufacture, no idea or symbol or concept, can adequately contain Him. Concepts are one-dimensional. Images are better at conveying what He is like. But all are inadequate. He is an incomprehensible mystery, a bottomless abyss, an infinite horizon, the ground of all being, the realest of the real.

Somehow in that darkness, I sensed the resonance of His being, the immensity of His presence, and somehow I knew He has a mind, a luminous intellect that pays attention to me, that orders my life and gives it meaning and purpose. And somewhere in that darkness, I felt a warm heart beating, and I sensed a smile. Somebody out there liked me. And suddenly I felt drawn by the power of that mind, the sweetness of that love. I did not fight it. I decided to go with it, to dive into this ocean, immersing myself in its richness, losing myself in its immensity. I just wanted to hug the horizon.

But I did have a problem. I could no longer move ahead under my own power. The tunnel had ended. The mountain had given way to open space. There's nothing to walk on. I came up short. I wanted to get to God. But I couldn't. I felt like catapulting myself into His arms. But I couldn't do it. And the more I tried, the more frustrating it became. So I did the only thing I could do. I gave up trying. I sat on the ledge at the end of the tunnel, looked out on the starless night, and waited for God to come and get me.

The waiting was very tough. But after a while I got used to it. I let the currents of His love wash over me. I tried to respond to them. And then I learned to commune with the sky from where I was. It was not everything I wanted. But it was a lot better than anything else around. So I opened myself to the sky. I breathed it in, filling my lungs with its oxygen, my soul with its strange kind of joy.

And I waited. And I prayed. And I said, "Lord, it's been a long time. Don't you think you should come and get me?"

As I sat on that ledge and contemplated the sky, I became aware of something else, too. I was not alone. Not only was God with me. But on this four-foot ledge, all of humankind was with me, too. I was not only communing with God, but I was also communing with all the other people who now inhabit this planet regardless of where they lived. And I was also communing with all the people who had ever lived, back to the very beginning of human history, and with all the people who will ever live until the very end of time. They were present to me and I was present to them. We were with each other. Place and time, the where and when of our living did not seem very important. Only our humanity was important, because that is where God lived, and it was through it that He gave Himself to us and drew us together.

I sat on the edge of the ledge on the side of the mountain and I looked at the black sky and I experienced no thunderclaps of awe, no trumpets of wonder, just a deep and chastened peace. I was in the presence of the real, the Realest of the Real, and I liked that. I felt good inside, quiet, together, and very, very alive. Good things were happening inside of me. And I began to realize that this was the beginning, the foretaste of what I had been made for. Not that I didn't yearn to see Him face to face. Not that I didn't, on occasion, get tired of all this darkness. But having to wait for vision, this seemed the next best thing. And sometimes the quiet breeze off the mountain was living breath and it swelled to become a mighty wind and it connected me to God and to every other person in the human family.

And then I realized I was not alone. I had never been alone. My loneliness started to dissolve. I liked being here.

The experience at Big Sur at New Year's of 1978 was not a turbulent and thundering tidal wave that crashed itself once against the rocky coast of my life and then receded into the depths of the sea, never to return again. At different times, in different ways, it has come again and again in the intervening years. It is sometimes luminous in its mystery, but more often it is dark and murky. On occasion it bursts into consciousness and pushes everything else out. At other times it is shunted aside in the press and push of daily business. But always it is there. It has become the subtext of my interior life.

And always when I need to think deeply about important things or make decisions that will significantly affect my life or that of other people, I try to make my way along that narrow tunnel and get to that ledge on the side of the mountain and look into that starless sky. I go there because that's where I am most real, most free of illusion, most in touch with myself . . . and with God. In that darkness I like to think I am clear-sighted and have perspective, and with perspective I can see how things fit together and what God wants for me.

The ledge has become my home. I have pitched a tent there. I go there to rest and refresh myself, to be re-created, nurtured, and energized. I enjoy my time there.

I have tried to write this book from there.

What do things look like from the ledge? What, in particular, does the journey that is my life look like from that vantage point?

It does not cease to be a mystery—that's for sure.

Yet I do notice a certain rhythm to the journey as certain moments seem to repeat themselves again and again.

I find three distinct stages in my life—from the middle years of high school (1943–1944) to my early years as a priest and producer (1963–1964), from the Vatican Council and Genevieve (1965) to the full flowering of "Insight" and the Humanitas Prize (1977), from the inner trip to the ledge and the exterior trip to India (1978) to the present (1995).

These three stages roughly correspond to Erik Erikson's identity, intimacy, and generativity crises.

In each of these three stages, five moments seem to recur: a time of disintegration when things fall apart; a time of crisis when I flounder around and grope for a solution; a time of decision when I decide where I want to go and perhaps more importantly who I have to be to get there; a time of reintegration as I plot this new direction and put together this new identity; a time of living out the new direction and expressing this reborn self.

In the first stage, the spiritual experience of being called and the death of my mother demolished my boyhood identity. During the latter part of high school and most of college, I floundered, trying to figure out who I wanted to be, where I wanted to go, what I wanted to do with my life. By the end of college I had decided to give the priesthood a try. By the end of the novitiate, the ambivalence had evaporated and I was sure I wanted to be a priest. The years in the seminary were spent putting together this new identity. The early years of my priesthood—at the parish and at the medical center, teaching inquiry classes and making "Insight"—were spent living it out.

In the second stage—from 1965 to 1978—the loneliness of my life apart from the parish, the inadequacy of the theology I had been given in the seminary, and the seismic shifts in my psyche produced by the Vatican Council and my love for Genevieve, caused the cerebral and voluntaristic identity I had put together in the seminary to collapse. In the latter part of the sixties, I floundered. Finally I decided to take the steps necessary to become an integrated and fulfilled priest (and human being) in the post-conciliar Church. I joined Jesu Caritas, went for psychotherapy, and enrolled at GTU. I pursued this new orientation and expressed this new identity from 1973 to 1978, when things started to come apart again.

In the third stage—from 1978 until the present—the impending demise of "Insight," excessive concern for my own fulfillment, and the spiritual experience I have just described combined to cause my post-conciliar identity to come apart. Through most of 1978, I floundered. But India was the bracing shock I needed. Its desperately poor yet spiritually rich people shattered my illusions, peeled away my narcissism, and revealed to me where the Realest of the Real was to be found. As a result I decided to scale back my desires and forget about myself as I tried to opt for the poor and open myself to the Lord who lives so uniquely in them. The trips to famine-ravaged Kenya, Somalia, and Ethiopia in the early eighties helped me put together the psychological wherewithal to follow through on this. Which is what, with varying degrees of success, I have been trying to do ever since.

Each of these stages has a time when a very important part of me dies and a time when an even more important part of me is born. It is the death and resurrection of Jesus working itself out in my life. The grain of wheat has to fall into the earth and die before the full stalk can spring up. I have to die with Christ before I can hope to rise with Him.

Looking back now, I can see how I resisted the dying process. It was painful and confusing and frightening and I wanted none of it. Yet now, with the wisdom of hindsight, I can also see how necessary those pain-filled times were, how stunted I would have become without them. The boy had to die that the priest could be born. The religious warrior intent on conquering the world for Christ had to die before the deeply flawed witness of Jesus's love and promoter of human values could take his place. And the missionary to main street had to die before the stripped human being, the servant of the poor, had a chance to take over.

Because of what has emerged from them, I can honestly say I am glad I went through these dying periods. I like what they have produced. I like what God has done for me through them. But, in all honesty, I must also say I would not want to go through any of them again.

Does this mean I have gone where I needed to go, done what I needed to do, seen what I needed to see, decided what I needed to decide; that, as a result, I now have it made? I need no more stripping, no more pain, no more dying?

It does not mean that.

To say so would be to tell myself the worst kind of lie.

I think the capacity for self-deception and the hunger for illusion are the essence of original sin. They do not die easily, and I suspect for this son of Adam they will not die at all this side of the grave.

Which is why, in recent years, I have needed to make a conscious effort to stay in touch with that side of me that is weak and needy, scared and guilty, lonely and empty, confused and dying. Whenever I have trouble doing this, I go down to skid row or take a walk through the veterans' cemetery at Sawtelle. There is nothing like a soup kitchen filled with the homeless or acres and acres of gravestones to shatter the illusions of Hollywood and return me to the real world of flesh-and-blood human living.

I still have a long way to go. The cycles of dying and rising are not only behind me. I am sure there will be more. At least the last and most important one—the ultimate stripping before the ultimate reckoning.

One thing is crystal clear: God has not called me to be a successful motion picture producer. Being a producer is not a bad thing to be and may even have a place in God's plan. But it is no justification for a life.

Success is nice. And it, too, may have its place in God's plan. But it is largely outside your control and does not last long even when you do get it. It cannot make or break a life.

No, God has called me to be a priest, a faithful servant of His people, faithful to myself, to the truth as He reveals it to me, to His love as He shares it with me, to the people He has put in my life and asked me to serve, to the kind of service He wants me to render to them.

He will not judge me by how successful a producer I have been.

He will judge me by how faithful a servant I have been.

The payoff is fidelity, not success.

A realization I find chastening and freeing.

Acknowledgments

Saying thank you to all who have helped with this book is difficult, since it includes all who have loved me and contributed in any way to the richness of my life.

But special mention must be made of the Paulists in Westwood, whose encouragement sustained me and whose gentle humor kept me from taking myself too seriously during the arduous months of composition.

The same must be said of the committed team at Paulist Productions who graciously put up with my prolonged absences without complaint.

I am also greatly indebted to those good friends—Merrit Malloy, Jim McGinn, John Furia, Liz Bugental, Bob Rivers, C.S.P., Stewart Stern, Frank Desiderio, C.S.P., Dennis Burke, Genevieve Sifransky, Jim Houston, Paul Robichaud, C.S.P., Peter Cameron, O.P., and Terry Sweeney—who read the manuscript and made many valuable suggestions.

And I am especially grateful to my consistently cheerful and loyal assistants, Terry Vaughn and Lucy Giles, who struggled with my handwriting and put the innumerable drafts into the computer.

And special thanks are due to my editors—Pat O'Connor, who helped get the project started, and Pat Golbitz, who gave some crucial encouragement along the way—and to my loyal agent, Charlotte Sheedy.

Without the continuing generosity of these beautiful people, this book would not have been written.